CITY, COUNTRY, EMPIRE

CITY, COUNTRY, EMPIRE

Landscapes

in

Environmental

History

Edited by
Jeffry M. Diefendorf
and
Kurk Dorsey

University of Pittsburgh Press

Published by the University of Pittsburgh Press, Pittsburgh, PA 15260
Copyright © 2005, University of Pittsburgh Press
Manufactured in the United States of America
Printed on acid-free paper
10 9 8 7 6 5 4 3 2 1

Library of Congress Cataloging-in-Publication Data

City, country, empire : landscapes in environmental history / edited by Jeffry M.
Diefendorf and Kurk Dorsey.
     p. cm.
   Includes bibliographical references and index.
   ISBN 0-8229-4257-7 (cloth : alk. paper) — ISBN 0-8229-5876-7 (pbk. : alk. paper)
   1. Human ecology—History. 2. Urban ecology—History. 3. Landscape changes—
History. 4. Economic development—Environmental aspects. 5. Social history. I.
Diefendorf, Jeffry M., 1945- II. Dorsey, Kurkpatrick.
   GF13.C58 2005
   304.2—dc22
                                          2004027713

Contents

Acknowledgments

We are very grateful to the many people who contributed to the production of this book and the conference that generated it in April 2001. The most credit must go to the Dunfey family, particularly Ruth and Julie Dunfey, who have so generously supported the History Department at the University of New Hampshire, particularly through the creation of the William L. Dunfey Endowment for the Study of History. This fund provided the support to bring to campus the distinguished scholars whose work you see on these pages, and it continues to support history education at the university.

Our colleagues in the department were also vital in making the book possible, from shaping the original idea to suggesting participants to serving as chairs and commentators at the conference. Our dean, Marilyn Hoskin, joined the department in providing financial and institutional support for the conference. Tom Kelly of the university's Office of Sustainability Programs supplied financial support for the conference and a generous subvention to assist in the publication of this book.

We would also like to thank the editors and anonymous readers at the University of Pittsburgh Press for their feedback and assistance along the way. They have helped to make this a better book.

Finally, we acknowledge the following publications for allowing us to reprint material included in this book:

Joel Tarr's "The Metabolism of the Industrial City: The Case of Pittsburgh" first appeared in the *Journal of Urban History*, vol. 28, issue 5, and is reprinted by permission of Sage Publications.

Nancy Langston's "Floods and Landscapes in the Inland West" is adapted from her work *Where Land and Water Meet: Transforming a Western Landscape*. Copyright © 2003 by Nancy Langston. Reprinted by permission of the University of Washington Press.

Andrew C. Isenberg's "The Industrial Alchemy of Hydraulic Mining: Law, Technology, and Resource-Intensive Industrialization" is an excerpt from *Industrial Frontier* by Andrew Isenberg to be published in June 2005 by Farrar, Straus and Giroux, LLC. Copyright © 2004 by Andrew Isenberg. Reprinted by permission of Farrar, Straus & Giroux, LLC.

J. R. McNeill's "Yellow Jack and Geopolitics: Environment, Epidemics, and the Struggles for Empire in the American Tropics, 1650–1900" is adapted from an article that appeared in *Review*, A Journal of the Fernand Braudel Center, vol. 27, no. 4, and is reprinted by permission.

Paul R. Josephson's "When Stalin Learned to Fish: Natural Resources, Technology, and Industry under Socialism" is adapted from *Industrialized Nature* by Paul R. Josephson. Copyright © 2002 by the author. Reproduced with permission of Island Press, Washington, D.C.

Challenges for Environmental History

Jeffry M. Diefendorf and Kurk Dorsey

I N THE June 2002 edition of *The American Historical Review*, Ted Steinberg's forum essay urged historians to take environmental history more seriously.[1] Nature, he argued, had too often been marginalized, either as mere scenery for human actors or as the foundation upon which humans built things of historical interest. Steinberg's lament, while perhaps a bit overstated, had the ring of truth to it. Nature has not penetrated the mainstream of historical thinking to the same extent that race, class, and gender have, even though all four were being hailed as "new" fields of history about the same time. Further evidence of his point can be seen in the fact that very few people participated in the online forum that allowed readers to discuss the merits of his article.

This situation is odd, if for no other reasons than the prominence leading environmental historians have attained and the increasing specialization within the field. The careers of Donald Worster and William Cronon illustrate both points. Each has gained increasing fame among historians and the general public for a series of influential books and articles. Each has also published an edited collection of articles that shows the state of the field. Worster's 1988 contribution, *The Ends of the Earth: Perspectives on Modern Environmental History*, covered a wide range of topics, from climate change

1

in early modern Europe to modern Soviet conservation. It served as an introduction to the field for a wide array of scholars who could find something of relevance to their own regions and timeframes. Seven years later, William Cronon was the editor of a book titled *Uncommon Ground: Rethinking the Human Place in Nature*. The fifteen authors in this collection focused on a common theme, the way that human societies—especially in the United States—create concepts of nature. Both of these books have been influential among environmental historians, and Cronon's even sparked something of a backlash among environmentalists.[2] But seven years after *Uncommon Ground*, Steinberg could argue persuasively that most historians were still not paying attention.

We share many of Steinberg's concerns, and we set out to invite to our conference at the University of New Hampshire a wide range of historians working to expand our ways of thinking about cities and landscapes. Most of the scholars represented in this volume are established environmental historians, but a few specialize in other fields, such as urban history. Together, they demonstrate how human and natural forces collaborate in the creation of cities, the countryside, and empires. Environmental historians will find here a set of chapters that further enhance the field's renewed interests in the interconnections among places and environments, whether for specific cities or large empires. Other historians of a wide range of regions, periods, and fields should find in this collection new ways to think about their work, which ultimately is what Steinberg asks of environmental history. In these chapters, nature is a force that cannot be overlooked.

Cities, countryside, and empires might seem disparate topics for one collection, but we hope that readers will see a continuum among the three. We move from specific urban settings, to broader suburban and rural areas, to an international context. As William Cronon persuasively demonstrated in *Nature's Metropolis*, cities and countryside—and by extension empires—are not distant from one another, but they are in fact closely intertwined.[3] Joel Tarr opens with a story of Pittsburgh, a city that owes its very existence to an imperial struggle 250 years ago and a city that owes its industrial rise and decline to the interaction of resources from the countryside and markets throughout the world. In the last chapter, Tom Dunlap focuses on empire but uses cities and rural landscapes to draw comparisons across time and space.

Beyond the continuum readers should also find connections among the book's three parts. The hills and rivers of northern California's gold mining territory might seem completely unlike the slagheaps of the Ruhr Valley, but in fact both were industrial landscapes altered by technology. In the end, both included parks that covered up the changes wrought by humans. Likewise, one might not see any relationship between the various Soviet fisheries and a valley in Oregon. But as Paul Josephson and Nancy Langston suggest, Soviet use of "brute force technology" was not that different from the Fish and Wildlife Service's attempts to poison and stab invasive fish as a means of managing a wildlife refuge. And one might find the intersection of politics and science in the debate over Los Angeles's smog not that different from the problems of politics and science in a West African maize rust outbreak.

The collection of chapters in this volume, then, combines the goals of both Worster's and Cronon's collections. Just as *Ends of the Earth* showed that environmental history can be done for almost any time and place, so too the authors here show a remarkable range, from the Malheur basin to the Ruhr valley. But, like Cronon's authors, they also allow the reader to focus on particular themes, such as the way in which humans and nature interact in the creation of landscapes and the influence of industrialization on an array of resources, from fisheries to gold-bearing streams. We hope that this collection will take its place alongside theirs both in documenting where environmental history now stands and in serving as a challenge to scholars to find ways to incorporate the ideas and insights of environmental history into their work.

Let us suggest but a few of the challenges that these chapters make. If the Gold Rush utterly changed the river valleys of California, what has happened during mechanized mining for diamonds, precious metals, or valuable ores in Africa and Latin America? How does the attempt to find environmentally sensitive solutions to the problems of the Ruhr compare to what has happened in the American rust belt? "Following the money" helps account for the victories of American mall developers over environmentalists. Does this explanation hold as shopping malls go up around Europe? Planting new strains of maize, introducing new grazing patterns, and attempting to apply an industrial model to fishing produced unexpected environmental consequences. How can this illuminate the processes of economic innovation in rapidly changing economies like China or India? What other tales of war and conquest, so commonly told purely in terms of human agency, should be recast in ways that resemble the impact of yellow fever on European soldiers in the Caribbean?

Environmental historians will find here a range of familiar scholars pursuing innovative work. Other historians, though, may benefit from a quick sketch of some of the trends in the field that are reflected—and built upon—in this book. In its early years as a field, environmental history was disproportionately connected to the history of the American west and the American frontier. It was also driven, to a certain extent, by the environmental movement, which seemed to provide much of the energy and moral force behind the field. But over the last fifteen years, scholars have opened up four approaches that had not been especially influential in the past. First, the field has become increasingly international. Also, it has incorporated many of the concerns of urban and social history. Moreover, environmental historians are now much more willing to question the environmental movement, from the very definition of terms like "nature" to questions of environmental justice. Finally, some scholars are wrestling with the notion of agency in the interactions on the fuzzy border between nature and culture.[4]

The internationalization of the field is perhaps the strongest sign of its vitality. A glance at the programs from recent meetings of the American Society for Environmental History demonstrates that people from around the world have presented at the meetings. The new European Society for Environmental History holds meetings that grow in size every year, and scholars debate what is unique about Europe's environmental history.[5] Not surprisingly, researchers' geographical foci have become increasingly diverse, with more attention paid to African and Asian history, for example. At one level, this might reflect simply an acknowledgment by historians of these regions that they have long been environmental historians, even if they did not use the term.

Likewise, historians are doing a better job of seeing that environmental history is often by definition international. Political boundaries rarely match ecological boundaries, and ideas, trade, and pollution all cross both types of boundaries with ease. Two recent books, Richard Tucker's *Insatiable Appetite: The United States and the Degradation of the Tropics* and Thomas Dunlap's *Nature and the English Diaspora*, show the potential for U.S. environmental historians to internationalize their research.[6] Tucker demonstrated how the sheer size and appetites of the U.S. market had global environmental ramifications long before anyone protested against globalization. Dunlap's book showed how ideas that flowed out of England influenced settlement in lands from Australia to Canada and then those ideas were themselves shaped by the environment that the settlers encountered. Beyond these two, one could point to the fertile interactions between environmental history, on one hand, and borderlands history and diplomatic history, on the other.

The best evidence of the internationalization of environmental history came, though, with the publication in 2000 of John McNeill's *Something New under the Sun: An Environmental History of the Twentieth-Century World*.[7] Mc-

Neill was able to undertake such an ambitious project because he had a vast body of scholarly literature from around the world upon which to draw, and he assembled an account of the planet's ecological change and its human causes, as well as its impact on human societies, over the course of a century. It seems likely that such a comprehensive study would not have been possible much earlier.

The focus on the international context of environmental change has paralleled an important shift within American environmental history toward studies of cities. It was very tempting for the environmentalist community to see the city as beyond its concern, and for many years most environmental historians agreed. But such crucial works as Andrew Hurley's *Environmental Inequalities* and Bill Cronon's *Nature's Metropolis* made it impossible for a reader to miss the connection between cities and nature, hammering home the point that cities had to be included in any complete understanding of environmental history.[8] Hurley's book, an investigation of the relationship between U.S. Steel and Gary, Indiana, owes its power in part to the ways in which he connected social history to environmental history. Class and race were important parts of the environmental history of Gary, and Hurley brought them into the mix in a way that no historian had done before.

Cronon's book, which has won praise from many quarters, helped open the field in a new direction, first by complicating the definition of nature and second by demonstrating the connections between cities and their hinterland. The metropolis in question, Chicago, was founded and grew so rapidly in part because of natural advantages of its location, but it also benefited from the ability of its citizens to gather resources from a broad hinterland, commodify them, and ship them on to consumers. Together, Cronon's and Hurley's books remind us that the environment encompasses cities, both in the sense that urban dwellers are confronted with environmental problems and in the sense that there is no fixed border between nature and culture. Work has also begun on understanding the place, and costs, of suburbs, which have so often seemed to be literally the interface between culture and nature in U.S. environmental history.

Two important books have developed that idea in the last decade. Jennifer Price's *Flight Maps: Adventures with Nature in Modern America* and Cronon's *Uncommon Ground* both argued that nature is a construct, not a concrete thing.[9] Price dug deep into American culture to find how Americans defined and valued nature, from millinery and malls to passenger pigeons and plastic flamingos. She concluded that nature had come to have a specific meaning in American culture as a place away from where people live and work. In creating that definition they had, she argued, lost sight of nature all around them—and even in them. Whether for sale in the Nature Company or on their television screens, nature had come to mean the exotic far away, not the toxics next door.

Cronon's collection included chapters from a number of leading scholars from different disciplines that analyzed, as they said, the human place in nature. Beginning with two basic premises—that the natural world was more complex and less stable than popularly assumed and that nature "is a profoundly human construction"—the authors set out to explore the complexities of nature from a variety of angles. Perhaps the most compelling analysis came from Anne Whiston Spirn, in her chapter on the legacy of Frederick Law Olmsted in such places as Niagara Falls and Yosemite National Park. Spirn demonstrates that places that many people take for granted as pristine nature were literally constructions, works of landscape architecture at their core.[10]

Two other chapters from this collection stood out for their arguments that distanced environmental history from environmentalism: Richard White's provocatively titled "'Are You an Environmentalist or Do You Work for a Living?': Work and Nature," and Bill Cronon's "The Trouble with Wilderness; Or, Getting Back to the Wrong Nature." Together, these two chapters challenged some of the basic assumptions of environmentalists; Cronon argued that wilderness was not a separate, real place, but instead "the creation of very particular human cultures at very particular moments." White challenged environmentalists to see how they had stigmatized physical labor, and its attendant environmental costs, while ignoring how they too had benefited from such work—and how their own work affected the environment. Environmentalism, he concluded, had become too entangled with our leisure and our play, while deprecating the work that all must undertake in some form.

That these chapters drew the ire of environmentalists marked, in fact, another important development in environmental history, a move away from close association with environmentalism. While it would be an oversimplification to say that environmentalism drove environmental history, it would be true to note that most environmental historians have been quite sympathetic to environmentalism and drew some of their inspiration as historians and desire to protect nature from the same sources. Therefore, it has been easy for scholars to let their political inclinations color their analysis, sometimes to the extent that they seemed as interested in advancing the movement as in rigorous scholarship.

But, as historian Andrew Isenberg noted, environmental historians no longer see the environmentalist movement "as a guide for interpreting the past, but as a historical artifact itself, to be studied and critiqued."[11] To that end, historians such as Isenberg in *The Destruction of the Bison: An Environmental History, 1750–1920*, Nancy Langston in *Forest Dreams, Forest Nightmares: The Paradox of Old Growth in the Inland Northwest*, and Joseph Taylor III in *Making Salmon: An Environmental History of the Northwest Fisheries Crisis* have knocked conservationists and environmentalists off their perches.[12] Instead of treating them largely as heroes fighting for the common good, these authors have also emphasized their prejudices and shortsightedness. Hurley showed how conservationists in Gary were deeply divided and sometimes tainted by racism. And Giovanna Di Chiro's chapter in *Uncommon Ground* further examined the problems of social justice in the environmental movement.[13]

Finally, historians have become increasingly interested in questions of nature's agency in human history. In 2002, both Isenberg and Ted Steinberg published essays that addressed changing notions of agency in historical scholarship.[14] Both noted that historians had gravitated toward two poles: environmental determinism, the notion that the broad outlines of human history were controlled by factors beyond human control, or environmental passivity, the belief that nature was largely static except when people did things to it. Both men argued that natural agency had to be understood as somewhere in the middle. Basing their insights on the work of ecologists, who for some time have been undermining the notion of a static nature (most explicitly framed in the concept of a climax community), Steinberg and Isenberg emphasized the notion of a dynamic nature that could change on its own even as people affected it too. Without undermining the concept of human agency, they emphasized that environmental change was often the product of complex forces. Steinberg, in particular, was building on his previous work, *Acts of God: The Unnatural History of Natural Disaster in America*, which challenged the whole concept of "natural disasters," events beyond human control.[15] Instead, the human toll from hurricanes, floods, and earthquakes was often in fact a product of a combination of a natural force and human decisions. A particular tornado or flood might be an act of God, but the lack of a warning system might be an act of bureaucratic incompetence and legislative cupidity.

Readers of this volume will see that the key trends of the past decade are apparent in these chapters. Internationalization is most prominent. Contributions from Ursula von Petz and Paul Josephson focus on Germany and the

Soviet Union, while James McCann, Thomas Dunlap, and John McNeill examine the interaction of Western peoples and ideas with nature and peoples around the world, from the Caribbean to Australia. Likewise, urban and suburban environmental history are central to five of the ten chapters. Joel Tarr's examination of Pittsburgh and Sarah Elkind's study of Los Angeles pair up well with Elizabeth Blackmar's study of suburban sprawl. Petz covers the industrial urban agglomeration of the Ruhr valley. The complexities of scholars' various approaches to agency in environmental history are also apparent in this collection. Alfred Crosby's conclusory remarks reflect something close to environmental determinism, while the urban history chapters tend to see nature as less of a force. Along the spectrum in between, McNeill and Dunlap reveal how human and natural factors worked together to break up human plans for imperial expansion, and McCann shows how a disease arose, spread, and disappeared before humans could understand it, much less control it. The challenges of defining nature are clear in the chapters by Nancy Langston and Andrew Isenberg. A tourist traveling from the old gold-mining district of northern California to the Malheur wildlife refuge in southern Oregon could be forgiven for thinking she is seeing relatively untrammeled nature, but these two chapters show the extent of human manipulation of these landscapes, even as they have different approaches to the importance of nature's agency. Finally, it is striking how unimportant Progressive-era conservationism and modern environmentalism are to the chapters in this collection. Certainly, the authors reveal sympathies for the movement's general goals, whether in its efforts to control sprawl or its critique of industrial mining, but the analysis reflects the impulses that William Cronon called for in his chapter in *Uncommon Ground*.

The volume opens with a part on cities. Joel Tarr explores the impact of industrialization on Pittsburgh and the passing of its industrial heyday. Sarah Elkind discusses how Los Angeles sought to come to grips with the problem of air pollution. Concluding this part, Ursula von Petz examines the decades-long evolution of a regional approach to addressing the problems caused by heavy industry in the Ruhr valley, an approach that has culminated in an attempt to create a new, environmentally friendly landscape in a deindustrializing area.

Petz's chapter is a useful bridge to the second part, on changing suburban and rural landscapes. Elizabeth Blackmar leads off by considering both the financial forces that are a cause of urban sprawl and the relationship between sprawl and the suburban landscape. Nancy Langston then explores the complex interaction among farmers, ranchers, biologists, and the landscape of the Malheur Basin in Oregon. Andrew Isenberg closes the part by analyzing the striking changes to California's river valleys brought about by hydraulic mining, an industrial process that displaced the lone prospector in reality, if not in the popular imagination.

The final part addresses the interaction of environment and empire. Paul Josephson builds on Isenberg's chapter about the transformation of an occupation and resource by industrial technology as he focuses on Soviet efforts to make fisheries more productive. Jim McCann then tells the tale of a plant disease that flourished and passed before Western science could even comprehend it—and the implications of that failure to comprehend. John McNeill specifically addresses the place of nature in shaping imperial struggles for control in the Caribbean. And Tom Dunlap closes out this part with a discussion of the ways in which empires shape and understand the landscape.

The volume concludes with some remarks by one of the founders of the field of environmental history, Alfred Crosby. After thirty years of work in the field, Crosby offers his perspectives on environmental history and a commentary on the chapters in this book. We share his view that, far from being a marginal activity, environmental history is and will remain an exciting, and challenging, field within which to work.

PART ONE

Cities

■ The chapters in the first part of this volume cover a range of locations in the industrial era, from Pittsburgh to the Ruhr, but they share some common themes. The impact on the environment of industrial development and large human populations runs through all three chapters, as each author attempts to explain how nature and culture came together to shape a particular urban area. The three chapters fall along different points of a spectrum but all focus more on human decision-making than on environmental forces. Pollution is a common problem in Pittsburgh, the cities of the Ruhr Valley, and Los Angeles, and in each case urban leaders preferred to wait for external solutions to their dilemmas.

Joel Tarr sees the modern city as an organism that consumes the water, air, and land that make up its environment. Pittsburgh appears in "The Metabolism of the Industrial City" as a classic example of a city that grew in the heyday of heavy industry, and, like other industrial cities, it took a very long time to come to grips with issues of environmental quality. A central function of city government during the middle half of the nineteenth century was development of waterworks to supply river water to the city's inhabitants. Increased water use, in turn, led to the need for an underground sewer system to handle both waste water and storm runoff. While such a system was built in the late nineteenth and early twentieth centuries, sewer discharges into rivers by Pittsburgh and other towns produced serious water pollution and high rates of disease and mortality, especially in districts inhabited by workers and immigrants. Water pollution was not just a local problem but a regional problem that crossed political boundaries. Even though the city then invested in filtration and treatment plants, it was still discharging some raw sewage into the Allegheny River in 1959.

Pittsburgh was also a city long noted for serious air pollution resulting from smoke produced by burning bituminous coal for energy both for industrial use and domestic heating. A massive civic effort to change behavior and obtain both regulation of smoke and voluntary compliance with smoke reduction goals did not bear fruit until the end of the 1940s, and a part of the gain in air quality was due to increased use of imported natural gas instead of local coal. The decline of the steel industry, which had dominated the landscape and closed most of the riverfront to private access, also accounts for the recent successes in land reclamation. Progressive reformers had begun a campaign in 1909 to reclaim at least the Nine Mile Run valley for parkland, but the steel companies wanted to use the area for slag dumps. Only in the 1990s, when slag dumping ceased, was the city able to launch a redevelopment plan that called for residential and retail development that would be sensitive to land restoration and environmental quality in Nine Mile Run. This plan is an important but still modest step toward achieving a sustainable environment rather than one in which nature was simply consumed by an expanding city.

Like Pittsburgh, Los Angeles is another city famous for its air pollution. In "Los Angeles's Nature: Urban Environmental Politics in the Twentieth Century," Sarah Elkind shows that local officials and businessmen first saw the cause of the city's bad air as industrial smoke—the same cause of air pollution in cities like Pittsburgh and St. Louis. The appearance of severe air pollution in 1943 was blamed on a Southern California Gas plant producing butadiene, which was used in the production of synthetic rubber, a vital strategic material in the war effort, and there was talk of closing the plant. Industry responded by pointing out its essential and patriotic contribution to the war effort and suggested that it was not solely to blame. The focus then shifted to nonindustrial sources of pollution, including private citizens who burned trash, used boilers, and drove motor vehicles. The county created the Los Angeles Air Pollution Control District (APCD) to deal with the problem, since smog affected the entire Los Angeles basin and not just the city proper.

Elkind argues that the Los Angeles Chamber of Commerce played an essential role in mediating between the interested parties, even though there was widespread suspicion that both the APCD and the Chamber mostly sought to protect business interests rather than seek a workable solution to the problem. Only gradually in the 1950s did officials and private activists recognize that invisible exhaust fumes from motor vehicles and not just visible smoke caused smog. But even with scientific proof of this fact mounting, the Chamber of Commerce continued to defend local industry. Motor vehicle exhausts provided an opportunity to shift responsibility from both local industry and local consumers, who were dependent upon their vehicles, to the more distant auto industry. The solution had to come from Detroit in the form of new technology (catalytic converters) rather than real changes in the behavior of Californians.

In Ursula von Petz's chapter on Germany's Ruhr basin, "The Environmental Transformation of the Ruhr," one can quickly see parallels with the experience of Pittsburgh. Like Pittsburgh, the Ruhr was steel and coal country, and in the nineteenth century it became the heart of German heavy industry. Industry dominated the region, and the decline of steel and coal production after World War II brought both problems and opportunities in its wake. The Ruhr was characterized by polluted water and air, by large slagheaps, and huge steel plants. Its reputation was one of bleakness, not harmony with nature. Petz notes that calls for reform came from many directions, starting in the nineteenth century, but what is most important here is the development of a regional approach to planning in order to ameliorate some of the worst conditions. Planners and reformers believed that measures to improve environmental quality would in fact also help the economy, particularly by encouraging activity that would ease the region's dependence on heavy industry.

A key figure was Robert Schmidt, a water engineer who became Essen's planner from 1901 to 1920. Before World War I, Schmidt, a member of the German Garden City Society who viewed cities as living organisms, wrote a proposal to create a regional planning authority. Such an organization could help create healthier housing and generally improve public health by caring for existing green spaces and creating new ones. Contact with nature, managed or wild, would strengthen both urban and human bodies. The pioneering Ruhr Regional Planning Authority was created in 1920, with Schmidt as its head. The authority published a regional plan in 1927 that devoted considerable attention to green spaces, and it also issued a building and zoning code for the entire Ruhr basin.

The efficacy of this regional agency was vitiated by the Third Reich, which made economic growth and military production a higher priority than greenery, and the Nazis put the eugenic ideas of the public hygiene movement to their own racist uses. After 1945, the Ruhr Planning Authority was reestablished under Philip Rappaport, and regional thinking about common problems was revived. Responding to increasing concerns about environmental quality, the authority published a second regional plan in 1966 that placed new weight on green areas, including reclaiming some of the notorious brownfields. New regulations addressed the issues of water and air pollution. Though the regional planning agency was abolished in 1975, district- and state-sponsored efforts to address environmental quality continued. Most important was the ambitious International Building Exhibition Emscher Park (1989–1999), which called for renaturalizing the Emscher canal and nearby brownfield sites, turning abandoned industrial sites into technology parks and generally promoting an ecologically sound redevelopment of the area. Though clearly the environmental damage left behind by the age of coal and steel has not been undone, the Ruhr now presents visitors and residents with an increasingly "green" face.

1

The Metabolism of the Industrial City
The Case of Pittsburgh

Joel A. Tarr

THE CONCEPT of *metabolism* has been adopted from biology and refers to physiological processes within living things that provide the energy and nutrients required by an organism as the conditions of life itself. These processes can be described in terms of the transformation of inputs (sunlight, chemical energy, nutrients, water, and air) into biomass and waste products. While essentially a concept originating in science, I have found it useful as a means to comprehend the environmental history of cities. Just as living things require the inputs of light, energy, nutrients, water, and air, so do cities. That is, cities cannot exist without those inputs—urbanites require clean air, water, food, fuel, and construction materials to subsist while urban industries need materials for production purposes. These materials may initially come from the area of the urban site itself but increasingly over time they are derived from the urban hinterland or even further. That is, as the city grows, it extends its *ecological footprint* further and further into its hinterland.

The ecologist Eugene Odum has written that "the city is a parasite on the natural and domesticated environments," since it does not grow food and dirties its air and water. One can also note that it reshapes and consumes the land. Odum observes that a parasite "does not live for very long if it kills or damages its host." Therefore, for a parasite to survive, it must develop systems of exchanges that benefit both its host and itself.[1] While some may object to characterizing the city as a "parasite" on the environment, thus raising the ancient specter of the evil city and the natural countryside, from a purely descriptive perspective, the concept is a valid one. Cities do consume their environments and cannot survive unless they reach a point of equilibrium with their sites and their hinterlands in regard to the consumption of air, water, and land resources.[2] Today we call such a goal "seeking a *sustainable city*."

Cities and their metropolitan areas have had major effects on the natural environment since their appearance, but these impacts have accelerated over the past two centuries with the development of industrialism and rapid urbanization. In the United States urban development has advanced, and today a large majority of the population lives in sizable metropolitan areas. These metropolitan areas are growing not only in population but also in terms of aerial extent. In these habitats, city builders have reshaped and often destroyed natural landscapes and eliminated animal, bird, marine, and insect species, while urban demands for resources have profoundly affected hinterlands.

The relationship between the city and the natural environment has actually been interactive, with cities having massive effects on the natural environment, while the natural environment, in turn, has profoundly shaped urban configurations. Nature has not only caused many of the annoyances of daily urban life, such as bad weather and pests, but it has also produced natural disasters and catastrophes such as floods, fires, volcanic activity, and earthquakes. Often, however, the actions of urbanites—such as building on flood plains and steep slopes, under the shadow of volcanoes, or in earthquake-prone zones—have exacerbated the dangers they are exposed to from natural hazards.[3]

This essay will focus on the metabolism of one major industrial city—Pittsburgh—in the years from about 1880 to 2000. In doing so, it will explore issues relating to the resources of water, air, and land, and the ways in which they were used, misused, and remediated. That is, the essay will consider the ways in which the city has moved from a lack of concern with environmental goods toward a more sustainable level.

Pittsburgh is sited in southwestern Pennsylvania, west of the Allegheny Mountains. The physical geography of the region consists of an uplifted plateau about 1,200 feet high that has been dissected by an extensive river and stream network flowing from the Allegheny Mountains. The cutting action of rivers and streams carved a complex topography of hills and steep valleys with a general relief of five hundred feet but also sharp variations. Human action as well as natural forces have shaped and reshaped the landscape. Development has taken place especially along the floodplains and terraces in the major valleys as well as in interior valleys and hollows. The region's greatest mineral resource is bituminous coal, but it also has natural gas and petroleum deposits that were historically important. The city's population reached a high of approximately 676,000 in 1950, but today (2004) it is down to about half that total. The six-county metropolitan area is at a plateau of about 2.25 million, where it has remained for several decades. Territorially, through annexation, the city grew to fifty-five square miles during the nineteenth and twentieth centuries but has remained stagnant since about 1930. Conversely, the urbanized area of the mature metropolitan region has continued to expand along its periphery. During this period, the city and the region's environment—its water, air, and land resources—has undergone dramatic changes.

Water Supply and Wastewater Disposal

Cities require fresh water in order to exist. These supplies fill a number of functions, such as domestic needs, commercial and industrial purposes, street flushing, and fire fighting. One of the most serious environmental problems Pittsburgh has faced throughout its history is pollution of its neighboring rivers.[4] As a riverine city, Pittsburgh has been both blessed by abundant supplies and cursed by extensive pollution of these supplies. This pollution, from both domestic and industrial sources, has severely impacted the quality of the water drawn from the rivers, as well as from wells, for both drinking water and industrial uses. In addition, pollution has sharply curtailed the availability of the rivers for recreational purposes.

Like other urbanites at the beginning of the nineteenth century, Pittsburghers drew their water from local sources such as wells, rivers, and ponds, and from rainwater gathered in cisterns. Both private and public water suppliers provided water to the city almost from its very beginnings. In 1802, for instance, the city councils passed an ordinance allowing the borough to construct four public wells and for the purchase of private wells "in useful and necessary parts of the Borough."[5] Private vendors peddled water in the streets, and the 1815 city directory listed five water carters. As the city grew, its water needs increased rapidly, requiring more ample sources.

The debate over improved water supply focused initially on the issue of public vs. private provision. In 1818 the councils refused to approve an attempt by private interests to obtain a municipal water franchise, and in 1821 sixty-one prominent citizens successfully petitioned the councils to provide new wells and to make all existing pumps public. In 1822, citizens again petitioned the councils, requesting that the municipality build a waterworks to supply Allegheny River water to the city. The petitions maintained that municipal ownership was required to guarantee improved fire protection and to secure lower fire insurance rates, to service domestic and manufacturing needs, and to meet public health requirements.[6] The insistence on public rather than private provision highlights the widespread belief that water was too important to city life to be left to the private profit-making sector.

In 1826 the Pittsburgh Select and Common Councils responded to citizens' demands and approved the construction of a waterworks that would, according to the councils' presidents, provide protection against fire and "beneficial effects to every manufactory and . . . family in the city." The city completed the waterworks in 1828. The system utilized a steam pump to draw water from the Allegheny River and raise it to a million-gallon reservoir for gravity distribution throughout the city. Responding to new demands caused by a major fire and the annexation of contiguous towns, the councils expanded the system in 1844 and in 1848. By the end of 1850, the city had laid twenty-one miles of water pipe, with the system serving 6,630 dwellings, stores, and shops. System expansion continued, especially after the major annexations of territory in 1868 and 1871. In 1879 the city opened a new waterworks that pumped water from the Allegheny River and stored it in two reservoirs for gravity distribution throughout the city. From 1895 to 1915, the city expanded the water supply network from 268 to 743 miles.[7]

The funding of the waterworks was the single largest expenditure made by the city during its first fifty years. Pittsburgh was not unusual in the extent to which waterworks costs constituted a substantial part of the total municipal budget. The building of New York's Croton Aqueduct in 1842, for instance, increased that city's debt from $500,000 to over $9 million and caused many citizens to predict financial disaster.[8] Pittsburgh's willingness to make such a large expenditure for a public good can be explained by the joining of a variety of interest groups—merchants and industrialists, homeowners, fire insurance companies, and those concerned with the public health—to demand the construction of an adequate waterworks. Waterworks were ordinarily the most expensive capital project undertaken by nineteenth-century American cities, indicating their importance to urban metabolism.

Access to water services, however, was unevenly distributed throughout the city, an important issue of what today we call environmental justice. Working-class districts had poorer water supplies than did affluent neighborhoods, often relying on local springs or wells, subject to pollution. Piped water was frequently accessed through a spigot in the back yard (frequently located near the privy vaults) rather than through indoor plumbing. The infamous Painter's Row, tenements owned by U.S. Steel on the South Side, had one spigot in the yard serving ninety-one families.[9]

An administrative ruling exacerbated the situation regarding water access. In 1872 the City Water Commission ruled that the size of the pipe laid on a particular street would be determined by the amount of potential revenue. This ruling resulted in either insufficient supply or no supply to poor neighborhoods. Such a policy, however, was not unusual for American cities. Robin L. Einhorn has called it the "segmented system"—a system that provided benefits to those who paid for them but which also "made the American urban landscape a physical expression of political inequality."[10] Typhoid death rates were high throughout the city, but were highest in working-class immigrant and African American areas.[11]

A supply of potable water was only one part of the city's metabolic system—wastewater from households and industries as well as storm water had to be disposed of. Household wastes and wastewater were usually placed in cesspools and privy vaults, and these were a frequent source of problems.[12] Many portions of Pittsburgh's heavily industrialized South Side, for instance, utilized springs for water that were located close to neighborhood privy vaults. Private scavengers under contract to the city were responsible for maintaining sanitary conditions by cleaning privy vaults and removing garbage. In the process of performing this task, however, they frequently fouled the streets and polluted the rivers. As the city grew, domestic waste disposal problems increased; in the late nineteenth century the Pittsburgh Board of Health identified privy vault nuisances as the major health issue facing the city.[13]

The provision of running water to homes and householder adoption of water-using appliances such as sinks, showers, and water closets exacerbated the nuisance problem. On the one hand increased water supply in the home was a benefit, but on the other hand it often had a devastating effect on public health. Pittsburghers made use of the availability of a supply of running water to adopt a number of water-using appliances such as sinks, showers, and water closets. In many cases, in order to dispose of the wastewater, householders connected these appliances to the existing wastewater disposal sinks—cesspools and privy vaults. In 1881, for instance, householders had connected 4,000 of the city's 6,500 water closets to privies and cesspools; only about 1,500 were connected to street sewers.[14]

Increasingly, it became obvious that only the construction of a sewerage system would alleviate wastewater disposal problems. A variety of public and private sewers existed. Until the 1840s, all municipal sewers were above ground and made of wood or brick. These sewers were intended to provide street drainage and to eliminate pools of water that could breed miasmas, but the conduits often became receptacles for decaying wastes. In June 1832, concern over epidemic disease, especially cholera, led the council to establish the Sanitary Board to "direct all such measures as they think necessary for averting the introduction of the frightful epidemics." The board had the power to "cause the streets, lanes, alleys, buildings, lots and shores of the rivers to be explored, cleansed and purified in an efficient manner." It proceeded to organize the city into sanitary districts and to exercise its sanitary duties. The councils also, in these crisis years, enacted ordinances to improve waste collection and to extend the water system.[15] But the city's response to the public health threat remained limited, and conditions soon reverted to their normal unsanitary state. Fear of epidemic disease alone could not persuade the councils to make the large expenditures necessary to build a sewerage system. In addition to costs, confusion over disease etiology as well as uncertainty about the technical and design requirements for an efficient system had a discouraging effect.

By midcentury, however, demands for improved services, particularly from the city's commercial interests, persuaded the municipality to construct underground sewers in the business district. By 1866 this district possessed a "fairly adequate" system of main sewers. Other sections of the city were provided with services in a more uneven and haphazard fashion. By 1875 the city had constructed about twenty-five miles of sewers, mostly for storm water drainage. These sewers, however, suffered from design faults and were often either undersized or oversized and subject to constant clogging. The city had no topographical maps until the 1870s, and sewers did not conform to topography; neither did they follow an overall engineering plan. Rather, the municipality built sewers as a result of council members' attempts to meet their constituent demands. In addition, householders often constructed their own sewers, many of which went unrecorded. In 1881 a noted New York civil engineer, J. J. R. Croes, hired to consult on improving the system, commented to a meeting of the Western Pennsylvania Engineers' Society, "You have no sewers; you don't know where they are going, or where they are to be found." Without sewers, the great majority of households in the city continued to depend on cesspools and privy vaults for disposal of domestic waste.

Debate raged about possible designs of the sewer system. Should it be a separate, small pipe system that carried only domestic and industrial wastes, the technology advocated by the famous sanitarian Col. George E. Waring, Jr.? Or, should it be a larger, combined system that could accommodate both waste water and storm water, a design favored by many noted sanitary engineers?[16] The city's public health and engineering professionals divided over this question. Physicians argued that the separate system was preferable because it would protect health by removing wastes from the household before they had begun to generate disease-causing sewer gas. Storm water was a secondary matter and could be handled by surface conduits.

Sanitary engineers took a different position, maintaining that sanitary wastes and storm water were equally important and that a large pipe system able to accommodate both was more economical. The superior virtues of the combined system in terms of both health and storm water removal convinced city officials, and by the late 1880s Pittsburgh had begun to build such a system.[17] Between 1889 and 1912, civil engineers from the new Bureau of Engineering of the Public Works Department constructed over 412 miles of sewers, almost all of the combined type. The construction of the planned centralized sewerage system signified a movement away from the "piecemeal, decentralized approach to city-building characteristic of the 19th century."[18] In constructing a large centralized combined sewer network, Pittsburgh was following the lead of other large American cities such as Boston, Chicago, and New York.[19]

Many citizens resisted connecting to the new sewer lines and attempted to keep their old privies and cesspools. The Board of Health used the sanitary code to compel connection. In a series of acts in the late nineteenth and early twentieth centuries, the councils barred the construction of cesspools where sewer service was available, outlawed water closets from draining into a privy vault, and prohibited the connection of privy wells to a public sewer. Resistance to connecting to the system continued, particularly in working-class areas, because of householder resistance to paying sewer assessments.[20]

Building the sewer system reduced nuisances but increased contamination of the city's water supply. By 1900 most of the Pittsburgh population received its water from either the Allegheny or the Monongahela River, and over the years the watersheds of these streams had become increasingly populated. By 1900, for instance, more than 350,000 inhabitants in seventy-five upriver municipalities discharged their untreated sewage into the Allegheny River, the river that provided water supplies for most of Pittsburgh's population. Some of Pittsburgh's own sewers discharged into the river at sites locat-

ed above water supply pumping stations. The resulting pollution gave Pittsburgh the highest typhoid fever death rate of the nation's large cities from
1882 to 1907—well over 100 deaths per 100,000 population. In contrast, in
1905 the average for northern cities was 35 per 100,000 persons.[21]

Typhoid fever death rates were highest in working-class immigrant and
African American living areas. The Health Department advised that drinking
water be boiled but new immigrants often ignored such advice since they
viewed the water as uncontaminated. "You cannot make the foreigner believe
that Pittsburgh water is unwholesome," observed one physician, noting that
roughly half of all foreign-born men sickened with typhoid within two years
of arriving in the city.[22] Pittsburgh had one of the highest rates of bottled
water consumption in the nation, but these supplies were out of reach for
most working-class people. Thus, as a 1909 Pittsburgh Survey article observed, "those who could not afford to buy bottled water continued to drink
filth." According to the municipal Health Department, Pittsburgh appeared
"as two cities, one old and congested with a high mortality, and the other new
and spacious with a very low death rate."[23]

Beginning in the 1890s, agitation increased among women's groups, engineers, and physicians about the need to protect the water supply from infectious disease. The new science of bacterial water analysis had convinced
many of these citizens that mortality and morbidity from infectious waterborne disease could be prevented. In the 1890s, engineers and civic groups
cooperated to investigate the quality of the water supply using the new methods of bacterial science. These studies conclusively demonstrated the relationship between typhoid and water quality, and in 1896 the councils
approved an ordinance authorizing the mayor to create a Pittsburgh Filtration Commission to further study the matter and make public policy recommendations.[24]

The commission's investigations reconfirmed the link between water and
disease, and its 1899 report recommended construction of a slow-sand filtration plant as the most economical means of dealing with the threat to the
public health. In 1899, voters approved a bond issue for plant construction,
but factional political battles over control of construction contracts and issues of technological choice necessitated a second vote in 1904 and delayed
final completion of the filtration plant until the end of 1907. Once in operation, the filtration system had dramatic effects, and by 1912 Pittsburgh's
death rate from typhoid fever had fallen to the average for the largest American cities.[25]

Water filtration provided one safety net in regard to polluted water, but many sanitarians and public health physicians believed that it was also necessary to treat the city's sewage for maximum protection. Professional, business, and medical groups protested against sewage disposal by dilution only. They demanded that municipalities treat their sewage and agitated for state laws against stream pollution.[26] In the years after the turn of the century, states such as Connecticut, Massachusetts, Minnesota, New Hampshire, New Jersey, New York, Ohio, Pennsylvania, and Vermont, responding to a series of unusually severe typhoid epidemics, gave state boards of health increased power to control sewage disposal in streams.[27]

The Pennsylvania act "to preserve the purity of the waters of the State for the protection of the public health," passed by the state legislature in response to the severe Butler typhoid epidemic of 1903, typified these laws. It forbade the discharge of any untreated sewage into state waterways by new municipal systems. While it permitted cities already discharging to continue the practice, it required them to secure a permit from the state commissioner of health if they wished to extend their systems.[28] Engineering opinion largely disagreed with these prohibitions. As the *Engineering Record* noted in 1909, "it is often more equitable to all concerned for an upper riparian city to discharge its sewage into a stream and a lower riparian city to filter the water of the same stream for a domestic supply, than for the former city to be forced to put in sewage treatment works."[29]

Although Pittsburgh was filtering its own water after 1907, the city continued to dump its untreated sewage into its neighboring rivers, endangering the water supply of downstream communities. In the beginning of 1910, the city requested the State Department of Health to grant it a permit allowing it to extend its sewerage system. The department, headed by a physician, Samuel G. Dixon, first responded by requesting a "comprehensive sewerage plan for the collection and disposal of all of the sewage of the municipality." In addition, the department argued that in order to attain efficiency of treatment, the city should consider changing its sewerage from the combined to the separate system. F. Herbert Snow, the department's chief engineer, maintained that the plan was needed to protect the public health of communities who drew their water supplies from rivers downstream from Pittsburgh. "The baneful effect of Pittsburgh's sewage on the health of the brightest citizens at her door," wrote Snow, "admonishes city and state authorities alike of the futility of defying nature's sanitary laws."[30]

The city of Pittsburgh responded to Dixon's order by hiring the engineering firm of Allen Hazen and George C. Whipple to act as consultants for the required study. Hazen and Whipple were among the nation's most distinguished sanitary engineers and were already known for their espousal of water filtration as an alternative to sewage treatment to protect drinking water quality. Hazen had actually served as chief consultant on the construction of Pittsburgh's sand filtration plants. The engineers based their study primarily upon an evaluation of the costs of building a treatment system and of converting Pittsburgh sewers to the separate system.

In their report, issued on January 30, 1912, Hazen and Whipple argued that Pittsburgh's construction of a sewage treatment plant would not free the downstream towns from threats to their water supplies nor from the need to filter them, since other communities would continue to discharge raw sewage into the rivers. The method of disposal by dilution, they maintained, sufficed to prevent nuisances, particularly if storage reservoirs were constructed upstream from Pittsburgh to augment flow during periods of low stream volume. Hazen and Whipple argued that there was no case "where a great city has purified its sewage to protect public water supplies from the stream below."[31]

Hazen and Whipple's most powerful argument concerned the lack of economic feasibility of converting Pittsburgh's sewerage system to separate sewers and building a sewage treatment plant. There was no precedent, they claimed, for a city replacing the combined system by the separate system "for the purpose of protecting water supplies of other cities taken from the water course below." They calculated that financing such a project would have caused the city to exceed its municipal indebtedness level and thus violate state law. Moreover, because the sewage treatment plant was intended for the protection of the downstream communities, it would not give Pittsburgh any direct benefits. Furthermore, downstream cities would still have to filter their water to protect against waterborne pathogens. No "radical change in the method of sewerage or of sewage disposal as now practiced by the city of Pittsburgh is necessary or desirable," they concluded.[32]

While the engineering press received the Hazen-Whipple report with enthusiasm, Pennsylvania Health Commissioner Dixon found it an insufficient response to his original instructions requesting Pittsburgh to develop a comprehensive sewerage plan based on long-range planning. He maintained that he had envisioned a report that would take a regional rather than a local approach to Western Pennsylvania water pollution problems. He argued that water pollution had to be viewed from a health rather than a nuisance perspective and that the immediate costs of sewage treatment would be outweighed by the long-range health benefits. The time had come, Dixon stated, "to start a campaign in order that the streams shall not become stinking sewers and culture beds for pathogenic organisms."[33]

Given the political context, however, and the financial limitations upon the city, Dixon had no realistic means by which to enforce his order. In 1913 he capitulated and issued Pittsburgh a temporary discharge permit. The city continued to receive such permits until 1939, and it was not until 1959 that Pittsburgh and seventy-one other Allegheny County municipalities ceased discharging raw sewage into the abutting rivers and began treating their wastes.[34] Thus, nearly a half century was to pass before Dixon's vision of sewage-free rivers would even begin to be realized.

This particular case has implications larger than those that relate only to Pittsburgh. The dispute pitted public health physicians against sanitary engineers and illustrated their different conceptions of the choice dictated by the urban environment. Sanitary engineers believed that they had a superior conception of the "relative needs and values" of cities in regard to public health because of their understanding of municipal financial limitations—thus sewage treatment was a luxury, less critical than other urban public health needs. Many public health officials believed, on the other hand, that sewage disposal was not a proper use of streams, especially if drinking water quality was involved.[35] From the perspective of urban metabolism and urban sustainability, the short-term nature of the engineering option is clear, however driven by fiscal necessities.

Smoke and Air Pollution

A vital part of the urban metabolism is clean air, but effective metabolism also requires a constant source of energy, which often conflicts with the goal of maintaining clean air. The primary air quality concern of cities before World War II was smoke pollution, which consisted primarily of particles generated by the burning of fossil fuels, especially bituminous coal. These particles blocked the sunlight, irritated the lungs, discolored clothing and other materials including building facades, and threatened the public health.

Heavy smoke pollution was a problem for many cities, but especially for those like Pittsburgh and St. Louis that were located close to large deposits of bituminous coal. Smoke pollution in Pittsburgh resulted from a conjunction of the factors of topography, urbanization, industrialization, and the availability at low cost of large sources of high-volatile bituminous coal. The coal was used for domestic and commercial heating purposes, for processing raw materials and manufacturing goods, and for providing fuel for transportation systems.[36] Early in the nineteenth century Pittsburgh gained the reputation as the "smoky city."

The increase of smoke pollution as Pittsburgh grew and industrialized compelled public authorities to make some gestures at control. In 1868 the city councils passed a statute banning the use of bituminous coal or wood by railroads within the city limits, and in 1869 they forbade the construction of beehive coke ovens. Neither statute, however, was strictly enforced. During the 1880s, the discovery and exploitation of local supplies of natural gas provided the city with approximately six years of clean air. Exhaustion of the local gas supply, however, caused a return to soft coal as a fuel and to heavy smoke palls, stimulating various elite and professional groups to press for smoke control.[37] The Women's Health Protective Association joined with the Western Pennsylvania Engineers' Society to push for smoke control statutes. The city councils responded by passing a series of ordinances in the 1890s and in the beginning of the twentieth century that regulated dense smoke from industrial, commercial, and transportation sources, but not from domestic sources. In 1911, the city council created the Bureau of Smoke Regulation for enforcement purposes. Rather than legal sanctions, the bureau's director believed that education, training firemen to operate furnaces and boilers more efficiently as well as retrofitting with various smoke-consuming devices, would persuade polluters to stop producing smoke. Fuel efficiency, it was argued, provided an incentive, since smoke was a sign of incorrect firing and fuel waste.[38]

Although it had some limited success, the smoke control movement failed to control the smoke nuisance to any appreciable degree during the first third of the century. During the 1920s and 1930s, therefore, smoke and fuel researchers and regulators redefined the problem. They agreed that industries and railroads had made advances in eliminating dense smoke through technological and fuel improvements, by care in firing methods, and through cooperation with smoke bureaus. The smoke problem persisted, smoke investigators held, because of a failure to control domestic furnaces. Experts argued that smoke from household furnaces was especially objectionable because "the amount of black smoke produced by a pound of coal is greatest when fired in a domestic furnace and that domestic smoke is dirtier and far more harmful than industrial smoke."[39]

Domestic furnaces had not been regulated for several reasons, the most important being the political and administrative problems involved in controlling the heating habits of a multitude of householders. In 1940, there were 175,163 dwellings in Pittsburgh, of which 141,788 burned coal and 30,507 consumed natural gas; 53,388 of those burning coal had no central heating plant and used stoves to heat their homes. Smoke regulators lacked an effective administrative mechanism to control domestic smoke without hundreds of smoke inspectors. Politically, the issue was difficult because control threatened to impose higher costs for capital equipment and fuel on householders. And, because of a historical equation between smoke and prosperity in Pittsburgh and other industrial cities, it was difficult to develop a public consensus for stringent controls.[40] In short, the problem was one of devising a strategy to change individual behavior in regard to fuel use in the name of the collective social goal of clean air.

The climate of opinion in Pittsburgh in the late 1930s, however, discouraged discussion of smoke control. A city dependent on heavy industry, Pittsburgh was badly scarred by the Depression; clear skies suggested closed factories and unemployed workers. In addition, many local businesses were related to the coal mining industry, which also suffered severely from the Depression. As a sign of its belief that smoke equaled prosperity and its relief at the return of full employment, in 1939 the Pittsburgh City Council actually eliminated the Bureau of Smoke Regulation. "You'll never get elected again," said one politician to a member of the city council who supported antismoke legislation. "Don't you know, the poor people, they don't want smoke control. It's going to cost them more money." "We like to see smoke," added another politician; "it means prosperity."[41] Many working-class people held opinions such as these—although they found smoke a nuisance and an annoyance, they were concerned that smoke control would cost them jobs. Pittsburgh, therefore, appeared an unlikely environment for the passage of substantive legislation controlling smoke emissions from either industries or homes.

At the end of the decade, however, the Pittsburgh smoke control forces received a dramatic assist from the city of St. Louis, also an industrial center dependent on bituminous coal. During the period 1937–1940, under the leadership of Smoke Commissioner Raymond R. Tucker, St. Louis took major steps to reduce its smoke pollution. Tucker realized that the key to solving the city's smoke problem was to persuade inhabitants to use either a smokeless fuel or improved combustion equipment.[42] In April 1940, the St. Louis Board of Aldermen approved an ordinance requiring the use of smokeless fuel or smokeless mechanical equipment by fuel consumers, including homeowners. The essential control mechanism was city licensing of fuel dealers in order to control the quality of fuel at the source. The result of the first test of the ordinance in the 1940–1941 heating season was a series of smokeless days that city officials claimed was the result of the smoke ordinance.[43]

In February 1941, the *Pittsburgh Press* began a concerted series of articles and editorials pointing to St. Louis's success and asserting that Pittsburgh could also achieve clean air.[44] Most effective in mobilizing opinion were two pictures published on the *Press's* front page showing a smoke-darkened St. Louis street before smoke regulation and the same street sunlit after the control ordinances had become operative. Egged on by the paper, readers, especially irate housewives, began bombarding Pittsburgh Mayor Cornelius D. Scully with hundreds of letters a day demanding action. Delegations of civic officials and politicians visited St. Louis on a "civic pilgrimage" to examine the administrative machinery of smoke control and to assess its potential political costs. Most returned convinced of its technical feasibility.

Three individuals who might be called "entrepreneurs" for the collective social good—Abraham Wolk, a lawyer and city council member who supposedly became involved in the campaign because of the effect of the smoke on his asthmatic son's health; Edward T. Leech, editor of the city's most influential newspaper, the *Pittsburgh Press;* and Dr. I. Hope Alexander, director of the Pittsburgh Department of Public Health—provided leadership for smoke control efforts.[45]

The antismoke campaigners stressed the achievement of St. Louis in achieving clean air and emphasized that the benefits of smoke control would outweigh the costs both for the community and its citizens. In February 1941, the mayor appointed the Commission for the Elimination of Smoke, which represented a broad spectrum of the community. In his charge to the commission, Mayor Cornelius D. Scully declared that "Pittsburgh must, in the interest of its economy, its reputation and the health of its citizens, curb the smoke and smog which has made this season, and many others before it, the winter of our discontent." The commission included representatives of business, labor, government, the media, the health professions, and voluntary associations with a civic and a welfare orientation; the inclusion of three women reflected the campaign leadership's perception of the importance of women in achieving smoke control. A technical advisory group stood ready to present recommendations concerning control of specific sources such as railroads and metallurgical companies and to gather information on questions such as the availability of smokeless fuel and smokeless equipment.[46]

While the commission was holding its hearings, the Civic Club and the League of Women Voters conducted a countywide campaign of public arousal and education through a network of voluntary associations. While voluntary organizations of all types were represented in the network, women's groups were most numerous, reflecting the deep involvement of women in the smoke elimination campaign. As homemakers, women of all classes knew how much extra cleaning smoke necessitated, with the burden falling most severely on working-class women who lived close to the mills. Middle-

and upper-class women in the Civic Club and the League of Women Voters coordinated luncheons and lectures and provided speakers to interested groups.[47]

Eventually, the Smoke Elimination Commission held twelve closed meetings and four public meetings. The purpose of the public meetings was to give interested groups a chance to be heard but even more to "get across to the public something which . . . still needs more hammering—the need for smoke control. . . . It gives the papers and the Commission a show. It gives the people a chance to be part of [the] . . . meetings."[48] While the public meetings served the function of public arousal and information transmission about smoke's negative effects, the closed meetings provided information on the more policy-relevant questions: smokeless fuel and technology supply; costs; effects of the policy on the coal industry, coal miners, and the poor; and administrative procedures and timetables for enforcement. The discussion within the commission clearly reflected the conviction of its members that, with the right policy, the socially desirable end of smoke elimination could be achieved without excessive costs to individuals or to industry. As Chairman Wolk noted early in the commission's proceedings, "We want to make this city smokeless without hurting anybody."[49]

Controlling smoke, however, would not be costless. Among the groups that would be most affected were coal miners and low-income workers. The representative of the Mine Workers on the commission, however, appeared to accept the argument that smoke control would not substantially impact mine employment because the need for smokeless coal would actually result in the mining of larger amounts of bituminous.[50] As for working-class consumers, the commission took the position that smoke control would bring more benefits than costs to the working class because it suffered the most from the effects of smoke pollution.[51]

In spite of disagreements within the commission, all members, including coal industry and labor representatives, signed the final report. The report listed the names of two hundred voluntary organizations, including fifty-six women's clubs, twenty-four business organizations, and many labor and civic groups as supporters of smoke control. The report held that smoke elimination would "bring about a new era of growth, prosperity and well-being" for the city and would impose "little or no additional burden on the low-income groups of the city."[52]

The commission report recommended a strategy based upon control of smoke at the source. Over a staged two-year period, all fuel users would have to either burn smokeless fuels or utilize smokeless mechanical equipment. By controlling the quality of the fuel inputs into the city's metabolic engine, air quality would improve.[53] The commission also recommended the creation of a Bureau of Smoke Prevention to be housed in the Department of Health and headed by a "qualified engineer" with the power to impose fines and to seal equipment in case of law violations. Only public opinion, concluded the report, would determine if the city would become smoke free.[54]

After a delay caused first by the war and then by a shortage of smokeless fuels, the smoke control ordinance was implemented in October 1947. The most critical question in terms of implementation continued to be enforcement against domestic consumers. The Bureau of Smoke Control solved the enforcement problem, as had St. Louis, by focusing on the coal distribution yards (approximately thirty) and the coal truckers. It forbade yards to sell high-volatile coal for use in hand-fired equipment and forbade truckers to deliver it. Truckers hauling coal for consumption in the city had to be licensed and to have license numbers painted on the side of the truck for easy identification. Those caught hauling illegal high-volatile (or bootleg) coal were subject to fines, as were dealers who made illegal sales.[55]

Successful implementation, however, would not have taken place without the support of the newly elected mayor, David Lawrence, and the efforts of two newly created and allied organizations—the United Smoke Council (USC), consisting of eighty allied organizations from Pittsburgh and Allegheny County, and the Allegheny Conference on Community Development (ACCD), formed in 1943. The council's function was to continue public educational efforts about the need for smoke control.[56] The mission of the Allegheny Conference on Community Development was the development of "an over all community improvement program" for Pittsburgh, in which smoke control played a vital part. The ACCD was especially critical because of its concentration of corporate power and its help in providing the planning essential for policy implementation.[57]

In spite of many difficulties with fuel supply, the heating season of 1947–1948 showed a considerable improvement in air quality compared to previous years. An unusually mild winter aided in reducing the smoke palls. "PITTSBURGH IS CLEANER" reported the *Press* on February 21—the worst smogs were gone, homes were cleaner, and white shirts did not have black rings around the collars.[58] Because of the visible improvement in Pittsburgh air quality, public opinion shifted from limited to strong approval of the law.[59] During the next few years, heavy smoke nearly disappeared from the Pittsburgh atmosphere. In 1955, for instance, the Bureau of Smoke Prevention reported only ten hours of "heavy" smoke and 113 hours of "moderate" smoke compared with 298 hours of "heavy" smoke and 1,005 hours of "moderate" smoke in 1946.[60]

The improvements in Pittsburgh air quality that occurred after the implementation of the smoke control ordinance, however, were not necessarily the result of the type fuel and equipment substitutions projected by the 1941 policy makers. In 1941, and also to an extent in 1946–1947, those involved in formulating and implementing the ordinance assumed that coal would continue to be the city's dominant domestic heating fuel for some years. The price of natural gas and oil was higher than that of coal through World War II and supplies were erratic.[61] Clean air would thus result from the use of smokeless coal produced from local bituminous or the use of equipment permitting smokeless combustion of bituminous.

While the use of low-volatile and processed coal (Disco) and smokeless coal-burning equipment did play a role in reducing smoke in 1947–1948, they steadily declined in significance. Increasingly, low-priced natural gas, furnished by pipelines from the Southwest and stored in underground storage pools, became the dominant fuel used for Pittsburgh domestic heating.[62] The rates of change for the city are striking. In 1940, 81 percent of Pittsburgh households burned coal and 17.4 percent natural gas (from Appalachian fields); by 1950, the figures were 31.6 percent for coal and 66 percent for natural gas. This reversal represented a change in fuel type and combustion equipment by almost half the city households, most of which took place after 1945.[63] In addition, railroad conversion from steam to diesel-electric locomotives between 1950 and 1960 also greatly reduced railroad contributions to the city's smoke burden.

Because of the shift to natural gas in Pittsburgh, the reduction in smoke pollution would undoubtedly have eventually occurred without the smoke control law. The price of natural gas made it very competitive with coal from an economic perspective and heating with gas was much more convenient. But, while not as critical as some Pittsburgh boosters would have one believe, the Pittsburgh smoke control ordinance undoubtedly accelerated the rate of change to clean fuel. Comparisons in rates of fuel change made between Pittsburgh and other cities make this clear. The clear air initiative was also important as a motivating factor in the famous Pittsburgh Renaissance, convincing Pittsburghers that positive change was possible.[64]

The movement for smoke control in Pittsburgh also produced a similar drive in Allegheny County. Here, industry and the railroads played a much more prominent role in standard setting and timetables for implementation than in the city. The 1949 county law omitted some of the region's key industries, such as steel and coal, from having to meet any specific performance standards for air pollution. The County Bureau of Smoke Control had only a handful of inspectors and was not capable of monitoring and enforcing air-pollution restrictions.[65]

The resulting system of business-government cooperation in the county brought very uneven progress. While fuel substitution and improvements in technology reduced county air pollution, progress was negligible in several key areas. To a large extent, emissions of fumes, gases, and odors, especially from by-product coke ovens and open hearth furnaces, were not regulated, and high levels of industrial pollutants plagued steelmaking areas. It could be argued that the actual success in controlling visible smoke actually masked the importance of regulating the other elements present in air pollution. By the 1960s it was obvious to clean air advocates that achieving clean air in the Pittsburgh region required control of all activities that affected the metabolism of the city and the region rather than a selected few.[66]

Uses of the Land

While water and air are commonly thought of as inputs into the metabolism of the city, the land also needs to be considered as an input. The building of a city creates a new landscape fitted into and imposed upon a preexisting landscape. As geographer Ian Douglas notes, while the foundations of the built environment have to be designed in congruence with the rock structures and soils beneath them, city development can drastically change conditions.[67]

Over the course of the nineteenth and twentieth centuries, industry usurped the Pittsburgh area river banks, building on the flat land along the flood plain. Integrated steel plants constituted the largest installations, sited especially on the flat land as the river meanders between river and rail lines. Some observers of the Pittsburgh scene, such as Robert Woods, writing in *Survey Magazine* in 1909, admired the development of the site—the "involved panorama of the rivers, the . . . long ascents and steep bluffs, the visible signs everywhere of movement, of immense forces at work,—the pillar of smoke by day, and at night the pillars of fire against the background of hillsides strewn with jets of light."[68] Others, such as R. L. Duffus, writing in the *Atlantic Monthly* in 1930, bemoaned the landscape alterations:[69]

> From whatever direction one approaches the once lovely conjunction of the Allegheny and the Monongahela the devastation of progress is apparent. Quiet valleys have been inundated with slag, defaced with

refuse, marred by hideous buildings. Streams have been polluted with sewage and the waste from the mills. Life for the majority of the population has been rendered unspeakably pinched and dingy. This is what might be called the technological blight of heavy industry.

The devastation witnessed by Duffus was dramatically illustrated by the fate of the beautiful valley of Nine Mile Run (NMR), located at the city's eastern boundary. Nine Mile Run is one of Pittsburgh's major urban streams, named for its distance from the Pittsburgh Point. Its watershed drains the city's East End, winding its way southward down steep slopes to the Monongahela River. Throughout the late nineteenth and early twentieth centuries it had some minor development, serving as the site for a salt works, a few farms and houses, a golf course, and a natural gas field. Most significantly, it represented Pittsburgh's last remaining access point to the Monongahela River, since industry and railroads had already occupied the rest of the waterfront.[70]

Because of its beauty and its location close to densely populated mill areas, the valley attracted the attention of reformers concerned with Pittsburgh's environmental quality and social stability during the first quarter of the twentieth century. These Progressive Period reformers were largely the same elite individuals who had driven the campaign for water filtration and smoke control. Along with other urban reformers, they embraced the philosophy of Frederick Law Olmsted that a healthy environment would directly improve the well being of urban residents and reduce urban pathologies.[71] Their campaign was a part of a larger effort to exert control over the region's degraded environmental resources.

In 1909, George Guthrie, a Democratic reform mayor, appointed a Civic Commission composed of the city's leading business and professional leaders to deal with the deteriorating urban landscape. The commission interpreted its mandate broadly, embracing many aspects of urban and environmental reform. It employed landscape designer Frederick Law Olmsted Jr., son of the great designer of Central Park, as one of the commission's three major consultants. Olmsted prepared a plan for the city entitled *Pittsburgh Main Thoroughfares and the Down Town District 1910,* published in 1911. He recommended a new system of downtown roads as well as making suggestions for riverfront improvement, steep slope development, and transportation improvements. He also explicitly noted the value of Nine Mile Run:[72]

Perhaps the most striking opportunity noted for a large park is the valley of Nine Mile Run. Its long meadows of varying width would make ideal playfields; the stream, when it is freed from sewage, will be an attractive and interesting element in the landscape; the wooded slopes on either side give ample opportunity for enjoyment of the forest, for shaded walks and cool resting places; and above all it is not far from a large working population . . . and yet it is so excluded by its high wooded banks that the close proximity of urban development can hardly be imagined. If taken for park purposes, the entire valley from the top of one bank to the top of the other should be included, for upon the preservation of these wooded banks depends much of the real value of the park.

Unfortunately, a new mayor, Chris Magee, ignored many of Olmsted's recommendations for land use changes. While the city issued bonds throughout the 1910s for playgrounds and to maintain the city's four parks, it did not attempt to acquire Nine Mile Run, reflecting a preference for active recreation rather than open space.[73]

The next attempt to preserve Nine Mile Run for public use occurred in the early 1920s as a result of the activities of the Citizens' Committee on Civic Plan. The Citizens' Committee was originated in 1918 from the decision of a group of Pittsburgh elites to create a city plan and to develop "city planning in all its aspects in the Pittsburgh district." The committee established six task forces to examine a range of urban problems, including recreation. In 1923, the Recreation subcommittee issued its Report on Parks. The subcommittee noted that there was only one place in the whole Monongahela River valley—Nine Mile Run—that could serve as the location for a waterfront park since in all other locations railroad tracks or industry blocked access to the river. The subcommittee recommended that Nine Mile Run become an active waterside attraction, with a botanical garden, athletic field, camp and picnic grounds, tennis courts, a theater, and a lake with a small beach. Because the site was close to working-class residential locations, it would provide open space to groups otherwise distant from such amenities. By providing healthy recreation, the park could supply physical and moral stability in the community.[74]

The Citizens' Committee also recommended that the city adopt a zoning ordinance to control land use, a recommendation that various civic groups had made several times in the past. In 1923, the city council approved legislation providing for zoning including separate zoning for heavy and light industrial and commercial areas and for low-density and high-density residential areas. It also limited building heights in certain zones. The river banks were largely zoned as heavy industrial, with light industrial in back of the heavy industrial. The zoning board, however, designated the 238 acres of Nine Mile Run valley as residential, providing exceptional access to the river.[75]

But the zoning ordinance provided only limited authority to the community to control development, and it did not prevent spoliation of the valley. In September of 1922, the Duquesne Slag Products Company had purchased ninety-four acres in Nine Mile Run Valley for the purpose of disposing of the wastes of Pittsburgh-area steel mills, especially those of the Jones and Laughlin Steel Company, located in the city several miles down the Monongahela River. This purchase grandfathered the industry in the valley, since it took place before the city council approved the zoning ordinance.[76] For the mills, the location of NMR valley close to their operations was ideal, since it kept transportation costs low and provided them and Duquesne Slag with a competitive advantage.

Over the years from 1922 to 1962, Duquesne Slag acquired further land within the valley, gradually filling it with slag, often leaving sharp slopes as steep as 80 percent. The slag generated by the iron- and steel-making process and dumped by the company consisted of silica and alumina from the original ore. For every ton of iron more than a half ton of blast furnace slag was produced, while steel making produced a quarter ton of slag for every ton of steel. By the time of the cessation of dumping in 1972, over seventeen million cubic yards of slag were deposited in the valley, forming a mountain of slag that was up to 120 feet high. Although the land was zoned residential, because Duquesne Slag had purchased property in the valley prior to the passage of the zoning ordinance, their industrial use of the land was categorized as a "nonconforming use" and they were allowed to proceed. Protests over the years by neighboring residents did little to control the nuisances created by the slag deposition.[77]

When slag dumping ceased in 1972, city officials and developers began thinking of possibilities for site development. As one of the city's last undeveloped sites it had great potential, especially because of its location between Frick Park and the Monongahela River. The City Planning Department completed a site development plan in 1982. Following this, over the next decade, several private interests prepared development proposals suggesting a mix of residential, retail, light industrial, office, research and development, and parks development. The complexities of site development, however, were large, and funding and developers were hard to find. Issues relating to traffic and neighborhood opposition were especially significant, and none of these plans became a reality. [78]

In 1995, however, the Pittsburgh Urban Redevelopment Authority (URA), at the initiative of Mayor Tom Murphy, purchased the land in Nine Mile Run for $3.8 million for possible residential neighborhood development. Murphy believed that attracting a residential population back into the city from the suburbs was critical for urban revitalization. New homes in Nine Mile Run would be located next to the stable middle-class residential neighborhoods of Squirrel Hill and Point Breeze, providing a powerful magnet. Environmental assessments and planning soon began, and in 1996 Copper Robertson & Partners, a New York design consulting firm, released a master plan. This plan proposed creation of a new community with 950 to 1,150 "new urbanism" housing units (since reduced to 713 units) including a mix of stand-alone homes, town house–type units, and apartment dwellings. The development was also projected to include 114,000 square feet of retail space, an elementary school, and fifty-four acres of open space. The plan was to be developed in four stages. Not only would the city's housing stock be substantially incremented by development, but it also involved converting a brownfield into a new residential neighborhood. [79]

Community involvement in the city's design and management of the site increased after the original proposal. Public meetings on both the housing design and the extension of adjoining Frick Park were held. An important public-private partnership formed involving local groups, the developer, the city, and a team of experts from Carnegie Mellon University. A dramatic change in the original plan, driven by the ecological perspectives of an interdisciplinary group from Carnegie Mellon University's Studio for Creative Inquiry, provided for daylighting rather than culverting the NMR stream and creation of a green corridor reaching to the river. Other changes were made to meet neighborhood concerns expressed at public meetings about construction and traffic nuisances and possible environmental hazards. [80]

The successful development of Nine Mile Run through a partnership involving the city, Carnegie Mellon University, developers, and the neighborhoods reflects a sharp change in attitudes toward the urban environment and land restoration. Prior to the 1990s, the history of Nine Mile Run had reflected a failure on the part of both civic and elite leadership to take steps to protect land and water resources. In addition, the history reflects the reluctance of the city to take steps to protect both natural areas and residential neighborhoods against industrial interests. Thus, as Andrew McElwaine notes, it favored industrial interests over ecological and preservation values.[81] Values, however, do change, and today a new administration and a city population that increasingly thinks in terms of urban ecology have moved to restore the site and to bring it to a state of environmental sustainability. Whether such ecological development will continue on other Pittsburgh brownfield sites has yet to be seen.

This essay has developed the concept of metabolism in relationship to the environmental history of the city of Pittsburgh. In so doing, it has examined the domains of water, air, and land in regard to their use, misuse, and restoration. The use and misuse of environmental resources was largely predicated upon a value system that emphasized production and material progress rather than environmental protection. Restoration of environmental quality in domains such as the air and the land has also been spurred mostly by economic development concerns, although, ironically, significant recent improvements have occurred because of the collapse of the steel industry. Concern over environmental values has been playing a larger role in driving change, but progress has been halting, and many aspects of the environment wait to be redeemed. Thus, although the city's metabolism has begun to move toward a point of balance, further environmental leadership and policy is required to help it reach sustainability.

2

Los Angeles's Nature
Urban Environmental Politics in the Twentieth Century

Sarah S. Elkind

I N THE summer of 1943, an acrid cloud settled over downtown Los Angeles. On the streets below, cars collided as "lacrimous fumes" blinded drivers. City officials received letter after letter complaining that the smoke destroyed the community, "depressed . . . [the] spirits," interfered with vital war production and the pursuit of happiness, and threatened the public health.[1] A municipal judge found conditions so unbearable that he considered adjourning court until the fumes lifted, while the tuberculosis ward at General Hospital reported increased hemorrhages and death. As one angry resident complained, the fumes threatened to turn Los Angeles into a "'stink-a-roo' neighborhood."[2]

The location and character of these first "gas attacks" led most of Los Angeles to blame a Southern California Gas plant. As evidence mounted that this one plant could not possibly cause all the air pollution experienced across the city, a protracted debate emerged over the causes and consequences of air pollution. One side blamed industry. Angelenos living in communities hit hard by air pollution but without much heavy industry observed that air quality declined suddenly, and that this decline coincided with rapid wartime industrialization. They lobbied for aggressive regulation of industrial pollution by writing letters to elected officials, mobilizing their service organizations, women's clubs, and improvement associations, and eventually creating new civic groups to fight smog.

The diffuse group seeking aggressive industrial controls encountered powerful and politically well-connected opposition. The industrial and commercial communities recognized that aggressive smoke regulations could severely limit prosperity and development. The Los Angeles Chamber of Commerce and, later, the Western Oil and Gas Association used their considerable resources and clout to shape a policy that would not hinder growth. The chamber of commerce and the heads of major oil refineries worked together to develop uniform air pollution regulations across the county, and to enforce air pollution controls on the trucking, railroad, agricultural, and marine shipping industries. They also agreed that city and county officials should target small manufacturers for aggressive regulation, rather than enforcing rules just on the largest firms. Eventually, they would also lobby for control of air pollution from rubbish and garbage disposal, automobiles, and other residential activities. Nevertheless, these groups did not always act in concert. Indeed, by the late 1940s, debate over the role of oil refineries in creating smog opened a significant rift between the oil producers and the Los Angeles Chamber of Commerce.

By the 1950s, air pollution split Los Angeles into three very uneven camps, each of which believed that some other group caused air pollution, and, with varying degrees of consciousness, each of which sought to displace the costs of air pollution control on to the others. The least effective was made up of the civic groups and individuals that sought aggressive regulation of industry. This group was marginalized in the arenas where smog policy was actually formulated. However, it was also the group that most clearly articulated the priorities and frustrations attributed to the general public by elected officials, the chamber of commerce, and the news media.

Of the three groups, the chamber of commerce clearly wielded the greatest influence over smog policy. In contrast with Western Oil and Gas Association, for example, a membership that included many different business sectors protected the chamber from being labeled a special interest group. The prominence of that membership, the assistance with policy formation they gave the city council, and their strategy of cooperating with the city government all gave the chamber of commerce far greater access to and influence with elected officials than the other groups that competed to shape public policy.

The chamber of commerce secured its influence by cooperating with local officials and by providing the city council with policy recommendations, draft ordinances, and the research to support them. The chamber's emphasis on voluntary smoke reduction and on cooperation between industry and regulators seemed to promise improved air quality without lengthy political or legal battles. Also significantly, the chamber moved more quickly than could elected officials. Just a few weeks into the 1943 "gas attacks," the chamber began formulating its voluntary industrial pollution control program, a program that has been credited by historians with contributing significantly to the ultimate success of Los Angeles's air pollution control efforts.[3] Cooperation secured for the business organization a privileged place in politics unavailable to most civic groups. As the chamber assumed its status as the principal public voice in smog policy, it consistently directed official attention toward automobile exhaust and other nonindustrial sources of air pollution.

Industrial Controls

Smog afflicted Los Angeles as much because of its geography as its industrial economy or enthusiastic embrace of the automobile. The same atmospheric conditions that bring Los Angeles its celebrated sunny weather also create temperature inversions in which a layer of cold air traps warm air close to the ground. Particularly during the summer, these temperature inversions act as a lid on the Los Angeles basin, preventing polluted air from dispersing over the mountains to the west and north of the city.

Temperature inversions trapped thick haze in Los Angeles several times in the 1920s and 1930s. Most Angelenos did not recognize these as anything more than quirks of weather. At the time, Americans had no frame of reference that would cause them to identify this haze as a serious air pollution problem. By the 1920s, antismoke campaigns had targeted soot and sulfur from industrial and domestic coal use in many European and American cities. By the 1930s, two of the most polluted cities in the United States, Pittsburgh and St. Louis, had dramatically cleaned their air by replacing soft bituminous coal with cleaner burning anthracite. Even so, in 1947 Los Angeles's experts noted that St. Louis remained "far dirtier . . . with respect to dust and grime resulting from the products of combustion" than Los Angeles. The Southern California metropolis escaped the grubbiest aspects of air pollution by fueling its industries and heating its houses with electricity and petroleum rather than coal. Nevertheless, "no other metropolitan area . . . [had] a fume or noxious gas problem as intensely acute as that faced by local residents" of Los Angeles.[4] Los Angeles "faced . . . a totally different problem" from America's other industrial communities, which meant that neither the smoke-control programs nor the explanations of air pollution developed elsewhere applied in Los Angeles. It also meant that for many years Angelenos thought themselves exempt from smoke problems.

All Los Angeles's illusions about its sunshine and healthy air shattered in 1943. Five times between July and November of that year, inversions trapped industrial fumes, smoke from burning rubbish, and automobile exhaust in the L.A. basin, creating "daylight dimout[s]" and widespread respiratory and eye irritation.[5] The fumes concentrated downtown, near a Southern California Gas plant that manufactured butadiene for the federal Rubber Reserve Corporation. Los Angeles's first air pollution control efforts all targeted this plant. First, Mayor Fletcher Bowron and the city council negotiated plant slowdowns or shutdowns when weather conditions increased chances of "gas attacks."[6] When this failed to bring satisfactory relief, Bowron sought an injunction to halt butadiene production at the Southern California Gas plant. After an investigation of the fume problem, the Los Angeles County Grand Jury supported Bowron's injunction.[7]

George Uhl, the city health officer, endorsed the plant closing as a start but never believed that closing the butadiene plant would end the crisis. In September 1943, he reported that other industrial and vehicular emissions contributed to the city's fume problem. He urged the city to develop a "long-term program for atmospheric pollution prevention and abatement" and pressed for enforcement of countywide smoke ordinances.[8] Although Los Angeles's elected officials and the chamber of commerce soon echoed Uhl's demands for a regional approach to air pollution control, the rest of Uhl's analysis did not immediately receive much attention.

In fall 1943, Los Angeles experienced several severe fume events even though the Southern California Gas plant had temporarily ceased operations. Even so, Uhl's warnings about other causes of air pollution received surprisingly little attention.[9] Newspapers during these months did report other sources of fumes; however, complaints sent to Bowron and the city council during this period almost universally blame the butadiene plant. The Jewelers Union Local 33, for example, begged the city council for relief from eye-stinging fumes that caused "untold hardship and suffering" and "loss of working time and wages."[10] A stenographer in the U.S. Engineers Office compared "that screwy synthetic plant" to a piggery that "nice people . . . can't be around" and demanded "Why can't *you* do something about it? Aren't you important at all?"[11] The city council received additional letters from a real estate agent who protested the invasion of Echo Park by noxious fumes, and several complaints from individuals who felt that the industrial fumes exacerbated breathing problems or endangered their health.[12] Newspapers noted the growing and voluble public indignation, too.[13] Angelenos pinned most of the blame on the Southern California Gas Company.[14] The possibility that fumes might come from sources other than that plant had little impact on their perception of the fumes problem.

Southern California Gas did take significant steps to reduce butadiene fumes. In addition to immediately changing plant operations "to minimize . . . odors and fumes," in August the company began installing a new cooling tower to eliminate the fumes entirely.[15] In the eyes of Southern California Gas, these actions did not to amount to an admission of responsibility; the firm insisted, much as Uhl had, "that the general fume and haze condition over the widespread area is a combined result of all industrial operations, plus the motor vehicle traffic."[16] Ultimately, the war, rather than these arguments, protected the plant from more aggressive regulation.

During World War II, the American military rolled into battle on rubber tires. Truck transport was equally vital to civilian production. The war, however, had closed off the United States' access to rubber plantations in Asia. So the United States Rubber Reserve Corporation built a number of facilities, including a Southern California Gas butadiene plant, to manufacture synthetic rubber. When Mayor Bowron filed an injunction to prevent the plant from operating, the director of the Rubber Reserve Corporation, Bradley Dewey, responded immediately, flying out to Los Angeles to plead with the city to reconsider. Dewey insisted that Los Angeles should not close the plant unless the fumes interfered with other types of war production.[17]

The Southern California Gas Company weighed in with a massive public relations campaign in October 1943. The company took out full-page advertisements in all major local newspapers, including those most critical of Los Angeles industry. The ads reproduced a telegram from the secretary of commerce urging continued butadiene production for the war effort.[18] In one public statement after another, the Reserve Rubber Corporation, Southern California Gas, and plant workers all reminded Angelenos that butadiene was essential to synthetic rubber, and that rubber itself was a strategic material.[19] When Bowron suggested that the nation had a surplus of butadiene, and that Angelenos might benefit more from the gasoline that the plant used, one Rubber Reserve Corporation official snapped, "Do you want to ride around in your cars or do you want the Nazis to take over?"[20] As the Los Angeles Chamber of Commerce saw it, "precipitate action at this time could seriously hamper war production."[21] This analysis eventually prevailed. The city council withdrew the injunction just days after filing it, apparently convinced that any limits on butadiene production were "contrary to the best interests of the war effort."[22]

Given that fumes had nearly shut the butadiene plant down, Los Angeles's industrial leaders had reason to fear the political consequences of unchecked air pollution. On one hand, Angelenos clearly blamed industry for declining air quality. On the other hand, they accepted the fact that war required unusual sacrifices, and this made them less likely to challenge industrial pollution. By linking industrial production to the war, business leaders could portray smog as a mere annoyance and could dismiss those complaining about the fumes as unpatriotic. Connecting smog to the war effort allowed industries to shift the blame for pollution, and any number of other production-related social costs, to the federal government.

Through 1945, the war became L.A. industries' best protection from aggressive smoke regulation. In July 1943, Southern California Gas insisted that it would have halted production to prevent the fumes problem, but for the "urgent requirements of the United States Rubber Reserve." The company insisted that the Rubber Reserve Corporation, not corporate self-interest for example, demanded "that production be continued regardless of any annoyance to the public."[23] Standard Oil likewise blamed "government pressure to increase the production of 100 octane gasoline for war purposes . . . for their inability to operate their plant in a way that would avoid . . . nuisances."[24] Representatives of General Chemical "frankly admitted" that wartime operations increased noxious smoke.[25] Even H. O. Swartout, the head of the county office of air pollution control, noted that the demands of war production forced operators of trucks and trains to overload their machines and to keep trucks and trains in operation even when they needed maintenance.[26]

Newspapers also promoted the idea that the federal government and the war were responsible for L.A.'s problems. In early coverage of the butadiene fumes, for example, the Los Angeles Times not only explained the importance of butadiene to the war effort but also referred to the plant as "Uncle Sam's big butadiene plant" and to Southern California Gas as a company operating the plant for the Reserve Rubber Development Corporation.[27] Rather than targeting this one plant, the Times insisted that Los Angeles needed county-wide investigation of "all the fume-makers" inside and outside city limits.[28] All but one of the Los Angeles papers helped to diffuse public anger at industrial polluters by repeating manufacturers' arguments about the importance of the war industries. In the media, the war argument demoted smoke from a potential health emergency to a mere inconvenience.[29]

The war trumped both health concerns and public skepticism about the official analysis of air pollution. By the middle of 1944, the county health department concluded that wartime conditions made it too difficult to pursue aggressive smoke abatement, in spite of reports from city health officials that the city had received "too many authentic complaints resulting from continued and prolonged exposures to ignore the potential or actual health hazard" from irritating fumes.[30] Even Fletcher Bowron, who attacked industrial pollution more aggressively than most, hesitated to interfere with the war effort.[31] Meanwhile, the classification of smoke and fumes as yet one more temporary wartime sacrifice made it extremely difficult for Angelenos to challenge proposals to delay aggressive smoke controls until after the war ended. The war argument also obscured the role of private industry in causing pollution, or in designing regulations that shielded polluters.[32] The logical conclusion of this argument was that federal policies, not local businesses, both caused smoke and interfered with local smoke reduction efforts. Blaming the federal government for this and many other inconveniences experienced on the home front contributed to the campaign to dismantle the federal bureaucracy after 1945.

Angelenos did not entirely accept the "war emergency" argument. Civic groups and individuals refused to accept that the war made smoke inevitable or excusable. As one activist insisted, "Manufacturers who are profiting from the war effort should take it upon themselves to abate the nuisance they cause. We've done the impossible in the war. Don't tell me nothing can be done to get rid of this smoke."[33] However, as the desire to protect war-related production was generalized into a mandate against stifling L.A.'s industrial economy, smoke officials had few options.[34] Caught between a vocal minority that demanded immediate and aggressive industrial smoke controls, and industries that insisted such controls threatened first the war effort and then the city's economy, Los Angeles area officials sought alternatives to strict industrial regulations.[35] The chamber of commerce's program of voluntary smoke reductions provided one attractive approach; controlling nonindustrial pollution offered another.[36]

Nonindustrial Pollution

The winter of 1944 brought a brief respite from the gas attacks and from the bitter rhetoric that accompanied them. Summer's return, though, brought with it both the eye-stinging clouds and public demands for relief. Los Angeles's major industries continued to drape themselves in the flag. The chamber of commerce's voluntary smoke reduction program and the economic importance of industry also served to moderate elected officials' reaction to protests. So, from 1944 on, Los Angeles air pollution policy increasingly targeted garbage dumps, household incinerators, automobile exhaust, and other types of "consumer" pollution.

This is not to say that official smoke-control efforts turned from industry entirely. Mayor Bowron, caught as he was between public outcry and the need to protect the industrial sector, advocated aggressive industrial regulation—against small firms and minor industries. Thus, in 1944, the Los Angeles city attorney charged five companies, including two metal foundries, a freight carrier, and a lumber yard, with emitting excessive smoke.[37] Emulating St. Louis's strategy, the city council debated a mandatory change in railroad fuels.[38] Bowron now blamed L.A.'s problems on factories outside the city limits.[39] Many of Los Angeles's industrial communities had no smoke ordinances. Bowron and the Los Angeles Chamber of Commerce understood that inconsistent regulation in the Los Angeles basin both impeded pollution control and threatened their city's economic future. Their solution, uniform countywide smoke controls, put all industries on an even footing. This suggestion did more to protect all communities from smoke and, not coincidentally, delayed aggressive industrial regulation in Los Angeles.

The Los Angeles County Board of Supervisors responded to calls for countywide smoke rules by appointing a five-member Smoke and Fumes Commission to "get rid of the fumes without closing down the plants."[40] In September 1944, the Commission blamed the city's smog problem, as the newspapers now called it, on a myriad of causes, including locomotive smoke, automobile exhaust, and household incinerators, in addition to war industries.[41] This conclusion closely resembled the chamber of commerce's own 1944 analysis linking smog to "burning rubbish heaps, home incinerators, automobile exhaust gases, diesel engine smoke, boiler smoke, sewage and municipal rubbish heaps."[42] Other experts, such as the United States Public Health Service, confirmed the chamber's and the county's analysis, suggesting in 1944 that Los Angeles "authorities . . . can approach the problem from three angles, the factories, the lachrymatory haze in the air caused by automobile and bus gases, weed and rubbish burning, and a condition created by dust such as is sent into the air from rock and metal grinding plants."[43] The second county smog agency, the Los Angeles County Air Pollution Control District (APCD), replaced the Smoke and Fumes Commission in the late 1940s. The new district continued the Smoke and Fumes Commission's multifaceted approach. The APCD did pressure gray iron foundries and oil refineries to help them curb emissions, but the district's policy of working with industries to reduce smoke, rather than imposing sanctions on them, overshadowed industrial regulations in the public mind.[44] In all, county administration, despite its merits, institutionalized cooperation with the L.A. business community as well as the shift in regulatory focus from industrial to nonindustrial pollution.

The Los Angeles Chamber of Commerce was crucial to county smog programs, acting as a liaison between industry and regulators, and defending embattled air pollution control officials. When the county Air Pollution Control District's director was nearly fired to assuage an angry public in 1954, for example, the chamber's was one of the few voices raised in his defense.[45] Chamber representatives regularly attended city and county meetings on air pollution. In addition to the voluntary smoke reduction program, chamber leaders repeatedly invited "responsible members of the community . . . [to] take care of the recalcitrant members of industry," to pressure them, in other words, to do their part.[46] The organization did not stop there but also pledged to assist official smoke abatement efforts by informing all industries of anti-smoke laws, and urging compliance with those laws.[47] The APCD and its predecessor agencies welcomed the chamber's activities, embraced cooperation with industry, and judged both crucial to the success of smoke reduction in Los Angeles.[48] Major newspapers also credited industrial cooperation with significantly reducing smog. One editorial argued that only industry contributed appropriately to smoke-control efforts. Los Angeles's many residents, even those most critical of the APCD, neglected their responsibilities by burning rubbish in their backyards and operating filthy trucks.

Fostering cooperation with Los Angeles industry was, indeed, necessary, as many manufacturers fought even the county's limited smoke controls. Sometimes they insisted that regulations placed an unfair burden on their companies or gave competitors an unfair advantage. This concern undergirded uniform county smog controls from the very beginning. Some industries continued to take "advantage of their war status to keep from installing smoke-control equipment."[49] The American Cyanamid company, for example, closed its doors to civilian inspectors, citing military secrecy.[50] Other firms, Los Angeles oil refineries among them, argued that they had already spent so much on air pollution control that they could do no more, or that other polluters should bear the regulatory burden for a while.[51] In the face of this resistance, smog officials welcomed anything that increased compliance.

The chamber of commerce lauded "the cooperation of industry with the [Air Pollution Control] District, and the results which have been obtained."[52] Even Mayor Bowron celebrated voluntary cooperation between the city and industry.[53] That cooperation, and the chamber's role in building and enforcing it, together with the chamber's other smoke-control activities, gave the organization a great deal of influence over official smog policy. The chamber further shaped policy by sending representatives to speak at public hearings and at meetings between local officials and federal delegates. When the Los

Angeles county supervisors drafted air pollution legislation, they began their debates with a model ordinance prepared by the chamber.[54] The chamber's zoning committee consulted on smog and industrial zoning.[55] The chamber sent additional policy recommendations and research to the county supervisors through the 1950s.[56] Just as crucially, the chamber consistently praised the city and county for their cautious and "reasonable" approaches in the face of near universal public criticism from individuals, the Western Oil and Gas Association, and other business groups.[57] This support ensured that city and county officials treated the chamber as a valuable ally in the battle against smog. All these activities ensured that Los Angeles smog control reflected chamber priorities.

The chamber's activities did reduce industrial pollution and smog in Los Angeles. Ironically, these same activities earned the chamber more public criticism than gratitude. Even as media coverage of the chamber's findings shaped public understanding of the relationships between industry, automobiles, and smog, the alliance between the chamber and public officials left many Angelenos deeply suspicious that industry wielded too much influence over smog control efforts.[58] From 1944 on, newspaper reports and letters received by elected officials reflected a growing sense that the chamber did not, in fact, speak for the public in smog control. As the *Los Angeles Times* put it, "the question is the welfare of millions of residents here versus the selfish interests of a few major industrial concerns."[59]

Public impatience and suspicion of industrial influence on smog policy came to a head in the late 1940s, during the first years of Air Pollution Control District administration. Louis McCabe, the first director of the APCD, promised to reduce smog by curtailing emissions from "oil refineries, chemical plants, oil burning industries, and rubbish dumps."[60] He set pollution-reduction targets based on the district's research, and on the smoke-reduction technology then available. What emerged was a broad shotgun approach that satisfied no one. Industries, particularly the oil industry, criticized APCD research and rejected McCabe's emission standards as arbitrary because the APCD could not definitively prove which industries and which factories caused specific pollution problems.[61] State legislators criticized McCabe for neglecting his public responsibilities by basing pollution targets on available technology rather than on public health.[62] McCabe's plan to reduce pollution from garbage burned in open dumps and backyard incinerators led to accusations that he was "playing politics" with smog control, and that his proposals cost taxpayers dearly but did "nothing so far to eliminate smog conditions in Southern California"[63] McCabe, caught between public impatience and industry resistance, left L.A. under a cloud of public rancor in 1948.

Gordon Larson, the second director of the APCD, did not fare much better. The APCD finally won cooperation from the recalcitrant oil industry in 1948.[64] Following this milestone, Larson turned to automobiles. This change confirmed critics' suspicions that the oil companies had engineered McCabe's departure.[65] Where McCabe had dismissed as a myth the suggestion that automobile emissions seriously contaminated Los Angeles, Larson insisted that Angelenos' cars, not their industries, filled the skies with haze.[66] Even before there was conclusive proof of the connection between car exhaust and smog, Larson argued that invisible, not visible, pollution was L.A.'s real problem.[67] Although county supervisors received dozens of letters complaining that McCabe ignored the obvious problems caused by smoke-spewing buses, trucks, and poorly tuned cars,[68] the greatest challenge to Larson's policies came from people who did not see the connection between haze and internal combustion engines. Despite numerous newspaper reports of the hazards of invisible exhaust, even the Los Angeles City Council was frustrated and unconvinced by Larson's policies.[69]

Skepticism about the role of the automobile was justified. Properly operating cars emitted little visible smoke. Until the 1950s, all pollution control efforts, with the single exception of the 1943 proposals to eliminate butadiene fumes, focused on the visible black smoke produced by coal fires, inefficient boilers, burning dumps, and industrial operations. More to the point, there was no scientific proof that invisible fumes could cause visible haze, or that emissions not irritating to mucous membranes at their point of origin might somehow cause those symptoms later. In the late 1940s, A. J. Haagen-Smit of the California Institute of Technology theorized that Los Angeles's haze was actually the result of oxidation of hydrocarbon gases from car exhaust exposed to nitrogen oxides and sunlight. Larson embraced Haagen-Smit's photochemical theory of smog and campaigned relentlessly to convince Angelenos of its accuracy.[70]

Even after Haagen-Smit reproduced Los Angeles's characteristic smog in his laboratory, Angelenos doubted his findings. They dismissed photochemical smog as an unsubstantiated theory and "a lot of high-sounding nonsense." They accused Haagen-Smit himself of mixing random chemicals until he "came up with something that irritated the eyes and caused damage when sprayed on vegetation. He could have probably got the same results with Chanel #5, Seagrams-Seven, Seven-up or any of the fifty-seven varieties of Heinz pickles." These critics went on, insisting that Haagen-Smit and Larson had "no proof whatsoever that this reaction takes place in the streets and by-ways of Los Angeles."[71] The petroleum industry's aggressive campaign against Haagen-Smit and the APCD fed this skepticism, even though that industry's research eventually confirmed Haagen-Smit's findings.[72] Clearly, scientific proof alone would not convince critics to support Larson's automobile pollution policies. Shifting pollution regulations from smoky factories to consumers' automobiles seemed all too convenient for air pollution control officers whom critics already suspected of working too closely with industry.

Cars were a major problem; in Los Angeles their numbers increased at a rate twice that of the nation as a whole.[73] But those who rejected Haagen-Smit's findings did so at least in part because so little could be done about motor vehicle emissions in the early 1950s. Los Angeles could ban auto traffic, convince Detroit to build cleaner engines, or require L.A. drivers to install afterburners to reduce hydrocarbon exhaust.[74] The first of these options was, of course, impossible. As for the second, Los Angeles officials had little influence over the automobile industry; nevertheless, forcing Detroit to build cleaner cars or install "afterburners" to reduce tailpipe emissions was a major element of L.A.'s smog policy throughout the 1950s. The chamber of commerce "serve[d] notice on the automobile industry that this metropolitan area . . . must have automobiles with vastly improved fuel combustion" to reduce smog.[75] Engine designs did improve in the 1950s and 1960s, which helped some. The auto industry, however, dragged its heels on afterburners or other technological fixes; the Clean Air Act of 1970 forced the industry to install catalytic converters on all automobiles in the early 1980s.[76] Throughout the 1950s, auto executives disputed both their responsibility for Los Angeles's problems and any connection between car exhaust and air pollution.[77]

By 1955, most studies revealed that automobile exhaust contributed 50–60 percent of the pollutants making up Los Angeles's smog.[78] Whatever the numbers, the automobile industry was an easy political target for the APCD and other Los Angeles officials. Focusing on automobiles made smog, in the words of one L.A. county supervisor, "an engineering problem with the automotive industry bearing the primary responsibility."[79] Here was an industry that the APCD could blame without fearing that an aggressive stance would damage the local economy. Of course the chamber of commerce and public officials were not the only ones worried about the industrial economy. Even the most vocal antismog activists stopped short of condemning industry in general.[80] Only *The Citizen News* went that far, asking, "Why wouldn't this be a good time to adopt a policy against any more factories for Los Angeles?"[81] and suggesting that Los Angeles's fume problems were the just and predictable costs of unrestrained boosterism.[82] Industry might be a good scapegoat for public anger, but not one that most Los Angeles leaders would truly sacrifice for clean air.

The Chamber of Commerce and the Public Interest

In 1955, the chamber of commerce listed Los Angeles's polluters, in order, as cars, industry, and household incinerators.[83] But many Angelenos never found this assessment persuasive. Activists continued to blame refineries and industrial expansion, not auto exhaust, for smog and the Air Pollution Control District's apparent inability to eliminate it.[84] Why did these individuals so mistrust the scientific reports on car exhaust? In part because they did not want to bear the burden of smog reduction, and because blaming cars before the advent of the catalytic converter seemed only to provide an excuse for continued pollution. Critics also believed that industrial interests manipulated air pollution research and shirked their public responsibilities. As one letter writer protested to the county supervisors in 1954, "the question is, will entrenched greed and political climbers make the sacrifice necessary to remove this terrible plague?"[85]

In the eyes of those who enjoyed less influence, no one embodied "entrenched greed and political climbers" as completely as the chamber of commerce, and the chamber knew it. In 1944, the president of the chamber announced new smoke-control initiatives to prove the business community's good intentions "before the public gets too violent in its condemnation" of industry and the business organization.[86] The chamber leadership feared that such public condemnation endangered Los Angeles's future: "It is important that this thing be done smartly because if . . . smoke control is done unsmartly then it can be a source of harassment to Southern California industry of all sorts . . . and it can be used by cities elsewhere in Southern California as a good argument for not bringing industries here."[87] When the chamber's manufacturing and industry committee reported an urgent need for "adequate, factual publicity . . . to acquaint the people with the constructive voluntary program that has been and is being conducted by the Los Angeles Chamber of Commerce" to reduce smog,[88] an enormous gap persisted between the chamber's and the public's assessment of the business leaders' smog control activities. Angelenos nevertheless accused the chamber of "follow[ing] a very stupid, ignorant and selfish policy of placing private interests before the welfare of the citizenry."[89] Mayor Bowron and a number of newspapers reinforced this impression when they dismissed the APCD as lax and plagued with collusion.[90]

The chamber of commerce played a crucial role in the success of pollution control despite consistent public criticism. The chamber's insistence that industries reduce emissions contrasts sharply with the reactions of similar groups in other communities, and with Detroit's reaction to Los Angeles's appeals for cleaner cars, for that matter. The chamber's incorporation into the machinery of local governance, by drafting and reviewing legislation, for example, ensured that business was protected, even as industries reduced emissions. Meanwhile, scientific studies of air pollution made the smog problem appear ever more technical; this reinforced the chamber's role as mediator among the scientific, the economic, and the political worlds. Thus, the chamber was able to define public priorities—and therefore to reshape Los Angeles's image and landscape—to suit themselves, in spite of some persistent opposition.

Clearly, there were many publics in Los Angeles in the 1940s and 1950s. This fact complicates efforts either to assess public opinion in the past, or to examine the notion of the public good as anything more substantial than a rhetorical device. Likewise, it would be a mistake to see the business community as monolithic; the Western Oil and Gas Association and suburban chambers of commerce routinely opposed Los Angeles Chamber of Commerce policies. Regardless of the difficulties in finding the voice of the general public, the stream of newspaper editorials critical of smog policy in the 1940s and 1950s, the consistent references to public opposition to smog policy even in probusiness newspapers, and the emergence of a series of organizations critical of smog policy all indicate that a substantial number of Angelenos did not approve of the way Los Angeles city and county fought air pollution. The fact that so many of these protests were directed at the chamber or at the protection that the chamber secured for industry strongly suggests that a sizable public was also dismayed that the chamber exerted such influence in public affairs. For these Angelenos, the chamber tainted smog policy, and APCD policy protected industry and increased public costs of air pollution control.

3

The Environmental Transformation of the Ruhr

Ursula von Petz

VISITORS TO the Ruhr, expecting to find what has often been called a "black country," are today usually amazed by the remarkable amount of greenery that the region offers. This impression of green everywhere, combined with the lack of a continuous, high-density cityscape characterized by high-rise buildings and multistory housing blocks, apart from a few dense urban cores like the inner cities of Essen and Dortmund, makes the area as a whole seem rather like a large garden city.[1] Those who know it best, however, would still perceive the Ruhr as a worn-out urban landscape, with all its unused brownfield sites—land still contaminated by the defunct coal-mining industry. For decades the Ruhr basin had been an unpleasant place to live because of its crude settlement structure, its lack of a sense of a genuine natural environment, and its persistent bad image of dirtiness and ugliness. In fact, there is truth in both images of Germany's historic industrial heartland. Part of the Ruhr's interesting history is the effort to introduce greenery and improve the environment in which people live and work.

To some extent the Ruhr is an industrialized and urbanized territory where green is more or less what is left over in between the built-up areas, such as agricultural land that survived the period of industrial expansion. Different forms of unused land, such as that between railway tracks and the green strips running alongside the linear infrastructure of pipes, tubes, power lines, canals, roads, and motorways, help complicate the landscape. There is also open space in the form of derelict and temporarily unused, often contaminated land, where recently birch or ash trees have taken over, and slag heaps or waste tips are covered with bushes and grass. Large housing settlements and workers' colonies have gardens. Alleys, green and open spaces, sport fields, cemeteries, allotment gardens, and playing fields create their own network of greenery. Each of the many cities in the region has a park, but real forests are scarce or worse: they exist only at the area's margin.

Nevertheless, in comparison with its industrial heyday, the Ruhr agglomeration is now relatively green, although the original environmental conditions as well as the natural forms have been transformed fundamentally during the last 150 years of urbanization. Today, great efforts are being made to revitalize in an environmentally responsible way those areas that were heavily stressed by industrialization or badly treated by urban development. However, it is important to realize that these efforts did not simply begin with the famous International Building Exhibition (IBA) Emscher Park, which took place between 1989 and 1999 and which sought to transform the quality of this area. The battle to improve environmental conditions in the Ruhr must be traced to a long-standing confluence of economic, intellectual, and institutional developments. Some date back to before World War I, when planners and politicians first sought to better local living conditions. In the 1920s institutional structures were created that drew upon national and international planning models to find ways of improving the environmental conditions experienced by the working population as part of a larger goal of enhancing and preserving the economic wealth of the region. The very attempt to solve problems on a regional level was new. The collapse of coal mining and decline of heavy industry after World War II made initiatives combining environmental and economic recovery all the more imperative. The most noteworthy success in improving the environment depended upon solving problems on a regional level, and the Ruhr became an early role model.

Industrialization and the Origins of Regional Planning in the Ruhr

The Ruhr mining and steel industries started around 1850 and had a fast growth period in the 1880s. Industrial expansion was characterized by a feverish exploitation of natural resources, space, and people. The Ruhr area developed more or less according to the common profit-oriented behavior of entrepreneurs, who chose sites, built the necessary railway tracks, opened mines, and erected the supporting facilities, including one or two moderate housing projects for the workers and their families because existing settlements were not available. Most of these miners were migrants from foreign, mainly eastern European, countries, and the settlements, where some of them were housed, provided a small piece of land for each little cottage or house for growing vegetables and keeping chickens, a pig, or sometimes a cow to augment what for workers was a subsistence economy. These bits of land were not at all pretty gardens with shrubs, flowers, or a terrace. In contrast to the mining industry, the Ruhr steel industry preferred to use local workers, and steel mills were thus usually located near the existing cities and the existing housing market in the urban grid of multistoried blocks. Greenery was hardly to be seen, and then only in a few communal parks. Environmental arguments were not in the foreground, even if demands for better public hygiene were on the agenda.

To the north of the Hellweg—a former Hanseatic track running east-west from the Rhine River along the back of a range of modest slopes connecting the traditional towns—a little creek, the Emscher, meandered through marshes and muddy woods. From 1900 onward the Emscher was declared a regional open sewer and was canalized to flow for seventy kilometers from east to west until it passed a purification station and then flowed into the Rhine. At the same time the incredible rise in demand for fresh water by expanding industry and a growing population required an increased water supply, for which artificial lakes were constructed as reservoirs on the edge of the Ruhr region's hilly south. The sewer and the water systems, the first such projects of a regional scope, were organized by a special board with representatives from the local communities as well as from industry. But an improved water supply and a waste water system were only initial steps in addressing the problem of public health and environmental quality in the Ruhr.

Around 1900 a strong intellectual movement developed in Germany under the slogan of "Lebensreform," the desire for fundamental change in everyday urban life. Industrialization had come suddenly and rapidly to Germany after 1850, and its dynamics intensified after the Franco-German War of 1870–1871 and the proclamation of the German Empire, the Kaiserreich, in 1871. Cities like Berlin, Hamburg, Leipzig, Breslau, Frankfurt, and others developed with industrial areas of a dimension up to then unknown. Railway tracks were built everywhere, and high-density areas of multistory housing blocks on a grid road pattern formed barriers around the old, often medieval city cores. Straight roads only sometimes planted with trees were lined with rigid, schematically designed facades, usually at a height of about twenty-two meters.[2] Whole city blocks had no open space apart from small courtyards to give access to the fire brigade. These industrial cities grew through encouraging maximum speculation in the housing sector, but that process deprived their inhabitants of any access to an environment that most of them still remembered from times when they or their parents still lived in small and pleasant towns or even in the countryside.[3]

An urbanity that had initially been highly attractive, providing access to jobs, culture, education, and a modern lifestyle, was increasingly revealed as highly one-sided. "Aus grauer Städte Mauern zieh'n wir ins weite Feld, wer bleibt, der mag versauern, wir fahren in die Welt" (getting outside the grey cities' walls, we travel into the open country) became a famous song of the middle-class Wandervogel movement, which was one of the main reform groups of this time. Mostly the members of these different groups declared their desire to leave bourgeois civilization. They wanted to devote themselves to a nature-oriented life—to dress, eat, and live free from traditional family structures, experience the naked body in sun and fresh air,[4] but also to follow new political ideas, moral ideals, or aesthetic forms. They searched for contact with "real" nature; they wanted to return to a simple life, to compensate for alienation through the experience of nature.[5] This antiurban reform movement was certainly influenced by international debates about the English and American landscapes (John Ruskin and Frederick Law Olmsted) and by social utopian reformers like Robert Owen and Charles Fourier; but with Wilhelm Heinrich Riehl and Friedrich Nietzsche as probably the most outstanding figures, this reform movement acquired its own, distinctly German, character.[6]

The cultural historian and first German sociologist Wilhelm Heinrich Riehl (1823–1897), whose magnum opus, *The Natural History of the Nation* (1851ff),[7] made him famous, proclaimed that Europe—and certainly Germany—would have to endure great suffering because of the size of its cities.[8] From then on a strong anti-industrialization movement, idealizing in a romanticist manner preindustrial agrarian structures, can be traced back to Riehl's position about the value of the traditional social classes and their conservationist function within modern society. While it is true that, after Germany lost World War I and the empire collapsed, parts of this movement were transformed within the extreme National Socialist blood-and-soil ideology, the anti-industrial movement did provoke necessary social and cultural reforms before and after World War I. This reform movement was supported by many different parts of the society, ranging from proletarian organizations to anarchistic groups, advocates of land reform, agrarian romanticists, political parties, antibourgeois intellectuals, and reform-oriented specialists like the German members of the European-wide Arts and Crafts and Garden City movements, just to name the most important.

There were several lines of development here, but in nearly all cases there was some appeal to nature as articulated by Friedrich Nietzsche (1844–1900), who abbreviated his philosophy about the secular character of life in his formula of *homo natura*, which proclaims the identity of man *and* nature.[9] Indeed, *God* in Nietzsche's anthropology is identical with *nature*. Unconsciously or consciously virtually every German reform aimed to reapproach nature, be it on behalf of culture, art, architecture (light, air, and sun), fashion, philosophy, sport, agriculture, food, or science.

Reform programs could also be found in the Ruhr. Friedrich Alfred Krupp can serve as a representative of the conservative wing of the Ruhr reform movement. This great industrial magnate, based in the city of Essen, announced in 1900 a competition to solicit the best answer to the question how to apply the theory of evolution and hereditary change to national social issues and legislation. Krupp's initiative clearly derived from the enthusiastic reception given a prize-winning thesis about "the physical degeneration of the culture of mankind" (Über die drohende körperliche Entartung der Kulturmenschheit), written in 1891 by Wilhelm Schallmayer and based on theories of race and eugenics.[10] Schallmayer's work represents more or less the beginning of a small movement with pan-German, Aryan, and anti-Semitic contents that resulted in 1905 in the foundation of a regional branch of the Society for Racial Hygiene (Gesellschaft für Rassenhygiene).[11] Support for this racist movement grew in an area like the Ruhr, where the immigrant population was already substantial and increasing. The Society for Racial Hygiene existed right into the Nazi period, when it was transformed into a Nazi research institute.

While the pursuit of reform based on racial hygiene came to represent a perverted use of the ideal of nature, more moderate and progressive social reformers could also be found in the Ruhr. An important example is Karl Ernst Osthaus, son of a rich banker from Hagen, a city at the southern fringe of the Ruhr area. Osthaus did not want to succeed his father as a banker but preferred to use his money to sponsor the cultural development of the region. In his opinion the industrialized Ruhr suffered greatly from a fundamental lack of art and culture. Being an enthusiastic collector of modern art of his period (including works by van Gogh, Matisse, van der Velde, and Gauguin), in 1902 Osthaus opened in Hagen the Folkwang Museum, which he intended to make into an educational institution for the general population of the region. He also pursued plans to establish a modern dance theater in Hagen and to combine this with a reformed school system. As a member of the board of the Deutscher Werkbund (the German Arts and Crafts movement) and cofounder of the German Garden City Society (DGG), he not only started to build a garden city at Hagen (which subsequently became an artists' colony) but also invited members of the main office of labor welfare[12] to discuss the design quality of workers' houses. For the purpose of this meeting, Osthaus organized an exhibition of model housing that was to be inexpensive, architecturally sound, and sensitive to the environment.

Another key figure was Robert Schmidt, who in 1901 became head of the planning and building department of the city of Essen, where Krupp had established his huge enterprise, famous for its extensive armament industry but also for its worker-oriented programs, which included settlements featuring hospitals, schools or kindergartens, and a pension system. Copying English enterprises like the Lever Company, Krupp wanted to bind his labor force to the firm and thereby prevent strikes or outright rebellion. In the late nineteenth century, about half of Essen was owned or occupied by the Krupp factory, mining, and related activities. Naturally, the economy of the city was tightly linked to the ups and downs of this local enterprise. Concerned about the one-sided industrial base of the city's prosperity, around 1900 Mayor Erich Zweigert began to encourage new economic activity, especially in the growing tertiary sector. He successfully attracted the headquarters of the north German railway, the regional coal-mining agency, and similar institutions, but he also modernized the city's administration. He enlarged the city staff to include a new legal expert (Paul Brandi), a new administrator to head the public records office (Otto Wiedfeld, who later became ambassador to Washington), and a new planner in Robert Schmidt.

Schmidt was born in Frankfurt, studied engineering at Hanover, and began his career in water engineering in Düsseldorf.[13] As planner in Essen from 1901 until 1920, he exerted a dramatic influence on the city's development through the application of new standards in town planning. As he wrote in 1912, he aspired to create an urban environment where "a new type of city was about to be developed. . . . Two city types traditionally opposite to each other, the industrial town and the town of housing settlements, now will be merged." Industry and housing will become one, "a unity supported by technical progress, the economy, the local administration, public engagement of private people, and a sympathetic population, a city which merges into the landscape and the landscape into the city and thus creates a soil-rooted settlement full of health and beauty, without tenement houses (*Miets-kaserne*), a perfect modern urban organism."[14] His first design in 1904 for a new quarter of the city already rejected the traditional grid road pattern and its infill with rectangular blocks. He instead drew a sequence of two widened blocks that embraced a generous open space with green and trees that gave people's apartments access to green space and fresh air and also served as a public walkway, an attractive alternative to the sidewalk along the noisy street. Like Karl Ernst Osthaus, Schmidt was a member of the German Garden City Society, and in 1906 he was involved in the creation of one of the first German garden cities, the Margarethenhöhe. In 1907 Schmidt introduced a new building code in Essen to replace the previous code, derived from that in Berlin, and in 1908 he pushed the acquisition of a huge wooded area, the preservation of most of its natural structure, and its integration into the local network of green spaces.

Schmidt and Osthaus, who were acquainted, both moved in the direction of regional planning. The latter's vigorous activities for the betterment of the entire industrialized Ruhr, and the inclusion of objects designated for historic preservation (one of his special interests), suggest that Osthaus was either the actual author of or at least behind a pioneering regional plan published in 1907 in a local newspaper. In either case, there is no doubt that he was a major figure in the project.[15] The presence in the 1907 plan of proposals for improving the overall road network and implementing a system of green areas in the region indicates that the author or authors must have been focused on general interests, not those of particular industries. The plan's authors were convinced of the need for open space within a dirty and smoky area and for ready access not only to the workplace but also to recreational spaces. The plan demonstrated real conviction about the need to care for nature, to maintain woods and green areas, and to be attentive to the *natural* needs of men and women.

Around the turn of the century regional schemes for green and open spaces were developed in Vienna (by Heinrich Goldemund), Boston (by Charles Eliot), Chicago (Daniel Burnham), Berlin (Hermann Jansen), and elsewhere.[16] Most of these proposals were presented on the occasion of the first international town planning exhibition, which was staged in 1910 initially in Berlin and Düsseldorf and then in London. Schmidt prepared Essen's contribution for this seminal exhibition, which gave his career a new direction. The exhibition's opening at Düsseldorf was linked with a series of papers on planning practice, and Werner Hegemann, the architect and organizer of the exhibition and a man quite familiar with urban and landscape planning in the United States,[17] was one of the guest speakers. One outcome of the Düsseldorf exhibition was the establishment of a special commission to examine the possibility of designing a regional or national park on the east bank of the Rhine River that would include the western part of the still-industrializing Ruhr area. Schmidt became not only a member of this commission but also had to collect the material and to write the report, which he finally delivered two years later in 1913.

This report probably reflected Schmidt's own thinking more than that of the entire commission. In fact, to the irritation of his colleagues, he published it as his doctoral thesis. The main arguments contained in the report are calls:

• to extend regional policies to include the eastern part of the Ruhr region, specifically the area east of the cities of Essen and Bochum, including Dortmund and Hamm,

• to keep building heights in the region low in order to avoid replicating the unfortunate nineteenth-century-style housing areas based on a grid and large blocks like those found in Berlin, Breslau, Leipzig, and elsewhere,

• to care for green and open spaces in order to improve the physical and mental strength of young people (Schmidt believed that "where the sun can shine the doctor doesn't need to go"),[18]

• to improve the regional road network in order to better connect—with the growing use of motor vehicles—industrial, commercial, and market sites, while at the same time providing better access to woods and open spaces, on the theory that recreation would improve the health of the region's workforce.

Schmidt's thinking here also reveals his sympathy for nationalistic demands to support the development of a strong economy that was focusing on intensified armaments production and at the same time to strengthen the military capacity of the male population through better housing, recreation, and sports. What was needed was "a vital organism" for "a happy, content and lucky nation," which only can be established "when [housing] settlements as a whole are faultless."[19] In other words, this comprehensive regional general plan sought to offer the basis for "a healthy, happy, and industrious population whose national pride and patriotism will be motivated and strengthened by the feeling of being part of a perfectly managed organization, which is based on the principles of public welfare."[20] Thus, Schmidt was one of the many planners and intellectuals of this era who understood the city as an organic ensemble, whose defects could be remedied through active planning, just as a sick human was cured by a doctor.[21] Similarly, they were influenced by Ebenezer Howard, who believed that the industrial city was not a "proper environment for a human body" and that bad housing conditions eventually made a nation become anemic and weak.[22]

From this time on, town planners were dedicated to maintaining existing and developing new green and open spaces and to caring for the environment. As planners increasingly adopted the concept of the separation of functions in the modern city, green spaces and leisure facilities were added to the list of urban necessities, and not only for the improvement of hygienic conditions for the population. Hygienic measures had formed the basis of the early building codes in the nineteenth century, and the regional boards controlling water supplies and sewers came from this tradition. Now, in the new century, the ideal of green and open spaces shaped a more general demand for planning a better environment: the desire to improve living conditions in the cities, to tighten physically the contact between urban inhabitants and nature, to integrate contact with nature into sociocultural habits, and to use nature as a remedy for the alienation brought by civilization all became part of a new agenda.

World War I, which began just a year after Schmidt published his report on Ruhr future development, meant that any discussion about a coordinated regional strategy was postponed. But immediately after the war, in 1919, the discussion was reopened for several reasons. Germany had to pay heavy reparations, a great part of which consisted of Ruhr coal to be delivered to France. Also, the personal constellation was favorable. Hans Luther, the mayor of Essen (and later chancellor of the Reich), was adroit at taking advantage of the historic situation, and he moved to strengthen the role of the city through strengthening its administrative position in the region by locating additional public authorities at Essen like the Siedlungsverband Ruhrkohlenbezirk (SVR) and the Treuhandstelle für Bergmannswohnstätten, thus further widening its tertiary sector. Robert Schmidt, author of the 1913 proposal, still was head of the Essen building department, and the city's lawyer, Dr. Bucerius, cooperated in developing the legal framework. Furthermore, the responsible Prussian minister at Berlin, Heinrich Hirtsiefer, was a born Essener and another committed supporter.

The 1913 proposal thus became the blueprint for a Ruhr regional planning authority, the Siedlungsverband Ruhrkohlenbezirk (SVR), which was created in May 1920.[23] Established under Prussian law, the SVR was the very first German regional planning authority. Its main task was to save open and free space and to define routes for new through roads within a region where an age-old, chaotic tangle of often still-unpaved country roads and small connecting lanes hindered an efficient flow of growing private and commercial motor traffic. The geographic borders of the new authority were defined by the catchment areas of the coal deposits and not by historic political boundaries.

It should be noted too that the regional scope of the new planning agency corresponded to another important phase of growth, which was to be foreseen already in the 1910s and in fact took place in the second half of the 1920s. Numerous small and unprofitable coal pits or mines (there was no iron ore in the region, so ore was imported) in the region's south were closed down, and fewer but much bigger mines were opened or extended in the north. The construction of new housing settlements and related infrastructure had to accompany this economic migration process. The steel plants, however, remained where they had been and in fact were expanded. An inland waterway, opened in 1900, connected the growing industrial area with the Rhine, and when the railway network proved inadequate for the mass transport of heavy goods (ore, coal, coke, and steel), this waterway became— together with the sewer system of the former river Emscher—the east-west axis for development. At the same time various companies merged to form monopolies. A huge new company, the Vereinigte Stahlwerke (or United Steel Works, literally copied from U.S. Steel), was established to make Ruhr heavy industry more competitive on the world market. It combined coal mining and steel production under a single roof while at the same time widening its product spectrum in general, producing finished goods using the Fordist model of conveyor belt production. At the same time, the sheer volume and complexity of production and administrative tasks mandated a specialization and separation of economic and urban functions. Planning became an indispensable strategic instrument both for organizing this economic and management process as well as regulating and ordering the spatial and functional needs of heavy industry.

The early years of the SVR were difficult. In 1923, French and Belgian troops occupied the Ruhr to enforce reparations payments in coal. German passive resistance both further disrupted the economy and set off hyperinflation, and the monetary reform of 1924, while stopping inflation, resulted in a scarcity of money, which also hurt recovery. As a consequence the mining industry started to reorganize, closing down many inefficient mines in the south and concentrating its efforts in the north. Declining international sales in the mid-1920s brought other consolidations in heavy industry, as entrepreneurs feared an end to export-oriented industry. These changes brought both the migration of labor within the Ruhr and new unemployment among miners. Town planners had to come up with new housing settlements and consider how some of the unemployed might be resettled in agrarian areas. To organize the return of people to the countryside (which never actually happened) while encouraging economic growth, regional planning also would have been needed.[24]

In 1927 the SVR published its first plan. For the traffic network two schemes were worked out, one showing the existing railway network with some newly added links, another the planned road system. The road system was extremely important because it foresaw a new regional network, premised on the idea of individual mobility, connecting all the main urban centers of the area. Also, the plan contained a map of regional green and open space based on a detailed survey, and it noted potential areas of value that ought to be preserved for the future in order to improve the Ruhr's environmental quality. The survey showed a detailed catalog of "green" and "agricultural zones," "alleys," and "gardens." Furthermore, the SVR published a booklet about the conservation of woodland. The booklet did not constitute a plea to develop artificial parks but rather favored the idea that the hard life of miners and steel workers and their families should be relieved by experiencing real nature in forests, which consequently required the preservation and maintenance of existing woodlands. To Schmidt, the design of a traditional park was more suited to a middle-class society; in the Ruhr this was a rather small group, and it already enjoyed better living conditions than the miners and steel workers.

Further, a program for reforesting about three thousand hectares was developed between 1924 and 1930. It was a courageous initiative, even if at that time a drop in the ocean. Through zinc processing, much of the Ruhr's soil had become highly contaminated by lead and cadmium. Initiatives were also taken to reduce industrial smoke emissions, including both soot and dust. The most harmful pollution came from the coke plants and from metal processing, whereby sulfur dioxide merged with atmospheric humidity to fall as acid rain. Smoking chimneys in the early phases of industrialization visually and literally demonstrated wealth, but they damaged the environment, the people who were living in the workers' colonies built next to the plants, and the soil in the attached gardens, where the workers grew their potatoes and their cabbage. Depending on the distance of the emitting source, harvests in formerly fertile lands diminished, the growth of the woods was disturbed, the fruit and corn crops declined or became more prone to disease, potatoes grew less abundantly than elsewhere, and the quality of grazing land for cattle worsened and led to reduced milk production, not to mention that the water in creeks, rivers, and ponds was contaminated. Even the rate of miscarriages went up.[25]

The SVR started to develop countermeasures. It published a booklet about smoke control similar to the brochure about the maintenance of woodlands. Model farms were started to train staff in gardening, and in a tree nursery horticulturalists tried to grow especially smoke-resistant trees! Publicity campaigns were started to persuade the public to care for the environment. Regulatory standards nevertheless were low because the dominant national interests stressed a growing economy and wealth. The people's focus in the debates was to reduce the environmental damage caused by industrial growth, but the principle of free economic development stood against the individual desire for an absolute healthful environment and the right of unrestricted use of the private land.[26]

In 1927 a general building code was published for the entire Ruhr area—another innovation in thinking toward a regional development strategy, a prerequisite tool for the formulation of the regional plan. The plan regulated zoning and a general separation of functions,[27] as well as building heights and densities to fulfill hygienic and moral standards, still understood by Schmidt and others in a traditional way. Environmental issues were not explicitly mentioned but were instead dealt with—inadequately—through various commercial regulations (Gewerbeordnung). Nevertheless, with the introduction of this regional building code the authors had managed to set mandatory standards for the entire region, and each town in the Ruhr agglomeration was asked—and was in fact empowered—to prepare a general, unified economic or land use plan that would outline future development. The goal was to combine these plans and construct a first comprehensive regional economic plan (Wirtschaftsplan) that would also include the regional transport network, as well as green and open spaces. However, because of the economic crisis of 1929, several towns were unable to get their local plans completed and approved by their town councils, and the larger project remained unfinished. Nevertheless, a preliminary set of these "land use plans" was available at the end of the 1920s and had some strategic value.

With Hitler and the Nazi Party coming to power in 1933, forces returned that had opposed the founding of the SVR. They now agitated for dissolution of the SVR, but instead a director was installed who favored the institution and succeeded in proving that the SVR had not misused public monies, a charge leveled against it. In 1936, however, the SVR became part of a national planning organization (Reichsstelle für Raumordnung), which was set up by the National Socialists. Hitler's armament programs after 1936 forced the Ruhr's heavy industry to expand production, construct new facilities, and extract coal at any cost. Even if Nazi propaganda and its "blood and soil" emphasized the importance of nature and a German landscape—as evidenced by the central role of natural landscapes in the construction of motorways and the layout of new settlements—preserving open space in the Ruhr was endangered by economic recovery and military expansion. Preservation of nature was jeopardized even though in 1935 a national law for the conservation of nature was promulgated.

Even worse, the Nazis took those ideas about eugenics and nature that had been around since 1900 and used them to develop, justify, and systematically carry out unutterably inhuman, radical racist programs under the rubric of science. Thousands of people were murdered,[28] as pseudoscientific arguments were offered to rationalize an attempt to strengthen the Germanic race. At the same time the perception of nature also played a dominant role in the ideological conception of Nazi buildings, whether for party meetings, cult ceremonies, special monuments, or Nazi youth camps. Both sport and education were linked to modern ideas about the positive effect that sun, air, and light would have for a healthy nation. In the early years of the regime, Nazi urban renewal programs adapted the decades-old interpretation of human settlement as an organic entity. Thus, in 1940 an urban renewal proposal in Frankfurt was praised as the correct way "to eradicate the sick structures [in order] to rescue the healthy and what is valuable for life."[29] But with the beginning of the war and then the bombing of Germany's cities, this discussion quickly ended.

Regional Planning and Environmentalism in the Ruhr since 1945

The Ruhr Regional Planning Authority was revived shortly after 1945 under the leadership of Philip Rappaport, who had served as the associate director since its founding in 1920. He had come to Essen in 1919, having worked in the Prussian welfare ministry under Minister Hirtsiefer, who had supported the activities that had led to the founding of the Authority. Rappaport's initial job in Essen was as head of the so-called Trust for Miners' Housing (Treuhandstelle für Bergmannswohnstätten), a new agency created parallel to the SVR because single industrial enterprises were no longer building housing projects by themselves. Throughout the Weimar Republic, the state had taken most of the initiative in housing construction because the private sector had failed so badly in providing a sufficient housing supply before the war.[30] Since the concentration process in the Ruhr mining industry continued, with the mines extending farther northward, circumstances favored a regional policy on public housing, and the new trust was better placed to decide about the location of new housing settlements than individual mine companies. Still adhering to the principles of the Garden City movement, housing of a more modern design could now be built at a healthful distance from the emitting industry, in an environment of sun, light, and air, with green and open space around the dwellings and a much better infrastructure than before.

When the SVR, as the authority responsible for strategic planning, was constituted in May 1920 by the legislative assembly, Rappaport was unexpectedly nominated, along with Robert Schmidt, as a candidate for the director's post. Schmidt got the appointment, but Rappaport—the newcomer from Berlin—got the position below him. Those two could not have been more different. Schmidt, the "artist," had been one of the social reformers; Rappaport, the "technician," was a conservative Protestant. Schmidt proved an excellent ambassador for the SVR, so that this institution soon became internationally known; Rappaport remained the practical planner, interested in traffic systems and road planning. During a journey to the United States in 1927, Rappaport studied road intersections, the separation of lanes, and other details for automobile traffic. As a specialist in settlement planning, he drew up land use plans for about thirty-six towns in the region. Schmidt became a founding member of the new German Academy of Town Planners in 1922, was elected its president in 1924, and in 1925 took part in the international conference of town planners in Washington, D.C., where he gained international recognition. Rappaport was less known to the public, although he was known to professionals in the United States as an excellent practice-oriented, technocratic town planner. Schmidt, who Berlin had sought to win away to take over planning in that city, was not reappointed when his term of the SVR directorship expired in 1932, and he died in 1934. Rappaport hoped to become director, but because of accusations that he had improperly made money in the planning process, and because he was half-Jewish, a prominent post was impossible under National Socialism. He had, in fact, for some years lived in a hiding place.

When the war ended, Rappaport quickly contacted the new political authorities at Düsseldorf, the capital of the newly created state Northrhine-Westphalia. In comparison with the more centralized prewar governments, the position of the federal states had been considerably strengthened. Prussia had been abolished, and authorities responsible for the Ruhr were no longer in Berlin, the capital of the former Reich and of Prussia, but Düsseldorf. Düsseldorf was Rhenish, the Ruhr Westphalian, a not unimportant difference. Untainted by any Nazi past, Rappaport seized the opportunity to revive both his career and the Ruhr Regional Planning Authority. The SVR was reestablished in April 1945; Rappaport became its director, a post he held until retirement in 1957 at age sixty-five.[31]

With Germany's economy in shambles in 1945, restoring coal production was crucial in supplying energy to slowly recovering industries and heat and electricity for urban populations. Hence, in spite of the Allies' program of dismantling German heavy industry, there was no question about the need for coal mining. Those who advocated a modernization and diversification of the monostructured production sector of the Ruhr were generally unheard, and Rappaport belonged to those who favored continuity with the old economy rather than change. But in the late 1950s the mining industries experienced a serious crisis in sales, which resulted in the shutting down of mines—mainly those that had managed to survive in the southern part of the Ruhr region. There was consensus between the mining industry, the unions, the chamber of commerce, the employment bodies, and the SVR that, while new industries should be established to substitute for the closed mines, the coal and steel industry would doubtless be the industries of the future. Between 1957 and 1961, the biggest coke plant ever, one kilometer in length, was constructed in the northern part of Essen—today it is part of a UNESCO heritage site. To replace the loss of mining in the city of Bochum, a branch of the Opel car company was opened. New small- and medium-sized industries were welcome. But even though the centrality of traditional heavy industry remained, there was once again growing attention toward environmental subjects. A variety of publications came out from the early 1950s onward concerning green and environment. Titles like "Grün im Revier"[32] (Green in the Ruhr Area) were published in 1953; articles were written about landscaping in the area (1954), the natural integration of gravel pits (1954), a new technique for deposit slagheaps (1955), public walkways (1958), the protection of woods as well as the protection of landscape (1957), landscaping slagheaps (1957) or transforming "grey slagheaps into green hills" (1965), recreation and water (1962), "greening" parking lots (1960), and the relationship between cities and landscape for the purpose of recreation (1961).[33] The strong movement to better the environmental conditions in the Ruhr motivated Willy Brandt, later chancellor of West Germany, as early as 1961 to demand energetically "a blue sky over the Ruhr."

These activities were based on or stimulated by a new planning instrument. In 1966, two decades after the end of the war, the SVR adopted a second major regional plan. This plan drew upon several overlapping theories or models, which were the internationally accepted tools of town planners.

These included: the Athens Charter and its theory of the separation of functions, the London plan with its green belt design of 1944, Walter Christaller's theory of central places, the newly developed system-theory techniques, and a Keynesian understanding of public planning with the state as a major player. A planned greenbelt for the Ruhr region was given a linear design, oriented north-south, in order to separate better the various urban settlement areas from each other and thus introduce green areas as new structuring elements into the "endless" urban agglomeration. Following Christaller's central place theory, hierarchically defined centers of leisure, leisure parks and leisure facilities, were located within the greenbelts and connected and coordinated with a public transportation system designed with system theory–based modeling. Additional greenery was to fill the spaces between high density housing blocks or developments, around single-family houses, and around new shopping areas and schools. It also accompanied walkways, parking lots, and all the different types of new roads. The new philosophy was to locate within any new settlement as much green and open space as possible, with adequate opportunities for leisure and education. Slagheaps were greened for the first time to improve the appearance of the mining sites. Moreover, the establishment of the newly built green areas and generously equipped parks for leisure was strongly promoted to the public and was widely accepted.

But despite these new SVR initiatives, the Ruhr's negative identity as a dreary region or "black country" remained. The forces that did not see or want to agree to the need for modernization were still too strong for any alternative economic scenario. In the late 1960s and early 1970s the idea that coal mining, steel production, and chemical by-products in their traditional forms might not have much of a future was not fully appreciated in the Ruhr.[34] In fact, oil and nuclear power were taking over the energy market, and information and communication technologies, rather than coal mines, basic chemical production, and steel mills, were driving the new economy.

Nevertheless, with the 1966 plan much more attention was paid to environmental questions. For the next decade the SVR was eager to fulfill its task of planning and building recreation facilities of different levels and size. A new department of leisure planning was established, and the Authority also became more severely concerned about dumping and disposal systems for industrial waste and contaminated materials. The awareness of negative environmental impacts, such as the negative effects of uncontrolled depositing of contaminated waste, grew. Noise as well as air pollution were restricted by special decrees or technical regulations, although these worked more through prescribing a greater distance between the emitting source and the location of affected people than in seeking a reduction in pollution. The measures taken in these years that concerned the environment were in a general sense technical and short term, aimed at preventing immediate damage, rather than part of broader, sustainable policies of the sort that came later.

The early seventies can be seen as a new era in terms of genuinely public discussion. In Germany, this development came out of the political turmoil of 1968, which was the product of the new generation of students responding to the first research that showed how many institutions as well as persons—some of whom had been their own professors or parents—had been involved in Nazi politics.[35] The rebuilding generation immediately after 1945 had gone to work, unable to come to terms critically with the National Socialist past. The students' revolt became linked with an international left-wing movement, mainly in France and Italy, and it also got heavily involved in the antinuclear movement. This cause became an important source for the debate about the growing negative ecological effects of old-style, large-scale industrialization. The publication of the Club of Rome Report in 1972 was a milestone in this development. In that same year, a new planning law was published in West Germany that gave top priority to renewing, through careful attention to urban quality (*behutsame Stadterneuerung*), parts of essentially nineteenth-century cities characterized by large tenements. This new direction was to replace the older policies of comprehensive redevelopment. Planning now also legally guaranteed citizens' participation in the process. In 1975, on the occasion of the European Heritage Year, the listing of an industrial site as part of a town's heritage was accepted as a conservation tool.[36] After intensive debates, the German Green party was founded in 1980, with its main objective the devotion of its political work to preserving a sustainable environment.

These political changes did not affect the Ruhr as a region as much as they did the big cities, but they nevertheless influenced developments in the decade between the early 1970s and 1980s.[37] The Ruhr area changed slowly, and the economic decline in coal mining and steel production was accompanied by a growing interest in seeing derelict industries as "historic sites" and understanding the era of industrialization as a historical period now over. It has turned out that this history has become part of the region's potential for revival.

In 1975, fifty-five years after its founding, the SVR was dissolved. Its responsibilities for designing regional plans were transferred to those bodies where they resided before the founding of the SVR.[38] Regional planning for the Ruhr is now done by district planning departments located in the district governments of Düsseldorf, Münster, and Arnsberg, all located on the far edges of the Ruhr basin.[39] In 1979, a successor to the SVR was established, but as a public relations agency, Kommunalverband Ruhrgebiet (KVR). Nevertheless, it still has a landscape planning department with coordinating functions for planning and establishing intercity parks and open spaces. The KVR also has some regional responsibilities for garbage collection, which has received considerable attention because waste disposal enterprises have closed down and left behind environmental damage at their dump sites.[40] The 1980s thus saw a weakened sense of regional responsibility at the same time that the economy experienced a further decline. The state government tried to support various financial programs, but the number of contaminated brownfields now increased quickly, without any hope for new use.

A New Approach

In 1989 the state of Northrhine-Westphalia announced a program named International Building Exhibition (IBA) Emscher Park. It followed the failure of the attempts to subsidize regional economic restructuring, which had had little impact despite large investments. The new program was based both on spatial planning and creating incentives for new development by rethinking regional perspectives on built-up structures, open space, and the environment.

This program was not only a new approach in regional planning but stood—following the economic change from modernism to postmodernism—at the margin of a new relation between man and environment, a relation in which the environment represents the point of reference instead of the human being.

The new vision in architecture presumes that man should be the focus, that he needs quiet repose in the rush of life, that his distracted nerves, so dangerously shattered by the intolerable noise of traffic and by the continuously changing scene of life, must be balanced by the harmony of his dwelling. Quieting surroundings, simplicity, and harmony of forms and colors, instead of a superabundance of bygone or meaningless forms and ornaments, prepare for his creative pause. They will fit him to relax, to contemplate, to think precisely, and to produce new ideas. . . . Meanwhile, we have another healthful way in which to overcome our bastard civilization or borrowed ornaments. If traditional form becomes hollow and insignificant, man must turn back to nature, his source of eternal renewal. Closer contact with nature will render us more productive. The forms of nature are never dull, can never offend as man's work may do. So the modern architect has started to open up our towns by letting nature reconquer the stony desert of our living places. He (man) is beginning to realize that, by blending architecture and vegetation, a truer way of enriching our surroundings may be found than by any ever so skillful application of so-called traditional ornaments. Growing trees and plants ingeniously interwoven on and between buildings, with vistas opened and shut out, enhance the mutual effects of plants and buildings. The shadows of trees, shrubs, and flowers, in sunlight or in artificial light, on exterior or interior walls, purposely combined with the various textures and materials of their surfaces, present to us a beautiful screen of patterns that impregnates our imagination with ever changing vivid impressions.[41]

With this statement in 1938, Walter Gropius placed man in the center of architectural design and planning. But by then the modern movement had already developed fairly far, and man controlled this modern world and made it fit for his use, for a "mankind world."[42] Probably the IBA, with its new understanding of a natural environment and the offer of new possibilities in its use, stands at the start of a new approach: instead of modern thinking that it is a human privilege (*Humanprivileg*) to use and exploit nature, an understanding might be possible to see man himself as a natural being and a part of nature. Wilderness and brownfields, with their aesthetic qualities, make part of this new environment.[43] This viewpoint might mark the beginning of a new understanding of human urban living conditions (*Menschenbild*) and future urban planning.

During the decade allotted to the IBA (1989–1999), various measures were developed for the improvement of the worn-out landscape and its revitalization. The implementation of these measures was carried out through a series of projects, which were of crucial importance. The list included such ideas as:

• renaturalizing the Emscher canal system, now that its use as a sewer for industry had declined,

• building a landscape park along the Emscher (using a master plan, section concepts, and local projects as planning tools and tools for implementation),

• improving living conditions and building new housing in the park,

• developing new forms of working in the park,

• considering industrial monuments as landmarks for cultural identity,

• requiring new construction to adhere to strict ecological standards.

Renaturalization of the Emscher system did not mean restoring the Emscher to its former character as a meandering creek. Instead, only small parts have been redesigned in this way, with the result that this "nature," artificially created at enormous cost, is a kind of fake. However, a start was made to transform a stinking open sewer running in a dreary open concrete channel into an attractively landscaped canal, with the contaminated water kept separate in an underground pipe system—a solution that became possible since the danger of land collapses due to subterranean mining had diminished. But even with the mining at its end, there will be a need for long-term sewerage. New footbridges and landings to improve the crossing facilities and to better the accessibility to both sides of the canal were designed as art objects rather than only technical structures.

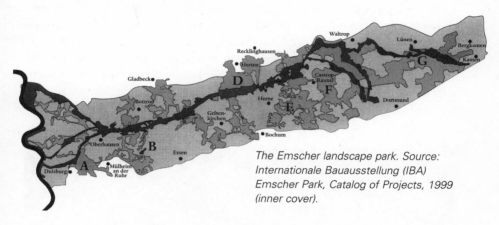

The Emscher landscape park. Source: Internationale Bauausstellung (IBA) Emscher Park, Catalog of Projects, 1999 (inner cover).

The Emscher landscape park uses the greenbelt system of the mid-1960s structure as its basic skeleton, adding a spinal park, oriented east-west, along both sides of the canal (see map above). This design has the effect that the park now works as a unifying grid instead of a separating linear system. Integrated in the park is a great variety of different types of green and open space, although many brownfield sites remain, along with derelict land where postindustrial vegetation has taken root and grown. Contaminated ground makes agricultural use impossible. But a variety of artificial treatments now function as a kind of laboratory for new approaches to landscape design, creating new forms of landscape, some sections that were designed by artists, and other areas where garden shows of various types have been organized during the last decade. Apart from those already greened in the 1950s, slagheaps that still had the image of the huge waste dumps that embodied the negative side of economic wealth, where access was strictly prohibited and only sometimes secretly used as playgrounds, were reinterpreted as objects that represent an important historical period of human sweat and dirt.

Art objects, objects of cultural or regional reminiscence, rather than real monuments, have now been erected on top of several of the highest heaps, where they offer some kind of orientation within a formerly diffuse spatial structure. Tetrahedrons, Bramme (a tall plain steel slash designed by Richard Serra), sundials, laser optics, and a reused gasometer are the new landmarks the people of the region are now becoming acquainted with: hundreds of people passed the Millennium night on top of or under the tetrahedron that crowns the slagheap at Bottrop, which has been turned into a "landscaped" hill of mining debris. (See figures 1–4.)

A great many brownfield sites still lie unused, but others have been converted into technology or industrial parks. A former mining area now houses a state academy, heated with solar energy and surrounded by a landscape park the design of which is intended to reveal the earlier history and the character of the site. New housing settlements were constructed under ecological standards and were mainly built for new social groups, like single parents with children or mixed households of young families and elderly people.

Figure 1. Art object: Tetrahedron on top of slagheap, near Bottrop. Source: Internationale Bauausstellung Emscher Park, Catalog of Projects, 1999, p. 348.

The regional housing market needed and still needs such diversification in an area where the housing stock is still largely dominated by traditional family-oriented flats or houses or miners' cottages. Visitors and residents encounter no landscaped park in the traditional sense, apart from the older ones surrounding a few old manor houses or a few traditional town parks. There are, however, new landscaping projects using colors, material, or forms derived from the period of the Ruhr's industrial glory. One of the outstanding examples is the landscape park Duisburg Nord, the site of a former huge steel plant, which would have been extremely expensive to pull down. The steel plant is now a combination of climbing frame, museum, and leisure area with a vast territory offering various sorts of "gardens," sometimes of very simple design or of unexpected aesthetics. A former ore basin is now a highly frequented climbing "garden." At night, the huge former steel plant is spotlighted with bright colors (designed by Jonathan Park, of Fisher Park, London), a tourist attraction known far outside the Ruhr. The biggest mine of the area, constructed in 1929 in Bauhaus style, together with the adjacent coke plant, fully one thousand meters in length, has just been designated a world heritage monument by UNESCO. It is now used for a variety of cultural events.

Figure 2. Cultural object: Sundial on top of slagheap, near Schwerin. Source: Internationale Bauausstellung Emscher Park, Catalog of Projects, 1999, p. 357.

There are about ninety single IBA projects of different sizes that have been realized within the last decade, mainly in the northern part of the Ruhr along the Emscher. Unfortunately, these projects have not been enough to fight successfully the Ruhr's continuing economic stagnation, but in their variety many of these projects demonstrate how the environment could slowly be improved to better the condition of life for the people who still live here as well as offer high-quality locations for a new economy in the region. The sky over the Ruhr indeed is now often blue, as Willy Brandt had wished forty years ago. And there are many more green and open spaces than Robert Schmidt might have imagined eighty years ago; far more attention to environmental matters in the process of planning and building housing settlements than thirty years ago; and a growing popular public consensus about accepting the remaining industrial structures as part of a history that only recently has come to be understood as a medium for regional identity. With the SVR dissolved, the IBA terminated, and a formally acting Ruhr Agency as a successor, the politically weaker KVR is more or less providing administrative leadership apart from direct political influence by the state (*Land*). The Ruhr, as defined by coal mining and steel production, is now gaining its iden-

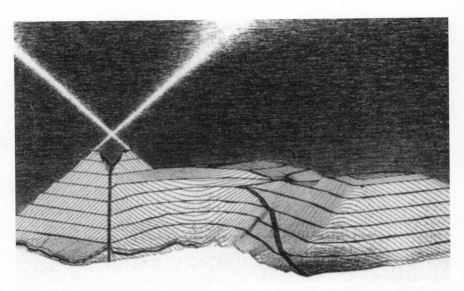

Figure 3. Laser light: Advanced technical installation on top of slagheap, near Rugenberg.
Source: Internationale Bauausstellung Emscher Park, Catalog of Projects, 1999, p. 363.

tity from its history. With this as a new background it certainly fights for regaining importance by attracting new economic activities.

Given the future needs of a knowledge society, the many universities in the Ruhr region, which have expanded considerably since they were founded in the late 1960s, are a positive resource in the region. This scientific backbone, concentrated mainly in the south (in the cities of Dortmund, Bochum, Essen, and Duisburg), together with the new landscape and cultural strength of the IBA Emscher Park in the north, certainly gives the region the potential to handle further development.

After roughly 150 years of continuous industrial use, the Ruhr area is seeking new possibilities of economic growth. Enterprises of the new economy demand a good environment, a pleasant landscape, and good housing. Culture and tourism are also important for the future. The IBA Emscher Park was conceived as a laboratory, with the region as its training area in a creative sense. Since the Ruhr remains the home and workplace for about 3.5 million people, the imaginative efforts of the past decade can help us to think not in terms of contaminated land without value but rather of an urban landscape that challenges us to think in new ways. Time and training are needed to get

Figure 4. Industrial reminiscence: Gasometro at Oberhausen. Source: Internationale Bauausstellung Emscher Park, Catalog of Projects, 1999, p. 364.

used to this urban landscape, but it also offers the challenge of understanding that an agglomeration the size of the Ruhr or Emscher region has the potential for future development. Very recently a "Masterplan Emscher Landscape Plan 2010—new perspectives for the conurbation" has been published.[44] It certainly is written in the tradition of the IBA philosophy when it says that open space is the platform for economic activity and innovation. With this goal it embodies the capacity for renewal where the creation of a new kind of green environment gives an old industrial region a new identity.

PART TWO

Countryside

■ Ursula von Petz's chapter in the previous part of this volume provides a useful bridge to thinking about the areas beyond the industrial cores. By addressing regional concerns, Petz reminds us that cities themselves are parts of larger geographical units. The chapters in this part extend the analysis beyond the city borders, first into the suburbs and then into the rural areas of the western United States. The three authors show how law and technology have allowed reconfigurations of the landscape, whether through suburban sprawl, hydraulic mining with its concurrent erosion, or attempts to regulate recurrent floods. In each case, human actors have tended to see the land both as something completely malleable and as something whose value is best measured in terms of economic productivity. In each case, too, there is something surprising about all of this, whether it is the role of investors in unwittingly supporting sprawl, or the way in which the costs of hydraulic mining have been hidden from view, or the belief system that concludes government agencies should spend exorbitant amounts of money to protect a small number of farmers from natural forces. The processes at work in the rural and suburban countryside are much like those in the cities.

As cities have grown, the sheer needs of a large, concentrated population have everywhere meant, as Joel Tarr put it, consumption of air, water, and land. In America that consumption of land has often taken the form of huge suburbs that have dramatically transformed the landscape. In "Of REITs and Rights: Absentee Ownership at the Periphery," Elizabeth Blackmar concentrates on one form of real estate development in detail, namely real estate investment trusts, or REITs. The projects of the big real estate trusts reflect absentee ownership, and actual development is often in the hands of corporations with little or no responsibility to the local community. REITs are democratized trusts, pooling the capital of millions of Americans, but without those investors taking a concrete interest in how their investments transform the environment in which they live. Just as the Federal National Mortgage Association and the Federal Home Loan Mortgage Corporation helped turn home mortgages into financial instruments no longer controlled by local lenders, REITs took commercial development to an equally abstract plateau.

Individual investors can buy shares in REITs like any other security without knowing anything about the actual properties under development, though of course large institutional investors do know. Among the latter, Blackmar notes that the Teachers Insurance and Annuity Association (TIAA), the largest pension fund for educators nationwide, has been a heavy investor in commercial real estate, including suburban shopping malls like the largest of them all, Mall of America. Large-scale developers command resources that enable them to fight off court challenges, including those raised on environmental grounds. The developers have their own environmental experts to prepare their own impact studies, and if need be they can wait out local opponents. In other words, in order to understand commercial development as part of the blight of suburban sprawl, one needs to follow the money—and the big, absent investors—to see how difficult it is for local citizens with environmental concerns to resist with success.

While land use is a central issue in the next chapter, conflicts over water rights are central in Nancy Langston's "Floods and Landscape in the Inland West." Here the issue is not torrents of water made and directed by man to extract mineral wealth but instead the varied responses to floods in the Malheur Basin in southeastern Oregon. Fed by the Blitzen River, the basin had been a frequently changed landscape shaped by seasonal water flows that ranged from floods to droughts. In the last quarter of the nineteenth century, this area was turned into the home of one of America's largest cattle empires by Peter French; though he drained swamps and built dams and ditches, he did not try to engineer the waterways as to prevent the spring flooding that enriched the land. When the seasonal grasses died, French used wild riparian hay to feed his herds. By contrast, homesteaders and small ranchers wished to prevent all flooding and use the water for irrigation, and this put them in conflict with French, who was killed by one of the homesteaders.

Beginning in the 1930s, much of the land in the basin, now reduced to dust by overexploitation, was bought by the federal government to create a wildlife refuge. But rather than simply allow the wild and irregular water flows to resume, the refuge's managers sought to manage both water flow and wildlife populations. This attempt at control led to major campaigns to poison invasive plants and animals, such as an invasion by carp. At the same time, studies were under way to determine whether an even more extensive system of dams and irrigation channels could control floods and increase agricultural productivity. Severe floods in the 1980s, however, overwhelmed the efforts to manage nature. Even the Army Corps of Engineers was unable to come up with a canal system that would both justify the cost of construction and satisfy the concerns of a public with new environmental concerns. As a result, the managers of the basin have been seeking a new compromise between the needs of human residents and ecological tourists and the forces of nature.

Drew Isenberg demonstrates in "The Industrial Alchemy of Hydraulic Mining: Law, Technology, and Resource-Intensive Industrialization" that the extraction of gold in California was in fact not the work of lone prospectors but rather that of large-scale hydraulic mining firms that had an enormous environmental impact on the river valleys of the Sierra foothills, the basin of the Sacramento River, and the area of San Francisco Bay. To control and utilize water flow, miners dammed rivers and diverted the water into ditches and sluices that fed pressurized water cannons. High-pressure water was deliberately used to erode river channels and embankments to wash gold into sluices where it could be recovered. Adding mercury to the water, which amalgamated with gold to form heavy deposits, increased the yield. Thus, hydraulic mining of gold stimulated auxiliary industries, like iron foundries for the manufacture of equipment, timber harvesting to produce the planks for the sluices, and mercury mining. In this way gold extraction became capital intensive, not labor intensive.

Since gold constituted only a tiny fraction of the material hosed out of the foothills, the remaining debris had to go somewhere, and Isenberg shows how debris deposits also transformed the landscape. In some of the stream valleys it was eighty feet deep. It raised and reshaped river beds, filled some of the Sacramento valley with silt, covered farmland, and polluted the water. The mud on river bottoms destroyed salmon spawning grounds, and mercury still contaminates some river bottoms. But even as the gold was extracted, contests appeared in the 1870s between mining and agricultural interests over water rights. These political and legal disputes initially favored hydraulic mining, but by the 1880s they shifted in favor of the growing large-scale agricultural industry of the Central Valley. Gold mining declined, and we are left with the mythological image of the lonely prospector, not the destructive machinery that in fact transformed large parts of the California landscape in such a short time.

4

Of REITS and Rights
Absentee Ownership in the Periphery

Elizabeth Blackmar

FOR MORE than thirty years environmentalists have identified suburban sprawl as a source of ecological degradation. Since the 1970s, half a million miles of new roads have paved the way to new houses, office buildings, industrial parks, and more than forty-three thousand shopping centers.[1] Between 1970 and 1990, developed land in metropolitan areas grew by 74 percent while population grew by 31 percent, an ongoing trend that can be verified by looking out the window during any transcontinental flight.[2] New phrases have been coined to characterize ever-extending suburban landscapes—exurbia, edge cities, urban fringe—which are widely understood to waste energy, destroy habitats, drain water supplies, erode farming as a way of life, and deplete a sense of connection to community.

Since the rapid conversion of farms into subdivisions became visible as a national trend in the 1950s, historians have offered a variety of explanations for Americans' gargantuan appetites for suburban real estate.[3] The expanse of land made it cheap, and taxpayer-funded highways made it accessible. Federal subsidies for low-interest mortgages and generous tax policies encouraged Americans to buy the homes that builders found most profitable to produce at the edge of settlement. Americans are said to be exceptionally attached to single-family detached houses and, in the postwar era, particularly mistrustful of the congestion, fiscal burdens, and social conflicts of central cities.

Debates over the environmental costs of sprawl, however, arose alongside new houses. As residents of postwar subdivisions encountered the strains that rapid development placed on water, sanitation, and clean air, the historian Adam Rome has argued, they formed a crucial constituency for the environmental movement.[4] To counter that movement, opponents of environmental regulations revived a nineteenth-century discourse of property rights, equating ownership with both freedom and stewardship. ("The truth is," Thomas Bethel typically writes, "private property is conducive to a more careful stewardship than public ownership."[5]) Funded by corporate backers seeking to dismantle policies protecting clean air and eliminating toxic waste, the architects of the property rights movement also challenged local zoning legislation and slow-growth initiatives. Development at the periphery was simply the demand-driven consequence of Americans' desires to "get away from it all." Freed of state impositions, homeowners, like Western ranchers or timber companies, would look after their estates out of enlightened self-interest. Moreover, commercial developers followed simple market logic and performed a public service by adding office parks and shopping malls to the communities that were emerging out of a shared individualist ethos. In legal challenges to environmental and zoning regulations in the 1980s and 1990s, the movement further propagated the purity of the twin American instincts of proprietorship and entrepreneurship by featuring as plaintiffs individual landowners or, in one key case, a church.[6]

If both critics and defenders of development at the periphery have long explained sprawl as the sum of individual landowners' desires and rights, historians and geographers have also begun to redirect attention to the "supply side" of the equation, observing that what makes it possible to develop land is capital, and the flow of capital into the American countryside in the last quarter century reached unprecedented heights.[7] Much of this concentrated capital investment in real estate has delivered its profits to beneficiaries far removed from a particular site. Absentee ownership, of course, is not new to the American landscape. Corporations are owned at a distance by stockholders; and large syndicates have acquired distant tracts of land for everything from cattle raising and oil exploration to the construction of resorts and vacation homes. Still, when it comes to suburban land, persistent images of homeowners and local developers have obscured something that is new in scale and scope. Institutional investors and especially pension funds, real estate investment trusts (REITs, pronounced "reets"), and deregulated banks—all using a panoply of new financial instruments—channeled vast amounts of capital into the American countryside to produce a landscape that not only embodied the art of the deal but also defeated local opposition.

The new institutions and modes of absentee ownership, whether stakes in a pension fund or shares in a portfolio of real estate securities, have transformed land not merely into a commodity—land has been a commodity in North America since the seventeenth century—but into a nonmaterial form of property, a claim on a stream of income abstracted from geography. Land values, of course, continue to rest on land use, but absentee owners seldom see that use, and not seeing land, they have little prospect of imagining themselves within a land ethic. That ethic, defined by Aldo Leopold as the foundation of any environmental movement, calls upon people to understand and preserve land's biotic or life-sustaining, and often noneconomic, value to themselves and to all species.[8]

There are particular and appropriately American ironies in the fact that absenteeism has found a home in the democratization of trusts, long associated with landed elites or plutocrats. The modern trust manager's fiduciary duty to make money, minimizing risks while maximizing returns, wreaks havoc with notions of personal stewardship over place. Trustees have no duty to care for land or buildings that have ceased to generate revenue. Land investments that pool risks, moreover, have attenuated conventions of entrepreneurship alongside those of ownership, eliminating the investor's need, for example, to personally evaluate the condition of particular properties. But opponents of environmental regulations link property rights to individualism and free enterprise in part to avoid talking about corporate forms or practices. And when environmentalists invoke concepts of social property or commons as alternatives to unchecked powers of private appropriation, they largely overlook the peculiarly socialized modes of real estate ownership that have, in effect, secured the retirement of millions of Americans by financing the production of a landscape they will not want to retire into.

This chapter illustrates how new institutions and instruments of absentee ownership have shaped real estate development at highway interchanges and suburban edges by looking briefly at the production of shopping centers, among the boldest markers of sprawl. Large commercial developers themselves defer to the narrative of demand-driven development. In order to obtain credit, they draw on sophisticated demographic and market surveys to show that sufficient numbers of tenants and customers exist in a particular region to sustain rents in stores and offices. In this sense, shopping malls are said to follow rather than propel outward movement. Such chicken and egg formulations, however, miss equally important issues of scale and cultural signposting, the self-fulfilling prophecy achieved when the location of key commercial institutions at interchanges brands a new territory for more intensive development. The "single best real estate investment in the world is a dominant regional mall," the vice president of one real estate investment trust told *Chain Store Age Executive*—"a mall is the center of its community and attracts millions of people each year."[9] They also have attracted other enterprises: as the geographer Michael Conzen put it when describing the Woodfield Shopping Center in Schaumberg, Illinois, "The original mall attracted all the other flies and insects around it."[10] At the end of the twentieth century, in response to close readings of consumer trends and competing returns, many institutional investors, in fact, turned their backs on retail development in favor of office buildings, luxury apartments, and storage facilities. But precisely because the absentee owners of shopping centers can so readily change their spots to fit into the larger investment environment, they reveal the contours of a new property regime in which land ownership, far from fostering personal stewardship, has lost its grounding in the natural world.

Real estate development is inherently local: buildings occupy land and define location, and the value of land varies according to very specific local economies. Through much of the twentieth century, speculative builders launched their ventures with the help of businessmen or bankers who knew the area. The first speculative builders to produce suburban shopping centers in the late 1940s and 1950s were often family firms. In Iowa, for example, Matthew and Martin Bucksbaum built their first shopping center for their father's four-store grocery chain in Cedar Rapids in 1956 and followed it with other centers in nearby towns, and then in nearby states—Illinois and Wisconsin. The brothers Melvin and Herbert Simon, originally from the Bronx, got their start with strip shopping centers, or strip malls, in Indianapolis in 1959 and built their first enclosed mall in Fort Collins in 1964. And Edward DeBartolo started building gas stations and supermarkets in Youngstown, Ohio, in 1944, followed by his first strip mall in 1948. In the 1950s, cultivating legends about his knack for identifying prime locations by flying his airplane over cornfields, DeBartolo declared himself the "plaza king" of the Midwest. By 1965, his company owned fifty shopping centers in six states. Similar stories can be told for other leading mall developers, including many who got their start in the 1950s or early 1960s in California.[11]

The first generation of mall entrepreneurs also quickly began collaborating with national retail chains to develop standard practices for the location and design of shopping centers. They mastered the use of market surveys to reassure creditors of the viability of their commercial speculations. Still, many lenders to untested large-scale retail outlets set tough terms. In the mid-1960s, independent grocers and pharmacists complained that they were shut out of shopping centers when financial backers required that tenants have a million-dollar net worth, as was true almost exclusively of chain stores.[12] The mall developers' trade organization, the International Council of Shopping Centers, founded in 1957, helped codify and publicize strategies of retail development, including different approaches to financing ever larger projects. Paying close attention to the industry's innovations, the Simons, De-Bartolos, and Bucksbaums moved from building strip shopping centers, or plazas around grocery stores, to malls with two facing rows of shops anchored by department stores at either end, to producing enclosed "regional malls" by the early 1970s. Through the first decades of growth, the family firms incorporated but most remained privately owned and heavily dependent on the goodwill of local creditors and planning boards as well as chain store executives.

Commercial real estate in outer suburbs was not a big draw for bankers in the late 1950s and 1960s. The high risks of speculative construction had long discouraged real estate lenders from venturing beyond local markets, closely watched by local managers.[13] Savings and loans concentrated on the housing market; and before 1970, many banks, headquartered in central cities, were fighting with state legislatures to gain greater access to suburban depositors and commercial borrowers through branch banking.[14] Business loans were thought to be more profitable and reliable than commercial mortgages. Several trends, however, encouraged investment beyond the fifty-mile radius that had traditionally marked mortgage lenders' territory. One trend, of course, was federal policies that not only spurred home purchases by guaranteeing mortgages but also established mechanisms for circulating mortgages far beyond individual home buyers and the actual property that secured their debt.

As the Federal Housing Authority and Veterans Administration helped underwrite suburban development in the late 1940s and 1950s by guaranteeing low-interest mortgages, Congress also nationalized the home mortgage market by establishing and funding the Federal National Mortgage Association (FNMA or Fannie Mae). Employing standard mortgage forms, Fannie Mae pumped money into suburbs by purchasing home mortgages from banks, which could then lend those funds to other home buyers. In 1968, when Fannie Mae was reorganized into a federally charted corporation that sold shares to private investors, Congress authorized it not only to purchase conventional mortgages but also to issue securities on pools of those mortgages. In 1970, Congress created the Federal Home Loan Mortgage Corporation (FHLMC or Freddie Mac) as another federally sponsored institution that could buy and sell home mortgages bundled into new financial instruments. The accelerated circulation of home mortgages among distant lenders offset the federal government's own promotion of longer terms, usually thirty years, instead of the short-term mortgages of the 1920s. In retrospect, we can see that the formation of a national mortgage securities market to provide Americans with easy credit to buy homes not only bolstered demand but also provided one rehearsal ground for the revolutions in real estate finance that intensified commercial development on the periphery in the 1980s and 1990s.[15]

Federal support for inexpensive, secure, and liquid financing for home ownership was accompanied by other policies that underwrote commercial building in the suburbs in the 1950s and 1960s. The historian Thomas Hanchett has shown how the 1954 federal tax law, which permitted owners to calculate and deduct the depreciation of investment properties on an accelerated schedule, drew into commercial real estate new investors seeking tax shelters. Indeed, Hanchett argues, these tax shelters helped speculative builders secure the capital to erect some thirteen thousand shopping centers by 1970.[16] Generous and fictitious depreciation allowances for suburban development accelerated the literal depreciation of central city neighborhoods. And because this tax policy rewarded investors in the early years of a building's life, it also accustomed absentee owners—whether prospering physicians, lawyers, and businessmen, or managers of philanthropic funds—to moving their money in and out of large real estate projects.

In 1986, Congress dismantled tax shelters in commercial real estate and thus shut down one stream of capital that fed suburban sprawl. But by then the largest mall developers, having grown in size and national distribution, had also established close ties to the country's leading institutional investors. Insurance companies like Prudential Life Insurance Company, Thomas Hanchett finds, "supplied the money for a surprising number of the landmark projects that redefined suburbia" in the 1940s and 1950s, including subdivisions, shopping centers, and industrial parks.[17] Managers of pension funds, like insurance companies, viewed real estate as a secure and reliable long-term investment, one that balanced portfolios of government and industrial bonds and provided a hedge against inflation. Equitable Life's commercial loans doubled between 1956 and 1965, in part because managers found "large-unit loans" cost less to service than residential mortgages.[18]

Among the most important strategic institutional alliances that shopping center developers made was with the nation's largest pension fund, Teachers Insurance and Annuity Association (TIAA). TIAA was organized in 1918 by the Carnegie Foundation as a contributory pension fund for the nation's educators. As was true of insurance companies, its investments during World War II were weighted heavily toward government bonds. But by the late 1940s, TIAA was taking up FHA-guaranteed and VA-secured mortgages, often for suburban subdivisions, which, the 1950 TIAA annual report observed, "enable[d] close supervision and approval of original plans and subsequent economical inspection and servicing."[19] Also in the late 1940s, the teachers' pension fund moved into commercial mortgages, backing stores, office buildings, and garden apartments. In 1952, TIAA lent $19 million on "shopping centers, super markets, and stores" and a half million dollars on "motor courts, restaurants, and service stations," together a small proportion of the fund's total assets but a harbinger of things to come.[20] Over the next decade, with fully half of its assets in mortgages, TIAA's managers gradually shifted the balance between secured residential mortgages and commercial mortgages. By 1965, loans for commercial development exceeded home mortgages, which paid lower interest rates precisely because they were federally secured.[21] TIAA's mortgage portfolio was diversified by region as well as by building types. Just as the 1952 annual report noted the advantages of wholesale production of subdivisions, so too did it announce the placement "of relatively larger proportion of its investments in those areas of the country that are developing most rapidly," meaning that New England received 2 percent of TIAA's investment capital in 1952 compared to the 13 percent that the Southwest and the Far West each received.[22] By 1960, its commercial mortgages served forty states and included such projects as a $2.5 million loan for Sacramento's innovative Southgate Shopping Center and $850,000 for an office building in Eddystone, Pennsylvania.[23]

TIAA's trustees and managers were proud of its status as a backer of shopping center development. Noting in 1972 that "only two or three financial organizations in the country have larger shopping center portfolios than TIAA," the annual report chose its mortgage for the Woodfield Shopping Center—130 acres in a Chicago suburb and anchored by the country's largest J. C. Penney and Sears stores—to illustrate the expertise of its investment committee, composed of a director of the Bowery Savings Bank; the chairman of a construction company; a former real estate executive with the Melville Shoe Company (parent of the Thom McAn chain, which had opened one hundred new stores in shopping centers since 1965); and an economist, Joseph L. Fisher, who was president of Resources for the Future, a nonprofit environmental think tank founded in 1952 with a grant from the Ford Foundation.[24]

In the context of the 1960s urban crisis, TIAA's trustees also supported James Rouse's new town project, Columbia, Maryland, "designed to avoid problems that usually accompany urban growth," and later backed Rouse's innovative Faneuil Hall project in downtown Boston.[25] But the $39 million that went into the utopian Columbia, or the $20 million earmarked for central city rehabilitation projects under the insurance industry's Urban Investment Program in 1971, was easily offset by the $41.5 million that went into the Woodfield Shopping Center and similar projects through the 1970s.[26] Far from seeing any environmental costs to their investments, TIAA's officers proudly looked back at (and even exaggerated) the institution's history of collaboration with leading developers: "TIAA was the first lender to finance the shopping mall business. We provided a start and we provided financing for the pioneers, for Al Taubman, for Ernie Hahn, Dick Jacobs, Ed DeBartolo, Herb and Mel Simon, Leonard Farber, Jim Rouse," recalled managing director Kathleen M. Nelson in 1998.[27] Those developers produced signature downtown malls—Ernest Hahn's Horton Plaza in San Diego, Rouse's Harborplace in Baltimore, the Simons' Circle Center in Indianapolis—that aimed to revive central cities; and together they built hundreds of shopping centers on the outskirts of cities that insured that most Americans would never have to go downtown again.

TIAA's financial backing of shopping centers as a portion of its total properties peaked at the end of the 1970s. In the 1980s, as analysts advised that the retail sector was overbuilt, loans to shopping center developers dropped from just over half in 1982 to one-third of the mortgage portfolio in 1986, with mortgages for office buildings and hotels picking up the difference. By the late 1980s, however, the scale of financing for any one suburban project had increased dramatically. When TIAA put up half the money to build the Mall of America in 1989, its stake of $650 million exceeded the amount of all of TIAA's commercial mortgages in 1968.

Although oil crisis and stagflation created financial problems for the Bucksbaums, Simons, and DeBartolos in the late 1970s, their courtship of institutional investors coincided with the rising visibility of pension funds within financial markets. In 1975, Congress passed new legislation to regulate institutional investors as they moved into the stock as well as bond markets; by 1990 insurance companies, pension funds, and mutual funds controlled more than half of the assets traded on the New York Stock Exchange.[28] It is perhaps significant that the journal *Institutional Investors* was established in 1975 for a new cadre of money managers who understood real estate investments less as landed property than as interchangeable financial assets. TIAA, proud of its acuity in backing the most reliable national retail developers, continued to provide whole mortgages for specific projects. But the inflation of the 1970s also pushed the fund's managers to pay more attention to the portfolio's mix of long-term and short-term mortgages, as well as to provide new hedges of variable interest rates or "contingent income" from future rent increases.[29] That is to say, profits derived from the "structure" of loans mattered as much as those derived from building structures that produced rents.

Pension funds and insurance companies were not the only means of mobilizing large amounts of capital for commercial development on the periphery. Historically, real estate's value as a secure investment, a tangible asset, and a hedge against inflation was always set against the difficulties of cashing in land for ready money. Thus, private trusts held real estate in order to generate annuities—a stream of rents—rather than to collect the profits of appreciating land values by selling. But if institutional investors first turned to real estate out of a traditional equation of land and stability, it was precisely land's intractability as an asset that had prompted Congress in the 1960s to create another institution that, it was said, would permit individual investors to enjoy the security of real estate while at the same time gaining a new ease in buying and selling it. Concerned that real estate on its own could never compete with the rapidly growing stock market, Congress authorized the formation of Real Estate Investment Trusts (REITs), which sold investors shares in either mortgages (mortgage REITS) or land (equity REITS).[30] Real Estate Investment Trusts were essentially holding companies, but unlike industrial corporations or trusts, the managers of REITs could not retain and reinvest their profits. The rules governing REITs were modified several times between 1960 and 2000, but REITs were bound to pay out 90 to 95 percent of their annual profits to shareholders. This requirement not only gave shareholders a stream of revenue from investment properties, it also formed the basis of a tax benefit. Because REITs paid out all their profits, they did not have to pay corporate income taxes; rather, shareholders paid income tax only once on the dividends. If tax policy enhanced the return from owning shares in REITs, their other significant distinction was to make ownership of real estate highly liquid, properties that could be bought and sold at an hour's notice. REITs were listed on stock exchanges where absentee owners could track the rise and fall of prices of shares in the production of rents just as they could for steel, cars, or candy bars.

REITs as a new investment vehicle for suburban commercial development, however, caught on slowly. In the 1960s and 1970s, the largest banks established mortgage REITs, which held debt largely on urban properties. Many suburban developers resisted going public with equity REITs that would require disclosing their company's financial operations. Nor did most large builders want to lose the option of controlling earnings, which they could roll over into the next speculative project. Nonetheless, some developers converted their firms into REITs during the rocky 1970s in order to stay afloat; and others joined them in the 1980s in order to gain the capital to expand.[31] Even then, the bulk of the publicly sold shares in development REITs remained concentrated in the hands of their founding entrepreneurs, whose absenteeism took the old-fashioned form of sending construction teams into distant communities on the strength of market profiles and strategic transportation nodes. Whereas in the 1950s and 1960s, retail companies, especially department stores looking to establish suburban branches, actively collaborated in the siting of shopping centers, by the 1980s, the developers proudly announced that they had taken charge of deciding where and how to build the ever larger regional malls.

Equity REITs organized by retail developers became primary institutions for structuring large-scale deals and joint investments to produce such monuments on the urban fringe as the Mall of America, the largest mall in the nation, opened in 1992 in a Minneapolis suburb. The Mall of America was initiated by Canadian developers, the Ghermezian brothers, whose Triple Five Corporation had opened the West Edmonton Mall on 121 acres in 1981, the first megamall to feature entertainment as well as shopping facilities. The owners of Triple Five proposed building the Mall of America on the site of a former municipal baseball stadium, and the town of Bloomington issued $80 million in bonds to pay for new roads and utilities. But sunk under the weight of financing the Edmonton Mall, Triple Five had to recruit other investors into the project, including the Simon Properties REIT and TIAA. Few commentators at the time saw anything anomalous in American teachers and scholars becoming, in effect, joint owners of a mall that offered five hundred stores and an amusement park to some forty-two million annual visitors a year. Anchored by four department stores, the Mall of America itself anchored one of the densest stretches of consumer institutions built over farm fields in the United States.

As real estate gained steam in the mid-1980s, pension fund and insurance executives and the directors of REITs found themselves competing with deregulated banks, savings and loans, and mutual funds for the opportunity to lend money to builders. Mall developers who chose to avoid the public exposure that came with REITs relied on loan syndicates to finance large-scale commercial projects. Commercial banks underwrote the downtown office building boom of the 1980s, but they hedged their bets by backing edge city development as well. A typical syndicate might consist of five or six financial institutions holding shares of a large loan. At the same time, some investment firms experimented with bundling and selling shares in pools of commercial mortgages, a process known as "securitization."[32] Ironically, perhaps, the creation of a secondary securities market for commercial mortgages got its biggest boost from the federal government's mopping up after the speculative frenzy triggered by deregulation. As savings and loans competed with commercial banks and institutional investors, credit managers moved capital into resorts, amusement parks, executive parks, and malls, only to watch the bubble burst in 1988–1989. Congress created the Resolution Trust Corporation to manage the assets of failed institutions, and the RTC pooled outstanding mortgages and issued securities worth $9.1 billion in 1992 alone.[33] By 1994, commercial mortgage-backed securities (CMBS) had been privatized, introducing a new instrument to institutional investors' portfolios.[34]

Like shares in REITs, shares in mortgage securities are highly liquid, one asset among many in the portfolios of leading lenders. And because a CMBS pools risk by setting one mortgage against another, it eliminates the need for individual creditors to know the nature or condition of the real property that secures any particular loan. In this sense mortgage securities represent a further attenuation of rights in land and hence of responsibilities toward it. The value of CMBS increased from $253 million in 1996 to $418 million in 1997, and has continued an upward surge since then. By 1998, two dealers in financial services and real estate securitization concluded that a "bridge" had been crossed in the techniques of "providing capital market financing to local borrowers nationwide." The goal on the other side of the bridge, they said, "is a totally liquid real estate market, with commercial property and mortgage portfolios traded in the same way as other financial instruments, including corporate debt." The fragmentation of individual ownership into "a piece of large portfolios designed to avoid concentration of risk" even altered the relation of value to land use or "property performance." As part of international financial markets, commercial mortgage-backed securities could gain or lose value quite apart from what was happening on the original site of a loan: financial upheavals in Bangkok could, the dealers observed, destroy the value of "an investment collateralized by a commercial mortgage in Wichita."[35]

The mobilization and concentration of capital in commercial development on the urban fringe altered the balance of power between local residents and absentee owners. Through the 1980s boom, as the Simons, DeBartolos, Bucksbaums, and other developers built regional malls, they also encountered, successfully fought, and outlasted resistance in towns across the country. Again and again local opponents argued that the new malls would destroy older downtowns, increase traffic, eliminate open space or farm land, and transform their communities. When these concerns did not provide zoning boards with sufficient grounds to withhold building permits, opponents turned to environmental arguments. In the late 1970s and early 1980s, for example, citizens of Appleton, Wisconsin, repeatedly tried to block the General Growth Properties' Fox River Mall, unsuccessfully going to court with environmental arguments when other tactics failed.[36] Yet the opponents of malls often raised environmental concerns less as matters of ecology affecting other species or natural resources than as defenses of residents' feelings about their own towns or way of life.[37] Environmentalism provided a ready language of opposition, particularly given its pairing with "protection" and its association with one of the few federal agencies perceived as retaining effective regulatory power after 1980. But invocations of environmental protection did not hold up well in court. Much of the damage new malls wrought was not measurable according to EPA standards, which protected qualities of air, water, and soil but had no bearing on problems of land use, traffic, or congestion that most readily mobilized opponents of sprawl. Nor could EPA impose sanctions on the habits of waste enshrined by consumer institutions.

The preservation of wetlands was one of the few areas of environmental regulation that did slow or stop new projects, a sensitive issue for mall developers who liked to buy easily accessible and relatively cheap lowlands as prospective sites. In the early 1980s, Edward DeBartolo sold a tract of swampland in South Attleboro, Massachusetts, to Pyramid Companies, a New York–based mall developer. Though Pyramid received a wetlands permit from the Army Corps of Engineers, EPA successfully blocked its efforts to build a mall on the site known as Sweeden's Swamp. After a fight that lasted nearly a decade, Pyramid moved on to join its competitor to build the Emerald Square mall in North Attleboro, fifteen miles from the first contested site. When Simon Properties acquired Emerald Square in 1999, one analyst observed that the company was smart to buy rather than build its malls in areas "where tough laws exist to restrict development, limiting competition from new supply." By the end of the 1980s, most developers had mastered the art of environmental impact statements, hiring their own experts not only to disarm opponents, but in a number of noteworthy instances to squelch the development plans of their competitors.[38]

In the long run, then, local opposition to commercial development did not constitute a risk that reached or discouraged investors. Overbuilding did. Amid the wholesale speculation of the late 1980s, even well-established developers found themselves overextended and forced to retrench. Simon Properties and the Bucksbaums' General Growth Property stabilized their finances not only by collaborating with institutional investors but by organizing their own real estate investment trusts in the early 1990s.[39] The last to go public was the eighty-four-year-old Edward DeBartolo; when he organized his family company into a REIT in 1994, he owned sixty-two regional malls in sixteen states and employed twenty-five hundred managers nationwide.

REITs provided the institutional framework for the dramatic consolidation of commercial real estate in the 1990s through acquisitions and mergers. According to *Business Week,* capital invested in REITs rose from $13 billion in 1991 to $131 billion at the decade's end.[40] Even as analysts warned that the domestic retail market was saturated, the leading trusts in that sector turned to an aggressive program of renovation and expansion of older malls, the introduction of entertainment facilities, and the conversion of some older strip centers to "power centers" for big box retail outlets (from Wal-Mart to Home Depot, which were by the late 1990s aggressively building at the edge of settlement across the nation). The tactics of retail REITs aimed to keep commercial properties viable, but the key to consolidation was market dominance. Toward that goal, REITs readily moved capital in and out of communities across the country.

The Bucksbaums' General Growth Properties, one of the top five REITs in the country, may have gotten their start in Iowa, but by the mid-1990s, they had left behind the fourteen malls they once owned in that state to become one of the biggest operators in Texas, while also building in Hawaii the highest rent-yielding mall in the country. When the company went public as a real estate investment trust in 1993, with twenty-one regional malls, it expanded rapidly through acquisitions, buying sixteen malls from Prudential Insurance Company and another twenty-six regional malls from Homart Development Corp., the retail real estate division of Sears. A decade after selling off the Iowa malls, General Growth, the company now headed by Martin Bucksbaum's son John, owned 134 malls in thirty-four states. At the end of the century, it even ventured back into Iowa.[41]

Not to be outdone by General Growth, in 1996 the Simon and DeBartolo REITs merged, placing 111 regional malls, sixty-six community centers, and six specialty centers in thirty-two states on one spreadsheet. The merger created, as one company officer observed, a "company of a size and scope never before seen in this industry. We believe the industry will experience continued consolidation among the entities and properties so there will be fewer and larger owners . . . the best way to compete and grow in this industry is to be of dominant size."[42] In 1999, Simon DeBartolo, now known as the Simon Property Group, led retail REITs in acquisitions, including its purchase of fourteen regional malls from Stephen Karp's New England Development Corporation. New Hampshire's one-million-square-feet Park Mall in Salem and the Mall of New Hampshire in Manchester were but two of the properties in the $1.7 billion deal jointly financed by the New York State Teachers' Retirement Association pension fund and the J. P. Morgan fund.[43] By 2001 the Simon Property Group had become the third largest real estate investment trust in the country, capitalized at nearly $5 billion, and the single largest owner of retail properties.[44] (The two largest REITs concentrated on office properties, always the generators of the highest commercial rent, balanced between downtown and suburban holdings.)

In 1998, one observer warned that REITs, under "increased investor pressure to perform," had few alternatives other than to expand through merger or to move into foreign markets. (Of course, foreign investors had long found REITs a convenient way to acquire American real estate. When Ernest Hahn, one of TIAA's favorite California mall developers, sold his Laguna Hills Mall in 1984, it was purchased by Pan American Properties, a REIT "owned by the pension fund for British coal miners."[45]) Mergers and foreign investment were not unconnected choices. Mergers like that of Simon and DeBartolo prompted TIAA to reduce the exposure that came from investments in the now consolidated properties of one company by, as one manager explained, working on European outlets, with new investments in shopping centers in England and Portugal. Still, analysts concluded, localism retained a place in the financial transformation of real estate development. Smaller local operators who "are good at what they do, understand local markets, and, as a result, enjoy access to buying opportunities that larger REITs might not even know about" could continue to develop on the edge of American cities, creating a "development pipeline" that would eventually turn "feeder" REITs into "merger candidates, feeding the growth of larger REITs."[46]

The development of the institutions and financial instruments that produced the commercial urban fringe was uneven and always vulnerable to the business cycle. But the power achieved through these new modes of absentee ownership is evident in three ways.

First, large national developers—whether family firms, real estate investment trusts, or combinations of the two—have the means to purchase land, structure financing, and build on a massive scale. Any given regional mall might cover from forty to one hundred acres, substantially less than most landscaped urban public parks, but they cost upwards of $100 million to construct, not including the rebuilding of roads. The scale of investment, while in some instances increasing risk, has also transformed older ideas about the stability of landed property into a matter of corporate tenacity, as managers dug in to see a particular project through to completion.

Also, REITs have the standing and influence to negotiate effectively with local officials and to hire experts when they need them. Substantial and experienced staffs carry large projects through zoning boards, environmental review processes, and county, state, and even federal courts. By contrast, the arrival of a major commercial developer is a new experience to each community, and residents seldom have adequate resources or legal know-how to mount a contest. Despite the carrying costs of large loans or of paying taxes on undeveloped land, REITs and large privately held development companies have also demonstrated remarkable staying power; again and again, malls open after ten, even fifteen years of delays, including those caused by local resistance. Rogue developers have been known to use their financial clout to buy local elections in order to gain support for a new galleria and to intimidate local zoning boards and town councils with threats of costly lawsuits.[47] But strong-arm tactics are not necessary in many places where zoning ordinances have already conceded the commercial use of interstate corridors that forecast more traffic and denser development.[48]

And finally, REITs and institutional investors have the power to divest and move their capital elsewhere. In the early 1990s in the face of saturated retail markets, when companies placed greater emphasis on renovating and expanding existing malls to include entertainment facilities, decisions to upgrade some malls—investment as "value added"—were frequently accompanied by divestment of others. And as is true in industry, mergers and acquisitions often trigger downsizing and closings. There is no more local accountability when a mall's backers leave town than when they arrived.

In the winter of 2001, the New Urbanism Institute commissioned a study by PricewaterhouseCoopers on declining malls.[49] The study found that 7 percent of existing malls were already failing and another 12 percent were vulnerable. Most of these "greyfield malls" had been built in the 1960s in the

Middle or South Atlantic region or the Upper Midwest. The New Urbanists looked to adaptive reuse, but the production and abandonment of shopping centers points to a dynamic that also produces malls themselves as, figuratively speaking, a form of hazardous waste. Even if new proprietors clean up and reuse abandoned malls, the impact on the natural environment is not reversible. Sprawl does not revert to woods or farmland.

Since the late 1980s, efforts to find alternatives to sprawl have coalesced into the "smart growth" movement in urban design. Environmentally conscious planners have recruited politicians and members of the Urban Land Institute to improve mass transportation and fill in already developed areas, rather than going further to the edge. They advocate density as a locus of community and more efficient resource use. Yet smart growth has also encountered the limits of investors' interest in alternatives to a well-established pattern. Thus, when the Department of Transportation in Oregon commissioned consultants to evaluate sources of capital for new environmentally friendly projects, their advisors concluded, "REITs are not likely to be a vehicle for financing new Smart Development" because they would invest in such a project only after it was built and had displayed a track record. "Since the project, unless over $15 to 17 million in value, would be pooled with other projects or a portfolio of properties, the individual project character would matter less than its record of financial success. New Smart Development would be extremely difficult to finance as a stand-alone REIT because of the speculative nature of new development and because of the same factors that make banks cautious about new or innovative development types."[50]

Even TIAA, which advertises the social responsibility *and* profitability of its investments, operates under the shadow of investor conformity. In the summer of 1998, TIAA sought to sell its 55.5 percent stake in the Mall of America but initially found no buyers. Quickly assuring the shopping mall industry that they had no intention of abandoning the sector, TIAA managers also revealed the disposition that governs investment in the periphery. Interviewed by a reporter for *Pensions and Investments,* a senior TIAA manager, Joseph Luik, said that the fund "has been buying and selling massive properties for its two real estate accounts during the past few years. 'We are continually churning the portfolio,' explained Mr. Luik. 'If properties no longer fit or if we think they have achieved their maximum value, we sell them. We do this every year.'"[51]

At the end of the twentieth century, TIAA's was the largest pension fund in the world and the nation's third largest financier of retail development with $1.5 billion dollars in project loans that ranged in 1999 from the Citrus Park

Town Center in Tampa, Florida ($115 million), to the Baybrook Mall in Houston, Texas ($95 million).[52] "As of December 31, 2000, TIAA's general account had a mortgage and real property portfolio of approximately $27 billion."[53]

In 1995, as part of a diversification of financial services for its clients, TIAA also set up a separate real estate account. With a portfolio that comprises mortgages and equity holdings in twenty-three states as well as shares in real estate investment trusts (including Simon Property Group and the Equity Office Property Trust, the largest office REIT), TIAA's separate real estate account held assets valued at $2.3 billion in the year 2000. The prospectus for the account offered the usual and necessary caveats for investors, noting "general risks of owning real property" that ranged from drops in real estate values or occupancy rates due to general economic decline to loss of income due to disputes and litigation. The prospectus also specified the "Regulatory Risks" of investing in real estate: "Government regulation, including zoning laws, property taxes, fiscal, environmental or other government policies, could operate or change in a way that hurts the account and its properties. For example, regulations could raise the cost of owning and maintaining property or make it harder to sell, rent, finance, or refinance properties due to the increased costs associated with regulatory compliance." The prospectus did not say that government policies could also enhance real estate values, as they had for nearly half a century. Nor did the prospectus linger on what it meant to warn investors of state regulations that aimed to enhance their lives and relation to the natural world.

Instead, the prospectus for the new real estate account warned investors of different kinds of "Environmental Risks" that arose from absentee ownership under the auspices of TIAA: "The account may be held liable for damages to the environment caused by hazardous substances used or found on its properties." Indeed, "the cost of any required clean up and the account's potential liability for environmental damage to a single real estate investment could exceed the value of the account's investment in a property, the property's value, or, in an extreme case, a significant portion of the account's assets."[54] It is true that real estate investment trusts and even pension funds are liable under the Superfund Act for officially designated hazardous waste sites. For this reason, a new branch of insurance—environmental insurance—has matured in the last few years. Environmental insurance companies in turn join the institutional investors who are also pouring capital into REITs and mortgage-backed securities to maintain their own profitable and balanced portfolios.[55]

Americans have entered a property regime that pits their stake in a comfortable personal future against their stake in securing habitable environments for themselves and other species. Absentee ownership gives lie to property rights advocates' invocation of stewardship of the land as a feature of proprietorship, but it is not incompatible with their vision of an ever expanding, unencumbered market as the gold mine of the new millennium. It is environmentalists who are confronted with the task of taking the measure of the rights and powers of absentee ownership that have turned millions of Americans, including ourselves, into rentiers while severing our connection to the land that sustains us.

Floods and Landscapes in the Inland West

Nancy Langston

CONFLICTS BETWEEN ranchers, irrigation developers, and government scientists over the control of flood waters have a long history at Malheur National Wildlife Refuge in southeastern Oregon. My focus is on the ways different groups have responded to floods. Floods shaped, and continue to shape, human responses to landscapes. One piece of land is never entirely separate from another, even if we think that a string of barbed wire forms an effective barrier between them. A bit of dirt kicked free by a cow finds its way into a stream and eventually gets deposited miles away. That sediment clogs the gills of a redband trout, far from where the cow grazed. Floods connect these places, weaving the threads of the landscape together.

For all the ecological benefits floods provide, most people hate them. Floods wipe out human signs of progress: they rip out roads, they destroy crops, they stink up basements, they drown children. Floods are a slap in the face of human industry, and for many people, floods have been a powerful source of frustration and anger. Yet human responses to floods have dramatically differed, and those responses have shaped both landscapes and identities.

Federal resource managers have often managed flood-prone landscapes in ways that confound outsiders. Since the 1930s, for example, managers at Malheur National Wildlife Refuge in southeastern Oregon have ditched wetlands, channelized rivers, sprayed Agent Orange over creeks, mowed down willows that managed to escape the poison, and repeatedly poured rotenone into the rivers and lakes to kill carp. Given that ecologists now consider these activities to be among those most harmful to watershed health, one cannot help but wonder: why did managers do this? What led them to make such decisions? What were the effects—ecological and social—of such decisions? And what can we learn from their successes and their failures? Examining the tangled history of flood management in one western watershed will suggest ways that a better understanding of history can lead to more effective resource management.

When bird watchers now flock to Oregon's Malheur National Wildlife Refuge—one of the nation's critical areas for migratory waterfowl—they find what looks like a teeming wilderness along the Blitzen River. Winding river channels, riparian meadows, willow thickets, ponds, and marshes create an oasis in the high desert of the northern Great Basin, used each year by up to twenty-five million birds. To the visitor, Malheur seems like a supremely wild refuge from both desert aridity and human industry. Yet wild as it seems, this landscape has been radically transformed by ranchers, irrigators, and wildlife managers.

Few whites settled in the region until the 1870s, put off by stories of marauding Indians, the area's remoteness from other settlements and transportation networks, and the nature of the land itself. The years from 1854 to 1869 had been particularly wet. While reports of northern Great Basin's grasslands had attracted California ranchers to eastern Oregon, they had avoided the Malheur Basin, for it seemed too wet, swampy, and flooded to be safe for unattended cattle.

In 1872, that isolation changed when a short, wiry young man named Peter French rode north out of the Sacramento Valley, searching for grass and water for cattle. Just two years earlier, French had been a hired hand breaking horses for the Sacramento "Wheat King" Hugh Glenn. Soon Glenn trusted French enough to make him manager for his expansion into Oregon, and so, with six Mexican vaqueros and twelve hundred cattle, French spent weeks riding across the northern California deserts, through dusty, dry lands where his cattle had a hard time finding sustenance. French kept heading north, until he rode up over a dusty ridge just west of the Blitzen Valley. What he saw over that ridge delighted him—an abundance of water in the desert. When the party stopped for the night, a discouraged prospector named Porter noticed the cook fire and came for a visit. Porter sold his few cows to French, along with the P brand. Since Porter's cattle were the only ones in the valley, French acquired informal rights to graze the land as well, to the exclusion of other cattle operations.[1] By the time French died twenty-five years later, murdered by a homesteader over contested riparian lands, he had built up those meager holdings into an empire of 45,000 cattle and 132,000 acres.

In the Blitzen watershed, French found himself within a watery world: a maze of streams, channels, wetlands, bogs, alkaline lakes, and lush riparian meadows—all fed by waters from the Blitzen River. Without that water, this would have been a barren desert, unable to support more than a few animals and even fewer people. With the water, it became the center for what was briefly the largest cattle empire in America, and what became some of the most bitter battles between cattle barons and Indians and homesteaders and irrigators and ranchers and environmentalists—all focused on who would win control of the flood waters.

French never wrote home describing what he found that night, but three years later, another rancher described the adjacent Catlow Valley as "one of the most beautiful valleys in southeastern Oregon, the bunch grass waving over its broad stretches like a grain field . . . in addition to the bunch grass the white sage stood two feet high, rendering it a veritable stockman's paradise."[2] The basis of this paradise was the natural wealth offered by the wetlands and riparian areas of the northern Great Basin, a geography of basin and range where the rivers flowed, not into the sea, but into briny lakes. Between each fault-block range lay a basin with a moist valley where streams wandered into a maze of wetlands, creating riparian corridors and ephemeral pools that fed into great blue-green salty seas teeming with life. When droughts came, evaporation dried up the lakes into playas, concentrating the salts into a white alkaline crust. These were places of extremes and sudden contrasts—desert interrupted by snowy mountains and great, shallow, salty seas.

For thousands of years before Peter French looked down at this abundance of life, the river had moved across the entire flood plain, using a set of sinuous channels that changed from decade to decade. These riparian communities were anything but stable; floods, changes in rainfall, and changes in animal activities led to dramatic annual changes in the bottomlands. Some years the marshes were lush and green and stretched from one end of the valley to another; the basin filled with water. Other years little snow fell on Steens Mountain, and by early summer the lowland streams ran down to a trickle, and the riparian meadows turned brown, and the marshes slowly dried. Some years the water was so high that numerous pools and ponds formed in the valley, perfect for brooding waterfowl. Other years few pools formed, and waterfowl rearing habitat was minimal. Yet because the Malheur Basin was embedded in a much larger network of wetlands stretching from California to Canada along the Pacific Flyway, when droughts struck Malheur, shrinking the ponds and pools, migratory birds could find other places to rest and feed.

Change was at the heart of the riparian landscapes that Peter French so admired. During spring snow melt, the waters rise over their banks and spread over the bottomlands, irrigating lush riparian meadows where wild rye waved six to eight feet high. Such floods could dramatically reshape the riparian lands, as winter storms pulled up entire forests, and spring snow melt swelled the streams, undercutting banks and reshaping sand bars. While destructive in the short term, these floodwaters helped to create the fertility that was soon to nourish Peter French's cattle, for they saturated the soil for weeks and washed organic sediments and nutrients from the uplands over the lowland meadows.

French was a progressive rancher for the times, determined not to follow the standard practice of letting one's cattle loose in the spring and then rounding them up in the fall. Instead, French had his vaqueros ride close herd on the cattle, which made it much safer to run cattle in the wet bottomlands, where untended cattle could founder in the mire. Manipulating water was the key to his success. Since the sagebrush uplands did not seem particularly productive to French, he drained tule marshes, using the water to flood out upland sagebrush, which dies when its roots are submerged. With his water systems, French set out to make the uplands wetter and the swamp lands drier, and both of them better for cattle production. Prim Ortega, a Mexican vaquero who had come up from Sacramento with Peter French on his first voyage into Oregon, testified that French had begun building dams and ditches "all over the place" long before any other settlers came to the Blitzen.[3] French, according to company documents, soon "laid out a plan for the drainage of the swamp by a main canal and the irrigation of all lands between the foothills and the canal, putting the water on the land along the highest lines and using the canal itself as a final drain ditch for the irrigation system."[4]

French succeeded not by attempting to engineer natural riparian systems out of existence, but rather by recognizing the abundance offered by riparian areas in all their messiness and uncertainty. What made the Blitzen Valley so fertile for cattle raising was not just the quality of its soil, nor the abundance of its water. The complicated connections between these two created the abundance, and annual flooding mediated those connections. Other ranchers looked at the annual flooding of the riparian landscapes along the Blitzen and saw something messy, troublesome, and inconvenient, a natural chaos that either needed to be avoided or engineered away. French looked at these same floods and recognized that they could become the source of his prosperity.

With simple methods of flood irrigation developed by observing and mimicking the natural overflow of water onto riparian meadows during spring floods, French spread water over his drier riparian meadows in the spring, increasing the growth of native hay that he could cut and store for the winter. Streams were encouraged to overflow their banks, just as they had done in creating the natural riparian areas. Rather than trying to reshape the riparian meadows into dry lands and reservoirs, French encouraged water to remain a little bit longer, to spread a little bit wider. These simple techniques of flood irrigation modified, but did not break, the connections between land and water.

Flood irrigation was an imperfect tool. If the field was not perfectly leveled, as no field ever was, water would fill the depressions and just sit there instead of spreading smoothly across the entire field, creating ephemeral wetlands. Even in the late summer, ranchers complained that they could not cross certain sloughs in their fields for fear of miring their horses.[5] To get all parts of the field wet, far more water than each plant needed would be let across the field, and that water might run off the land instead of sinking into the dirt.[6] Flood irrigation relied on snow melt early in the growing season, rather than stored waters from reservoirs. Such flood irrigation had little benefit for farmers trying to grow nonnative crops such as alfalfa or wheat, species that needed water later in the summer to survive. Riparian grasses, or "wild hay," however, thrived under the early flood waters. Rather than trying to introduce exotic grains as other ranchers were doing, French prospered by harvesting native riparian hay.

Within a few years after French's success in the basin, the area began to be settled by homesteaders, who soon came to hate him for his monopolies on riparian areas. Flood irrigation of riparian meadows gave French something critical in his quest to control access to grazing: a way to grow and harvest cheap hay for winter feed. As early as 1877, according to Ortega's testimony, French began putting up hay.[7] Other cattlemen scorned the very idea of winter feeding, believing that it made the cattle lazy and lifeless, or as one cattleman put it, "illustrating the ordinary results of charity to a street beggar."[8] After the harsh winter of 1879–1880, when most cattle in the region starved to death, winter feeding allowed French to buy out the holdings of his neighbors until he controlled nearly all the water sources and riparian areas in the Blitzen Valley.

The wealth of the cattle empires depended directly on the wealth of the riparian meadows. French's genius in manipulating riparian structure, and increasing the action of natural floods without destroying riparian function, was one keystone to the success of his empire. But while French did not try for complete control of the movement of water across the land, he did try for complete control of the movement of people across his land, and their use of water—he soon gained complete control of water rights in the basin. His control of water rights was only an illusion: powerful tensions were brewing in the basin between cattle barons, homesteaders, and irrigation developments.

Flood irrigation in Oregon was an alteration, but one that maintained the connectivity of the riparian area, mimicking and even extending natural riparian functions. Homesteaders and other critics of ranching attacked flood irrigation on these very grounds, arguing that such waste prevented efficient manipulation of the landscape. But the real abuses by ranchers were not ecological (wasting water on riparian vegetation, as homesteaders accused) but rather social (in preventing homesteaders from getting access to water). By the 1890s a few large cattle companies were dominating the irrigated acreage in Harney County. Between 1889 and 1899, the irrigated area of Harney County increased from 26,289 to 111,090 acres (a 322.6 percent increase) while the total number of irrigators dropped from 240 to 228, as large cattle companies bought out the water rights and irrigation systems of small operators.[9] While ranchers gained control of the riparian meadows and began turning the wetlands into what one observer called "giant hay ranches," homesteaders began attacking the very idea of flood irrigation.

By the 1890s, overgrazing and water projects, combined with a few dry years, had sparked an explosive situation among valley residents. As early as the 1880s, the water levels of Malheur Lake had begun to fall as more water was diverted for irrigation, and the lands between the high-water mark—the meander line—and the water line became contested territory. The central conflicts rested on what the boundaries between water and land meant in a place where those boundaries were never fixed, and how those shifting boundaries affected legal title.

Above the meander line was French's land, but between the meander line and the actual lake levels, ownership was uncertain, because the precise nature of that riparian landscape was uncertain: was it water or was it land? Large operators such as French claimed rights to those newly formed spaces because, in their view, it was not land but lakebed, and therefore part of their original riparian claim. Homesteaders, on the other hand, argued these new spaces were true land and therefore should be considered public domain open for settlement.[10]

As settlement increased in the basin, human interventions made the water levels increasingly unstable, thereby decreasing the stability of legal title as well. More water diversions from the Blitzen and Silvies rivers were built for irrigation, which lowered water levels further in Malheur and Harney lakes. In the spring of 1881, the sand reef separating Malheur Lake from its smaller neighboring lake, Harney Lake, broke (as legend has it, through the angry kick of a cowboy's boot). Water rushed from Malheur into Harney Lake, cutting a new channel two feet deep. Because Harney Lake's elevation is slightly lower than Malheur Lake, the new channel lowered the level of Malheur Lake, exposing more land bed for people to fight over. Not only did the new channel lower average lake levels, it also made them more unpredictable. In some years, erosion led the channel to become silt-clogged, blocking flow from Malheur into Harney and raising water levels in Malheur Lake, swamping out the squatters. Other years, heavy spring run-off washed out the silt in the channel so that Malheur Lake levels dropped precipitously, even though rainfall was high—exactly the opposite of what people expected.[11]

When homesteaders first moved onto the exposed lakebed in the early 1880s, French raised no objections. In 1894, however, he claimed riparian rights and informed the homesteaders they had to leave. When they ignored him, he started suits in the federal court in Portland, and when the first case was found against him, he appealed the verdict.[12] Some homesteaders cut French's fences, burned his hay, and killed his cattle; he retaliated by buying their lands when they could not make payments.[13]

The tensions between homesteaders and cattle barons over control of water escalated until finally, on December 26, 1897, a homesteader named Ed Oliver rode onto French's land. French and his crew were rounding up cattle and looked up to see Oliver galloping toward them. Oliver's horse struck French's so hard that the horse fell to his knees, and French struck out with his whip, beating Oliver about the head and shoulders. Oliver pulled out a gun and began waving it about, whereupon French turned his back on the man and rode off. And then, in front of all the crew, Oliver shot the unarmed French in the back, killing him.[14] The jury—made up of homesteaders and shopkeepers in Burns—found Oliver not guilty, agreeing with his claim that he acted in self-defense.

The empire French had built did not last long after his death. In 1906, the

French-Glenn Livestock Company was sold to Henry L. Corbett, the Oregon senator; he soon sold to Swift & Company, the meat-packing company, which reorganized the holdings into the Blitzen Valley Land Company. Hoping to subdivide their holdings and sell them off as small farms, the Blitzen Valley Land Company built extensive irrigation facilities and dredged twenty miles of the river. The development scheme never paid off, however. In 1916, the operation reorganized yet again, this time into the Eastern Oregon Livestock Company, running about twenty thousand head of cattle on the P ranch. Unlike Peter French, the managers failed to put up enough winter hay, and they lost 40 percent of the cattle in the next two winters. Feral hogs filled the tule marshes and bottomlands, and then sheep were brought into the valley, which did not exactly improve conditions. The effects of all this human, animal, and machine activity were soon apparent. In the early 1930s, drought hit, and combined with overgrazing, conversion to grain agriculture, dredging, channelizing, and elimination of much riparian habitat, much of the valley was reduced to dust. The land was sold once again, this time to the federal government, which wanted the Blitzen River water rights to protect water levels on the Malheur Lake Bird Reservation.

With the goal of restoring waterfowl nesting habitat in the valley, John Scharff, refuge manager from 1935 to 1971, began extensive engineering projects for the control of water. Scharff had grown up on a local ranch, and he was an enthusiastic proponent of management to increase production. With the help of the Civilian Conservation Corps, his staff bulldozed new ponds for chick-rearing habitat, built dams to hold water, dug ditches for irrigating meadows, and extended hundreds of miles of canals along both sides of the valley to supply water reliably to the entire floodplain.[15] Instead of a system of wandering channels, where in some years only part of the valley might be wet, they created a landscape where they hoped to control which meadows were wet, which ponds stayed full of water, and which meadows were allowed to dry out.

To understand these decisions, we need to remember the desperate conditions of migratory bird populations in the first decades of the twentieth century—and the equally desperate attempts ornithologists and conservationists were making to save those birds. In the early 1930s, severe droughts along the Pacific Flyway desiccated wetlands, habitat that had already been drastically reduced by three decades of drainage and reclamation. By 1934, the continental waterfowl population dropped to a low of twenty-seven million birds; only 150 egrets and fourteen whooping cranes remained.[16] Conservationists were convinced that preservation of habitat alone would ultimately be powerless against land speculators, reclamation engineers, and drainage districts bent on creating farmland out of wetland. The bleakness of the situation led conservationists to advocate what were basically engineering solutions for the restoration of Malheur, borrowing the same techniques that had helped devastate the marshes in the first place.

What John Scharff was doing with the Malheur Refuge waterways was not unusual for the era. The 1930s were a decade marked by national enthusiasm for wildlife conservation, and much of that enthusiasm was aimed at projects that actively manipulated habitat. In 1934, the Bureau of Sport Fisheries undertook the first nationwide program of stream surveys and habitat improvements.[17] Throughout the West, the bureau began to restore and improve streams on public lands. The program's major emphasis was on structural engineering solutions, what managers such as Scharff termed "improvements." Often using CCC camp labor, between 1933 and 1937 restorationists throughout the nation built a tremendous number of in-stream habitat structures, such as rock dams to create pools for trout, riprap to stabilize stream banks, and deflectors to force streams to meander. Soon, many managers came to assume that *all* water sources needed improvement: structural engineering was not just for damaged streams, but for all streams.

Although the water control system at the refuge did quickly increase waterfowl habitat, trying to maintain the system led staff into continued complications. Until Scharff retired in 1971, the refuge's emphasis was on maximum waterfowl production. Anything that seemed to detract from waterfowl production was eliminated. When coyote and raven populations soared, lowering duck nest success, refuge staff set out poisoned bait, and then had to contend with increased rodent predation on eggs. When beaver returned to the valley and blocked up the irrigation ditches, staff trapped them out, even though the irrigation system was trying to replicate what beaver had created in the first place.[18]

The post–Second World War hatred of beaver in the valley reflected changes in national attitudes about wetlands and riparian management. As the wetland historian Ann Vileisis argued, after the Second World War, the Fish and Wildlife Service, the Bureau of Reclamation, the Army Corps of Engineers, and, above all, the USDA's Soil Conservation Service did their best to drain and ditch American riparian areas and wetlands into machinelike landscapes. For the Fish and Wildlife Service, the purpose was better duck habitat; for the other agencies, the purpose was better agricultural land.

Across much of the country, drainage had swept agricultural practice during the first decades of the twentieth century, but the Dust Bowl made many question the practice. However, after the war, high agricultural commodity prices allowed many farmers and ranchers to begin draining wetlands again. This time, farmers had the help of the federal government, whose programs encouraged farmers to turn marginal areas into croplands.[19] Soil Conservation Service agents considered drainage a fundamental conservation practice and provided farmers with bulldozers and draglines to dig ditches. Moreover, agents considered drainage a way to bring farmers into their network; by helping them drain lands, agents felt they could develop rapport with locals and establish their advisory role for other soil conservation projects, such as those to reduce erosion. The USDA's Production and Marketing Agency shared costs of on-farm drainage projects, paying farmers 60 percent of the costs of drainage. This grant, along with price supports for surplus crops, meant that federal subsidies effectively removed much of the risk of investing in turning wetlands into agriculture.[20] Drainage became a patriotic mission, part of the postwar dream of using agriculture to feed a hungry world.[21]

In 1954, the Federal Watershed Protection and Flood Prevention Act was passed (known as PL-566), creating a Small Watershed Program that would help the USDA agencies work with state and local governments to reduce large floods by damming streams high in watersheds. Because years of erosion had left many streams clogged with sediment, the program was also intended to channelize waterways to carry away floodwaters faster and more efficiently.[22] Since the channelized streams would carry drain waters as well, drainage projects could also fall under this project. By 1955, 103 million acres of land had been organized into drainage systems, and $900 million had been spent on ditches, outlets, levees, and pumps. Soon, more miles of public drainage ditch than highway covered the country. During four years in the 1950s, drainage funded by the USDA converted 256,000 acres of waterfowl habitat into farms. The technology of the bulldozer accelerated channelization through the 1960s, for the machine made the work quick and cheap. The Soil Conservation Service undertook huge projects of what they termed "stream improvement"— straightening and deepening water courses, removing riparian vegetation, dredging sediments, and thoroughly altering hydrology.[23] Within the Malheur Lake Basin, as throughout the West, projects funded by the PL-566 small watershed program were particularly popular with local landowners, even in a locale that professed to hate government projects.[24]

By the 1950s and 1960s, weed control became another major objective for Scharff. Willows were cut, mowed down, and sprayed with herbicide for several reasons: to remove predator habitat, to make it easier for tourists to see the wildlife, to increase mowing efficiency in the hay meadows, to increase the number of acres that could be put into full cattle and duck production, and, most important, to decrease competition for water. Woody riparian plants are phreatophytes, meaning that they extend their roots into the water table and consume a great deal of water. As one 1967 federal report on the Malheur Basin argued, "Many people believe that the high consumption of limited water supplies by phreatophytes is one of the most serious problems in the West."[25] Phreatophyte removal accelerated with the introduction of new herbicides—the 1955 Yearbook of Agriculture recommended that for complete control, one must repeat six sprayings of 2,4-D and 2,4,5-T, which later became notorious as Agent Orange.[26] Water experts of the mid-1950s came to believe that they could create more water and control floods through such phreatophyte eradication programs.[27]

The plan, however, backfired. The very plants that managers thought drank too much of their water actually contributed to maintaining a high water table. Riparian hardwoods are thirsty plants, which was often why people cut them down, thinking they were stealing water from livestock and more useful trees. But using water does not always mean reducing the supply for everyone else. Instead, riparian vegetation can allow streams to continue flowing longer. Even while they steal water, those plants increase the available supply to other plants. Riparian plants make the boundaries between water and land more complex, slowing water flow and keeping dirt from flooding the streams. Their leaves shade the streams, reducing water temperatures. Their branches and deadwood fall into the water, creating deep pools of scoured gravel where fish can spawn, trapping debris, and forming dams. Refuge staff used to think all this was bad—the point of a stream was to move water from point A to point B as efficiently as possible. But the more people tried to simplify streams by channeling them and piping them and cleaning them up, the more the waters dwindled away. Riparian zones made the boundaries between water and land more complex, and John Scharff, like many other managers, believed that these complexities interfered with his efficient administration of nature.

The most spectacular of all programs that Scharff initiated was surely the carp control project. Pioneers had introduced carp into the nearby Silvies River during the late nineteenth century, hoping to create a reliable food supply.[28] Few people proved to like the taste of carp, however, and carp populations soon exploded, with a host of unintended effects. Carp made their way from the Silvies River into Malheur Lake, perhaps during the high-water year of 1952, when floods flushed carp into the lake.[29] Bottom feeders, carp churned up sediments and destroyed sago pondweed. Because sago pondweed was a critical food source for water fowl, duck populations plummeted at Malheur. By 1955, sago pondweed was almost gone from Malheur Lake, and by 1957 carp had made their way forty miles up the Blitzen River. This unruly bit of nature—an unnatural introduction, but profoundly natural in its unwillingness to abide by human rules—became a profound threat to the empire of ducks at Malheur.

Scharff responded by initiating a series of poisoning projects whose intensity and scope were made possible by two things: technological advances that had resulted from the Second World War and a worldview that had declared war on any aspects of nature that refused to accede to human control. Refuge staff set out to control carp by dumping and spraying the fish poison rotenone throughout the system—an enormous project, for it involved treating the Blitzen River, the Silvies River, all their tributaries, and the lake itself. Several dry years meant the lake levels had dropped quite low, shrinking the lake surface.[30] With an extensive dike that stretched across part of the lake, and with water control structures along the Blitzen River, the staff shrunk the lake even further, making carp control feasible.

In the fall of 1955, the poisoning began. With aerial applications of rotenone, then with drums of toxicant dumped into the water, and finally with staff wading out into the marsh and hacking the heads off dying fish, the refuge killed one and a half million carp.[31] But two thousand carp escaped, spawned, and within three years carp were more numerous than before—now that their competitors, native fish much less resistant to rotenone, had been poisoned out.[32] Control projects continued for several decades. Two more extensive aerial sprayings were undertaken during low water years, with equally limited success.[33]

What decades of drainage efforts had failed to do, carp managed quite nicely: they transformed Malheur Lake from a splendid duck habitat to something still magnificent but far less productive for waterfowl. Carp had inadvertently created another nature—a monster to some, a place of incredible fecundity and stink to others. Nature kept recreating itself, a many-headed hydra, escaping from the bounds people attempted to place upon it. People were responsible for these monsters, but they had little luck controlling them. Scharff, however, was not troubled by the prospects of failure. Torpedo bombers, undiluted poisons, hacking the heads off millions of carp: anything was possible in the war to create a better nature. Eventually, however, after Scharff's retirement, the refuge staff admitted defeat in the war against carp and focused instead on merely keeping carp populations from exploding to the point that they displaced everything else in the marsh.[34] Instead of complete control, the refuge staff realized they would have to find an uneasy relationship of give-and-take with this new nature they had helped to create.

In Scharff's era, refuge management was driven by visions of maximizing duck production, just as earlier management in the valley during the era of the cattle barons had been driven by hopes of maximizing cattle production. For nearly five decades, ranchers and refuge managers had, for all their conflicts, found common ground in the promises and hopes of progressive land management. Both groups believed they could reshape nature to increase production, thus engineering a brave new nature. Both groups believed that through water manipulations, the replacement of native riparian vegetation with exotics, the removal of competing animals and plants, and other forms of intensive management they could have cattle and ducks both.

In the 1980s, this faith began to crumble, largely because of floods that reshaped the face of the ecological and human landscape. Heavy snowfalls led to increasing water levels each spring, until by 1984 floodwaters filled much of the closed basin, wiping out farms one after another, washing out roads, ripping out culverts, and undermining the post–Second World War belief that riparian landscapes could be reshaped into an orderly agricultural and duck machine. What shifted with the waters were not just the boundaries between water and land, but cultural attitudes.

To understand the effects of the floods in the 1980s, it helps to step back and review local efforts at water development and flood control. Floods were nothing new: they had recurred for millennia. As ecologists had begun to argue in the early 1980s, floods were a critical element in the functioning of riparian landscapes. Yet while floods were certainly natural, the effects they had on the basin had changed dramatically in the past century. In presettlement conditions, many of the most damaging effects of floods had been buffered by abundant riparian vegetation. Riparian plants had slowed the speed of floods and reduced the erosive power of flood waters. Side channels, meanders, beaver dams, debris in the creeks, and the sinuous, meandering, swampy landscape had all worked to moderate the impacts of floods. But farming, grazing, and channelization of the Silvies and Blitzen rivers had reduced the riparian landscape's ability to absorb flood waters.

Those same human modifications also reduced people's willingness to live with floods. Early ranchers who had flood-irrigated wild hay meadows had been relatively willing to live with the inconvenience of annual floods. Benefits from flooding had been clear to ranchers: water, lush grass growth, subirrigation, and sediment deposition that increased the quality of basin soils. The ranchers had recognized that if floods were cut off from their meadows, sagebrush and other upland vegetation would move in, reducing ranch income. Early ranchers had protected their houses and barns from the spring waters, and they had tried to manipulate where the flood waters ran in the spring, but they otherwise had been willing to adapt to the floods, living with both the costs and the benefits.

But as ranchers made the switch from wild hay to alfalfa in the 1950s, effectively turning their holdings into what Scharff called "beef factories," they had been less willing to adapt to floods. John Scharff described this transformation approvingly: "The income is rising spectacularly on many ranches as the owners fertilize the meadows, replace sagebrush with grass, use water to better advantage, get higher calf crops, and perfect the hundreds of management factors that make a ranch a better beef factory."[35] To many locals who were struggling to "perfect" their beef factories, the problem seemed clear. Floods washed over the Silvies Valley early in the spring, making it impossible to get the heavy equipment needed for planting alfalfa into wet fields, while in the late summer, water needed for irrigating alfalfa ran out. Why not simply build a storage reservoir that would hold back the waters in the spring and release them in the late summer? Even though in the early twentieth century Bureau of Reclamation officials had spent many years writing reports that declared such projects unfeasible, the political landscape changed when the Army Corps of Engineers came into the picture.

In 1941, the Flood Control Act had authorized the Army Corps of Engineers to survey rivers across the nation for flood control.[36] In 1945, the district engineer of the U.S. Engineers Office had produced the "Report on Preliminary Examination for Flood Control of Silvies River and Tributaries, Oregon," which recommended an extensive survey for flood control. In 1957, the Army Corps of Engineers finally published the results from this survey, arguing that local water conflicts had become acute because very little water from the Silvies ever reached Malheur Lake. Most was used in irrigation, and the rest went to percolation or evaporation.[37] But while irrigation water was running short, the corps could write in 1957 that "irrigation practices are showing improvement on many of the ranches." Primitive flood irrigation was beginning to give way to more efficient projects, as "Large earth-moving equipment has been brought into the basin and is available at reasonable cost for constructing levees, clearing or reconstructing canals, and similar operations."[38] Bulldozers had begun to allow extensive and relatively cheap channelization of local streams and waterways, not to mention the construction of levees that would keep flood water off the land.

The 1957 army report made the case for a storage and flood control reservoir, arguing that floods threatened efficient ranching. From the perspective of army engineers, the "destructive effects of annual flooding" made it difficult to grow "the better types of hay, generally limiting crops to native grasses."[39] The army report argued that floods were being made worse by "lack of adequate natural channel capacity."[40] What this seemingly innocuous statement assumed was that channels were not incised or damaged enough. If only they had become even deeper and wider and more degraded—if only they were more like ditches and less like rivers—then those channels could have contained the floods, engineers believed. The over bank flooding that ecologists and hydrologists now see as the major benefit of high water, army engineers saw as the major problem. The incised channels that ecologists now see as the central problem, engineers then saw as the solution.

To decide if the reservoir could be justified economically, the army calculated a cost-benefit ratio. Cost-benefit ratios were supposed to be a quantitative, and therefore unbiased, way of measuring the value of a project. Army planners estimated total construction costs at $5,454,000, with annual charges of $292,000.[41] Annual benefits were estimated at $408,700.[42] The report claimed that the cost-benefit ratio showed the project would be economically beneficial for the basin.[43] The project did not go forward, however, because contested water rights derailed it, just as they had derailed every other reclamation project ever proposed for the basin.

Cost-benefit ratios were a favored tool for planners because they were seen as value free and therefore beyond attack. Numbers, rather than values or political alliances, surely had to offer a rational way of making decisions, planners believed. But values shaped the assumptions behind these calculations, and as values changed, the calculated cost-benefit ratio could also dramatically change. Twenty years later, in 1977, the Army Corps carried out another study on the same project in the same location, with new cost-benefit ratios that revealed some fundamental changes in values.[44] This time around, estimated project costs were calculated to be over $19 million, three and a half times the cost projection from twenty years earlier (far outpacing inflation). The annual charges for the reservoir increased from $292,000 in the 1957 projection, to $3.5 million (an increase explained largely by the need to service debt from initial construction costs). Most strikingly, total annual benefits decreased to $395,000, so the cost-benefit ratio dropped to 0.11.[45] As the report stated: "In view of the obvious lack of economic feasibility, it is recommended that this study be terminated and no action taken toward broad authorization of a project at this time."[46]

Where did these changes in calculated benefits come from? By 1977 the army had lost its optimism about the possible benefits from irrigation development. Rather than calculating the potential value of agriculture outputs from an entirely transformed basin, as the 1957 report had done, the 1977 calculations simply calculated the increase in value of irrigated hay. Planners therefore figured that the project would produce only $52,000 in annual agricultural benefits from irrigation (the rest of the $395,000 benefits came from flood protection).[47]

The Agricultural Research Station stridently opposed the army's calculations, arguing that the project could create a new agricultural machine in the basin that would produce, not $52,000 in annual benefits as the army calculated, but rather a $13 million profit each year. By using every drop of the average flow of the Silvies River each year to irrigate alfalfa, the Agricultural Research Station staff calculated farmers could produce 236,000 tons of alfalfa each year, worth at least $45 a ton or over $10.6 million. Farmers could then convert each and every acre of marshland in the entire basin to alfalfa. Once water was kept off the land, farmers could use groundwater irrigation to convert sagebrush to improved pastures. Cattle on those irrigated uplands would surely gain over seven hundred pounds of weight per acre, so farmers could get an increase of 10,545,000 pounds of beef over what they were currently producing. Then farmers could sell that beef for an extra $2,636,000 each and every year, leading to over $13 million in annual irrigation benefits, not a mere $52,000.[48]

The army responded by consulting with the Bureau of Reclamation, whose acting regional director gently pointed out some of the flaws in the station's projections: "The assumption that the entire runoff of the Silvies River, 118,000 acre-feet, would be available for crop production (available to the plants) is not valid. The requirement for minimum streamflows, losses from evaporation, and conveyance losses both off and on the farm would reduce this amount by perhaps 40 percent."[49] Conversion costs, the regional director added, to change wild hay meadows into irrigated fields, would not be the $30 per acre figure offered by the superintendent of Squaw Butte, but rather at least $1150 per acre, and probably far more. In addition, the regional director asked, did the Agricultural Research Station really believe that all farmers could produce as much as the station's scientists produced on their experimental farms?[50]

The Agricultural Research Station's calculations existed in a dream world of imaginary agricultural perfection—a world in which Scharff's fantasy of the landscape as a "better beef factory" had been realized. But the superintendent of the Agricultural Research Station did recognize one critical point: that the army's cost-benefit ratios reflected cultural assumptions. He accused the army of lying, writing in a bitter protest letter that "sociological pressures, pressures from others relying on water from the Silvies, and the reluctance of land owners to conform to the acreage limitation may be of greater impact on this project than it 'not being economically feasible.' Please do not confuse the real issues by inferring that the construction costs exceeded the expected increase in income unless it is a fact."[51]

While some locals residents applauded the Army Corps's decision to shelve the project, others felt betrayed. Decades of study had resulted once again in the failure to construct a dam that could save the basin from its own natural vicissitudes. Just a few years after the flood control project was turned down, the worst dreams of planners and ranchers and farmers came true: floods that kept rising, year after year, until water had rewritten the story of the human and natural landscapes.

Heavy snows began in 1982 and continued for several winters, leading to slow but inexorable rises in lake levels. No wall of water came hurtling into town and no great floods of meltwater ripped through the basin, tugging children from their mother's grasp. The waters rose slowly, spread slowly, and seeped slowly through the basin. By June 27, 1984, Malheur Lake had reached 4102.4 feet: nearly nine and a half feet above the normal lake maximum of 4093 feet.[52] Nine and a half feet of water may not sound like much, but in a flat basin, a little bit of water goes a very long way: each one-foot rise in lake levels submerged another 8500 acres.[53] Instead of dropping, the lake continued to slowly rise with each wet year that followed, until by 1986, the lake had reached 4102.6 feet high.[54] While an average lake surface area of about 46,000 acres had seemed normal for Malheur Lake, by June 1984, Malheur, Mud, and Harney lakes had merged, eventually covering more than 170,000 acres, becoming the largest lake in the entire Pacific Northwest.[55]

The local economy, already hurting, suffered tremendously. After a rail bed washout in March 1984, the Union Pacific Railroad closed its spur line between Burns and Ontario, Oregon.[56] This line had been used to transport lumber from the sawmill in Burns, and so lumber had to be trucked out, an expensive proposition.[57] Parts of two highways were submerged, along with fifty-seven thousand acres of marsh habitat. Twenty-five ranches were badly damaged, thirty families were displaced, power and telephone lines were destroyed, carp populations skyrocketed to some 80 to 90 percent of fish biomass, groundwater was contaminated with arsenic, and fifty thousand acres of hay were lost.[58] Much to locals' anger, the State of Oregon and the federal government refused to declare the county a disaster area and refused to release emergency relief funds, largely because the slowly rising waters of a Great Basin flood did not meet outsiders' perceptions of what a flood should be: a sudden, sharp mess.[59]

The Army Corps was called in once again to solve the problem, and after several years of study (and several years of mounting frustration among locals), the corps proposed three possible solutions to the flooding: a dam and reservoir; a canal system that would drain Malheur Lake into the Columbia River system; and a nonstructural solution that would move the railway line out of the floodplain and purchase flood-prone lands from the ranchers. The cost of the proposed reservoir had ballooned to $130 million (up from $19 million seven years before, largely because the army engineers realized a much bigger dam would be needed to control floods). The annual cost of this reservoir solution would be $13.1 million, which even for army engineers seemed a bit steep in a basin where the most profitable crop was hay.[60]

The army figured a much cheaper solution would be to drain water from Malheur Lake through a seventeen-mile-long canal into the Malheur River, which then flowed into the Snake River, then the Columbia River, and from there to the Pacific Ocean itself. The initial 1985 army reconnaissance report estimated the annual cost of the proposed canal at $4.4 million. The report estimated that the annual benefit of flood control would be worth $2,160,000. Malheur Lake water could be sold to the hydroelectric dams on the Columbia River system, planners figured, and those annual power benefits would be worth $4,332,000, leading to a cost-benefit ratio of 1.5:1. The 1985 reconnaissance study concluded that the canal "could be an effective solution to flooding around Malheur Lake and provide economic and social benefits."[61]

These estimates of costs and benefits, while seeming perfectly rational at first glance, proved insupportable even for the army. Most of the calculated annual benefits came from the sale of hydropower at dams on the Snake and Columbia rivers. But, as an army report published two years later admitted, power benefits would mostly occur only in the first two years, as drawdown occurred. After that they would be brief and intermittent only.[62] Moreover, the army had estimated annual flood benefits of over $2 million. Critics quickly pointed out that several years earlier, in the 1977 report, the army itself had estimated annual flood reduction benefits at only $277,000.[63] If the worst flood in one hundred years had produced $1.2 million worth of crop damage, how could flood benefits total over $2 million a year? In a basin that produced such low-value crops, how could it be economically feasible to construct a project that cost far more each year than the crops were ever worth?

By the time the army completed the full report in 1987, their new calculations revealed much higher costs for a much smaller project. The revised canal would hold only half as much water, preventing only about 58 percent of flood damages in the future while reducing hydropower benefits. It would be those power benefits, not flood protection, that might make the plan economically feasible.[64] The army calculated an estimated cost to complete the project at $20,900,000, with estimated annual costs of $1,846,000. The annual benefit would total $1,683,000—but the army calculated that annual benefits to farmers would be very small, and most of the annual benefits would derive from the hypothetical hydropower production sales.[65]

While economic calculations showed that the project was marginally unfeasible economically, what about the environmental consequences? By 1987, the Army Corps of Engineers was required by law to detail possible environmental consequences. The report reveals that, although planners did analyze possible effects, their own values prevented them from paying much attention to what those effects might mean for the ecosystems involved.

The primary environmental concern was that water quality in the Malheur River might suffer, eventually contaminating the Snake River and the Columbia River. Malheur Lake, as an inland sump basin, had the high levels of dissolved solids found in nearly all Great Basin lakes. Evaporation from Malheur Lake, as from most closed basins, concentrated dissolved solids, and the pH of the lake was usually above 7.0. Boron and arsenic concentrations were also high.[66]

What the canal system to save Malheur Lake from its own variability represented was not just an attempt to control a few floods, but an attempt to reshape nature in profound ways by changing a Great Basin watershed into a Pacific Ocean watershed. Malheur Lake is now part of a Great Basin watershed, closed from the sea. This system seems part of its essential nature: it is salty, stinky, filled with boron and arsenic and salts and fishes that have been trapped in their closed basins for many millennia. Intentionally changing the lake from one system to another would have led to a cascading set of environmental complications: What would carp do to the native fish communities in the Malheur River? Would they wipe out the native trout fisheries? If the proposed canal were to link Malheur Lake with Malheur River, the Oregon Department of Fish and Wildlife feared that the native trout fishery would be destroyed. The carp that filled Malheur Lake would find their way into the upper Malheur River, degrading the river as they had degraded the Malheur Lake. The Oregon Department of Fish and Wildlife estimated that the annual fisheries losses would amount to at least $500,000, an amount not figured into any army calculations, even though the potential economic loss far exceeded the potential estimated benefits to farmers.[67]

Would the alkaline, arsenic-laden water from the lakes destroy something essential about the Malheur River, a river that had already been profoundly altered by irrigation? What would those alkaline waters do to the threatened and endangered salmon runs in the Snake and Columbia Rivers? The Army Corps never constructed this canal system, but not because of environmental consequences. Construction costs had risen too high to justify the new cost-benefit ratio, so army economists finally advised against the project.

In this remote watershed, ranchers, irrigation speculators, homesteaders, and wildlife biologists competed for control of the uncertain boundaries between water and land. All the groups that have lived and worked in the Malheur basin have changed the connections between water and land, and all of these changes have led to unintended consequences. But the moral of this story is not that everything people have done has degraded the ecosystem. The effects of different groups were profoundly different.

Some groups tried to bring stability to these flood-prone landscapes, hoping to create a predictable machine that could maximize agricultural or waterfowl production. They cut the connections between water and land, often with disastrous effects. In the short term, this increased cattle, hay, and ducks. In the longer term, their efforts destabilized what they had been trying to stabilize.

Some people, such as the earliest ranchers and recent refuge managers, manipulated water's boundary with land without ever hoping to achieve complete control over either, and without trying to completely separate them. Although French and other early ranchers certainly simplified nature, they did so with surprising sensitivity to ecological conditions, as they sought to accommodate their grazing regimes to intermittent flooding. They manipulated water's boundary with land without ever hoping to achieve complete control over either, and without severing the connections between water and land. Rather than trying to lock rivers and streams within their channels, they learned to take advantage of the richness offered by periodic chaos. Rather than trying to regulate and engineer change out of existence, they learned to live with variability.

In the years since John Scharff retired, management of Malheur riparian areas has become less clumsy, but no less manipulative. Now, instead of using bulldozers to channelize the river, the staff is trying to figure out ways to use bulldozers to return the river to its old meanders. Willow are being planted instead of being ripped out, but herbicides still play a role, removing vegetation that might compete with desired native species. The irrigation and water control system grows ever more elaborate, since without it much of the habitat for rare and endangered birds would be lost. Flood irrigation still waters the meadows, but now it creates hay for bird cover, not just for cattle.

The most profound change in the Blitzen Valley is that refuge staff are no longer trying to fix a single pattern of ponds and meadows and wetlands in place. Instead, they are trying to manage variability back into the system by alternating which meadows are dry and which are wet. Yet, given the constraints of managing a wildlife refuge with extensive investments in structural improvements, this variability can be allowed only within strict limits. For example, the river is now encouraged to meander a little, but not enough to threaten the constructed canals and brood ponds.

Some critics of Malheur Refuge policy have recently argued that the water control system should be dismantled, and natural variability should be allowed to have full sway. But is this possible in a world so dramatically altered by people? Before extensive water control systems, some years water levels were so high that numerous pools and ponds formed in the valley, perfect for brooding waterfowl. Other years few pools formed, and waterfowl rearing habitat was minimal. This historic variability existed within an entirely different context, however. Malheur Refuge was once only one of a long string of fertile, vast marshes stretching up and down the Pacific Flyway. Much of the Great Basin was stopover habitat for migrant birds needing to rest and fatten up on their long journeys to the Arctic. If most of the Malheur Lakes Basin happened to be dry one year, the birds could stop elsewhere, because the Pacific Flyway consisted of numerous patches of desert, riparian, and wetland habitats.

Now, however, the vast majority of those historic riparian areas and marshes are gone, lost to agriculture, shopping malls, and highways. Malheur Refuge has become a critical habitat in a way it never was before. If natural variability were returned at Malheur, it might be disastrous for entire populations of ducks, sandhill cranes, and shorebirds. Until millions upon millions of acres from California to Canada have been restored back to wetland and riparian meadow, allowing natural systems to work entirely without human intervention is as unnatural as trying to gain control over every drop of water and every act of predation.

Refuge managers feel, in other words, that they cannot allow natural systems to be purely natural. Managers try to restore some natural variability, but not enough to threaten the water systems that have been painstakingly constructed. There is nothing ideologically pure about current refuge policy: it is not an attempt to return to pristine natural conditions, nor is it an attempt to gain complete control of nature.

Such a policy infuriates some environmentalists, who see little difference between John Scharff's regime and current refuge attempts to limit predators and regulate water. But this view misses crucial differences. Scharff, unlike current managers, did aim for ideological purity: his ethic was one of control and improvement. He rarely seemed to doubt that humans could and should take complete control of nature. Likewise, some modern environmentalists have an ethic that is equally ideologically pure: the ethic of naturalness. A thing is good when it is natural, bad when it is not. Controlling predators or water is unnatural, so therefore it is bad.

In the world that refuge staff actually have to work in, neither ethic is particularly helpful. Refuge staff muddle along, trying to find some reasonable path between extremes, zigzagging back and forth between trying to manage ducks and cranes, fish and magpies. The refuge managers are trying to act pragmatically, rather than ideologically. They are not trying to restore the refuge to some past set of pristine ecosystems; they are trying to adapt to change, making things work as best they can, while minimizing future complications.

Such pragmatic decisions are the key to adaptive management, which is the messy process of developing a management scheme that incorporates multiple human perspectives while also responding to changing scientific understandings of dynamic ecosystems. At its best, adaptive management is a way of paying close attention to what happens when we manage landscapes, and then altering practices when old ways no longer produce the desired results (or when the results that people desire change). This approach, at heart, is simply applying the scientific method to management. Everything managers do is nothing more, and nothing less, than an experiment. Experimentation means approaching the world with an open mind. As a scientist, you are supposed to treat your own ideas with humility, abandoning your hypotheses if the results are not what you expected. This process is never completely open-minded; initial ideas about how the world ought to work shape what you see. But there is an important ideal here, of allowing the natural world to shape your ideas, and not just the other way around. In other words, there is a kind of give and take, a willingness to be surprised. The critical step for management, however, comes after the research: the hard part is using all that information to change how you work with the land. Adaptive management does not necessarily mean big government programs; what it means above all is people on the ground being responsive to what the land is telling them, and being responsible for acting on that knowledge. It means a dialogue between people and land; it means people knowing the place they work. Adaptive management at its best is an interactive process that yields new information about ecological and human systems and then uses that information to develop policies that can respond to changing knowledge about a changing world.

Managers such as John Scharff long hoped that they could engineer the riparian landscapes to produce a stable output of what people most desired, but the watery landscape proved far too dynamic for this. In the 1930s, refuge managers made reasonable engineering decisions in a desperate situation, developing a set of powerful water manipulation techniques that make excellent sense in a particular context, given the challenges waterfowl populations faced at the time. But as Scharff gained power, those ideas became increasingly rigid. By the 1940s, refuge staff proved slow to respond to information that suggested their schemes were leading to trouble. When events at the refuge began to spiral out of control, managers did not question their own basic assumptions but instead tried to hold the system under increasingly rigid control. Management techniques at Malheur that began as experiments soon became orthodoxy. People found it difficult to challenge the developing orthodoxy until outside events—floods, litigation, and pressure from environmental groups—forced refuge managers to take new perspectives seriously. Conflict forced people, institutions, and states to incorporate new ideas into their worldview.

At Malheur National Wildlife Refuge, management's path is now as indirect as the river's course once was. Legal battles constantly reshape refuge policy, much to the eternal frustration of staff who are trying to get their job done. But such outside influence is a good thing in the long run, however annoying it is from day to day. Without criticism and political pressures and court cases, refuge management would be far more efficient—and in the end, far more problematic.

When managers work in isolation, they can come to operate with the ideological certainties that drove John Scharff's plans. Recent managers at Malheur have had a far more difficult time getting things done than Scharff ever did, for they have been bogged down in court cases, tied up in endless negotiations with different stakeholders, distracted by petitions to list native fish, and dragged into fights with hot-tempered neighbors. While these are all enormous hassles, they offer a way for federal agencies to chart a responsive course in a changing political, social, and ecological landscape.

6

The Industrial Alchemy of Hydraulic Mining

Law, Technology, and Resource-Intensive Industrialization

Andrew C. Isenberg

INCE THE 1850s, the popular icon of the California gold rush has been the lone prospector panning by a stream. In American iconography, the prospector is mining's version of the homesteader: a symbol of simple, virtuous labor, coaxing wealth from a bountiful nature. In 1893, Frederick Jackson Turner incorporated the prospector into his central narrative of American history: settlers' transformation of (in his terms) "wilderness" to "civilization." While the icon of the prospector fit nicely into Turner's frontier thesis, a narrative that centered on farm families progressively moving westward as they established homesteads, the gold rush itself was less well suited. Turner made an allowance for mining in a thesis heavily weighted toward agriculture, but nonetheless California's gold rush was too sudden, too urban, too much undertaken by non-Anglos, and too quickly overtaken by industrialization to fit comfortably into his paradigm.[1]

Nor does the prospector fit easily into the paradigm that replaced Turner's frontier, the regional model of the New Western Historians. Walter Prescott Webb, the intellectual godfather of New Western History, first articulated that model in 1957, defining "the Heart of the West" as a desert region of defeated expectations between Nevada and Colorado.[2] Donald Worster, Webb's chief intellectual heir, extended this interpretation of the desert West to California, characterizing the state as a "hydraulic society," a modern

Mesopotamia of bureaucratically centralized irrigated agriculture.[3] If Turner's vision of nineteenth-century California folded the state back into the agricultural settlement of the trans-Appalachian West, Worster's pressed it forward into the irrigated landscape of the twentieth-century West.

The disappearance of a distinct nineteenth-century California from both of these historical paradigms is not all that links them. In the minds of most historians, the frontier and the desert were basically agrarian places. Yet nineteenth-century California was neither a typical frontier nor entirely a desert province. California was more accurately an emerging industrial place, where the industrial exploitation of minerals began within a few years of the discovery of gold.[4] The production of almost $1 billion in gold between 1849 and 1874 spurred industry in the state; California manufacturing excluding gold mining rose from a value of under $4 million in 1850 to well over $100 million in 1880.[5]

The industrial development of California was by no means inevitable. Like all industrializing nations, the United States achieved its economic growth in the nineteenth century through the combined exploitation of the three so-called factors of production: capital, labor, and natural resources.[6] Yet the nineteenth-century United States was chronically short of the first two of these three ingredients of industrial growth, capital and labor. At great cost, the United States imported a significant proportion of its capital and labor from abroad. At the end of the nineteenth century approximately one-third of American investment capital came from Europe and one-fifth of American wage earners were immigrants. In California these two commodities were still scarcer. Only a fraction of manufacturing capital was invested in the West.[7] Labor is harder to measure: at particular times and places, labor exceeded the demand, but in mid-nineteenth-century California laborers were unruly, transient, and, most important, expensive.[8]

While capital and labor were scarce and expensive, natural resources were abundant. California lacked significant deposits of the two key natural resources of nineteenth-century industrialization—coal and iron ore—yet it possessed a wealth of timber, ranchlands, and precious minerals. Law and technology worked in concert to shift the burden of industrialization to the exploitation of these natural resources. Because most mineral deposits were on public lands, the exploitation of California gold was hardly an autonomous economic development. State and federal authorities enacted legislation that liberalized access to mineral resources. Laws permitted miners—first independent prospectors and later industrial mining companies—to enter upon the public domain to dig, tunnel, log, and dam in their search for gold. These laws funneled natural resources from public lands into the control of entre-preneurs.[9] In California and elsewhere in the West, state and federal courts fa-cilitated the transfer of natural resources in the public domain to the control of private industrialists through a series of friendly rulings.

Precisely because industrialization relied disproportionately on cheap natural resources, it exacted heavy environmental costs. By the end of the 1850s, labor-intensive and thus expensive means of exploiting gold deposits such as pans and rockers (the tools of the prospector) had given way to the industrial techniques of hydraulic mining. Industrial technologies ordinarily require a substantial capital investment, but the technology of hydraulic min-ing was relatively inexpensive.[10] High-pressure water cannons washed hill-sides into sluices constructed to trap gold but let soil and gravel wash away. The sluices flushed these tailings into the streams that flowed out of the Sier-ra Nevada. However inexpensive, hydraulic mining technology created ex-tensive industrial pollution. By the mid-1860s, debris from hydraulic gold mining had fouled and flooded rivers that drained into the Sacramento River, and ultimately into San Francisco Bay, destroying both fish and farmland. By one estimate, between the mid-1850s and the early 1880s, hydraulic mining deposited 885 million cubic yards of debris in California rivers—over three times the amount of earth moved to make way for the Panama Canal.[11] Min-ing sediment discolored the water of San Francisco Bay so extensively that in the 1870s it was visible in the Golden Gate.[12] Moreover, hydraulic miners used mercury, a toxic mineral mined and processed near San Jose, as an amal-gam in their sluices. Large amounts of mercury also found its way into the river environment. In short, as Californians transformed the environment in the pursuit of wealth, they created costly ecological problems.

Law and Technology

Unlike lode deposits, in which precious minerals are encased in solid rock, California gold was located primarily in placer deposits, in which the surrounding rock had been partly or entirely eroded. Some of the greatest erosion was in river valleys. In 1849, in certain places in the streambeds of the Feather, Yuba, American, and other rivers, flakes and nuggets of gold were visible to the naked eye.[13] The river valleys were thus the ecological cen-ters of the gold rush.

Gold in placer deposits was only *relatively* accessible. The flow of water in the streams on the western slope of the Sierra is torrential in the spring, as winter snow melts, but a comparative trickle in the summer. Unpredictable river flow alternately impeded and permitted miners' search for gold. High water in the spring prevented miners from working the streambeds. Not until the summer, when the streams had receded, were the miners able to begin. Companies of miners engaged in the back-breaking work of damming or diverting streams to scour the riverbeds for gold.[14] In a letter home in May 1850, Joseph Pownall described this labor-intensive process:

> You have come to the conclusion it may be that we can pick up a chunk of gold whenever we choose on the surface anywhere. This is a gross mistake. Imagine to yourself a stream between two mountains full of rocks and trees and stones and grass. . . . What is there to be done? Why you have to strike for the rocky bottom or ledge on which the stream runs and on which the gold is deposited . . . which often requires a tremendous deal of extremely laborious work. Picture to yourself your humble servant pulling at one end of a pump endeavoring to keep a hole free while some 3 or 4 companions are at work in it.[15]

If too much water obstructed the miners' access to gold, so too did too little. Miners relied on flowing water to wash gravel through wooden sluices. Low water made it impossible for miners to wash gravel for gold.[16]

The unpredictability of the river valley environment impeded not only the search for gold but the search for outside capital investment to support mining in California. One of the ironies of 1850s California was that, despite producing roughly one-third of the gold in the world, the state was chronically short of investment capital. Many successful miners and merchants took their gold and left California after only a few years. Because so many goods were imported, considerable bullion flowed out of California in the 1850s. Once the most obvious and accessible gold deposits had been exhausted, few investors from outside the state were willing to commit capital to the speculative venture of California placer mining.[17] Stipulations of the state constitution and certain state laws exacerbated the shortage of investment capital. Mindful of the financial panic of 1837, California in the 1850s forbid bank notes to circulate as specie. Californians thus relied on a currency of gold dust, nuggets, and foreign coins. In 1854, much of the California economy operated on credit and in early 1855, several of California's few private banks closed.[18] Following the opening of the Comstock silver lode in Nevada in 1859, much of the available investment capital in California moved there.[19] Investment capital was so scarce in California in the 1850s and 1860s that some mining companies sought funds by offering clerical positions in return for loans.[20] In short, California was chronically short of capital for investment in placer mining. Thus, when miners began in the early and mid-1850s to build reservoirs and canals to control the unpredictable river flow of California, they sought not only to regularize the environment and thus gain easier access to placer deposits, but by imposing predictability on the rivers, to attract investment to placer mining.

The first reservoirs were shoddy and unreliable. Eventually, a few successful miners cobbled together their capital to construct more stable (and profitable) reservoirs. Joseph Pownall, seeing the centrality of the control of water to mining operations and probably weary of laboring in the mines, joined a group of investors that eventually called itself the Tuolumne County Water Company. Beginning in 1853, the company constructed a system of reservoirs and ditches on the Stanislaus River. By 1855, the company had built four large dams. A system of distributing ditches supplied water—for a fee, of course—to mining camps in the area. A typical agreement with a miner in California was for 10 percent of the net proceeds arising from the use of the company's water.[21]

Impounding water was a necessary precondition for the development of the single most important technology in the exploitation of placer deposits: the machinery of hydraulic mining. As early as 1852, engineers used pressurized water from a reservoir to flush gravel into a sluice. Water shot out of the hoses at enormous speed. At the North Bloomfield mine, water left the nozzle at a speed of one hundred miles per hour; the force of the water carved large craters out of the foothills.[22] The water flushed everything—soil, boulders, tree stumps, and gold-bearing gravel—into plank sluices designed to separate heavier gold from lighter material. Every week or two, the miners stopped the flow of water to "clean up" the sluices, or in other words to extract the gold. In the early 1860s in Nevada County, the center of the hydraulic mining country, clean-ups every eight or ten days yielded from $1,000 to $3,000 worth of gold.[23]

Hydraulic mining's advantage was not in its ability to extract gold. As much as 20 percent of the gold that entered the top of the sluice washed out the bottom with the debris.[24] Rather, the technology was astonishingly successful in reducing the costs of labor. According to the Whig journal the *Marysville Herald* in 1854, hydraulic mining allowed one laborer to do the work of six.[25] An 1873 study of mining techniques calculated that handling a cubic yard of gold-bearing gravel cost $15 employing a pan, but a mere $.15 with the hydraulic process.[26]

For investors, hydraulic mining imposed regularity on the nonhuman natural environment and on laborers; these benefits justified its initial costs. By reducing the high costs of labor, hydraulic mining initiated the transformation of the gold country from a place dominated by independent prospectors to an industrial place characterized by wage laborers. The key to this transition was the replacement of *tools* such as pans, picks, and shovels, which were owned and used by independent laborers, with the *machines* of hydraulic mining, which were owned and directed by investors.[27] Moreover, the hydraulic system extended a measure of human control over the dynamic hydrology of the California gold country. By the end of the 1860s, six thousand miles of ditches paralleled the streams of the Sierra, supplying water—controllable and measurable—from the reservoirs to the mines.[28]

Mining companies sought to regularize the legal as well as the natural environment. Through the 1850s and early 1860s, California judges extended the protection of the law to hydraulic miners. To do so, they had to transform a legal system initially constructed to protect the rights of independent prospectors. California's earliest mining laws were improvised by prospectors themselves. In 1849, riverbank prospectors could stake out claims to the minerals below the earth without holding title to the land; most of the land in question belonged to the federal government. These claims were bounded, of course, by certain restrictions. Prospectors' claims were both limited in extent and number (usually no more than one). If unworked, a prospector's claim lapsed entirely. The regulations thus both drew upon and supported the mid-nineteenth-century notion of free labor: each prospector was entitled to a single claim of limited extent so long as he labored at it.[29]

As early as January 1855, when hydraulic mining had just begun to take hold in California, the California Supreme Court extended to hydraulic miners the same rights enjoyed by prospectors who worked their claims, ruling "that however much the policy of the State, as indicated by her legislation, has conferred the privilege to work the mines, it has equally conferred the right to divert the streams from their natural channels." Hydraulic miners were bound only to respect the rights of prior appropriators of a river's water. Because hydraulic mining companies often held such rights themselves—sometimes by succeeding to the claims of the first prospectors—the doctrine of prior appropriation extended hydraulic mining companies' privileges more than it limited them. Those privileges were extensive. In an October 1855 case the California Supreme Court ruled that prior appropriators, who in many cases were hydraulic mining companies, acquired a "*quasi* private proprietorship" to the use of a river.[30]

In several cases, California jurists eroded the ability of lawyers to categorize hydraulic miners' ditches, which frequently overflowed and flooded neighbors' lands, as nuisances.[31] In 1858, the California Supreme Court overturned a district court ruling that had awarded damages to plaintiffs whose lands had been flooded by a break in a Tuolumne County Water Company reservoir. In overturning the lower court's ruling, the state supreme court held that the lower court judge had erroneously instructed the jury to hold the water company to ideal standards of construction and safety. The lower court judge had instructed the jury that "if they believe that . . . the defendants could have constructed [the dam] in a better or more substantial manner as to prevent its breaking, then they are liable." Such standards, the court ruled, imposed impossibly high burdens on water companies and hydraulic miners. Instead, they ruled that water companies were required only to construct their dams using the far weaker and more nebulous standard of "ordinary care and diligence." It was not a question, they ruled, of what the company "could have done," but rather "what discreet and prudent men should do."[32] Later using that same term, the court overturned another district court ruling in a similar case against the St. Louis Independent Water Company, in which the company's flume had collapsed in a storm, flooding neighbors' lands. The judges of the California Supreme Court charged that the lower court judge had improperly instructed the jury to find the company liable unless it had built its flume to the standards of a "*very prudent* man" rather than merely the standards of "ordinarily prudent men."[33] Such rulings made it nearly impossible for injured parties to demonstrate negligence on the part of hydraulic mining companies.

The transformation of the California legal environment was an extension of a process of legal change that had started in the northeastern United States decades earlier. Judges shifted away from reliance upon English common law, which largely protected agricultural uses of land and rivers and discouraged industrial development. They came to regard the law not as a body of immutable principles but as a social tool that could promote change. By the middle of the nineteenth century court decisions increasingly favored industrialists, reflecting industry's increasing economic weight.[34] California's legal transformation also paralleled the economic transformation of the state: from independent, technologically rudimentary prospectors to technologically sophisticated industries. The legal change did not merely reflect the industrialization of mining; rather, its relationship to economic change was reciprocal: it both reflected ecological and economic change and it furthered those changes.

Industry and the Environment

Hydraulic mining exacted startling environmental costs. If, as one geologist has maintained, the rivers of the Sierra foothills are the results of a geologic contest between the mountains and the erosive effects of the water-rich atmosphere, then hydraulic mining tipped the balance of that contest decidedly in favor of erosion.

At the mines, the erosive power of water cannons left the landscape blasted and worn. To reach deep deposits of gold, large mines sunk a shaft from one hundred to two hundred feet deep to the channel of gold. Miners then dug a nearly horizontal tunnel called an adit, graded slightly downward, from the bottom of the shaft to the bank of the nearest river. In the adit, which could be several hundred feet long, the miners constructed a plank sluice. For valuable mines, the adit was wide enough to accommodate two sluices side by side, so that miners could stop the flow of water and extract gold from one sluice while continuing to flush gravel through the other.[35] By the early 1880s, large hydraulic mines kept the monitors running and sluices flowing day and night, using water power to generate electricity that flooded the mines with light.[36]

The wilderness advocate John Muir observed that in the gold country, "the hills have been cut and scalped and every gorge and gulch and broad valley have been fairly torn to pieces and disemboweled, expressing a fierce and desperate energy hard to understand."[37] Another horrified observer wrote in 1868:

> By no other means does man so completely change the face of nature than by this process of hydraulic mining. Hills melt away and disappear under its influence. . . . The desolation that remains after the ground, thus washed, is abandoned, is remediless and appalling. The rounded surface of the bed rock . . . strewn with enormous boulders too large to be removed, shows here and there islands of the poorer gravel rising in vertical cliffs with red and blue stains, serving to mark the former levels, and filling the mind with astonishment at the changes, geologic in their nature and extent, which the hand of man has wrought.[38]

Hydraulic mines also consumed or destroyed large amounts of timber. The mines needed large supplies of wood for flumes and sluices. Wooden blocks used to pave the sluices were replaced every few weeks. Reservoirs submerged the trees at the bottom of valleys.[39] Altogether, according to the

California State Agricultural Society, by 1870 one-third of the timber in the state was already gone—almost all of that deforestation occurred in the sugar pine forests in the Sierra gold country.[40]

The environmental costs of hydraulic mining were not confined to the gold country. Thousands of tons of debris traveled through the sluices to be deposited in the river valleys directly below the mines. Debris piled so high in the Bear and Yuba rivers that all but the tops of pine trees on the banks were submerged. On the Yuba, debris piled up beneath twenty-foot-high telegraph poles until only the top four to six feet remained above the surface.[41] Downstream, debris filled river channels; the channel of the Yuba was filled so completely that by the 1870s the stream ran a mile away from its original course.[42] Debris spoiled salmon spawning grounds: in 1878, the California Commissioners of Fisheries reported that hydraulic mining debris had destroyed half of the salmon habitat in the state.[43]

Debris raised riverbeds, causing spring floods to inundate farmlands with a watery mixture of sand and gravel that farmers called "slickens." The mixture was poisonous to humans, other animals, and soil. It was high in alkali and deficient in phosphorous and nitrogen; nothing would grow in it.[44] In order to confine the waters of the spring floods, farmers raised levees. As new deposits of sediment accreted on the riverbeds, they raised the levees further. By 1878, stretches of the Bear River's bed were actually higher than the surrounding countryside: the waters of the river were held in place only by the artificial levee.[45]

Sediment poured all the way to the mouth of the Sacramento River and beyond. Steamboat pilots reported in 1878 that at the mouth of the Sacramento so much sediment had accumulated that the bottom showed at low tide. Likewise, the secretary of the Navy reported extensive shoaling at the naval base on Mare Island in San Pablo Bay by the late 1870s. In short, industrial mining did not extract wealth from the nonhuman natural environment so much as it rearranged the distribution of natural wealth.

Much of the debris that mining companies flushed downstream contained large amounts of mercury. By the 1870s, California had become not only a leading producer of gold but mined one-third of the mercury in the world. Much of the mercury came from the New Almaden mine outside San Jose in Santa Clara County.[46] The production figures of New Almaden's Quicksilver Mining Company from 1850 to 1885, though incomplete, indicate an average yearly production of nearly two million pounds.[47]

Laborers at New Almaden, particularly those below ground, were largely Mexican-Americans. They dug the dark red mercuric sulfide ore, called cinnabar, and packed two-hundred-pound loads of ore to the surface. Above ground, workers heated the cinnabar in furnaces to transform it into elemental mercury. The odorless, colorless vapors escaping the furnace were highly toxic. According to William Wells, who visited New Almaden in 1863, the vapor from the chimneys killed every tree on the mountainside above the furnace. Cattle sickened if they grazed within a half-mile radius of the furnace. The furnace was likewise poisonous to the laborers at the mine. Employees worked at the furnace for only one week out of four. Wells wrote: "Pale cadaverous faces and leaden eyes are the consequence of even these short spells. . . . [T]o such a degree is the air filled with the volatile poison . . . that gold coins and watches on the persons of those engaged about the furnaces become galvanized and turn white. In such an atmosphere, one would seem to inhale death with every respiration."[48]

Indeed, mercury vapor is quite poisonous. Between 75 and 85 percent of inhaled elemental mercury vapors are absorbed by the human body and are rapidly distributed throughout. Short-term effects, likely familiar to the workers at the New Almaden furnace, range from tremors to fatigue to nausea and vomiting. Because mercury easily transcends the blood-brain barrier, it is particularly toxic to the nervous system. Chronic nervous system effects include mental instability, personality changes, memory loss, and speech impairment.[49]

For the industrial laborers of the Coast Range, quicksilver production was debilitating, but for the hydraulic mining companies of the Sierra, the close availability of mercury was advantageous. As the degradation of gold coins and watches by mercury vapors at New Almaden demonstrated, mercury's ability to readily amalgamate with gold allowed hydraulic miners to harvest greater amounts of gold from their sluices. Accordingly, the addition of copious amounts of quicksilver to the sluices quickly became an integral part of the hydraulic mining process. An 1885 treatise on hydraulic mining recommended that a "charge" of quicksilver consisting of 225 pounds be put into the upper two hundred to three hundred feet of a sluice, with a further amount distributed farther down the sluice. The North Bloomfield mine put between one thousand and thirteen hundred pounds of mercury into its main sluice every twelve days. The Blue Tent mine charged its sluice with two tons of quicksilver.[50] According to an 1869 estimate, the mines consumed over one million pounds of mercury a year. An 1874 estimate put the yearly consumption at nearly one and a half million pounds.[51]

Cleanup crews could not recover all of the mercury-gold amalgam from the sluices. Much of it washed out of the sluices with the rest of the debris.

Large clay boulders rolled through the sluices, carrying off significant amounts of gold and mercury.[52] Owing to the inefficiency of the sluices in capturing gold, the debris contained such large amounts of precious metal that enterprising engineers contracted to mine it. Debris prospectors included Thomas Edison, who formed a company to mine tailings in 1879.[53] Edison and other debris prospectors had ample material with which to work. The eighty feet of debris on the Bear River in 1872 contained large amounts of both gold and mercury.[54] The Bear River Tunnel Company, which proposed to mine it, estimated that the canyons below the largest hydraulic mines contained twenty tons of mercury every mile. Each pound of mercury contained one dollar's worth of gold.[55]

Much of the mercury in the rivers downstream of the mines, together with mercury in vapors that returned to the Earth's surface in rain and snow, was likely converted by bacterial microorganisms in rivers to methyl mercury, an organic compound. Methyl mercury moves readily through the food chain, from microorganisms to the fish that consume them, to the larger fish that eat the smaller fish. As methyl mercury moves through the food chain, it concentrates at higher levels in the bodies of animals. Human beings, when they consume such fish, absorb nearly 100 percent of methyl mercury through the gastrointestinal tract. Methyl mercury poisoning produces the same ill effects as the inhalation of mercury vapors.[56] Many Californians doubtless consumed contaminated fish in the 1860s and 1870s. Canneries continued to fish the Sacramento and San Joaquin systems heavily: in the mid-1870s, fisheries extracted over nine million pounds of fish from the Sacramento and San Joaquin rivers for markets in San Francisco, Sacramento, and Stockton.[57]

Reckoning with Hydraulic Mining

Anonymous Californians' destruction of corporate reservoirs as early as the 1850s demonstrated their recognition of the concentration of economic power in the hands of those who controlled water. Their destruction of the reservoirs presaged the legal challenge to the hydraulic miners in the 1870s and 1880s by a Sacramento Valley farmers' organization, the Anti-Debris Association.[58] Some historians have portrayed the Anti-Debris Association as a protopopulist organization, but the Anti-Debris Association represented not hardscrabble homesteaders but large-scale commercial farmers. The group was organized at the behest of one of the largest and most influential engines of economic development in California, the Southern Pacific Railroad. The owners of the Southern Pacific conglomerate had determined by the late

1860s that California's economic future was in commercial agriculture rather than mining. They employed the newspaper they controlled, the *Sacramento Record-Union*, to editorialize against hydraulic mining. In the summer of 1878, the editor of the *Record-Union*, William Mills, was instrumental in organizing the Anti-Debris Association, whose purpose was to pursue a lawsuit against hydraulic miners.[59]

The legal system provided no easy solution to the conflict over water rights. Statutes favored the miners. The California water code of 1872 embraced the notion of "prior appropriation," or "first in time, first in right." The judiciary, however, tempered these statutes by recognizing the older, common law doctrine of riparian rights. This doctrine protected farmers' vested rights to the undisturbed, natural flow of the river.[60] The guiding purpose of the common law was to restrain uses of the land to agricultural purposes. Instrumental uses of the land such as dams and mills, for instance, ran counter to one of the common law's cardinal principles: "use your land without harming another's" (*sic utere tuo ut alienum non laedas*).

The confusion of the legal system was evident in an 1857 California Supreme Court case involving a dispute between two hydraulic mining companies over the diversion of water from the Bear River. Associate Justice Peter Burnett complained that "The mining interest of the State has grown up under the force of new and extraordinary circumstances, and in the absence of any specific and certain legislation to guide us. Left without any direct precedent, as well as without specific legislation, we have been compelled to apply to this anomalous state of things the analogies of the common law, and the more expanded principles of equitable justice." He concluded, "in these mining cases, we are virtually projecting a new system." Nonetheless, he wrote, "we are compelled to decide these cases, because they must be settled in some way, whether we can say after it is done, that we have given a just decision or not." Unable to untangle the claims and counterclaims of the mining companies, the justices opted to affirm the simple expedient of prior appropriation. While the doctrine provided clarity, the justices, despite their general inclination to support the economic interests of entrepreneurs, were clearly unnerved by its potential for concentrating power in the hands of a single corporation.[61]

Ironically, the plaintiff in the suit, the Bear River and Auburn Mining Company, whose prior right to divert the waters of the Bear River the court ultimately affirmed, unintentionally provided the court with the opportunity to express its misgivings over the "new system" that hydraulic mining had created. Overreaching in its arguments before the court, the company maintained that, by its prior appropriation, it had acquired "a positive vested right" to an undiminished and unaltered flow of water in the Bear River, just as a farmer or rancher had a right to an uncorrupted flow of water to irrigate crops or water stock. The court rejected this contention in unequivocal terms. Burnett wrote: "The use of water for domestic purposes, and for the watering of stock, are *preferred uses,* because essential to sustain life. Other uses must be subordinate to these. . . . in our mineral region we have a novel use of water, that cannot be classed with the preferred uses."[62] In 1857, agriculturalists' rights to water in the gold country were largely hypothetical; rather, the court asserted those rights as a check on the otherwise absolute rights to divert water that the hydraulic mining companies held under the doctrine of prior appropriation.

Economically and politically, California was likewise divided between agricultural and mining sections. Representatives to the California Assembly from the agricultural districts of the Central Valley were the leading opponents of hydraulic mining. By 1878, Valley representatives had achieved a majority in the Assembly and created a special Committee on Mining Debris. Hearings before the committee in early 1878 publicly discredited hydraulic mining companies, which sought to blame debris on natural erosion and claimed that slickens contributed to the fertility of the soil.[63]

Too politically astute to endorse the mine owners' transparently disingenuous denials of responsibility for the debris, the minority—representatives from mining districts and urban areas—adopted a more persuasive defense of the mines. The minority report argued: "The industry from which a large part of the damage proceeds gives employment and sustenance to a considerable portion of the State."[64] This argument prevailed when the Assembly considered a bill prohibiting the dumping of mining debris in rivers. The Assembly rejected the bill by a ratio of five to one. Every member of the Assembly from the urban districts of Sacramento and San Francisco voted against the bill.[65] San Francisco's reliably pro-mining *Alta California* celebrated this result, editorializing that the bill was "properly killed." The editors argued that "The miners have a legal right to use the natural channels for the outlet of their sluices, and even if they had not, it would be policy to give them that right, for the State could not afford to do without the $10,000,000 or $12,000,000 obtained from the hydraulic mines annually."[66]

As a compromise measure, the legislature passed the Drainage Act providing for the building of dams to minimize downstream pollution. Unfortunately, the dams built under the auspices of the Drainage Act failed utterly to contain mining debris. A fourteen-foot-high, two-mile-long log dam across the Yuba River broke in three places during the rains of 1881. The water poured through with such force that it crushed the ten-ton boulders used to construct the dam. During the dry summer that followed, much of the remainder of the dam caught fire and burned down.[67]

Farmers thus turned to the courts to challenge the hydraulic mining companies. Their challenge to hydraulic mining became more powerful in the 1880s, as steam-powered tractors, reapers, and threshers manufactured in Stockton spurred the exponential expansion of wheat cultivation in the Central Valley. In 1879, according to the federal census, California's wheat production had been seventh in the nation; in 1884, California led the nation in wheat production.[68]

The expansion of agriculture undercut the hydraulic miners' claim to be economically indispensable to California, the claim that had always forestalled regulation of the industry. By the mid-1880s, the economic landscape had changed markedly: the wheat farmers who opposed hydraulic mining debris had become one of the leading economic sectors in the state. The biggest wheat farmers emerged from the same groups of investors that included the hydraulic miners. Edward Woodruff, for instance, a wheat farmer who owned an agricultural estate of seventeen hundred acres, was in the late 1870s also a speculator in Marysville real estate and in mining claims in the Ophir District in Utah Territory.[69] In 1884, Woodruff sued one of the largest mines in the state for inundating his lands with slickens. Judge Lorenzo Sawyer of the Ninth U.S. Circuit Court ruled in Woodruff's favor. He declared mining debris a nuisance and perpetually enjoined miners from discharging debris into rivers.[70] The decision was not unanticipated: California lower-court decisions had paved the way, and Sawyer's ruling drew on evidence of pollution from the mines that had been part of the public record for over a decade. In short, it was not a sudden awareness that hydraulic mining created pollution that urged the court to act, but the knowledge that the pollution harmed another important economic interest in California. Sawyer had ruled against one part of California's industrial economy, the hydraulic miners, because their mining debris harmed the economic interests of another, and increasingly important, part of the industrial economy, the heavily mechanized farmers of the Central Valley.

By the early 1880s, hydraulic mining had transformed the river environments of the Sierra and the Sacramento Valley. Thirty years of hydraulic mining overturned the ecological order of these environments: it unearthed long-buried minerals; it washed away hilltops and flushed them to the bottom of San Francisco Bay; it raised riverbeds above the level of their banks.

No less significant than the extent of these changes was their rapidity. Hydraulic mining left large mines such as North Bloomfield as steeply eroded "badlands," not unlike the Badlands of South Dakota or Wyoming. The badlands were created by a geologic process similar to that of hydraulic mining: as one geologist called it, the "cutting action" of water on a slope.[71] A process that in South Dakota took two million years was complete in California in a mere three decades.

Hydraulic mining had social as well as environmental costs. The industrialization of mining closed off opportunities for independent prospectors. Hydraulic mining diffused its pollution widely, endangering the health of Californians well downstream of the mines. In effect, the operators of hydraulic mines profited by extracting valuable commodities from nature while passing along the costs of extraction to less powerful members of the community in the form of industrial pollution. The transformation of nature to make possible the extraction of gold was extensive, invasive, and, when one considers the damages to river lands, forests, fisheries, and human health, arguably as costly as the wealth extracted from the mines was valuable.

Nineteenth-century environmental history is often told as a story of the short-sighted plunder of natural resources. Hydraulic mining in California was, ironically, an effort to impose order on the environment, to make the extraction of resources regular and predictable. That effort, and the large-scale transformation of the environment that resulted from it, reflected the larger economic, cultural, and ecological context of California industrialization: a shortage of capital and labor and an abundance of natural resources. Hydraulic mining in nineteenth-century California was emblematic of the industrialization of the nineteenth-century West in general. The effort to shift the burden of industrial development to the environment characterized not only the mining West but logging, industrial ranching, and "bonanza farming": not capital- or labor- but resource-intensive.

This extraction of gold meant the rearrangement of other parts of the environment, often to the detriment of Californians, such as foothills rock and soil to river bottoms, and mercury to the bodies of fish and human beings. This extensive alteration of the environment was premised on the belief that nature was a storehouse of resources that could be extracted as commodities. The environment, however, contradicted that assumption at every turn. The California environment was an interconnected system that embraced the human economy and human bodies. Minerals did not cease to be part of nature when they passed from the environment to commodities in the human economy. The flow of commodities through the market was inseparable from the flow of energy and materials through the environment: think of the passage of mercury from mineral to commodity back to the environment as debris. Human beings were part of that flow of material both as economic actors and as biological entities: in the transitions from mineral to commodity to debris some mercury lodged in the bodies of Californians. To borrow a phrase from the California naturalist John Muir, "When we try to pick out anything by itself, we find it hitched to everything else in the universe."[72]

PART THREE

Empires

■ The processes of resource use and the power of nature to alter human plans that were so evident in the first two parts have a place in the final part as well. Here, four authors tackle the problems of empires and the environment, whether the ability of disease to wreck imperial military plans in the 1700s or the problems of a huge totalitarian state seeking food in international waters. Together, they provide interesting perspectives on the interaction of culture and nature on a larger scale. The Soviet state believed that it could control nature through heavy applications of applied science, and natural systems crumbled under the onslaught. Disease hindered European armies working in the Caribbean, but Europeans had made decisions that unwittingly helped spread that disease. The British took ideas about nature and certain expectations with them on their colonial missions, but they also were forced to adapt those ideas in the face of new ecosystems. And in West Africa a new disease sprang up, ran wild through the maize crop, then faded before humans could even understand it, much less control it.

The first two chapters, by James McCann and Paul Josephson, examine the impact of science and technology on what might be called the food industry. The next two chapters, by John McNeill and Tom Dunlap, address different aspects of the histories of the European empires from the perspective of environmental vectors and change.

In his chapter "West Africa's Colonial Fungus: Globalization and Science at the End of Empire, 1949–2000," James McCann uses the brief but devastating appearance in Africa of a strain of maize rust as a vehicle to examine how the scientific and economic institutions of the former imperial powers managed to continue to dominate the political ecology of Africa, even as their empires waned after World War II. Maize, imported into Africa in the sixteenth century from the New World, had attained a dominant position in the food system, and the cultivation and consumption of maize had found an important place in African cultural practices. The rust that appeared suddenly in 1950 brought a loss of 40–50 percent of the crop in many places, with a rapid rise in the price of this basic staple. The response was an international scientific effort to develop resistant strains of maize, an effort funded and led not by Africans but rather by Europeans and Americans, and it did not rely upon the knowledge of local farmers. The irony is that the rust disappeared by 1954, without any new maize strain having been introduced, and international agricultural research has yet to come up with an entirely satisfactory reason for its sudden disappearance.

At the time of its creation, the Soviet Union was a vast country rich in natural resources but underdeveloped industrially. The Bolsheviks sought to change this. Paul Josephson shows, in "When Stalin Learned to Fish: Natural Resources, Technology, and Industry under Socialism," how they sought to apply science and technology to create a highly productive fishing industry. However, Josephson argues that the use of what he calls brute-force technology, namely the insensitive application of "technologies on a massive scale," led over and over again to failure. Centralized, authoritarian planning and management both overreached the technological capacities of the Soviet system and neglected long-term consequences for biodiversity and the environment. Under Stalin, biological, scientific thought yielded to industrial models, and "resource scientists . . . became [in effect] . . . engineers." Massive funding for scientific research was supposed to result in massive gains for the fishing industry, as fishing shifted over the decades from inland to coastal to distant, high-seas locations. Damming rivers for hydroelectricity and agricultural water use created vast new bodies of water that opened the possibility of fish farming, but reengineered rivers harmed spawning areas and migration routes. Poor management and failure to realize the consequences of changed water temperatures and chemistry had catastrophic consequences for fish stocks in inland waterways, as did industrial pollution. The only option was scouring the high seas with huge trawler fleets and floating fish factories, but here too unrestrained, mechanized fishing exhausted the fish supply. This fish plunder was brute force technology par excellence. Economic policies with dire, perhaps irreversible, environmental consequences produced processed fish products that Soviet consumers found inedible.

The successes and failures of European domination of the Caribbean islands have usually been recounted in terms of the interplay of political, military, and economic forces and interests. In "Yellow Jack and Geopolitics: Environment, Epidemics, and the Struggles for Empire in the American Tropics, 1650–1900," John McNeill shows that one can understand the imperial and anti-imperial contests "in the lowland tropics of Atlantic America" only by revealing the links to environmental and epidemiological history. He argues that the European exploitation of the islands through the introduction of intensive sugar cultivation produced conditions that favored the mosquitoes that carried yellow fever. That disease, in turn, proved central in turning back the full Anglo conquest of the sugar-producing islands. To understand this history requires understanding the interdependencies between the life cycle of the relevant mosquito species, the agricultural cycle and economics of sugar planting and refining, the relative immunities of different human populations, the demographics of military expeditions from Europe, and the nature of siege warfare. Were it not for huge casualties caused by yellow fever, northern Europeans would have enjoyed much greater success in their conquests. In fact, the fever was a chief weapon working against them.

Tom Dunlap, in "Creation and Destruction in Landscapes of Empire," offers a picture of the interaction between Anglo-American settlers and the environments of North America, Australia, and New Zealand that is sweeping not only in its geographic scope but in its conceptualization of change. His chapter can thus serve as a survey of a particular part of environmental history and as an introduction to the large themes that underlie both this volume and the field itself. Dunlap argues that settlement and its impact on nature is still an ongoing process dependent on both natural and mental processes. The progressive conquest of these areas was premised on beliefs in individual opportunity, the application of practical knowledge to create wealth, and an eventual desire to be simultaneously "Western" and "native." Becoming native, developing native roots, meant claiming native landscapes and flora and fauna as their own. This embrace, in turn, helped feed the new environmentalism, which fundamentally has come to reject what Dunlap calls "settler culture and history" and the idea of the "conquest of nature."

The new environmentalism demands that the human culture that evolved in the past five centuries must change radically. This demand is perhaps too radical and too idealistic, since it requires great changes that will do great harm to current ways of life. At the same time, it has also revealed new challenges, namely the need to resolve the dichotomies between understandings of nature and of culture and between what is considered natural and what is in fact urban or suburban.

7

West Africa's Colonial Fungus
Globalization and Science at the End of Empire, 1949–2000

James C. McCann

N SEPTEMBER 1949, a colonial plant pathologist at Sierra Leone's Njala research station reported with alarm the presence of a brownish-red fungus on the leaves of that colony's maize crop. He thought it to be a variant of the fungus *Puccinia sorghi* and called it the "American rust." Within the next three years this highly virulent crop disease had spread throughout West Africa's humid zone to Gold Coast, Ivory Coast, and Nigeria, and then across the entire African maize belt west to east, destroying as much as 50 percent of vital maize harvests. In 1950 the effects of this new disease in some areas caused maize prices to rise by 500 percent. By 1956 the disease had spread across the globe's southern hemisphere, infecting maize in Madagascar, Australasia, and as far east as Christmas Island in the western Pacific.

Beginning with the 1949 report from Sierra Leone, colonial officials mobilized a network of applied scientists and research institutions linked within the British colonial administration to respond to this immediate threat to the food supply of their colonial possessions. But shortly thereafter the limits of the colonial science infrastructure gave way to a new postwar reality. By the height of the "American rust" crisis in 1952 crop scientists, geneticists, and plant breeders from around the globe had begun a frenetic effort to identify the fungus, to find resistant maize germplasm, and to set up breeding programs to solve the threat to colonial food supply and economic stability. Joining practitioners of colonial science were powerful new American institutions, and a new array of multilateral agencies, progeny of the postwar world. By 1953 this self-confident global network had produced new strains of resistant maize but found to its surprise that the threat of American rust to the world's food supply had vanished as quickly and mysteriously as it had come.

What happened? And what can we learn from this seemingly narrow and now-forgotten episode of crop disease? The purpose of this chapter is to use the short-lived American rust crisis to understand the nature of science, political ecology, and globalization of power at the end of Europe's formal global empires and the beginning of the postcolonial multilateral world. The American rust itself was an intense but short-lived threat to the colonial food supply, but the response to it was a globalized empiricism that had gestated from within a mature imperial world that was on its way to becoming a world dominated by a modern development industry and invasive multilateral organizations. In the 1950s the organizations and economic philosophies that would dominate the political ecology of development were only in embryonic form, but their global reach was increasingly evident.

Maize and West Africa

The response to a mysterious but imminent threat to West Africa's maize crop stemmed from the key role that this New World crop had come to assume in Africa in general and West Africa in particular over the course of the four and a half centuries since its introduction via the Atlantic trade system. It is worthwhile tracing maize's rise from a farm-level curiosity to its current dominant status in twentieth-century African food systems.

After the opening of the Atlantic basin to trade, cultural exchange, and violent exploitation of human labor, the Old World was for maize a tabula rasa. The plant *Zea mays* arrived in Africa after 1500 as part of the massive global ecological and demographic transformation that historian Alfred Crosby calls the "Columbian Exchange."[1] The great irony, of course, is that the same Atlantic economy that wrenched captive labor from Africa to the preindustrial economies of scale in the New World also provided to Africa new cultigens (cassava, beans, potatoes, and maize) that reinvented the continent's food supply. There is, however, little documentary evidence of what must have been a conscious process of Europeans and Africans introducing the maize plant to Africa and installing it into the existing farming systems that had originally evolved around the Old World crops of sorghum, millet, and rice. Historical sources are maddeningly silent on this process, and the importation of the maize seeds to various parts of Africa generally went unremarked, though it certainly was not unremarkable.

The first reference to maize's introduction to Africa may be that of an anonymous Portuguese pilot in 1540 who described its already well-established cultivation on the Cape Verde Islands: "At the beginning of August they begin to sow grain, which they call subaru [zaburro], or in the West Indies mehiz [sic]. It is like chick pea, and grows all over these islands and along the West African coast, and is the chief food of the people."[2]

On the island of São Tomé another Portuguese pilot in the mid-sixteenth century reported that the island's slave traders fed their captives on "zaburro, which we call maize in the western islands and which is like chickpeas."[3] By the middle of the seventeenth century European references to maize in settings in coastal West Africa were commonplace. French scholar Dominique Juhé-Beaulaton cites in great detail historical "recit[s] de voyage" that chronicle the appearance of maize on West Africa's Gold Coast beginning in the early seventeenth century. She notes that by the late seventeenth century both millet and sorghum declined dramatically, replaced by maize, which had at that point become the dominant food source in the region. By the eighteenth century maize was the principal *céréale cultivée* in the region. Only in two areas, the Volta River delta and at coastal Axim, did rice remain the dominant cereal.[4]

West African farmers from the Akan region (Gold Coast) to Dahomey to Yorubaland found maize's early maturation and low labor requirements ideal for intercropping with cassava (another New World innovation) and as a pioneer crop in forest clearance. Maize proved to be a key component for what Kojo Amanor calls forest fallow cultivation.[5] Depending on its New World provenance and the maritime links that originally imported it, maize arrived in Africa in three distinct cultivars (flint, dent, and floury) and in a wide range of colors. Each of these maize types reflects many generations of selection and adaptation of maize germplasms by farmers (mostly women, of course) in Mexico, the Caribbean, and Latin America who selected for genetic traits to increase yield, reduce risk, and thrive in specific ecozones. These various maize types differ in agronomic characteristics: flints are early-maturing hard starch, dents tend to a higher yield and tolerate warmer temperatures, and floury maize has soft starches favored by women who grind flour by hand. Yellow maize has beta-carotene in its seed coat, white does not;

red, brown, and blue maizes offer aesthetic choices and seed selection markers. Red flint maize dominated the eastern Mediterranean and Nile Valley until the mid-twentieth century.[6]

By the twentieth century West African farmers, processors, and consumers had established distinctive tastes and aesthetic preferences. In Nigeria, for example, C. L. M. Eijnatten describes an elaborate geography of preference in Nigeria by mid-twentieth century:

> In northern Nigeria most of the maize cultivated is of the pale yellow colour and is flinty, although white flinty varieties do occur quite regularly. Around larger towns white floury varieties are regularly cultivated, but these only on a small scale and invariably only for sale to "southern" inhabitants of these towns. In the northern and eastern parts of this region the occurrence of dark brown, red or blue coloured grains is quite common.
>
> In the whole of southern Nigeria the people have a strong aversion towards brown, red, or blue grains. A definite preference for white colour does exist in Oyo, Abeokuta, and Ijebu provinces of Western Nigeria and in the eastern part of Eastern Nigeria, both of which produce mainly white varieties. It is in these areas that type and colour preferences are very pronounced, especially in the Yoruba communities of Western Nigeria. In most other areas colour preference is of little importance. Either of the two colours, white or yellow, will be acceptable, provided the grain type is suitable for the preparation of the foodstuffs. The preference for flinty or floury grains is less pronounced than the colour preference even in the "white floury" areas of Western and Eastern Nigeria. When colour preferences were plotted on a map of Nigeria a mosaic is obtained, of intermingled preferences, varying from one town to the other. Outside of these areas flinty grains were normally judged more acceptable than soft, floury types, apart from Niger province. In Illorin province just north of the distribution area of white floury maize varieties, the white floury "Yoruba maize," as it is called, was definitely not acceptable.[7]

By 1950, the temporal setting of our story, maize had achieved prominent status in the African food supply in what had become key British colonies in West Africa (Gold Coast, Nigeria), East Africa (Kenya), and in southern Africa (Malawi, Northern Rhodesia, and Southern Rhodesia). In South Africa itself the mining economy increasingly depended on cheap black labor fed on

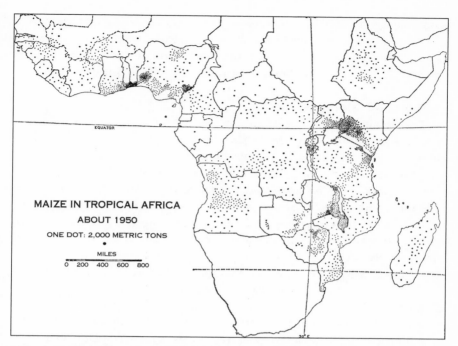

Maize in Tropical Africa, about 1950. Source: Marvin Miracle, *Maize in Tropical Africa* (Madison: University of Wisconsin Press, 1966), 82.

stiff maize porridge washed down with maize beer. French West Africa (especially Dahomey, Ivory Coast, and Togo), the Belgian Congo, and the Portuguese colonies of Angola and Mozambique were equally dependent on stable supplies of food at stable prices. Moreover, the trend of maize's expansion into African diets in the decade of the 1950s would continue and by the end of the century become in some cases a monoculture dominating all other food sources.[8]

In the postwar decades the European empire was in the process of building urban economies, a stable labor force, and political institutions, all of which relied on stable food prices at the farm gate, at the mine head, and in urban markets. The map of maize in tropical Africa indicates what colonial officials and agricultural scientists already knew about relative dependency on the crop, its levels of production, and long-term trends.

Despite maize's growing importance in much of colonial Africa, agricultural research had neglected the crop, concentrating research investments on cash crops such as coffee, cotton, palm oil, groundnuts, and cocoa that linked African economies more directly with emerging world commodity markets. It is not surprising, therefore, that at the time of the outbreak there were no maize specialists within the colonial agriculture service in British West Africa.[9]

Rust and Global Scale

The seemingly random arrival and impact of one of the New World maize rusts in Africa in precisely September 1949 is an environmental and historical puzzle. The line of infection that began somewhat innocently in Sierra Leone moved quickly within the region along the coast to Ivory Coast, Gold Coast, Dahomey, and Nigeria where prevailing westerly winds may have carried the aecidospores (transfer spores) along continuous maize-growing zones from Sierra Leone east to Dahomey and Nigeria. But the rust also spread within two years of its arrival to southern Africa and East Africa where there had previously been no evidence of it. What accounts for the geography of its spread? The best guess is that the spores, like the Spanish flu virus of 1918–1919, had traveled along newly emerging lines of colonial communication that presaged globalization of the late twentieth century.

Rust is the common name applied to any of a group of parasitic fungi that form orange-red spores on the stems and leaves of the seed plants they parasitize.[10] The genus *Puccinia* has some of the most complex life cycles of any fungi, including several different spore stages; these stages include uredospores ("summer" spores) that form as a result of the infective aecidospore stage. Reddish brown pustules (and thus the term rust) burst through the host maize leaf epidermis and disperse in the wind to other maize plants. The fungus does not kill the plant but causes leaf lesions that decrease photosynthesis and other metabolic activities and thus reduce grain yield. The fungus then overwinters as dormant teliospores that then go through a sexual phase and infect the maize.[11] The rust thus spreads rapidly from plot to plot and from region to region, appearing in each place to be episodic. Tropical rusts infect maize only in humid conditions where the temperature exceeds 80 degrees (27–28 Celsius) and thus take on a seasonal character consonant with the bimodal seasons of wind and rainfall that predominate in Africa and the tropics in general.

What its first observers called the "American rust" thus traveled global paths created by the world of late-colonial empire. So did the attempts to forestall its effects. In 1949 maize was only a minor crop in Sierra Leone (rice predominated), but its moist tropical climate was ideal for rust infection. After the 1950 crop season, however, the mysterious rust leapt across colonial boundaries, appearing all along the West African coast, this time in Gold Coast, southwest Nigeria, and the French colonies of Dahomey and Ivory Coast, all economies where maize was a central item in the food supply. In Nigeria and Gold Coast British colonial officials estimated crop losses to be 40–50 percent, and in Dahomey, perhaps West Africa's most maize-dependent colony, maize prices increased to 124 shillings per hundredweight, a 500 percent rise.[12]

In the spring of 1951, there was a further rust outbreak, this time spreading throughout the maize-dependent regions of Nigeria, damaging crops there. In Gold Coast the results were even more alarming. Losses to the maize crop drove the Gold Coast price to eighty-nine shillings per hundredweight, an all-time record. The maize shortfall there in 1950 had required the import of 12,300 tons of grain and the projection for 1951 was for a further 15,000 tons.[13] In June, Secretary D. Rhind of the Department of Agricultural and Forestry Research offered a pessimistic forecast in a memorandum circulated by the West African Inter-Territorial Secretariat to the governors of Nigeria, Gold Coast, Sierra Leone, and Gambia:

> Maize rust disease has been known in many parts of the world for a long time, but it has rarely assumed epidemic proportions and generally the damage done is negligible. There are records of previous outbreaks as epidemics in America and West Africa but they appear not to have been as bad as the present epidemic in West Africa. At first it was thought that the West African outbreak in 1950 might be due to unusual weather conditions favouring the fungus, though there was no proof of this theory and not all the facts were in conformity with it. In 1951 the attack has again been extremely severe in Nigeria and the Gold Coast. At present I have no information from other West African territories but they are unlikely to escape. The idea that the disease was related to the weather conditions seems no longer tenable.

Failing to find evidence of a climatic cause, Rhind came to a much darker hypothesis reminiscent of a Michael Crichton (*Jurassic Park*) dystopia:

> The other explanation, and much more probable, is that the epidemic is due to the appearance of a virulent biological strain of the parasite. American research some 20 years ago showed at least 7 biological strains of the parasite existed in America and rust fungi are capable of changing their physiological form and of hybridizing, one strain after

another, giving rise to forms having different degrees of virulence. It is feared that something of this kind has happened in West Africa and that we now have to deal with an extremely dangerous disease which has come to stay.

He went on to express his exasperation with the difficulty of controlling the still-mysterious rust:

There is only one satisfactory way of dealing with this disease and that is to find or breed a variety resistant to it. Removal or burning of old maize plants or infected leaves might control the disease if every single farmer throughout West Africa carried it out, not missing a single scrap of the diseased maize. This is quite impossible. Accidental maize plants occur round habitations or even in the bush and those could carry on the fungus from season to season. The spores by which it is propagated can be blown by wind for immense distances, several hundred miles having been proved possible. Each diseased leaf produces enormous numbers of these spores, which are microscopic in size. Once a focus of the infection starts it can spread at a very rapid rate, miles per day if there is only a gentle breeze to carry the spores. It is therefore quite useless to try to control it by plant sanitation methods. Equally, spraying with fungicides is impracticable. The maize plants will need to be sprayed repeatedly, every fortnight at least, as each new leaf produced by the plant is not spray-protected. . . . The fungus can get actually inside the sheaths of the cob where spray or dusts could not penetrate.[14]

Rhind's memorandum concluded with a proposal to begin a full-scale effort to focus the regional resources of the British colonial administration in West Africa to address the threat to the region's food supply and economic stability. Over the course of the next two years the effort to control the strange and virulent American rust mobilized the resources of the late-colonial research capacity and reached beyond to include the emerging postwar world of science, multilateral institutions, and the new American hegemony. Science thus became part of a new postwar world order that recognized the global nature of the rust outbreak itself and put the response to it on global terms.

The first stage of the response was to set up a West African research consortium made up of elements of the West African departments of agriculture to begin a breeding program to create a rust-resistant maize cultivar:

The breeding of a resistant variety (which must also be agriculturally satisfactory for such characteristics as yield, life period, palatability, etc.) requires concentrated and continuous research by well-trained and experienced maize breeders and mycologists. It is a problem which is likely to take some time, being limited by the cropping seasons and complexities arising from the maize plant's method of reproduction. It affects all maize-growing areas of West Africa, and may even spread to other parts of the continent. It is therefore a problem particularly well suited for research by a team of scientists working on behalf of all the West African Governments whose results could be expected to find wide application. I therefore consider it a matter of urgent necessity that there be set up, with the least delay possible, a research project to undertake the study of rust disease on maize and the search for resistant maize varieties. It should be funded for 5 years in the first instance. Tentative, preliminary estimates are attached in which it is assumed that support from Colonial Development and Welfare funds will be forthcoming to cover the capital cost and half the recurring costs for five years, the balance to be found by the British West African territories in the usual ratio.[15]

Rhind proposed four possible sites for the research facility: the Ibadan University College of Agriculture (Nigeria), the Kwadaso Central Experimental Station (outside Kumasi in Gold Coast), the Njala Agricultural Research Station (Sierra Leone), and the Moor Plantation (Ibadan, Nigeria). In July 1951 in a joint memorandum from the Committee for Colonial Agriculture, Animal Health, and Forestry Research the governors of Gold Coast, Nigeria, Sierra Leone, and Gambia assessed the situation and agreed to fund a research project at Moor Plantation. The governors agreed with Rhind that the Moor Plantation's location outside Ibadan offered water, electricity, gas, land for test plots, and housing suitable for a resident European (British) research team.[16]

The previous month on, June 18, 1951, Rhind had also written to S. P. Wiltshire, director of the Commonwealth Mycological Institute, broadening the scale of the colonial response and indicating the work done to date:

Dear Wiltshire,
    The maize rust in West Africa about which you have no doubt heard last year has again appeared in epidemic form in Nigeria and the Gold Coast. I have no news yet from other territories in West Africa about the present position but will be visiting Sierra Leone and the

Gambia in the next month. The damage which this disease has done and is doing to the present crop is very serious indeed. There are no precise figures of loss of crop but I have seen many fields totally destroyed while less severe loss is inevitable at all places in Nigeria and Gold Coast wherever maize is grown.

In Nigeria they have a trial of 45 maize varieties going now but all are infected. A few varieties tried last year in Gold Coast were all killed by the rust. Waterston, the botanist at Ibadan (Nigeria), has just been to the Gold Coast and will be sending you specimens shortly for confirmation of the species, but it appears to be a form of P. *sorghi.* . . .

At first we hoped the outbreak of 1950 was due to unusual weather conditions and that it was a flash in the pan; but it is difficult to accept this idea because of the widespread nature of the outbreak (Gambia, Sierra Leone, Liberia, Ivory Coast, Dahomey, Gold Coast, and Nigeria) and the fact that it appears to be just as bad this year though weather conditions have been distinctly different from 1950. Reluctantly, we are coming to suspect that we have to deal with a very virulent biological strain of the parasite, though of course we have not been able to type it yet. Nigeria have put some work in hand with one botanist on the job, but I feel that the problem is so very serious, causing a real scarcity of maize and food shortages in some areas, that something more is needed in fundamental research into this disease.[17]

At about the same time, an American agronomist, O. J. Webster, in July 1951 was touring Nigeria on behalf of the Economic Cooperation Agency (ECA), an adjunct program of the Marshall Plan. Webster's presence expanded the international networks further when he proposed that the ECA could help fund a maize breeder from America through the American Point Four program and noting that he had also contacted a maize breeder in Venezuela and another in Mexico.[18]

Despite some hesitation about opening the door to American expertise and institutional involvement, Geoffrey Herklots at the Colonial Office in London noted Webster's idea and proposed a strategy to contact Dr. M. C. Jenkins at the U.S. Department of Agriculture's Bureau of Plant Industry in Beltsville, Maryland.[19] Herklots held out hope, nonetheless, that British imperial resources would be sufficient to cope with the crisis. His strategy was to avoid involving American expertise but to obtain U.S. maize varieties for testing at the Nigerian research station and, further, to enlist a British member of the West African staff to be responsible for writing "to other parts of the world where maize is grown as a commercial crop." He also wished to appoint a mycologist from Britain who could, if necessary, visit specialists in the United States. To find the British mycologist, Herklots suggested contacting the universities of Cambridge, Birmingham, and Oxford as well as the Rothamsted Experimental Station in Hertfordshire.[20] But despite official reluctance to reach beyond British colonial resources, the networks had already stretched throughout the British Isles and across the Atlantic.

P. sorghi, P. polysora, and the Global Infrastructure of Science

F. C. Deighton, who in 1949 was the first scientist to identify the outbreak of a virulent type of rust, was a crop pathologist working for the Sierra Leone Department of Agriculture at its research station at Njala. The uredospore samples he had found in 1949 on rust-infected maize plants appeared to be the common rust *Puccinia sorghi*, though the spores were unusually large and the damage to the plant far greater than he had seen before. Deighton wondered if this rust was a new variety or mutation but dutifully passed on a rust-infected leaf to the Commonwealth Mycological Institute at Kew Gardens, southwest of London. In October 1951 the important news reached the Colonial Office (via West Africa) that mycologist G. R. Bisby at the Commonwealth Mycology Institute had determined by examining the heretofore missing samples of the dormant teliospore phase that the West African rust was not a variant of the common *P. sorghi*, but *P. polysora*, an entirely new rust never before reported outside of America. Moreover, retrospective study of earlier samples of rust on West African maize confirmed that the new fungus had not been present in Gold Coast or Sierra Leone before Deighton's report of 1949. Trans-Atlantic science expressed itself when the American G. B. Cummins at Purdue University in Indiana who had first identified the *P. polysora* rust in Alabama in 1941 confirmed Bisby's research at Kew.[21]

A new game was afoot. And thus spring 1952 reports from field agents at the Mugugu agricultural research station in Kenya of a rust outbreak along the Kenya coast and in the Taveta highlands could confirm that the new *P. polysora* American rust had appeared there as well. From February through March 1953 reports of new outbreaks came in from Katanga (Belgian Congo), Bas Congo, Nyasaland, Yagambi (Congo), and Reunion Island near Madagascar.

By the 1953 crop year an expanding international network of individuals and institutions was actively engaged in the search for a solution. That network included the newly formed West Africa Maize Rust Unit at Moor Plantation in Nigeria, the East African Agricultural and Forestry Research Organization, the U.S. State Department's Economic Cooperation Agency, and several institutions in Britain, especially the Commonwealth Institute of Mycology at Kew Gardens and the London School of Hygiene and Tropical Medicine. In March 1953, W. R. Stanton, director of research at the West Africa Maize Rust Unit, received funds to travel to Lake Como, Italy, to attend the International Congress of Genetics and to visit the Italian Istituto di Cerealicultura in Bergamo. This visit and Stanton's contacts expanded the professional networks, which previously included only plant breeders and fungus specialists, by engaging European and American geneticists to join the effort to deal with the rust threat. During 1953 the network broadened to include the New World and the new multilateral agencies of the postwar world: the Food and Agriculture Organization, the Iowa Tropical Research Center in Antigua, Purdue University, the U.S. embassies in Rome and in Caracas, and the Rockefeller Foundation (see appendix B).[22]

In effect the reconstruction of postwar Europe had global implications that included African colonial networks of agricultural research. Communications between these groups, the British Colonial Office, and even French colonial officials were surprisingly seamless. In the case of the Rockefeller Foundation, its European offices were located, ironically, with the Colonial Office in London itself.

From early on in the fight against the American rust (after October 1951 known to be *P. polysora*) colonial crop scientists and mycologists had agreed that the best strategy to combat the disease was to breed on test plots a resistant variety of maize suitable to West African conditions. To do this required two sets of activities: first, researchers had to find maize varieties that resisted the rust, provided acceptable crop yields, and tolerated tropical field conditions. Very early on in the process they concluded that no West African maize types had any resistance whatsoever (see appendix C).[23] Therefore, their search for genetic varieties for crossbreeding would have to call upon a massive international effort to assemble genetic materials from biomes all over the world, and especially the New World and North America, where *P. polysora* has long existed in balance with maize. A sign of the times: no one proposed a farm-level survey of fields in West Africa or an inquiry into local knowledge of African farmers.

Second, to develop a resistant variety would take many successive crop cycles, including multiple test plots cultivated in a given year. The problem was that the *P. polysora* rust reached its infectious uredospore stage only once a year and then receded into its dormant teliospore stage. Infecting a test plot only once a season would be far too slow a process to yield the quick results needed. How artificially to infect successive test plots within a single season to identify resistant cultivars and to breed resistance? In September 1953 J. M. Waterston, research advisor from the Moor Plantation Maize Rust Research Unit, announced a breakthrough, that is, a payoff for the investment in the colonial science infrastructure. The Moor Plantation research team had developed a method of preserving *P. polysora* uredospores in vitro, thus allowing the team to induce infection of different maize varieties on multiple test plots for rust resistance over the course of a single calendar year.[24]

The primary concern now became the need to assemble as much genetic diversity as possible to develop resistance in a maize variety that would also provide viable yields in West Africa's humid and semihumid conditions. In August 1953 early results at Moor Plantation on twenty-nine assay plots to compare eight Mexican types and one South African variety showed promising results. Yields compared to the local susceptible Lagos White variety (as 100) showed the results in the following table.

White Tuxpan	125
Tsolo	124
Yellow Bounty	120
Mexican 1	167
Mexican 4	159
Mexican 5	203
Mexican 13	118
Mexican 21	132
La Creole	127

Source: Committee for Colonial Agriculture, Animal Health, and Forestry Research, November 3, 1953, Colonial Office, Public Records Office, Kew, England 927/276.

Not surprisingly, lowland Mexican varieties showed very promising resistance to the rust that had its origins in that New World ecology. But the resistance of Tsolo brought to West Africa in 1941 from the dry Eastern Cape region (Griqualand) of South Africa was especially encouraging, even though the seed was less well adapted in yield to West Africa's humid zones.

On the East African side the results were less encouraging. Reports of maize rust outbreaks from East Africa (Tanganyika, southern Kenya, and coastal Kenya) had reached West African agricultural officers. In late 1952 the research efforts intensified as rust infections, confirmed as *P. polysora*, appeared in East Africa and spurred the development of a parallel research effort by the East African Agricultural and Forestry Research Organization at its research station at Mugugu in Central Province. None of the East African varieties showed any resistance.

With research underway on two sides of the continent the international links of late-colonial empire came into play, pioneering the fledgling links between colonial structure and postwar multilateral agencies emerging in Europe and across the Atlantic. Global science flexed its newly forged geographic muscle and undertook the task of transporting plant genetic materials across global biomes, in essence retracing the historical expansion of maize and *P. polysora* itself.

As early as December 1950 and proceeding apace in 1951, 1952, and 1953 varieties of maize had begun arriving in West Africa from Ontario, Michigan, Maryland, North Carolina, and South Africa. Small shipments of seed corn, a few ounces at a time, arrived in Nigeria by post and courier from private seed companies, university faculty, embassies, research stations, and farmers' associations around the globe. Once the research stations began formal trials (after 1953) the flow of genetic materials to West and East Africa research stations changed from a trickle to a flood. By May 1953 Harold H. Storey, secretary for East African Agricultural Research, claimed that multilateral sources and his personal contacts in Central America had provided more than two hundred sample seed types. Institutional sources for these maize varieties included:

West African Maize Rust Research Unit, Ibadan, Nigeria
Agricultural Experimental Station, Medellin, Colombia
Purdue University School of Agriculture, Indiana
Imperial College of Tropical Agriculture, Trinidad
The Rockefeller Foundation, New York
Department of Agriculture, Salisbury, Southern Rhodesia
Director of Agriculture, Zomba, Nyasaland
Department of Agriculture, Pretoria, South Africa

Agricultural science had become global.

An Anti-Climax

In a sense this story has no real conclusion since after the 1953 crop season the enigmatic American rust receded as quickly as it had appeared on the scene three years earlier. A rust-resistant maize cultivar produced by global science networks was ready for release in 1957, but colonial Africa agriculture authorities never in fact released it. The danger to West Africa's crops had seemingly vanished. Internationally, however, *P. polysora* continued to expand its territorial range, appearing here and there in Africa and continuing eastward into Asia and the Pacific (see appendix A). British colonial records for maize rust in West Africa end abruptly after 1953, though Kew Gardens' mycological program continued to record minor *P. polysora* outbreaks and to collect maize leaf tissue samples from around the globe into the 1970s.

We are left with the question of how to account for the virulence of the original outbreak and its sudden decline. There are several possible explanations for the sudden decline of *P. polysora's* effects on Africa. Nobel Laureate Norman Borlaug speculates that a long dormant "fossil gene" from its West African maize's New World ancestry emerged among local African maize varieties to reassert resistance to the fungus as a result of the mass selection of maize genotypes that survived the rust. In Borlaug's hypothesis the American rust (*Puccinia polysora*, now more commonly called Southern rust) has origins in the same New World ecology that spawned its host crop, maize. Two species of rust exist as parasites on maize in Latin America and the Caribbean, *Puccinia sorghi* and *Puccinia polysora*. The former predominates at higher altitudes and lower temperatures and the latter at lower elevations and higher temperatures. One or another of these rusts infects virtually every plant of maize throughout maize's natural range in Mexico, Central America, the Caribbean, and northern South America. In areas of the New World where both rust types exist local maize types have evolved resistance to both. Therefore, because of a biotic balance between host and parasite, damage to New World maize has been rare.[25] The rapid commercial spread of maize around the globe in the last half-millennium, however, apparently disrupted this balance and set the stage for the emergence of the American rust in Africa in the second half of the twentieth century.

In the process of maize's first import to West Africa in the sixteenth century, *Puccinia sorghi* (common rust) traveled with it, and West African maize coexisted in a balance between the host and rust from the beginning. Examples of *P. sorghi* rust existing benignly on African maize was reported for decades, and pathologists assumed it to have been present for much longer, presumably since maize's first arrival. The second rust *Puccinia polysora* (Southern rust), however, appears to have remained behind in the New World until the mid-twentieth century when about 1949 it encountered African maizes. Once unleashed to Old World tropics, the American rust spread like wildfire onto Old World tropical and subtropical maize land-scapes that had no resistance and whose conditions of humidity and temperature encouraged the rust's life cycle of infection, dormancy, and transfer.

If the infectious aecidospores could not travel by wind across expanses of ocean, they could exist on living host tissues that traveled by sea and air, that is, food shipments (maize grain and maize transported with husks) that went from the New World to colonial possessions in tropical Africa during and after World War II.[26] Spores that arrived in Sierra Leone thus found a tropical climate and host maize that had long lost resistance to it. Over four hundred generations of maize and ten thousand generations of the pathogen West African maize varieties had lost their resistance.[27]

Borlaug also speculates, with even less evidence but with a populist sentiment, that African farmers themselves directed the emergence of resistance genes by selecting seed of surviving plants that displayed evidence of resistance.[28] Confirming Borlaug's speculation would require extensive field studies among an older generation of West African farmers, a worthwhile project but one well beyond the scope of this chapter.

The third possibility is simply ecological serendipity: fungi or insects that assert themselves with great virulence at certain times and in certain places often recede inexplicably. Environmental history is not linear, but more often conjunctural, resulting from a critical mass of factors and their interaction at a specific place and time. This happenstance is the case with the groundnut (*Senecio vulgaris*) fungus *P. lageruphorae* and with the Sri Lankan "brown bug," which the conjuncture of local conditions and ecologies seem to have brought into balance on their own terms.[29] Science and farmers as well seem to accept such anomalies, even if they cannot fully explain them.

Finally, the American rust has more recently taken a new name and a new persona. Now known as Southern rust, *P. polysora* is no longer an unwelcome stranger, but an endemic risk, a familiar foe, especially in tropical maize fields where its sporadic reappearance is unpredictable and almost quixotic. It is one of many threats to Africa's food supply that both farmers and scientists face from season to season.

Appendix A

Chronology of the Spread of *Puccinia polysora*

Location	Date Collected
AFRICA	
Njala, Sierra Leone	September 1949
Mandu, Sierra Leone	October 1949
Newton, Sierra Leone	April 1951
Calabar, Nigeria	May 1951
Abeokuta, Nigeria	May 1951
Accra, Gold Coast	June 1951
Ouidah, Dahomey	July 1951
Sierra Leone	September 1951
Mombasa, Kenya	June 1952
Taveta, Kenya	July 1952
Tonga, Tanganyika	December 1952
Adjam, Ivory Coast	1952
Katanga, Belgian Congo	February 1953
Bas Congo	February 1953
Taengg, Nyasaland	February 1953
Yagambi, Congo	March 1953
Reunion Island	May 1953
Njuli, Nyasaland	May 1953
Yambio, Sudan	October 1954
Agalega Island, Seychelles	1955
Mascarene Island	1955
Ivory Coast	1957
Luapula, North Rhodesia	April 1961
Abeokuta, Nigeria	May 1961
Mauritius Island	April 1962
Zaria, Nigeria	1963
Kwanda Tea Estate (Uganda)	July 1964
Zanzibar	February 1966
Togo	1975
Gambella, Ethiopia	1976
AUSTRALASIA	
Oomais, Papua	November 1955
Bomana, Papua	January 1956
Bougainville, N. Solomon Islands	November 1958
N. Queensland, Australia	May 1959
New Caledonia	1961
Tonga	April 1964
Guadalcanal, Solomon Islands	January 1970
ASIA	
North Borneo	April 1955
Mindinao, Phillipines	January 1956

Selangor, Indonesia	January 1956
Christmas Island	1956
Malaya (four locations)	April 1956
Los Banos, Philippines	September 1956

Notes on the chronology of *Puccinia polysora* samples in the Mycology Specimen Collection, Royal Botanical Gardens at Kew. Permission granted by Dr. Brian Spooner, taxonomic mycologist, June 16, 2000.

Appendix B
Agencies and Institutions Involved in American Rust Outbreak in West Africa

J. M. Waterston
The Research Advisor
Department of Agriculture
Moor Plantation
Ibadan, Nigeria

Dr. F. Yates, F.R.S.
Head of Statistical Department
Rothamsted Experimental Station
Harpenden, Hertfordshire

Secretary for Agricultural and Forestry
    Research
West African Inter-Territorial Secretariat
Accra, Gold Coast
Research Department

The Colonial Office
Sanctuary Buildings
Great Smith Street
London

G. R. Bisby
Commonwealth Mycology Institute
Kew, Surrey, UK

W. R. Stanton
Senior Scientific Officer
Maize Rust Research Unit
Department of Agriculture
Ibadan, Nigeria

Istituto di Maiscultura
Bergamo, Italy

Istituto di Phytopathologica
Rome, Italy

Food and Agriculture Organization
Rome, Italy

Dr. J. G. Harrar
Rockefeller Foundation
Division of Natural Sciences and Agriculture
New York, NY

Central Research Organization
Department of Agriculture
Moor Plantation
Ibadan, Nigeria

Dr. A. J. Ullstrup
Department of Genetics
Purdue University
West Lafayette, Indiana

Dr. J. A. Logan, D.Sc.
London School of Hygiene and Tropical
    Medicine
London

H. Tempany, editor
World Crops
Stradford House
London

Norris H. Evans Co. (seed company)
Upper Montclair, NJ

Dr. G. B. H. Bell
Plant Breeding Institute, Cambridge
    University
School of Agriculture
Cambridge, UK

Dr. H. H. Storey
Deputy Director
East Africa Agriculture and Forestry Research Organization
Kikuyu, Kenya

Dr. R. German
U.S. Embassy, Rome

Dr. Paddock, Director
Iowa Tropical Research Center
Antigua, Guatemala

Dr. Panze, Statistical Advisor
Central Council for Agricultural Research
India

Dr. R. F. Jones
Connecticut Agricultural Research Station
New Haven, Connecticut

Dr. S. P. Wiltshire
Commonwealth Mycological Institute
Kew, Surrey, UK

F. C. Bawden
Plant Pathology Department
Rothamsted Experimental Station
Harpenden, Hertfordshire

Agricultural Experimental Station
Medellin, Colombia

Imperial College of Tropical Agriculture
Trinidad

Department of Agriculture
Salisbury, Southern Rhodesia

Director of Agriculture
Zomba, Nyasaland

Department of Agriculture
Pretoria, South Africa

Appendix C

Country Sources for Maize Seed Used at Moor Plantation, Maize Rust Research Unit

Country of Origin	Seed Types Tested	Test Results
West Africa	31	No resistance found
East Africa	7	No resistance found
South Africa	2	No resistance found
India	18	No resistance found
Ceylon	7	No resistance found
Malaya	2	No resistance found
United States	20	Of variable resistance
Mexico	22	Several tolerant and highly resistant varieties
Caribbean	3	Several tolerant and highly resistant varieties
Venezuela	2	Several tolerant and highly resistant varieties

Source: Adapted from W. R. Stanton and R. H. Cammack, "Resistance to the Maize Rust, *Puccinia polysora* Underw.," *Nature* 172 (1953): 505–6.

When Stalin Learned to Fish

Natural Resources, Technology, and Industry under Socialism

Paul R. Josephson

8

NO LESS than other branches of the economy, Soviet planners intended the fishing industry to become mechanized, modernized, and functioning according to plan. Building on the research of oceanographers, limnologists, ichthyologists, and other specialists, planners sought to harness fish to the engine of socialism, making them contribute to the national diet on a greater scale than in the Tsarist era. To achieve this end, a revolution in all manner of fishing was required. Whether inland bodies of water such as rivers, lakes, and ponds, or on the high seas, the Soviet state had to introduce fundamental changes in the training of fishermen, the technology of the catch, and the nature of the finished fish products delivered to the consumer, as well as the science behind all three. Because of the need to focus on other sectors of the economy, planners turned to the fishing industry later than they did to other agricultural and forestry resources. Even if good weather and warm water ports had enabled them to do so, they did not have the technology to stray far from the Soviet Union's coasts.

The modernization of the empire's fishing industry involved three stages that reflected the economic and political desiderata of Soviet history. In the first stage that lasted until the early 1930s, Soviet scientists and planners sought to resurrect fisheries located primarily on rivers and inland lakes and seas. These had foundered since World War I. Toward this end, biologists had the ear of a government interested in cooperating with them, and they conducted the first systematic researches on the USSR's rich fisheries from the Caspian Sea to the Siberian rivers. Difficult economic circumstances—the recovery from war, revolution, and civil war—prevented far-reaching application of the results of research to the modernization of fisheries.

In the second stage, which lasted until the mid-1950s, officials tried to use the same techniques that were employed in other branches of the economy to create a modern fishing industry: modern technology, cutting-edge science, and Stalinist propaganda techniques. They ordered the construction of a motorized fleet, which still lagged by Western standards owing to the need to start essentially from scratch. They undertook scientific research to make fisheries operate all year long instead of according to seasons and weather, even when scientists pointed out their research as yet did not permit such conclusions. And they exhorted managers of canning factories, captains of boats, and crew members to establish superhuman targets for tons of fish caught and processed.

In the third stage, taking advantage of the shipbuilding industry that grew out of the war effort, and of such military technologies as sonar and radar, new materials such as plastics for use as nets, and a burgeoning refrigeration capability, the Soviet fishing fleets turned to the oceans and pelagic fishing. At the same time, the scientists pushed for the construction of modern hatcheries to seed the dozens of huge reservoirs filling up behind massive hydroelectric power stations along the Volga, Don, Ob, Angara, and other rivers. In each of these periods, even under Stalin, fish scientists publicly fretted about the impact of industrialization, deforestation, pollution, and the destruction of natural spawning waters that accompanied the effort to turn the USSR into a fish superpower. But since planners saw nature's resources as inexhaustible and nature itself as an enemy, scientists' concerns were pushed into the background.

The scientists themselves contributed to this state of affairs by believing in their ability to turn fisheries into industrial enterprises and to overcome the problems created by transformative technology with technological solutions. They were mistaken in this belief as the experience of the scientists connected with the development of the Volga River and the Murmansk-based ocean fisheries industries demonstrates. Striving rapidly to move from cottage to modern industry, they overestimated resources and their ability to manage them, especially in the face of state pressures to increase harvest and the inadequate catch, processing, and distribution technologies to do so.

The most important reason for the failure to create a fish's paradise in the USSR was the adoption of a new technological style for resource management that can be called brute-force technology (BFT). BFT refers to overemphasis on unforgiving technologies of massive scale, and to the premature search for monocultures based on incomplete understanding of the biological impact of human activities. In natural resource management, the driving force has been the effort to determine where production and biology meet. Brute-force technologies exist in all economic systems. They are based on standard engineering practices applied in several areas of human activity without considering at length potential exogenous costs (for example, prefabricated forms from apartment construction for use in dams, canals, and hydropower and nuclear power stations, with only modest modifications). Those standard techniques delay incorporation of the knowledge of climatological, geophysical, hydrological, and biological differences in decisions to apply BFTs. BFTs often have rapacious harvesting capabilities (e.g., ocean trawlers) that overwhelm undercapitalized processing equipment and inadequate infrastructure.

BFTs raise crucial issues about the relationship between the periphery of society and its core—between undeveloped regions and cities, for example. Modern scientific and engineering decisions concerning resource management tend to be centralized and coercive, with investment requiring armies of employees including researchers, thousands of laborers and their machines, and tons of building materials. The decisions tend to exclude consideration of the impact of brute-force technology on biodiversity—including indigenous people. While BFTs are universal, a crucial difference regarding the USSR was the absence of public participation in its genesis, diffusion, and reception. There was, furthermore, the significant impact of uneven economic development that resulted from the stress on producers' preferences, heavy industry, and the imposition of industrial paradigms on the development of natural resources.

The Russian Revolution and the Soviet Fishing Industry

Russia's coast, by far the longest in the world, is icebound for much of the year, so her inland fisheries were more important than ocean fisheries until the 1950s. Before the Russian Revolution, 80 percent of fishing was concentrated in internal bodies of water where rapacious capture—often out of season—accompanied destruction of spawning grounds, especially of sturgeon. Hatcheries existed on a small scale, more as a curiosity than a scientific endeavor, and were often connected with pond farming on individual noble land holdings. The inland fish included perch, pike, salmon, salmon-trout, char, carp, sturgeon, and thirty-five kinds of white fish. The Russian Court developed the floating fishmonger's shop for the Neva and the canals of St. Petersburg, shops fitted with floating tanks to keep fresh fish alive, and others in which fish was kept frozen in ice and snow. Mostly, however, fish was salted. Aquaculture commenced in the 1850s, but with modest results.[1] Caspian herring and sturgeon were the central industry before the Russian Revolution. Of course, during the late-Stalin period, fish specialists argued that Russians had been the first in the world to mechanize the fishing industry, as a reading of *Vestnik rybopromyshlennosti* in the 1890s would show, but that Tsarist capitalists were not interested in technology because of an oversupply of cheap labor.[2]

The few coastal fisheries remained backward. Fishermen used small row boats and sailing vessels on which small crews labored, unchanged from a century earlier. Occasionally there was a steamship. Usually ten to fifteen boats fished together within fifty to one hundred kilometers of the coast. They averaged nine thousand tons of cod in good years. But the British and Norwegians, both already with motorized fleets and more fishermen, harvested more in the very same waters. If thirty thousand Norwegians were fishing the Lofoten Islands, only four thousand Russians worked the Murmansk region.[3] Attempts to modernize the Russian trawling fleet relied on the acquisition of decrepit foreign trawlers.

Nikolai Mikhailovich Knipovich (1862–1939), the founder of modern Russian oceanography and fisheries research, hoped to provide a scientific basis to this modernization.[4] Like other scientists of the Tsarist era, he remained convinced of the power of science to solve the nation's problems. He thought that scientific activity in and of itself was apolitical and that it was the scientists' task to provide his nation with good science to tame natural resources for the benefit of the nation's citizens.[56]

Knipovich became infatuated with the Russian north in the late 1880s. The harsh weather of the northern parts of Archangel province made extensive agriculture nearly impossible; the growing season might last three months. So many peasants had turned to the sea for sustenance. An increasing number of inhabitants inland to the south, including from Vologda province, were also engaged in fishing along the many rivers and glacial lakes of the region. They caught enough to ship from Archangel to St. Petersburg and other ports on the Baltic Sea. But there were very few fishermen whose boats were well equipped, and their "captains" judged by gut feeling, not any kind of knowledge of the riches of the sea.[7] Knipovich desired to change this situation.

In 1887, Knipovich turned to the study of hydrobiology and zoology of the White Sea, where he collected data over the next five years in connection with the Solovetsk Biological Station. A freak windstorm in 1894 destroyed twenty-five ships with great loss of life. Local and national government officials formed the Committee for Assistance to the Russian North, which provided funds for the families of the fishermen and for study of meteorological conditions. Knipovich joined the committee. In addition to funds, the committee determined to undertake research to prevent the repeat of the tragedy, turning to the Bremen Vulcan firm in Germany to build a special research ship, the *Andrei Pervozvannyi*. Knipovich nearly single-handedly organized and carried out the scientific fisheries expedition on the *Andrei Pervozvannyi*. Connections in government, university, and academy enabled him to put the venture together. In 1897 he went abroad in pursuit of equipment. He acquired otter-trawl, winches, and ship-based hydrological and biological laboratories. The expedition from 1898 to 1902 along the Murmansk shores and into the Barents Sea drew scholars from Norway, Denmark, and Germany, for it was one of the first attempts to combine the study of fish with that of oceanographic conditions. Knipovich's expedition resulted in detailed maps of the Barents Sea, its currents, and rich marine life.

A three-volume study and a series of articles resulted from Knipovich's expeditions. Knipovich determined that fish reserves were far more extensive than previously believed. Their economic significance demanded "putting them on rational ground." Yet these resources were not limited. Knipovich warned of "bitter experience with the illusion of unlimited natural resources." He insisted upon the necessity of carrying observations out periodically over the years and comparing these results with those collected in other countries. Knipovich wrote: "Only with in-depth, universal knowledge of the nature of fishery waters will it be possible to give a firm foundation for the full and rational utilization of their natural wealth."[8] Knipovich's work had tremendous applied as well as theoretical importance, for it showed the great potential for trawl fishing in open seas instead of the craft industry that predominated along Russia's shores. While the governments of England, Norway, and Germany recognized the importance of his work and provided support to expand their own research and trawling efforts, only after the 1917 revolution did Russia develop a powerful trawling fleet.[9]

Fortunately, the Bolsheviks provided Knipovich and other scientists with modest support. Agriculture, forestry, and fisheries were in shambles, so they had nothing to lose and much to gain by giving scientists modest support. Lenin knew of Knipovich; they met in the 1890s. Lenin signed decrees giving Knipovich the authorizations to continue his work in Caspian, Azov, and Black Sea expeditions. On March 10, 1921, the Council of People's Commissars ordered the commissariat of enlightenment to support the formation of a Marine Scientific Institute with biological, hydrological, meteorological, and geological-mineralogical departments to focus on the resources of the Arctic Ocean and river deltas entering into it. Lenin cut through the red tape, ordering that Knipovich be supported and calling him "not only a scientific force of the first rank, but, without question, an honest human being." Recognizing the importance of this research for the economy, the new institute received special rations of coal, petrol, equipment, and food. Known then as Plavmorin, and a very rudimentary "institute" at that, Plavmorin was to become PINRO, the All-Union Polar Research Institute of Fish Economy in Murmanski where Knipovich finished his career.

Knipovich continued to focus on Caspian research, which he considered a sad reminder of the poor state of knowledge of Russia's natural resources. Russia lagged far behind England and Norway, smaller countries whose fisheries were far more modern. The laws regulating catch were poorly drafted and even more poorly enforced. Fishermen caught illegal catch at the wrong time in the wrong place using the wrong equipment. It was cheaper to pay fines and keep fishing. The revolution damaged much of the anadromous fishing industry. As the civil war escalated, Red and White deserters fished and overfished with impunity in the regions they took turns conquering. They and others destroyed nature preserves (*zapovedniki*) that took years to recover. Recognizing the need to preserve fisheries from rampant poaching during the civil war, Bolshevik officials established a new bureaucracy, the Main Fisheries Administration (Glavryb), to protect resources and establish a scientific basis for controlling fisheries. Glavryb had the responsibility to regulate the fishing industry by enacting limits and laws for fishing implements and seasons, establishing *zapovedniki*, and charging local officials with enforcing laws. Those officials lacked the resources needed.

For Knipovich things could not be worse. He wrote:

We do not know our own motherland well. Its diverse nature is still far from sufficiently studied. Those natural resources which in abundance are spread to all ends of Russia, from the desolate cold north to the fertile heat of the south, and on the surface of the land and in its bowels, and in the depths of the waters, are all poorly understood. And that which we know, we do not use rationally and widely. The huge sums of money that are paid by other governments for that which we could and ought to produce ourselves places us in power-ful economic dependence on them. The difficult experience in the last war shows clearly how significant this dependence is. And that which we already have studied, researched at the present time, that which we know, remains primarily the province of scholarly specialists, and the broad masses of people are as poorly informed as before.[10]

But Knipovich dreamed of the establishment of a modern fisheries indus-try in Murmansk. He and a research team set out for the Barents Sea in a boat named after him and had conducted four measurements, when the ship broke down and they had to return to port. Knipovich himself returned to Murmansk only in 1935, which in the intervening fourteen years had become a small city.[11]

The Foundations of Soviet Ichthyology

One of the major goals of Russian foreign policy for centuries has been the creation of a warm water port. Murmansk, situated at the end of the Gulf Stream, freezes over very rarely and so became an area of intense interest of Soviet planners for the fishing industry. Yet until the early 1930s, the Mur-mansk region industry was based in Archangel, which is on the White Sea and frozen over for at least four months of the year. The desire to develop and protect Murmansk grew stronger during foreign intervention and the Russ-ian civil war of 1918–1920, when a joint American-French force captured the city. Western leaders approved foreign intervention to keep Russia in the war against Germany and to undermine the Bolsheviks whom they saw as pre-tenders to power. Intervention had a long-lasting impact on the fishing in-dustry in Murmansk. Many fishermen left for the south. The catch in 1920 was half the 1913 level, and only twenty-five hundred people remained in the town.[12]

At the beginning of War Communism (1918–1920, when the Bolsheviks used harsh military measures to subjugate the economy and society to their rule), the Bolsheviks nationalized most major industries including the em-pire's small trawler fleet in March 1920. At this time the Archangel fleet boasted only eighty-five employees and a one-hundred-ton trawler with a three-hundred-horsepower engine that carried fewer than two dozen fisher-men on board. By 1924 the fleet had grown to fifteen trawlers, but they man-aged only ninety voyages. Fishing in the Archangel region was seasonal work, only after the neck of the White Sea was freed of ice. Scientists and party officials shared the belief that the only way out was to establish a Murmansk base. In 1924, the government and fishing industry organized the Northern State Fishing Trust (Sevgosrybtrest) with responsibility from the Vaida Inlet to the Pechora River. Construction on Murmansk harbor began the next year in the village of Aleksandrovsk, where a maritime academy was established.[13]

The stability of the New Economic Policy (1923–1928), which permitted small trade and a moneyed economy to prosper, enabled a growing trawler fleet to increase its modest catch. The Barents catch was 3,650 tons of salted fish in 1922; by 1929 it reached 21,100 tons. By then they had established nearly year-round fishing out of Murmansk, but trawlers rarely strayed far from port. Specialists initially encountered skepticism from planners that their studies of water conditions might help Sevgosrybtrest undertake industrial fishing. A March 1925 report based on studies of a fishing expedition fell on deaf ears. Scientists criticized both technology available and methods of catch. Exploitation was "primitive" and unmechanical. They used tides, nets, and sticks. Salmon fishing lagged. Herring were caught exclusively in the winter and in a limited area through ice fishing. There were no large size implements.[14] Researchers were invited to undertake new extensive research on the high seas only in 1932 after repeated failure of the fleet to meet targets.

At last the Leningrad Northern Shipbuilding Yards began construction on the first of twenty-eight Soviet-made trawlers. By 1945 there would be only fifty of them since the war effort required battleships. The trawlers ranged from 40 to 340 meters and had large holds for sorting, processing, and keeping fish on ice. The shipyard engineers dreamed of diesels, not the standard steam engines, to increase the size of the catch both by extending time at sea and using more space for fish. Even with these small trawlers, the technology of harvest overwhelmed the technology of processing and the training of personnel capable of serving on ships. They had few electric motors for cutting fish. Only two institutes offered training for the fishing industry: the Economic Polytechnic Institute in Leningrad and the Archangel Marine Technological Institute.[15]

Until the mid-1930s the Russian fishing fleet was based on Western technology, as were other sectors of the economy (iron and steel, construction, electrical equipment). But under Stalin the Soviet state attempted to achieve autarky, which it promoted through the slogan "Socialism in one country." During the first five-year plan of rapid industrialization, the USSR added thirty-four steam and ten diesel trawlers to the fleet, and in January 1932 the first of the new domestic contemporary designs left Leningrad shipyard dry docks. Unfortunately, the new fleet had young, inexperienced fishermen, so that in 1931 there were seventy-two serious accidents, and in the winter of 1931–1932 four ships were lost at sea. Overall catch was growing, but it was still only one-half the 1928 level in 1931. There were growing pains on shore, too, where there were not enough slips—this shortage remained a problem through the 1980s—so that ships waited in line to unload. The second five-year plan saw the same problems. In 1933 sixty trawlers brought in 750,000 tons, still only twice the 1926 catch with a fleet four times larger.[16] Only a scientific and technological revolution helped fisheries meet targets.

Total horsepower of all electric motors in the Soviet fishing industry—for trawlers, seiners, boats, factory buildings, and refrigerators—grew ninefold from 28,000 to 240,000 horsepower between 1928 and 1932. This increase was a small amount in comparison with other nations' fleets, reflected in a catch of only 1.3 million metric tons in 1933. Nine-tenths of the catch was categorized as being shore catch. The second five-year plan called for an increase to 1.8 million metric tons, which would be a hard-fought battle. In the northern provinces the schooner trapping and trawler catch, according to a contemporary Soviet study, was at a very low technological level. Two contemporary observers wrote, "The fisherman just as in the old days sits on the shore and waits for the fish to enter the inlet or the river and it seems that the majority of traps are in place on shore itself."[17]

A crisis in the catch connected with technological backwardness rekindled interest in science. In 1931, when the catch was only two-thirds that of 1928, Murmanryb, the main northern fishing trust, decided that there must have been a decline in the number of fish in the Barents Sea and therefore concluded against expanding the fleet. But the reasons were poor fishing methods that were inadequately tied to scientific data. Foreign trawlers had located huge schools closer to Bear Island, while Soviet fleets were too far south. The initial rapid growth in the fleet had masked the problem, for the captains had persisted in fishing in precisely the same way, focusing on the same areas and the same depths. Leningrad party leader Sergei Kirov put an end to this problem, forcing Murmanryb and Sevgosrybtrest to adopt "scientific" methods.[18] This dictate meant listening to researchers from PINRO and reviewing their hundreds of measurements of depth, flora and fauna, water composition, currents, and seasonal changes.

PINRO scientists commenced research in 1921. Starting from simple measurements, they added information on fish populations, spawning, and migrations. In 1926 they began studying cod and herring. At the beginning of the first five-year plan the institute had acquired two research boats and a trawler. The most important research vessel was *Persei*. It was 41.5 meters long with a displacement of 550 tons and an engine of 360 horsepower with speed of 7.5 knots. Scientists began using *Persei* for research in 1923. During its eighteen-year life, the *Persei* undertook ninety-one voyages through the Barents, White, and Karsk seas, creating over fifty-seven hundred scientific stations—sites for regular measurements of water mass, chemistry, fish populations, currents, and so on—and contributing to the formation of a school of oceanographers. On July 10, 1941, German fighters sank *Persei* in the Eina inlet. The postwar years saw rapid rebuilding of PINRO's research fleet with several new scientific research ships including *Persei II* and several deep diving underwater research vessels. This research enabled them to locate fish and determine when the catch would be best.[19]

When Stalin Learned to Fish

Stalin's revolution from above, the self-proclaimed "great break," changed the nature of scientific research, organization of industry, and technological development in all regions of the economy and society. Scientists who had managed to achieve a degree of autonomy now felt compelled to demonstrate how their research had immediate applicability for economic development programs. They had to provide research plans to indicate step-by-step how their research would be of economic benefit. The Communist Party orchestrated a series of show trials of so-called bourgeois specialists and wreckers in the late 1920s and early 1930s to demonstrate clearly that scientists and engineers were fully accountable to the state. Mere ichthyological data gathering and analysis were inadequate. Data had to indicate economic possibilities, and under Stalin these possibilities concerned industry. In part as a result of this requirement, industrial phrases and words replaced biological concepts and terms in scientific journals. Fish, too, would become an industrial activity, and resource scientists, some wittingly, others unwittingly, became their engineers.[20]

Many scientists were willing participants in these changes in research emphasis and approach, for they received massive infusions of funds for their programs and institutes, which subsequently expanded. They established new branches of institutes and extended their horizons of interests, both literally and figuratively. A series of biological stations, in some cases initially little more than shacks on the shoreline that housed nascent fisheries research, thrived owing to increased funding associated with industrialization policies. In 1921 the Institute of Fisheries was founded in Moscow, and the Murmansk Biological Station was reorganized into the State Oceanographic Institute. The institutes were joined in 1933 into the All-Union Scientific Research Institute of Fisheries and Oceanography (VNIRO), the leading such institute in the country. By the 1950s it had branches in the northern Baltic, Caspian, Aral, and Azov-Black seas, and in the Far East fisheries basins. Research on reservoirs, lakes, and rivers fell under the All-Union Scientific Research Institute of Lake and River Fisheries (VNIORKh), established in Leningrad in 1932 under the auspices of the Leningrad Ichthyology Institute. By the Khrushchev era, the institute had twelve laboratories covering such areas as ichthyology, hydrobiology, and hydrochemistry, and also pond fisheries, acclimatization, and pollution, with branches in Pskov, Tatarstan, Saratov, Volgograd, Ural, Novosibirsk, Karelian, Ob-Tazov, and Iakutsk.[21] The Institute of Hydrobiology in Kiev conducted similar research for Ukrainian rivers and lakes. Branch institutes for pond fisheries were established in Russia, Ukraine, and several other republics. The Ukrainian Scientific Research Institute of Fisheries (UNIIRKh, under the Ukrainian Academy of Agricultural Sciences), focused on pond aquaculture on state and collective farms and had seventy-seven ponds under active development by 1959. The Academy of Sciences, including the Zoological, Oceanography, Limnology, and Morphology of Animals Institutes; the Borok, Sebastopol, White Sea, Baikal, and Murmansk scientific research stations; and Leningrad, Moscow, Tomsk, and Saratov universities were all involved in fisheries research. The Ichthyology Commission of the Academy played an important role in coordinating research and responding to various queries from the fishing industry.

Not only scientists but also laborers were reoriented toward Stalinist norms. Through Stakhanovism, socialist competitions, and other forms of exhortations, fishermen and other marine laborers were expected to treat fish as no different from bricks, something to gather, process, and stack as quickly as superhumanly possible. At a 1930 meeting of workers of the fishing industry, Anastasios Mikoyan, a protégé of Stalin who rose to the top of Soviet leadership, declared, "The fishing industry is one of the lagging industries here. It is necessary to transform it from a backward into a progressive, technically advanced, socialist industry. We need to make the forces of nature serve the interests of socialism, not be a slave to nature." But the Stalinist effort to rebuild fish enterprises from one end of the fishing process to the other (catching, processing, refrigerating, canning) was no easy matter. The construction of an industrial fleet capable of fishing in any weather and on any sea would take decades. Party officials believed they could establish an MRS (motor fish station) like the MTS (machine tractor stations in agriculture) to serve as a pool for machinery and equipment, simultaneously acting as a political arm of the party at sea (like the MTS in the countryside). But a resolution of 1932 to create the MRS did not result in stations equipped with enough motorized boats and nets and fishermen to operate them.[22]

Unable to rely on agriculture alone to feed the cities, and lacking modern technology, the country's leaders turned to exhortation of commercial fishermen. In a speech to representatives of the Commissariat of the Food Industry on October 20, 1935, Mikoyan lectured the attentive throng about the need to embrace the Stakhanovite movement. Stakhanovism—named after a miner from the Don River basin, the richest coal region in the USSR at the time, who many times overfulfilled the norm for pulling coal out of a seam—was a kind of Soviet Taylorism, intended to maximize output, that is, increase productivity of labor, with minimum investment in capital, by exhorting workers to achieve to the glory of the proletariat. (It must be assumed that Stakhanov had few friends among his fellow workers.) As Mikoyan stated, Stakhanovism was a movement from below of the most progressive proletariat who "extracted from technology the maximum that it was possible to extract from it." Its results had been felt in heavy industry and now had to be felt in the food industry. Stakhanovites in all phases of the fishing industry (catching, processing, navigation, and ship repair) and from all regions (Murmanryb, Volgo-Caspian, and Azov-Black Sea) would be included. The problem was that ships were too long in port, nearly 40 percent of the time, under repair. Through Stakhanovism a number of trawlers, notably the *Kirov*, named after the Leningrad party chief and rival whom Stalin had had murdered in his office, had begun to increase catch and processing much faster than existing norms, and mechanics had sped up repairs, cutting days off time ships were tied up in port. Through Stakhanovite whaling, the captains increased harvest of whales by 162 percent and in terms of total weight of blubber 170 percent and of bone 172 percent.[23]

Stakhanovism remained crucial to the trawling and processing industries until the early 1950s. Stakhanovism faded away with the Khrushchev era. Khrushchev recognized that Soviet society needed more than coercion and fear of arrest to raise the productivity of labor. He offered the incentives of higher wages and better working conditions. These helped combat the problems of accidents and high labor turnover. But technological innovation for the fishing industry was the crucial ingredient. It ranged from refrigerated trawlers capable of mechanized on-board processing and cleaning of fish to new nets. This technological revolution was combined with geophysical engineering on a scale impossible in any other nation, to transform nature into a machine in order to control its flora and fauna.

The Stalinist Plan for the Transformation of Fish

In October 1948 the Communist Party unanimously voted to adopt the "Stalinist Plan for the Transformation of Nature." Having subjugated human enemies to Soviet power in the 1930s through industrialization, collectivization of agriculture, and the purges, and having fought off the invasion of the German armies, Stalin had no intention of resting. It was time now to push onward in creating the great socialist fortress. One last formidable obstacle remained, however—nature itself. Although the hated *kulak* (the bogeyman of the Bolsheviks, a peasant who was generally a bit wealthier than his neighbors) had been eliminated, agriculture continued to perform poorly. Industry, which was being rebuilt at a furious pace, required copious amounts of water for cooling, distilling, and cleaning. And there was never enough electricity. The transformation of nature would solve these problems. By treating nature, too, as an enemy of the people, Stalin and the party leadership mobilized the nation to turn it into a machine that operated according to plan using the appropriate tools of nature transformation: armies of workers (many of them gulag prisoners), steam shovels, tractors, graders, dynamite, huge dams, hydropower stations, irrigation ditches, and canals to subjugate each molecule of water to the engine of the plan. Gone would be seasonal ebbs and flows. Over the next fifteen years, all European rivers would be dredged and straightened, and massive hydroelectric power stations—so-called hero projects, larger than any the United States could build—would extract all of the kinetic energy in them. The reservoirs filling up behind them, also the largest in the world, would provide water for agriculture, industry, and municipalities on demand, not as capricious nature had offered in the past. Within a decade the hero projects would create twenty new reservoirs with total surface area of 2.2 million hectares (three times the previous total), including the Tsimlianskoe, Kuibyshevskoe, Gorkovskoe, Kamskoe, Cheboksarskoe, and Stalingradskoe (later renamed Volgogradskoe).

There were additional benefits of Stalinist transformation to the fauna. Just as in the United States, where reclamation, flood control, irrigation, and hydroelectricity projects encouraged fish farming, so in the USSR the projects led to pond and reservoir aquaculture. No less than the TVA, Bonneville Power Authority, and Army Corps of Engineers, so Minvodgeo (the Ministry of Water Geology), Gidroproekt, and other Soviet water engineering organizations saw unexpected benefits to nature of their massive projects, even as they moved earth and channeled water ruthlessly. Gidroproekt, the major Soviet water-engineering institute, was initially a part of the Stalinist labor camps or gulags but metamorphosed into a "legal" design and construction organization under Sergei Zhuk, its director during both incarnations.

At the nineteenth party congress in 1951, Mikoyan addressed the delegates and called for the fishing industry to organize on an industrial basis throughout the USSR, taking advantage of huge reservoirs now filling up on the Don, Volga, Dnieper, Kura, and Amu Dar'ya rivers. These reservoirs, Mikoyan acknowledged, had changed seriously the hydrology of the Caspian, Aral, and Azov seas, in specific natural spawning grounds and capacities. But, he apparently had on good authority, all could be put in order through the construction of industrial hatcheries to counter the decimation of sturgeon, sevruga, and other important fish. Unfortunately, Zhuk's engineers were so concerned about construction deadlines that they overlooked the destruction of spawning areas and the creation of barricades to anadromous fish, which seemed unable to climb ladders. Since the party focused attention on the reconstruction of heavy industry after World War II, many sectors of the economy that seemed distant from heavy industry got short shrift of investment funds. Iron, concrete, and electrification all merited huge infusions of funding, while the food and housing sectors suffered—and would suffer until the late 1950s. Fish were left behind.

What did the fish and the fish specialists think about the Stalinist plan for the transformation of nature? They recognized that the massive reconstruction of rivers and reclamation of wetlands destroyed spawning areas and prevented anadromous fish from migrating. But specialists were expected to take advantage of the opportunity presented by the transformative melioration projects by developing new aquacultural techniques. Try as they might, their efforts fell far short of goals. The reasons for this failure, as in other countries and projects, rapidly became clear: the construction projects had priority, they caused irreversible damage to ichthyofauna, none of the seeding or hatching projects came close to meeting expectations, and, as usual, while fish specialists assumed they might figure out how to reverse declines in fish populations through some other technological advance in the long run, in fact they never would. They hoped through closer cooperation with engineering organizations to pursue river transformation more carefully to minimize the damage. They would teach fish new tricks with hatcheries, fisheries, ladders, ponds, seeding, and acclimatization.

On the eve of World War I there were perhaps 3,500 hectares of pond fisheries in the Russian empire, but most of them were in Ukraine and White Russia. There was some rebuilding of pond fisheries after the revolution, but only during the second five-year plan (1933–1938) did these fisheries contribute significantly to production. During that time seventy new fisheries and hatcheries and 23,000 hectares of farms were added that could produce 340,000 metric tons annually. At first specialists grudgingly recognized the "positive" influence of man on nature when they noted with surprise how nonendemic fish appeared in the first reservoirs "naturally." They began to conduct small-scale seeding studies in the Veselovskoe reservoir in the late 1930s with sazan (a kind of carp), bream, pike perch, and sea roach. The studies ended when the Germans blew up the dam during the war before results might reveal their expected successes. Only in 1947 when the reservoir was rebuilt could acclimatization studies resume.[24]

On the eve of World War II pond aquaculture had grown to 120,000 hectares but produced mostly bony carp. The postwar transformation of nature led immediately to the construction of tens of thousands of ponds—virtually every usable body of water—for fish farming. They were stocked by hatcheries producing fifty million eggs and fingerlings—three times the 1945 level. Specialists attempted to farm pike, pike perch, silver carp, and trout but with less success than carp, for they could not seem to get the right mix of oxygen, feed, circulation, and temperature in the ponds.[25]

The fifth five-year plan (1950–1955) involved an extensive effort to take advantage of the new reservoirs and to understand what might be accomplished in internal bodies of water, both natural and artificial. Yet specialists all too rarely considered how fish would react to frequent changes in water level, chemistry, and temperature owing to hydroelectricity, irrigation, and other uses. There was no doubt that the huge dams going up on the Don, Dnieper, and Volga had interrupted the swim of anadromous fish who strove with genetic determination to return to their spawning grounds. Another problem was the push to finish filling reservoirs as quickly as possible, which precluded proper bed preparation. Water poured in, inundating swamps, streams, creeks, and so on, creating uneven relief that varied as much as six meters from one spot to the next. These spots encouraged the accumulation of muck and silt in which plant life dangerous for fish blossomed. The reservoirs and dams destroyed the gravel beds and slowed current significantly in any spawning areas that managed to survive, making them of no interest to the fish. Further, the plants prevented the use of seines or drift nets. In the Rybinskoe reservoir alone, summer seining declined by 40 percent and winter by 80 percent.[26]

Nor, when filled, did they release or add water with the proper thermal or hydrochemical characteristics for aquaculture. Study of the Gorkovskoe and Kuibyshevskoe reservoirs revealed great fish losses because the water was drawn down and then refilled from upstream dams, taking water from the depths of reservoirs. This interference meant that the level, temperature, and chemical characteristics of the water were constantly changing. These haphazard practices resulted in low temperatures, low oxygen levels, and fish freezing or suffocating.[27]

If they included the design and expansion of breeding ponds nearby during the excavation or concrete-pouring stages of hydroelectric projects, might this conserve fish resources? The director of Gidrorybproekt (the Hydrofish Design Institute), G. N. Mikhalchenkov, believed it could. He argued that pond aquaculture was crucial for the burgeoning industrial centers that were feeding off hydroelectricity but needed fish to provide balance to their diets and take pressure off underperforming agriculture. Gidrorybproekt engineers designed a series of projects in the Moscow, Ulianovsk, Orenburg, Riazan, Kuibyshevsk, Vladimir, Cheliabinsk, Stalingrad, and Kalanin regions where there were but 2,180 hectares of fattening ponds and 350 hectares of hatcheries producing only 143,600 kilos of fish annually. Reconstruction and building of new fish farms would increase production capacity astronomically, including new farms in Omsk, Kurgansk, Ivanovsk, and Iaroslavl provinces.[28]

To take advantage of huge reservoirs for the fishing industry specialists urged the design institutes to take aquaculture into consideration before construction, not as an afterthought. One of the major requirements was saving and stocking such valuable fish as sturgeon, white fish, and lamprey in holding ponds for up to two years before construction destroyed spawning areas. The Teplovsk Fisheries in Saratov had begun work along this line, but the State Fish Trust clearly could do more. On the southern reaches of rivers they were losing sturgeon, sevruga, and sterlet. Pond raising for two years seemed to lead to high weights and survival rates.[29] Hero projects, in a word, offered great possibilities for aquaculture, but only if the design institutes thought about fish before they destroyed them.

Technological solutions to technological problems also failed. The ladders they designed to provide passageway upstream did nothing. In one year only six sevruga and two sturgeon climbed the ladders around the Tsimlianskoe reservoir. The only solution, it appeared, was seeding beluga, sevruga, and sturgeon in the massive reservoirs. Lacking funds to do a good job of this, they caught fish and hurriedly transported them upstream. For the Tsimlianskoe reservoir, Azdongosrybvod (the Azov-Don State Fisheries Factory) personnel trapped four hundred fish for trucking upstream. The long and difficult journey over Soviet roads meant that most were in no condition to survive when released; virtually all perished soon after hitting the reservoir. In 1957 Stalrybtrest—a name doubly interesting for celebrating Stalin's contribution to fisheries and the joys of steel (*stal'*)—caught and released another 142 fish without success. In 1958, Rostoblrybtrest released 314 fish some of which they thought to tag beforehand. This experience was more successful, although a few fish escaped the reservoir through spillways, locks, and pumping stations—the latter in mangled bits and pieces. The fisheries personnel concluded that, pollution and other obstacles notwithstanding, industrial sturgeon fishing in the reservoir would be possible if no fewer than 500 were released annually. But this number turned out to be much too small for a reservoir extending 240 kilometers to the northeast whose surface area was 2,700 square kilometers.[30] Scientists at the Saratov branch of VNIORKh were more circumspect about the potential of transplanting, calling for further study to determine whether it made sense to release sturgeon into upstream reservoirs; many of the fish at first lay on the bottom of the reservoir in shock before swimming away.[31]

Not only ichthyologists attacked the engineers of nature. Forestry specialists also criticized the huge water works. They worried openly that the scale and speed of construction of the hero projects on the Volga, Kama, Dnieper, and Siberian rivers had destroyed valuable lumber. The reservoirs were largely in steppe and forest-steppe regions where forest had been preserved precisely along the flood plains of rivers. The reservoirs thus sharply reduced the forested areas of those regions. For the Kuibyshev station, 18,500 hectares disappeared under water before the trees were felled; under the Tsimlianskoe, 14,000 hectares; in the Saratov region, which was only 5 percent forested, the reservoirs destroyed nearly 70,000 hectares of forest-steppe; and in the Stalingrad region 33,000 hectares. Gidroproekt specialists apparently did not understand the need to remove lumber more systematically, prepare the bottom, and cart off the rubble of homes.

Even more, the reservoirs frequently caused significant erosion, created huge ravines, triggered landslides, and precluded use of the land for farming or other purposes. Reservoirs were so poorly constructed that they often had whitecap waves two meters and higher, like those in the oceans. As a result, for example, along the Tsimlianskoe Sea, millions of cubic meters of soil were lost annually. On the Ob River reservoir, built in the late 1950s, scientists observed two-meter-tall waves moving along for twenty to thirty kilometers, destroying the shoreline. A railroad along the shore had to be moved inland. Forest plantings along the shore provided a modest defense. The forest industry recommended an extensive program of planting projects, of five to ten thousand hectares of trees, along denuded reservoir shores to fight erosion and landslides and reclaim the area for agriculture.[32]

On the southern reaches of European rivers—the Volga, Don, Dnieper, and Dnester—the damage wrought by hydroprojects was greater still. The chemistry of the Caspian, Black, Azov, and Aral seas changed for the worse. Brackish water increasingly penetrated the deltas of the rivers. The valuable sturgeon, beluga, and salmon all suffered. On the Caspian and Azov seas, catch of valuable fish was down 200 percent because of overfishing, dams, pollution (paper, chemical, oil, metallurgical), and reservoirs. In addition to hydroelectricity, planners envisaged various canals, irrigation systems, and forest belts in the south to turn the fertile but relatively arid land of the southern steppe into an oasis. Yet as one fish specialist observed, "Every violation of the flow and hydrological regime of rivers that flow into the Caspian under the influence of climatic factors or the activities of man (hydroconstruction, irrigation, etc.) destroys in the first place conditions for the reproduction of anadromous and semianadromous fish." The huge Stalingrad and Kuibyshev stations along the Volga prevented sturgeon and sevruga from reaching their spawning grounds. As for the deltas, reduced flow meant than many of the semianadromous fish had stopped swimming upstream, for the signal to migrate was the spring run-off that was now controlled, and its height, length, and intensity had all changed. Fifteen years of research demonstrated that a series of measures was required to preserve fish and ensure their reproduction. At the very least, hatcheries and fisheries had much to contribute. As the first step, before any construction began, fish had to be protected. "Any industrial catch of beluga, sturgeon, sevruga, herring, salmon, and white fish in rivers that flow into the Caspian, beside the lower reaches, must be categorically forbidden."[33]

Soviet researchers also underestimated the ways in which modern large-scale technological systems were vectors for the transmission of various microbes, diseases, and pollution. For example, the irrigation ditches and canals associated with the Amu Dar'ya River had lowered flow into the Aral

Sea, leading to lower water level, higher salinity, changes in ichthyofauna, and the destruction of the Aral barbel.[34] Crosby and others have pointed out the ecological imperialism of technologies of transportation, communication, and immigration.[35] So, too, some Soviet researchers called for "biological melioration" measures to accompany "hydrotechnical melioration (e.g., inundation of spawning areas)." They needed actively to fight the penetration of weed and predatory fish into inundated areas, and to acclimate and seed appropriate fish more diligently. They needed to build ladders and elevators to enable fish to get above dams. They needed hatcheries and fisheries.[36] When the engineers of nature advanced the great Siberian river diversion project in the 1980s, they also minimized the potential for disease, insects, and other vectors from Siberia into Central Asia and the European USSR.

Were acclimatization and seeding solutions? The Kuibyshev reservoir was the largest in the USSR when formed and had an interesting, elongated shape and unique characteristics owing to the fact that the Kama River entered it, as did several other smaller rivers through valleys. The reservoir was not very deep, with most of it roughly ten meters, with only one quarter of it to twenty meters deep. This depth and relatively long and hot summers created a good habitat for various fish species. However, extensive pollution from the Kama contributed to extensive winter fish kills. To prepare the reservoir for aquaculture, for two years before closing the dam, specialists forbid fishing of sturgeon, bream, perch, and sazan and removed "nonvaluable" fish; built hatcheries with pond area of 1,314 hectares; and left some trees and bushes behind as biomass for benthos (organisms living on the bottom). Specialists in the Tatar VNIORKh and Tatgosrybtrest were pleased with the results, although disturbed by delays in opening the hatcheries and holding ponds, and especially the extensive pollution from the Kama. They called for passage and enforcement of strict fishing laws above the reservoir on the Volga to Gorky, and on the Kama to the Votkinskaia hydropower station. The laws included prohibition of any kind of fishing during spawning. In addition, they urged expansion of hatcheries for sazan, bream, and pike, and work on acclimatization of such fish as white Amur.[37]

Another possibility was the creation of beluga-sterlet and other hybrids whose use lagged apparently only because the construction of fish factories and hatcheries along various Volga reservoirs also lagged considerably behind plans.[38] Some agribiologists recommended a kind of Larmarckian adaptation (the inheritance of acquired characteristics) of fish to new environments as a way around destruction of spawning grounds. The Saratov branch of VNIRO saw "great success" in the adaptation of fish that had settled upon unaccustomed but accessible spawning grounds below dams; they based these conclusions on limited numbers of beluga, sevruga, and sturgeon fingerlings they had caught while making hundreds of measurements during seven trips along the Volga over three summer months.[39]

Even if they had succeeded in developing aquaculture, systematic pollution along the Kama and Volga—millions of cubic meters and hundreds of tons of phenols, acids, heavy metals, and oil products entering the rivers annually—precluded saving the fish. No matter where you turned, pollution was the biggest problem. The Institute of Hydrobiology of Dnepropetrovsk University showed how the Kakhovskoe reservoir and hydropower station slowed the Dnieper's flow. This development permitted organic and heavy metal wastes to accumulate rapidly. Daily, some three hundred thousand cubic meters of virtually untreated waste from various industries filled the reservoir. A young specialist at the institute concluded that filtering equipment was not enough. He wrote, "On the basis of these experiments we firmly recommend that the authorities of Gosrybnadzor (the State Fisheries Inspectorate) demand categorically that directors of enterprises perfect filtering mechanisms, having promised by a specific time to cease entirely the release of industrial waste waters into the reservoir."[40] Laws to protect the fish had little effect for enforcement was lax, fines too small, and responsibility difficult to prove. All technological solutions—seeding, hatcheries, acclimatization, and even conservation—lagged, for the Ministry of Electrification was interested in kilowatts not carp, and the other ministries were interested in steel, pesticides, oil, and copper, not sturgeon.[41] There was, however, a solution: rapacious harvest on the high seas.

Taking to the High Seas

Postwar development of pelagic fishing contributed to the decline of the Volga-Caspian basin as a source of fish, so that the region dropped from providing one-third to one-tenth of total USSR catch. A. N. Baluev, chief engineer of Gidrorybproekt, called for continued attention to the basin to maintain shipbuilding and ship repair facilities, as well as fish resources—especially since Gidrorybproekt engineers had reduced the flow to the delta by 40–50 percent depending on the season, meaning that the delta had shrunk from five or six hundred thousand to four hundred thousand hectares. Gidrorybproekt developed an engineering scheme to establish and maintain spawning grounds of sturgeon, beluga, and herring on the Volga from Astrakhan to Kaluga, and on the Kama from Kazan to Molotov.[42] Time would show that engineering schemes to deal with the negative impact of other engineering schemes could not restore fish populations.

While pond aquaculture and seeding of reservoirs remained important in the 1960s and 1970s, the emphasis on capital investment shifted suddenly and significantly to ocean-going trawler fleets and floating factories. There appeared to be no need for limits on catch in the ocean; the captains brought on board everything they could. They did not have to worry about industrial pollution of closed bodies of water, about seeding, or about functioning fish farms. The world's oceans became the Soviet Union's fish farms with huge trawler and seiner fleets and floating fish factories to process the catch. There was a twofold increase in ocean catch between 1950 and 1957, and by the end of the sixth five-year plan (1960) the catch already constituted 82 percent of the USSR's total. This increase was made possible by the conversion of the shipbuilding industry and ships themselves from military to civilian purposes, the technological revolutions connected with military sonar and radar for locating fish easily, and larger, stronger nets. Mechanization of catch, refrigeration, and processing (canning) completed the revolution.

There would be new problems in the Khrushchev era. One was the adoption of brute-force technologies to catch and process fish. A second problem was the continuation, if not the exacerbation, of sectoral imbalances between harvesting, processing, and canning, even though the Khrushchev era is noteworthy for a redoubled effort to automate and mechanize all industries. But at least Khrushchevian peaceful coexistence had replaced Stalinist inevitability of war between the capitalist and socialist systems. Stalinist economic autarky, international uncertainties, and lack of technology had kept ships close to Soviet borders. This ideological revision gave impetus to the fishing fleet's ability to sail far from Russian shores.

The Soviet fleet rapidly pushed its trawling area to the coasts of Canada, Newfoundland, the United States, the banks of Greenland, western Spitsbergen, and Iceland. The ordinary steamships that earlier served the Murmansk industry could not exploit these fisheries. They had a limit of eighteen days at sea, including a few days devoted to traveling to industrial fisheries. A technological revolution of the fleet permitted the Soviets to go far and wide. The first advancement was the large freezer refrigerator trawler (BMRT), which included an entire fish-processing factory on board, enabling the delivery to port of a finished product. The BMRT also marked the transition to diesel engines and increased time at sea without refueling. The construction of a special fleet of transport refrigeration vessels, floating fish factories, and tankers accompanied the development of the BMRTs. BMRTs such as the *Altai, Pushkin,* and *Leskov* had top speed of 12.5 knots, were 85 meters long, 14 meters wide, and had 13,800 horsepower and displacement of 3,170 tons. BMRTs were brute-force technologies par excellence.

New refrigerated transport ships designated UM-2FV-8/4 developed by Rybosudoproekt seemed promising, for even in the summer they held temperature to two degrees Celsius. The holds were smaller than the previous generation (from 42 to 33 cubic meters), but since they used not ice makers but refrigerators, the total catch increased from 8.7 to 10.4 tons.[43] The Pushkin series of refrigerated fishing vessels appeared in the early 1950s. They were 75 meters long, had a 13.4-meter draft and 1,900-horsepower engines, reached a top speed of 12.5 knots, and had 1,450-cubic-meter holds. They were the best the USSR had to offer in terms of radio and ultrasound location, and elevators, cranes, and fish pumps to handle catch.

Another important component of the revolution in trawler technology was the midsized ocean-type trawler with cooled holds; processing equipment was added later.[44] PPRs, or industrial production refrigeration ships, such as the *Gurmant* and *Rembrandt,* were also added to the fleet. They had a top speed of 14 knots, were 102 meters long and 16 meters wide, with 3,100-horsepower engines and a 5,500-ton displacement. The trawling fleet sought cod and perch using the BMRTs at sea for three to four months at a time. The herring fleet—usually ocean trawlers—was most active from August to March, using drift nets for Atlantic herring, and in the summer moved to trawling for pelagic fish. By 1966 there were 157 medium-sized trawlers in the fleet including 26 of the ocean type, and 222 large ships of which 43 were BMRTs.[45] The ships were large and they were many, but they quickly became obsolete and fell apart. Constant repairs became the rule, and as the fleet expanded, so did the number of ships awaiting repair in drydock.

But they caught fish. During the first half of the 1950s, the trawl grew three times in Barents Sea, nine times in the North Atlantic, and there were big increases in the Far East. In 1955, the catch was approximately 2.7 million metric tons, a 190 percent increase over 1940. Specialists did not realize the need to avoid fishing during spawning seasons and were thrilled that unlike on inland bodies of water it seemed they could fish almost all year long.[46] Initially capable of fishing for three to six months without a port of call, by the late 1970s the Soviet fishing fleet had supertrawler fishing ships that could stay at sea for up to one year. The fishermen liked one-year tours of duty even less than three-month tours because, although they were paid more, the conditions were miserable.

There was always a disjunction between harvesting, processing, and distribution of the catch. When Soviet boats first ventured from the coast, fishermen dressed in shoddy clothes armed with knives and with little else manually cleaned the fish, then salted them heavily. There was no such thing as filleting, and no such thing as fresh fish. The fishermen had access only to rudimentary fish-processing machinery. This equipment was hardly mechanized, for the assembly line still ran by brute force, crushing fish for the consumer and for fish indiscriminately and mixing in too much bone and entrails. When refrigeration and freezers were installed on the high seas, fish were frozen in huge blocks. It was impossible once at shore to thaw anything resembling a fish. Consumers got "fish block" in the stores, which in fact was all the planners and trawler captains hoped for. Their incentive structures led them to trawl rapidly, deliver tons of mixed catch to so-called floating factories, and return to fish some more.

Fisheries Destroyed

There were three fishing fleets, the northern that sailed from Murmansk; the Baltic that sailed from Klaipeda, Lithuania, and other ports; and the Far East fleet that was centered at Vladivostok. The crucial relationship between Knipovich, PINRO, Sevryba, and the Murmansk fleet, like AtlantNIRO and Zapryba in the Baltic and Dalryba and TINRO in the Pacific Ocean, indicates how scientific research, technological development, and overfishing were inseparable. The Murmansk fleet grew on the research of PINRO and the shipyards of the Soviet nuclear navy. Murmansk had been on the outskirts of civilized Russia, at the end of a wild, cold peninsula extending into the Arctic Circle, an outpost of the intrepid until the late 1950s. Crucial to the genesis of the imbalance between catch and processing was a series of PINRO articles published in the 1950s and 1960s that preached the theory of the inexhaustibility of Barents fish stocks. Scientists from PINRO frequently went along on voyages to test new trawl-boards and conduct other forms of research to enhance the brute-force nature of the harvest.[47]

In spite of the strategic promise of a harbor open all year long (the Gulf Stream finally dissipates at Murmansk fjord), Murmansk grew slowly until Knipovich's research indicated the significant economic potential of Barents Sea fishing. Many of those persons who moved to Murmansk with the promise of a job or an apartment were Jews wishing to avoid anti-Semitism or others who had tired of Moscow and Leningrad intrigues. In 1915, the tsarist authorities began to build a railroad from Petrozavodsk in Karelia to the Kola Peninsula that reached Romanov-on-Murman in 1917 (later called Murmansk). The railroad contributed to a fourfold growth in population in the 1920s. People came from the interior, from the swamps and *taiga* (the northern forest) of Vologda, Riazan, Iaroslavl, and Viatka, people attracted by the summer sun and northern lights and the distance from Moscow. Fishermen arrived from the Azov, Caspian, and White seas. The Kola Peninsula was a province of only 23,000 people in 1926, but grew twelvefold to 292,000 in 1939. Most of the Kola Peninsula inhabitants lived in cities and towns, making isolated Murmansk surprisingly the most urban of all Soviet provinces. Murmansk, a region of great natural and mineral wealth, has 21,000 rivers and streams and 107,000 lakes, virtually all products of the ice age, which are filled with trout, bass, salmon, grayling, sig (a kind of salmon), loach (a kind of carp), and roach—114 species in all, 20 of which the Soviets considered "industrial." But lacking the manpower or the science, these resources remained undeveloped until Knipovich turned his attention northward.

Mikoyan and Kirov gained responsibility for turning Murmansk into a Soviet city in the 1930s; Stalin himself came in July 1933 to have a look. This was a strategic city. The German armies attacked from the air but never entered or took Murmansk, and Murmansk harbor was severely damaged by German bombs during the war. The bombs hit the docks, loading equipment, cranes, factories, store houses, and oil depot. Fishing, reconnaissance, and other activities had to go on. The fishing vessels had no guns, so they had to enter port at night, putting additional pressure on a city already short of fishermen and laborers who had been conscripted to fight at the front.

Rebuilding and modernization were extremely slow after the war. Crane capacity reached only 249 tons by September 1954. The slow rebuilding was curious because Murmansk was the most important link of the northern sea route along the Arctic coast to Kamchatka.[48] The route cut fuel use by 30–50 percent over the railroad and time to forty-five days down from seventy-five days on rail. A series of icebreakers named after ongoing hero projects—RionGes, AngarGes, KuibyshevGes, TsimlianskGes, Baikal, Severomorsk, Kavkaz, Lena, and Ob—worked hard to increase northern route freight threefold from 1954 to 1955. A half-dozen nuclear icebreakers entered the Arctic Ocean in the 1970s to keep fishing and freight lines open.

In 1949 the Kola Base of the Academy of Sciences became the Kola Branch of the Academy, a change in nomenclature that reflected both Murmansk's newfound importance and a trend to turn bases into branches and branches into republican academies throughout postwar USSR. In 1956 the first students were admitted to the first university, the Murmansk State Pedagogical Institute. Another university opened in 1966. In January 1954, prison laborers finished the railroad from Murmansk to Nikel, site of one of the most polluted regions and most polluting factories in the entire Soviet Union, superlatives of infamy, to be sure. Apatity, the site of diamond mines, was four hours by train to the south. In December 1961, construction commenced on the 2,535-kilometer Murmansk-Leningrad highway, a bumpy two-lane road. The *Lenin* nuclear icebreaker arrived in May 1960; industrial shipbuilding of the sort found in Leningrad, Klaipeda, and Vladivostok began in the 1960s. Hydroelectricity powered the city. By 1966 there were eight hundred thousand inhabitants in the province, including three thousand doctors and dentists, and thirty-three winners of the Hero of Socialist Labor award.

Murmansk's fishing industry grew rapidly in the Khrushchev era. Between 1946 and 1954 the number of ships in the fishing industry tripled. The herring industry, Murmanseld, was recreated in 1949; its poorly functioning predecessor of the same name dated to 1938 but accomplished little. Slightly more powerful steamships traveled to richer fishing grounds far from shore, then BMRTs and other modern trawlers replaced them.

Development of the Fishing Industry in Murmansk

According to other official statistics, which seem too large to be true—and it is impossible to reconcile them all—the Murmansk industry catch grew 228 percent from 1928 to 1932; 293 percent more by 1937; dropped 73 percent by 1940; increased 295 percent between 1945 and 1950; 282 percent in the next five-year period; 102 percent more by 1960; and 124 percent more by 1965. If true, it is surprising there are any fish left in the Barents Sea.

In 1957 Murmansk got only 5 percent of its catch from distant waters; in 1960 almost half came from those waters. Large vessels also meant increased

Development of the Fishing Industry in Murmansk

Year/index	1913	1932	1940	1945	1960	1965	1966
Total catch, 1000s of centners*	176	958	1783	760	6447	7971	7870
Food fish products, 1000s of centners	...	489	927	457	4121	5277	5516
Canned fish, 1000s of cans	...	659	1311	2198	34592	34894	43296

* one centner = 100 kilograms

Source: D. M. Skripal', ed., *Narodnoe khoziaistvo murmanskoi oblasti za 50 let Sovetskoi vlasti* (Murmanskoe: knizhnoe izdatelstvo, 1967), 41.

catch over shorter time periods. But the goal was to keep the fleet constant-ly occupied. The problem remained that the catch overwhelmed the ability to unload or process efficiently. Much of it spoiled, and frozen products often waited on refrigerated ships for days on end for a slip to open up to unload product. In 1956 there were only nine mechanized lines in the factories. At least they opened a repair yard, Sudoverf, and in 1958 an oceangoing mar-itime academy with twelve departments to teach captaincy and other spe-cialties. In 1965, seeing the problem not as one of rapacious harvest and inadequate processing capability but of administration, the planners estab-lished Sevrybkholodflot, a new northern fisheries refrigeration combine and fleet. In 1969 the Murmansk trawling fleet caught 7,000,000 tons of fish using 1,620 kilometers of steel cable; 13,000 tons of ice; 30,000 tons of salt; and 260,000 tons of fuel. In Murmansk alone there were 180 BMRTs and 300 smaller vessels registered. Usually, the fleet met plans, but when it did not, "The sea is the sea, and it often makes significant changes in our plans."[49]

To meet the targets set by planners in Moscow in the face of all this waste, inefficiency, and consumer indifference, the industry overfished. By the end of the 1960s, Soviet industrial ships trawled the Indian, Pacific, and Arctic oceans and the Antarctic region, day in, day out. The Far East fishing indus-try employed 160,000 persons, of whom 60,000 worked at sea on over two hundred trawlers and processors. Output grew threefold in the decade. Once they emptied coastal waters, they turned to pelagic fishing of mackerel, tuna, and sardines, using drift nets to harvest indiscriminately. Industry officials ordered retrofitting of seventy ships and built BMRTs and floating factories. They founded new scientific research institutes for fundamental ichthyolog-ical, hydrobiological, and hydrological research needed to calculate reserves on a scientific basis and make prognostications of harvest.[50] However, they ignored the consumer.

Let Them Eat Carp

In the effort to increase harvests, the ministries turned to the "assimila-tion of progressive technology." But as in forestry, whether it was technology for the catch or for processing, the result was either the diffusion of brute-force technology, or wasteful, undercapitalized processing equipment. There was a particular lag in mechanizing the hardest, most unpleasant jobs: lifting, carrying, and cleaning in spaces that rolled and shifted with the sea and stank to high heaven. Even simple cranes, elevators, and conveyors lagged in de-velopment. New machines were also needed to increase production of canned, frozen, refrigerated, and filleted fish.[51]

The effort to improve processing failed. First, scores of trawlers dropped anchor in harbors with rotting catch and inadequate port-handling facilities. Also, in those harbors they found outdated machinery and few well-motivated workers to run them. Finally, Minrybkhoz (the ministry of the fishing industry) did not provide enough capital for housing for workers and their families. Workers, therefore, understandably sought employment in other industries where the job was easier and apartments were available. The effort to attract students for part-time summer employment in the Far East, far north, and Siberian fishing expeditions fell short, for the ministry only belatedly offered to pay them for travel expenses or time in transit and initially failed to guarantee their place in school and scholarships upon return to university.[52] Convoluted but crucial coefficients, gross target numbers of tons (not mix, assortment, or quality), plans that provided disincentives to fish in a rational manner, not to mention low salaries pegged to those convoluted coefficients, all contributed to rapacious harvest. There were incentives, too, to salt fish, rather than provide fresh fish, because it was easier to deliver salt fish to lumberjacks and Vorkuta coal mine prisoners.

Consumers were unwilling to buy the products on three grounds: low quality, unfamiliarity, and poor assortment. Once it turned to pelagic waters, the fleet picked up everything and anything it could with huge drift nets. Scientists of fleet research institutes then explored ways to turn anything and everything into nutritious, edible products. Scientists spoke the new gospel: ground fish for fried cutlets was 25 percent cheaper than meat and had iodine and bromine. At one demonstration, Dalryba, Sevryba, and Zapryba specialists revealed eight appetizers, thirteen main courses, fish pies, and even fish desserts. Research published in *Problems of Nutrition (Voprosy pitaniia)* showed scientific success; *short* lines of disgruntled consumers showed olfactory disagreement. The chief engineers of the fishing combines blamed the scientists for failing to understand the consumers' taste buds. In the meantime, every fishing organization was responsible for inspection of the quality of the fish, and each one—Dalrybinspekstiia, Gostorginspektsiia Dalrybsbyt, and so forth—had its own opinion: This fish is good enough to sell.[53]

For example, when calamari first appeared in cans, it languished on the shelf. It took decades of concerted propaganda effort before every apartment served at one time or another calamari with vinaigrette or with mayonnaise. Old housewives and pensioners stood for hours in lines to buy fish they did not recognize. There had been pike, perch, salmon, sturgeon. "That's fish. What this other stuff is, who knows!" one woman exclaimed. "Where the hell is the herring?" consumers asked as the 1960s drew to a close. Familiar fish had simply disappeared from the shelves. This scarcity was shocking for a country that had increased its catch two- and threefold in the decade. After overfishing or killing the waters of the Caspian, Baltic, and Black seas, and the coastal waters of the Pacific Ocean, they moved into pelagic fishing in the Pacific, Atlantic, and Arctic oceans, as well as the Antarctic region. The Atlantic Scientific Research Institute of Fish Economy and Oceanography in Kaliningrad (AtlantNIRO) took responsibility for identifying dozens of tasty, appetizing, and tender fish with the philosophy "The consumer will have to adjust."[54]

In one five-year plan food scientists introduced over three hundred new products and canned goods. According to the deputy minister of the fishing industry, A. N. Gulchenko, it was regrettable that it took a long time for the consumer to become accustomed to the new products. The products resulted from overfishing cod, bass, and other fish, which required the fleets to trawl far into the open seas. New products were "unfamiliar in appearance and taste, but contained more protein and minerals like iodine than many fresh water fish." The problem before scientists and engineers was to create new products that the consumer would not reject, like tasty smoked sausage from tiny tunny (a fatty fish related to mackerel). There were no limits. Packaging, advertisements, and some hunger were the key.[55]

The fishing industry built one hundred "Ocean" franchise stores in Moscow, Minsk, Ivanov, Krasnodar, Rostov, Sochi, and other major cities to present the glories of the Soviet catch: shrimp paste, fish blocks, mackerel liver, cans of you-name-it in heavy sauces to cover the slightly off taste, and occasionally fresh fish. The Ocean stores also suffered from lack of refrigeration and grinding and packing equipment. They could not bridge the great divide between "shore and store." The Council of Ministers periodically passed resolutions calling for measures for "Raising the Effectiveness of Utilization of the Industrial Fishing Fleet, Improvement of the Quality and Expanding the Assortment of Fish Products." But the public rejected many products on the basis of quality and assortment. Citizens did not like unfamiliar fish, bony fish, frozen masses of fish, fish smoked and marinated to kill aftertaste. Even scientific studies to determine how to produce tasty, edible products of fish paste and culinary studies to suggest new recipes failed to win over the masses of people.[56]

Unbalanced modernization of the fleet contributed to the sad state of affairs, for catch increased rapidly, but the ability to process it did not. A typical floating factory took in seventy tons of fish daily, while BMRTs harvested over three hundred tons from the ocean depths, but then often waited days to transfer the increasingly odiferous catch. One captain reported early completion of catch, "but no where to give it. We lie at anchor. Other ships also waiting." They had no mechanized equipment to unload quickly, let alone adequate on-shore refrigeration capacity. The planners could not get it into their heads to design and manufacture smaller on-board and on-shore processing, cutting, and canning machines. When the *Gletchera* returned to port to celebrate early fulfillment of its five-year plan, there were thirty-three hundred rock-hard tons of fish in the holds, half of which were not cleaned. More than one-fourth of each fish was inedible, for the fishermen still used knives, not machines. The young fishermen had a hard time at first with all the entrails, their stinking hands covered with frozen blood. Even the most experienced man could process only a dozen fish a minute. For each tour of duty, half the workers were new. Finally, someone had a great idea: to cut the head off the fish in one operation. A trawler fleet signed a contract with PINRO to provide the experimental foundation for this startling research.[57] But much of the work remained manual.

As big technology improved, labor productivity declined, for officials ignored small improvements in the social and personal side of fishing. Only one factory in the entire USSR was designated to produce special gloves for fishing industry employees. It never met demand due to a shortage of latex. Fishermen looked like scarecrows because of their poor-quality work clothes. Their rubber overalls weighed sixty pounds and cracked, allowing the cold, wet weather in, and the boots were like sieves. Sweaters had buttons that were hard to handle with cold hands and never fit right. Poor-quality mittens could not handle the elements. Said one fisherman, "We have the most modern ships, but the mittens they send us remain primitive as always." When officials built new processing factories based on modern canning technology, they could not hire workers because they never built apartments, daycare, schools, or stores nearby. They were unable to retain skilled, experienced, and hard-working employees. Workers had no incentive to overachieve: They were paid 70 percent of their salary when in ports of call during unloading and repairs. Why would they work harder when at sea for a pittance more? On-board political propaganda meetings, films, lectures, and sketches only slightly improved productivity. Booze was more likely entertainment, but it had terrible side effects. The *Sovetskaia Kamchatka*, a huge floating factory, was gutted by a twelve-hour blaze started by drunken crewmen that cost many lives. They had been drinking pure spirits. After accidentally spilling some spirit on the floor they lit it to hide the traces. Many of the crew were so drunk that they panicked and jumped into icy waters and died of hypothermia.[58]

The Legacy of Soviet Power for Fish

From meager beginnings, the Soviet fishing industry grew to one of the largest in the world. The forces behind its growth include a strong foundation of scientific research with prerevolutionary roots; modest government support during the difficult years of revolution, civil war, and economic recovery; Stalinist insistence upon achievement of rapid increases in the level of catch; opportunities presented by plans to "transform nature"; and the new political and technological circumstances of the Khrushchev era. The political and economic desiderata of fisheries development—as for other regions of the economy—ensured that brute-force approaches would predominate in this area of natural resource development. On inland bodies of water and rivers, industrialization, construction, and pollution threatened indigenous populations of fish. Technological solutions to those threats—fish ladders, fish farms, incubators, hatcheries, pond aquaculture, and so on—proved to be inadequately funded. The scientific research behind those solutions was also necessarily rushed, for ichthyologists were hoping to save fish from hydropower stations, dams, and irrigation systems going up willy-nilly in the country.

Brute-force technology prevented specialists from selective harvests of fish, even if they had desired them. Hydrologists and geophysicists who designed dams, hydroelectric stations, reservoirs, and irrigation systems discovered that changes in water speed and temperature, sedimentation, and excessive evaporation accompanied their every "improvement." The quality and level of ground water declined. Pollution precluded any chance for recovery of inland fisheries. Significant artifacts of human history, such as churches and homes, were inundated by reservoirs. When scientists discovered that their research was inexact, it was difficult to retreat, for harvest and construction plans were everything, and retreat was not in the Bolshevik lexicon. There was in fact no technological solution, for political and economic pressures to harvest and process increasing tons of fish overwhelmed any effort to conserve resources. How could they overfish with 777,000 rivers and streams with a total length of 5 million kilometers, 3 million lakes and ponds with almost 500,000 square kilometers, and a growing man-made pond-fishing industry?

When they turned to the high seas new problems faced the Soviet fishing industry. Specialists overestimated the capacity of the oceans to provide all the fish the USSR needed. The fisheries industry grew accordingly. Nearly nine hundred thousand persons toiled on ships, at farms, in ports, and in processing plants, not to mention the scientists and engineers in institutes.

By the 1980s, 90 percent of the catch came from the ocean, although this catch was becoming harder to land owing to two-hundred-mile limits and overfishing. So rapacious was the harvest that international pressure grew to force the fleets to change their patterns somewhat. For example, in 1973 the Soviet Union finally agreed at a meeting of the International Commission for the Northwest Atlantic Fisheries (ICNAF) to reduce its wasteful catches off the New England coast by 25 percent to conserve world fish stocks, at the same time agreeing that the Canadian and United States shares would increase. Overall the catch on George's Bank off the Maine coast would drop to 924,000 tons versus 1,118,200 tons in 1973. The Soviet share would drop 30 percent to just under a half million tons, with the United States fishing roughly two hundred thousand tons and Canada twenty-five thousand tons.[59]

Yet the USSR was infamous for ignoring these kinds of international agreements. One reason, as should be clear from the foregoing, is that the Soviets created organizations that acquired significant bureaucratic and technological momentum in all areas of the economy. These were huge all-union fish associations in Murmansk, Archangel, Leningrad, Tallinn, Riga, Klaipeda, Kaliningrad, Odessa, Nikolayev, Sevastopol, Kerch, and Vladivostok, each with its own fleet, processing facilities, factories, packing and catching machinery and equipment, design bureaus, training schools, and research institutes.[60] These organizations and their brute-force technologies overwhelmed resources. They created something far from scientifically managed natural resources. Soviet policy makers seem to have decided that if it was inevitable to destroy fish stocks, they might as well destroy them off the shores of other countries than off the USSR's own coasts. Then they polluted the water. They would wash out the oil storage tanks of tankers at high sea and dump dirt, grease, and waste overboard.[61] The environmental damage caused by Soviet ships may never be reversed, and it will be decades before the Russian fishing fleet becomes modern and efficient. But the plan was everything, and the fish were another brick or cog in the Soviet economy.

9

Yellow Jack and Geopolitics
Environment, Epidemics, and the Struggles for Empire in the American Tropics, 1650–1900

J. R. McNeill

N RECENT years environmental history has enjoyed an enviable climb to respectability within the historical profession. That happy trajectory has allowed a measure of specialization among environmental historians, which carries the inevitable risk that other historians will cease to pay attention. For this reason, I think, environmental historians would do well to pursue the links between their findings and the concerns of other historians. In this chapter I attempt just that, joining ecological and epidemiological history to one of the most venerable of historical interests, international and military competition, in the context of European imperial struggles, and American anti-imperial struggles, in the lowland tropics of Atlantic America.

Today yellow fever is almost a trivial disease, perhaps accounting for about twenty thousand or thirty thousand deaths per year according to the World Health Organization (although the officially recorded figure is usually around five thousand). For comparison, malaria kills two to three million people per year today. But before the twentieth-century medical interventions that led to mosquito control and vaccination, yellow fever was a fearsome scourge in the tropical Atlantic world. It was above all else the ecological and social revolutions of the sugar plantation that opened yellow fever's reign of terror in the Americas.

The sugar revolution created new environmental conditions extremely propitious for the propagation of yellow fever, and in so doing, it created a new set of governing conditions for geopolitics in the American tropics. A lot of Latin America stayed Latin because of these new conditions, despite predatory ambitions of the British, Dutch, and occasionally French. Moreover, a lot of tropical America acquired independence after the 1770s because of canny exploitation of these conditions by people born and raised in the American tropics and hence often resistant to yellow fever. Those little Amazons, the female mosquitoes *Aedes aegypti*, vectors of yellow fever, underpinned the geopolitical order of the American tropics from 1660 to 1780. After 1780 they undermined it. But for mosquitoes and viruses to exert such influence over the course of history, governments, militaries, and people had to conduct their affairs in certain very specific ways: nature makes its own history, but it does not make it just as it pleases.

With decisive help from Eurasian diseases, Spain acquired a loose but lucrative empire in the Americas after 1492. By 1600, the lowland tropical segments of that empire were depopulated backwaters, but great riches flowed from silver mined in the Andes and highland Mexico. To get silver to Spain, it had to pass through choke points in the tropical lowlands and the Caribbean Sea, such as the Isthmus of Panama or the port of Veracruz, and always the port of Havana. That fact, and the hope that great wealth might lie elsewhere in the American tropics, inspired England, France, and Holland to contest these Spanish dominions. They acquired several Caribbean islands and a few stretches of coastline by 1655, usually via conquest and settlement involving, initially, only a few hundred people per adventure. This was the age of buccaneers, when even modest efforts with minimal support from European states could change the political map of the Caribbean. That age ended when three things came to the Atlantic American tropics: sugar, slaves, and sieges.

Sugar made its first major impact in the Americas in northeastern Brazil. When the Portuguese expelled the Dutch (who controlled part of Brazil 1630–1654), the Dutch (and Luso-Brazilian Sephardic Jews) brought sugar and the latest in sugar-refining technology to the Caribbean, beginning in Barbados in the 1640s. A social revolution followed, as the plantation complex (Philip Curtin's phrase)[1] spread throughout suitable lowland regions. Eventually, after an experiment with indentured labor from Europe failed, planters turned to mass importation of slaves from West Africa. Slavery ensured politically unreliable majorities on many islands and coastlands, changing the nature of war and politics. The comparative scarcity of whites and their appropriate fear of arming blacks led to a pattern of warfare by European expeditionary force. To protect their colonies, all European empires upgraded their fortifications. Spanish silver and everyone's sugar made it possible to afford such investments in the seventeenth century and made many colonies and ports too valuable not to fortify. Spain in particular relied on masonry and local militias, more than upon naval power, for imperial defense. Thus, the Vauban revolution in fortification (named for the French military engineer Sebastien le Prestre de Vauban, 1633–1707) came to the Americas, and with it, the pattern of prolonged siege warfare.

Siege warfare in the Atlantic American tropics proceeded under conditions very different from those prevailing in Europe, along its Ottoman frontier, or at the scattered European outposts elsewhere around the world. A Vauban fortress in Europe was intended to be able to hold out for six weeks, by which time, the theory went, relief columns might march to the rescue.[2] In the far-flung Portuguese, Dutch, and British strongholds in the Indian Ocean, relief could never arrive in time, and so besiegers often succeeded. But in the tropical Atlantic, siege warfare after 1655 favored the defenders.

In 1655 the English took Spanish Jamaica, part of Oliver Cromwell's "Western Design," intended to weaken Spain. This conquest involved a force of some seven thousand men, far more than had taken part in any previous campaign in the Caribbean. The days of buccaneers were passing, although another seventy years would elapse before they were finally extinguished. The era of expeditionary forces, of systematic and large-scale warfare around the Atlantic, was beginning. It took Cromwell's legions a day to take the main Spanish settlement on Jamaica, and a week to control the entire island (although guerilla resistance flickered on). But after this easy conquest, very few successful invasions took place in tropical America, despite repeated war and upwards of fifty attempts.[3] The main reason for this failure lies in another unsuspected consequence of the arrival of sugar: yellow fever.

Native to tropical West Africa, yellow fever[4] is a viral infection, of the genus flavivirus that also includes dengue fever, West Nile virus, and Japanese encephalitis, among others. It, like all others in its genus, is an arbovirus, meaning it is communicated by mosquitoes or ticks. Its symptoms can be mild or serious, and in fortunate cases consist of high fever, muscular pains, and headache that last for three or four days but then disappear. In serious cases, these symptoms abate, then recur, joined by jaundice, and internal hemorrhage. In the latter stages of lethal cases, the victim vomits up partially coagulated blood, roughly the color and consistency of coffee grounds, which symptom gave the disease one of its several nicknames: the black vomit.[5] When this happens, death is near. Yellow fever kills people through organ failure, normally the liver, and by circulatory collapse. Typically the immune system forms antibodies within a week, but that does not always help. Indeed "it is unclear whether immune mechanisms during the acute stage of the disease contribute to pathogenesis."[6] In vulnerable human populations in times past, case mortality may have been as high as 85 percent, although today the range seems to be much lower, never more than 30–50 percent.[7] Perhaps in the past reporting was so poor that many who had the disease but recovered went unnoticed; perhaps nowadays the virus no longer gets the chance to run amok among highly susceptible populations. Additionally, it may be that the virus has evolved so as to be less virulent in recent centuries, although the evidence from analysis of the virus's genome implies it has been genetically very stable: the American yellow fever virus is extremely close to the West African one, and the symptoms of disease are identical everywhere. This new evidence suggests the virus has remained genetically stable since its transmission from Africa to the Americas. It also confirms the West African origin of the virus, which had formerly been a controversial question.[8]

Young adults are the most at risk—which suggests that an overvigorous immune system response may indeed sometimes contribute to the lethality of yellow fever. Once one has the virus, even today there is nothing much doctors can do, and in the seventeenth and eighteenth centuries what they tried, such as bleeding patients, likely hurt more than it helped. Children normally experience it only mildly, a common pattern among infectious diseases, and their prospects for survival are excellent. In survivors, it produces lifelong immunity. Seventeenth- and eighteenth-century observers sometimes claimed the disease struck men more seriously than women, but this vulnerability was probably a matter of exposure rather than pathology. The modern medical literature makes no mention of any differential risk among males and females. A very effective vaccination has been available since 1936.

The yellow fever virus has long been endemic in tropical African forests and is now endemic in tropical American ones as well, circulating among monkeys and species of mosquito that are not much attracted to human blood. Today, as in the past, it is primarily a disease of tree-dwelling monkeys, lethal to howler monkeys but not to most other monkey species. Its mosquito vectors, which carry it from monkey to monkey, live in the forest canopy and rarely take a human blood meal. It strikes individuals who venture into tropical forests, especially loggers who cut down trees and stir up mosquitoes. Usually these are isolated cases (sometimes called "sylvan yellow fever") and do not trigger epidemics because too few people are within range of infected mosquitoes, and the forest mosquitoes prefer monkey blood anyway. Yellow fever becomes epidemic among humans when it circulates among urban populations via the vector A. aegypti, which does find human blood appealing. (Happily, no outbreak has occurred in the Americas since 1954.) Urban, epidemic yellow fever is the same disease as sylvan yellow fever, caused by the same virus, but communicated by a different mosquito and circulating among a larger human population.

Yellow fever's geographic range and distribution is determined mainly by characteristics of the vector. The virus spends most of its life in the salivary glands of mosquitoes; human bloodstreams and livers are merely the principle means by which the virus gets from mosquito to mosquito.[9] The A. aegypti, of African origin, is a domestic mosquito that lives close to humans and breeds mainly in water containers and, according to some reports, preferably clay-bottomed ones.[10] Unlike many mosquitoes, it needs clean, unpolluted water for its eggs to become larvae, pupae, and then to become fledgling mosquitoes. Once mature and aloft, it likes to stay close to the ground and bites people mainly on the ankles and calves, generally at dusk or dawn. Unlike its buzzing brethren, it is a silent mosquito. It can suck up two or three times its weight in human blood (only in desperation will it bite other mammals) in ninety seconds. It is attracted to motion, to heat, and to exhalations of water vapor, carbon dioxide, and lactic acid. A hardworking body low to the ground, say a sugarcane cutter or a digging soldier, was catnip for a female A. aegypti.[11] The mosquito rarely travels more than three hundred meters from its birthplace, except on ships (or airplanes). It needs temperatures above ten degrees centigrade to survive, above seventeen degrees centigrade to feed, and above twenty-four degrees centigrade to prosper. It also needs liquid every few days. Hence yellow fever is and always has been a disease of the humid tropics and especially of preferred habitats of the A. aegypti, although it used to make seasonal forays to temperate ports around the Atlantic basin, occasionally as far north as Quebec, in summer months when infected mosquitoes lodged on board sailing ships.

Epidemic yellow fever has other, more stringent, requirements. The virus must establish a cycle that allows indefinite transfer from mosquito to human host to mosquito. This cycle requires a lot of mosquitoes, the more so because only about 60 percent of A. aegypti are able to transmit the virus.[12] Without plentiful vectors, the virus will not move from person to person rapidly enough: people have the disease only seven to ten days, after which time they are either immune or dead, in either case no longer capable of hosting the virus. Victims' blood is infective for only three to six days. The transmission cycle also needs a favorable ratio of nonimmune to immune people available for mosquitoes to bite. To perpetuate the cycle, an infected *A. aegypti* must behave a bit like Count Dracula: it must find virgin blood and find it fast. The mosquito lives a few weeks at most. Immune people are virus killers: the cycle of transmission is broken when mosquitoes inject the virus only into immunized bloodstreams. So a yellow fever epidemic requires suitable vectors in sufficient quantity and susceptible hosts in both sufficient quantity and proportion. From the virus's point of view, its opportunities are sadly limited by the fragility of this cycle. Indeed, despite the warmth and rainfall, conditions in the Atlantic American tropics before 1640 left a lot to be desired: not enough water vessels, not enough (if any) *A. aegypti*, not enough human bloodstreams, and among those bloodstreams, not enough who spent their childhoods in places where cold temperatures precluded exposure and therefore immunity to the virus.[13]

But after 1640 sugar and geopolitics set the table very nicely for the yellow fever virus. Sugar wrought an ecological revolution upon dozens of islands and numerous patches of adjacent continental lowlands. Soon, armies of slaves hacked down and burned off millions of hectares of forest in order to plant cane. Their efforts led to multiple ecological changes.[14] Soil erosion accelerated. Wildlife vanished. More important from the human point of view, as plantations replaced forest, conditions came to favor the transmission of yellow fever. Falling trees brought canopy-dwelling mosquitoes down to ground level, where their chances of biting a person improved. These ecological changes, specifically more frequent mosquito bites, meant sylvan yellow fever, if it existed on the sugar islands at all, could more easily ignite an epidemic. Deforestation meant fewer birds, and fewer birds meant fewer predators for all mosquitoes.[15] However, for mosquito population dynamics breeding conditions matter more than predation, so by far the most crucial ecological development was what replaced the felled forests: the sugar plantations themselves.

Plantations made excellent *A. aegypti* incubators. Sugar production in the seventeenth and eighteenth centuries involved initial refining on the spot.[16] Part of the process required putting partially crystallized sugar in clay pots for a few months. The pots had holes in them to let the molasses drain out, leaving semirefined sugar. A small plantation needed hundreds of clay pots. A big one used tens of thousands of them. They were empty except for three or four months after the harvest. Presumably they often broke, as they were of clay and roughly handled by people who had no interest in their preservation. Clay pots and fragments of clay pots caught the rain and made ideal homesteads for *A. aegypti*.[17] Perhaps the pots' clay surfaces somehow helped improve the supply of nutrients for *A. aegypti* larvae. In any case, whether clay contributed to mosquito nutrition or not, clay pots contributed mightily to mosquito numbers. With the spread of sugar eventually many ports (and forts) were ringed by plantations producing tons of sugar and clouds of *A. aegypti*. The mosquito may have successfully colonized the Atlantic American tropics before 1640, but after 1640, thanks to sugar, appropriate breeding grounds were far easier to find.

So was good food. *A. aegypti* prospered after 1640 because human blood and sugarcane juice got easier and easier to find. Sugar meant slaves, and population growth. Caribbean population had crashed after 1492, and by 1640 was perhaps two hundred thousand. By 1800 it had surpassed two million, improving mosquito nutrition handsomely. Beyond blood, *A. aegypti* can also eat sucrose. It likes sweet fluids, the sweeter the better. It can live off honey or sugar alone, although that diet is insufficient for the female of the species to sustain ovulation. So while individual mosquitoes could live well tapping the abundant cane juice on Caribbean plantations, sustainable *A. aegypti* populations required human blood meals as well. After 1640 there was more and more sugar, more and more human blood, and more and more water vessels in the Atlantic American tropics. For that matter, there were more and more slave ships arriving from West Africa, bringing as stowaways more mosquitoes. Things were looking up for *A. aegypti* in the Americas.

Conditions for the yellow fever virus improved too, with one catch that geopolitics soon addressed. More mosquitoes, more human bloodstreams, and more ships from Africa favored the establishment of the yellow fever virus in the American tropics. Indeed, the first clear epidemic of yellow fever in the Americas came in 1647, striking Barbados—then the main sugar island—first, and over the ensuing months and years, Guadeloupe, St. Kitts, Cuba, the Yucatan, and the east coasts of Central America generally. It killed perhaps 20–30 percent of local populations. But after this outbreak, yellow fever disappeared for almost forty years.[18] Presumably, it worked its way through the susceptible hosts, leaving behind a higher proportion of immunes. It could not flourish again without a sufficient proportion of nonimmunes, which for the yellow fever virus was problematic.

The virus's problem was compounded by the resistance of West Africans. Yellow fever confers immunity upon all survivors. Almost all slaves arriving in the Caribbean from Africa had grown up in endemic yellow fever zones and hence were immunes and virus stoppers. Moreover, West Africans and people of West African descent may carry an inherited partial immunity to yellow fever whether or not they carry conferred immunity.[19] So while the population growth of the sugar zones helped the mosquitoes find food, it did not provoke many epidemics because so many of the people bitten by mosquitoes were West Africans (or, possibly, because of West African descent). Raging epidemics required an influx of inexperienced immune systems. This influx is what expeditionary warfare provided.

Participants and observers in the interimperial wars of the seventeenth and eighteenth centuries normally regarded yellow fever epidemics as acts of God. Modern military historians tend to see them as random events. But differential immunity made yellow fever decidedly and systematically partisan.

Yellow fever went easy on entire populations that included numerous individuals with either conferred or (if it existed) inherited immunity. In this way, a large contingent of Africans or, perhaps somewhat less effectively, of Caribbean-born whites, could serve as a shield for individuals highly vulnerable themselves to yellow fever, by interrupting the transmission cycle (known as "herd immunity" to epidemiologists).[20] Yellow fever strongly favored local populations over invaders and immigrants, strongly favored populations with West Africans as opposed to those without them, and even favored populations with children as opposed to those made up exclusively of adults. Yellow fever was most dangerous to unadulterated populations of young adult Europeans: precisely the composition of expeditionary forces.[21]

After the one-week conquest of Jamaica in May 1655, the English troops fell victim to disease. By November, 47 percent were dead, and half the remainder were ill.[22] Henceforth, British garrisons in Jamaica died off at a rate of about 20 percent annually in peacetime, almost entirely from diseases (malaria and others as well as yellow fever). This percentage was about seven times the peacetime death rate of British garrisons in Canada. But in 1655 English soldiers conquered the island before disease conquered them. After 1655, the reverse was the rule.

Beginning in the 1680s, in the context of the struggles between England and Louis XIV's France, expeditions to the West Indies became more frequent and thus so did yellow fever outbreaks. Before 1713, Spain often fought on the same side as Britain, but after the accession in Madrid of a Bourbon king, Philip V, Spain normally allied with France against Britain. Most West Indies expeditions were British, but some were French, especially before Louis XIV scaled back his navy in the 1690s. Almost all were failures. After the successes, victors usually evacuated quickly, suffering from epidemics, and at the next peace treaty conquered ports were restored to their previous masters.

In 1689 an English expedition against Guadeloupe failed, losing half its men to diseases. In 1692, Commodore Ralph Wrenn's force lost more than half its number to yellow fever sailing in waters around Barbados. In 1693, another expedition lost 50 percent of its soldiers and sailors in failing to take Martinique. In 1695 a combined English and Spanish force lost 61 percent of the soldiers it disembarked in a doomed effort to dislodge the French from settlements that would at the next peace treaty (Ryswick 1697) be recognized as Saint Domingue. In 1697 a French expedition under Baron de Pointis failed to take Cartagena from Spain, losing 24 percent of its men to disease.[23] Thus ended the inglorious history of expeditionary warfare in the American tropics during the War of the League of Augsburg (1689–1697). A deadly pattern had begun to assert itself. That it continued was due to a combination of ignorance and callousness on the part of those charged with crafting grand strategy.

The War of the Spanish Succession (1701–1713) was a Spanish success in the American tropics. France and Britain mounted nineteen cruises or expeditions; serious disease mortality hampered or destroyed at least fourteen of them, possibly as many as eighteen. Of only one is there clear evidence that less than 10 percent of the troops died from disease. The War of Jenkins' Ear and the War of the Austrian Succession (together 1739–1748) presented much the same picture. In a famous expedition in 1739–1742 Admiral Edward Vernon took Portobelo and Chagres, ill-defended ports each of which surrendered within two days of sighting Vernon's fleet. He arrived in November, well before the rains that always presaged a population explosion of *A. aegypti*. He had the largest force ever seen in these seas, nearly twenty-five thousand counting sailors and soldiers. In April 1741 he tried to take Cartagena but lost 41 percent of all men under his command, 70 percent of all disembarked soldiers, and 77 percent of those hailing from Britain (thirty-six hundred colonial troops fared slightly better). Only about 650 died in combat. Fleeing Cartagena, Vernon attempted to take Santiago de Cuba as a consolation prize and lost 50 percent of his surviving troops to yellow fever. In all Vernon lost about three-fourths of the men under his command in 1740–1742; fewer than one thousand of these died in combat.[24]

The Seven Years' War, the War of the American Revolution, and the Napoleonic Wars included numerous further episodes along these lines. I will mention only two, one for its anecdotal quality and the other because it is an important exception to the grisly rule. The anecdote comes from a British expedition against Fort San Juan in Nicaragua in 1780. Fevers, including yellow fever but probably not confined to it, killed 77 percent of its men and forced the abandonment of an initially successful campaign. One of the few survivors was twenty-one-year-old Horatio Nelson, future hero of Trafalgar: among his other strengths, it seems, was his immune system.[25]

The exception came in 1762, when Admiral George Pocock, Lord Albermarle, and fourteen thousand men besieged Havana. Havana was the key to Spain's strategic position in the Americas, the port from which ships bound for Spain departed the Indies, as well as the most important naval shipbuilding center in the Spanish Empire. It was well fortified and generally regarded in Spain as impregnable.[26] Spanish authorities anticipated an attempt on Havana and in the summer of 1761 reinforced it with about 1,000 men—of whom 138 promptly died of yellow fever. But the thousand reinforcements were too few to sustain an epidemic, and by late 1761 Havana's defenders and population—then about thirty-five thousand people—enjoyed good health. They were busily strengthening the city's fortifications, intent on slowing besiegers' progress and exposing them to the dangers of the local disease environment.[27] But when the British landed, on June 7, 1762, they were masters of the city in nine weeks. The Spanish governor, Juan de Prado, after a bombardment that tore a hole in the city's walls, surrendered just as yellow fever took hold among the besiegers.[28] Shortly after the conquest, Pocock had lost 41 percent of his men, 34 percent of them to yellow fever (only 7–8 percent died in combat or of other causes), and another 37 percent were ill. Only 21 percent were fit to bear arms. On October 18 the expeditionary force reported that 305 men had died in combat, 255 from wounds, and 4,708 from sickness.[29] More still would die before Britain evacuated Havana in mid-1763. The British army lost more men to yellow fever in thirteen months at Havana than in all the campaigns of the Seven Years' War in North America put together. Lord Albermarle had to abandon plans to move from Havana to a conquest of Louisiana because of a shortage of able-bodied men. Although they at first intended to remain and spent money rebuilding Havana's fortifications, they gave it back to Spain at the Peace of Paris in 1763 and evacuated in July of that year.[30] Samuel Johnson wrote: "May my country be never cursed with such another conquest!"[31] Yellow fever kept Cuba Spanish even though Havana fell before the virus could work its mischief.

The power of yellow fever was such that defenders, if comprised of local troops with hardened immune systems, generally had only to hold out for three to six weeks to be assured of victory. Their chances improved if the siege took place during the rainier parts of the year (May–November in the Caribbean) when A. aegypti strength peaked. Expeditionary fleets tried their best to avoid the hurricane season (July–October) in the American tropics.

Strategists in Europe well knew (at least from the 1690s) that prospects for success receded if one failed to get the troops to the scene between December and May. But organizing and victualing a force according to schedule was no easy business in an age of private contracting and uncertain stocks of food and ships. Finding men willing to take the king's shilling proved especially challenging if prospective recruits thought their destination might be the Caribbean. Hence, many expeditions arrived later than planned and suffered the consequences. At any time of year, one had to be quick. As Admiral Charles Knowles wrote in 1747, "Whatever is to be effected in the West Indies must be done as expeditiously as possible, or the climate soon wages a more destructive War, than the Enemy."[32] Amphibious expeditions and siege warfare worked in the Indian Ocean, where there was malaria but no yellow fever. In the Caribbean, with rare exception, they did not.

The geopolitical significance of yellow fever in the Americas changed toward the end of the eighteenth century. The restiveness of slave populations acquired more political forms and more often led to organized violence. An illustrative example came in Surinam in the 1770s. There, Dutch planters had lived sumptuously if unhealthily amid a slave majority, but by 1772 maroon communities had grown powerful enough to threaten Surinam's plantation society. The Dutch government sent about 1,650 men from Europe in two contingents to do battle with the maroons. They succeeded in driving the maroons deeper into the forests and away from the plantations, but only about two hundred soldiers lived to return to Europe.[33] A Scot who served with the Dutch in Surinam observed that by the end "not 20 were to be found in perfect health." He also detected the impact of differential disease immunity, noting that: "amongst the Officers and Private men who had *formerly* been in the West Indies, none died at all, while amongst the whole number of near 1200 together I Can Recollect one Single marine who Escaped from Sickness."[34] Once people of West African origin began to make war on their own behalf in the American tropics, their relative immunity to yellow fever (and to falciparum malaria), if shrewdly exploited, magnified their power. That power soon shook the foundation of the imperial order in the American tropics. The maroons of Surinam lived to fight another day but were too few to take over their country.

In the Haitian revolution, both the scale and the agenda were larger. In the French colony of Saint Domingue (as Haiti was then called) by 1790 there were about half a million slaves, forty thousand French, and thirty thousand free people "of color." Taking advantage of and inspiration from events in France, slaves and former slaves engineered a revolution against

French planters, beginning in 1791, which the French, then the British, then the French again attempted to undo. In 1792 slaves prevented a small French force from reestablishing control. In 1794 British redcoats occupied the major ports. They found themselves, together with their Spanish allies, at war with Toussaint L'Ouverture (1743–1803) and his ill-equipped Haitian army. In the course of their stay at Saint Domingue, British forces lost about fifty thousand men, the majority falling to yellow fever. Britain lost about sixty-five to seventy thousand in all West Indian campaigns, 1793–1796.[35] After the British gave up, the French tried to reclaim Haiti. In 1802 Napoleon sent his brother-in-law, General Charles Leclerc, and fifty-eight thousand soldiers to subdue Toussaint. Initially, they met with military success as Toussaint prudently refused to commit large forces in a decisive battle. Over the next eighteen months, some fifty thousand Frenchmen died in Haiti, the French surrendered, and the survivors departed. Toussaint was no fool: he knew that if he did not give battle yellow fever would destroy the French, as it had done the British. His lieutenant and successor, Jean-Jacques Dessalines, knew it too: he told his followers to take courage, "The French will not be able to remain long in San Domingo. They will do well at first, but soon they will fall ill and die like flies."[36] And this prediction is exactly what happened. Toussaint and Dessalines would have been poor commanders indeed not to shape their strategy to exploit the overwhelming power of their insect and viral allies. Napoleon's defeat in Haiti led him to sell Louisiana to the United States in 1803. France finally recognized Haitian independence in 1825.

In the cases of Surinam and Haiti, the military impact of differential immunity was especially strong, because one of the combatant forces in each case consisted mainly of West Africans. But American-born whites, called creoles in the Spanish empire, also enjoyed military advantages derived from the antibodies in their bloodstreams. Like Toussaint, they learned how to exploit it without understanding it.

When Napoleon invaded Spain in 1808, most of Spanish America took the opportunity to declare independence. Vicious civil wars followed in many settings. After the Spanish, with British help, ejected Napoleon from Iberia the restored Spanish monarchy sought to reclaim its American empire and to this end shipped out over forty thousand soldiers. Very few ever returned. The largest contingent, some ten thousand men under General Pablo Morillo, went to the former Viceroyalty of New Granada, today's Colombia and Venezuela, in 1815. They successfully besieged Cartagena in a fifteen-week campaign, but their luck ended there. By 1817 a third of Morillo's men were dead from disease. Reigning ideas held that yellow fever (and malaria) came from "miasmas" arising from swamps, but Morillo was ahead of his time. He wrote to the Minister of War, "The mere bite of a mosquito often deprives a man of his life," an observation that anticipated the discovery of the etiology of yellow fever by eighty years.[37] Of all the men who served Spain in Venezuela and Colombia, between 90 percent and 96 percent died there, mainly from disease.[38] Yellow fever and malaria also afflicted soldiers fighting for independence, but not nearly as seriously. Simon Bolívar, while lamenting the "infinite" illness that beset his troops, noted that royalist troops suffered even more from disease, on account of their "nature" and their positions. What he observed but did not recognize was that the soldiers' place of origin, rather than their nature, determined their level of susceptibility. But the result was the same: Spain could not maintain an army in New Granada, because soldiers died far faster than replacements could be found. Morillo recruited local men, but they deserted en masse, sometimes for political reasons, sometimes to avoid the epidemics that beset the Spanish troops. With its army melting away, Spain could not resist the revolution.

While it is true that the Spanish American revolutions succeeded in Buenos Aires and elsewhere in the absence of serious epidemics, the events in New Granada affected all of Spanish America. The Crown unwisely chose to concentrate its military efforts there and thereby exposed the greater part of its forces to tropical fevers, which meant fewer troops could be spared for Chile, Peru, and elsewhere. And it further meant that recruiting new soldiers in Spain would be even more difficult. Contingents bound for New Granada had to be told they were headed to Buenos Aires lest they mutiny. According to one British account, rebellious Buenos Aires was ripe for reconquest in 1819–1820. But Spain could not get an army to the scene in order to take advantage of the situation. An army of fourteen thousand assembled in Cadiz in 1820 threw its weight behind a revolution rather than go to fight in America. Its officers had the salutary experience of observing some of the few survivors of Morillo's Colombian campaigns (who apparently sparked a yellow fever epidemic in Cadiz) shortly before they joined the revolution of 1820.[39]

On several other occasions in the nineteenth century yellow fever affected military campaigns in the greater Caribbean. Perhaps its most significant impact was in preventing a French Panama Canal. In 1879 Ferdinand de Lesseps, the French diplomat who had organized the Suez Canal project a decade before, formed a company to build a canal across the Isthmus of Panama. After his bankruptcy in 1889, a successor company carried on the work. Between 1881 and 1903 de Lesseps and his followers recruited tens of thousands of laborers to Panama, half of them from Jamaica, many of the rest from elsewhere in the Americas, but a few thousand luckless souls from Europe. Among the Frenchmen who went to dig in Panama, 67 percent died there. An Inspector General, Jules Dingler, declared upon arrival in 1883 that only dissipated drunks died of yellow fever. Within months his son and daughter died of the disease, then his wife. Dingler returned to France in 1884. The annual death rate for all men on the canal project was about 6–7 percent, and in all twenty-two thousand died failing to finish a canal. In the hospitals the French built, more than three-quarters of all patients suffered from yellow fever or malaria. The hospitals were racially segregated, in keeping with medical practice of the time. This custom had the unintended effect of separating immunes from nonimmunes, preventing any herd immunity and maximizing the death toll among Europeans and others whose background left them vulnerable to yellow fever. In addition, to prevent ants and other crawling insects from feasting on hospital patients, French doctors tried to ensure that each hospital bed's legs were inserted into pots of water, creating ideal breeding habitat for the silent angels of death, the *A. aegypti*.[40] The French finally gave up, leaving a Panama Canal to the Americans. With the help of newly acquired knowledge of the transmission cycle of yellow fever, and with energetic mosquito control, the United States in 1914 succeeded where France failed, ensuring American control of the Canal for some eighty years to come.

10

Creation and Destruction in Landscapes of Empire

Thomas R. Dunlap

W E THINK of dreams as insubstantial, calling something a dream to place it outside the "real" world, and we see land as solid, giving property in land the special status of "real estate." In theory the two should not meet. In fact they do. Our dreams shape the land and the land our dreams, and the creation and destruction of landscapes on the ground and in our minds is central to our history. This thinking is particularly true in the Anglo neo-Europes—the United States, Australia, Canada, and New Zealand—the places where English-speaking immigrants so completely displaced the indigenous peoples that they could pretend the lands were new and empty and set about reproducing (with improvements, of course) the culture and even the political organization of "home."[1] Here the settlers could believe they had no necessary connections to the land, that with their technology they could make of it what they wished. Needless to say, reality was more complex. It had to be, for clearly we do not live in the New England of the patriotic literature or railroad company sales brochures. I want to comment on the interaction between lands and dreams in these countries with three points in mind. One is that we must see American history in the larger context of the expansion of Europe and in particular of Britain—hence my appeals to what happened in Canada and the antipodean countries. A second is that settlement is not an accomplished fact but an ongoing process. We are not the pioneers, but we are not done with exploring or settling, either. The result, my third point, is that creation and destruction, mental and physical, are our heritage and our future. Any peace we make with the land will be dynamic and unstable, remade by each generation in the circumstances of their lives and the conditions of the land.

To begin, look around. We live amid the wreckage of landscapes and dreams. In cities from New York to Sydney the commonest birds are English sparrows, pigeons, and starlings, the commonest mammals Old World rats (they do outnumber humans). Roadside ditches are full of European weeds; skylarks sing above Tasmanian fields; ring-necked pheasants strut through corn stubble from Alberta to New Jersey. The view from the air shows survey systems neatly parceling out the land into legal and social pieces. Everywhere, though, native species persist. Among the skyscrapers of New York and Toronto peregrines prey on pigeons; coyotes and dingoes range from suburbs out into the pastures; in the wild there may be exotics but much of the biota is native. The aerial view that showed our own divisions also reveals the ghostly remains of abandoned fields, irrigation ditches, and towns. Our mental landscapes are as mixed. National myths, from the American idea of the frontier to the Australian bush legend, use European concepts of Romantic nature to speak of a new people in a new nation. We make regional and local loyalties from our mixed landscapes with agrarian and rural ideals from eighteenth-century Britain. Individually, we organize memories of home and childhood around European ideals, modified by experience, and give them meaning with the sound of magpies (in Australia) or North American robins, the scent of pines or eucalyptus, and the feel of winds and seasons Europe never knew.

These mental and physical mixtures make both the official account of settlement (that story of human triumph) and the environmental tale (our fall from grace into ecological destruction) only parts of a larger narrative. The center of settler history is neither the destruction of the old landscape nor the creation of the new. It is the interplay of settlers and land. Its most important characteristics are not victory or defeat but ambiguity and unintended consequences. The settlers destroyed existing landscapes and displaced indigenous societies. The land, though, never quite became a New England. The indigenous peoples, despite the Anglos' fond hopes and repeated funeral orations, did not die out. The settlers ceased to be Europeans but did not become natives. Most important, the story goes on. The land still changes, the settlers still dream. I recount the events of the past, but the processes of now and tomorrow are the backdrop to our lives and our children's.

Like other peoples the Anglos reshaped their lands and looked for a place in them, but they did so with unprecedented speed and thoroughness. They changed the land much faster than it could change them; it was ours long before we were the land's. In 1800 Anglo settlements in North America lay scattered along the Atlantic coast and up the St. Lawrence, in Australia in a few spots in the southeast, and the Maori ruled New Zealand. By the end of the century more than eighty million people lived in Anglo-dominated North American towns and cities or on the farms and ranches that spread into the rain shadow of the North American Rockies and almost to the sub-Arctic (in both cases beyond the limits of European crops and farming practices). Most of the indigenous societies were gone or hopelessly scattered, and the survivors controlled only pieces of land, usually not in their ancestral range. Non-Anglo European settlements like the French in Quebec and the Spanish in the American Southwest came under cultural siege. The great herds of buffalo and vast flocks of passenger pigeons were only memories. In Australia what remained of the Aboriginal population lived on the margins while white farmers occupied the relatively well-watered southeast, and stockmen moving west from Queensland met those coming east from Western Australia. Only the arid Centre remained white space on the map. The wildlife dwindled toward nothing. By 1900 the thylacine was almost gone (and would become extinct by the middle of the twentieth century), the koala, platypus, and other species scarce across large parts of their ranges. In New Zealand graziers had to make new sheep stations on less fertile or otherwise undesirable lands. The Maori were a remnant. Hunters and collectors scrambled for the last specimens of many of the islands' unique birds.

Their rapid and apparently complete conquest encouraged the settlers to believe they could do anything. Though each landscape had its own possibilities, problems, and Anglo history, the core of settler dreams was everywhere the same, the vision of the land as a place for individual opportunity. Indeed, these societies defined themselves by the chance they offered to everyone (or at least every white man). Everywhere, people regarded science as the key to understanding. They praised practical knowledge and local experience but looked to the culture's authoritative knowledge for riches. They also sought—a dream at odds with their other visions—a place in the land, as individuals but also as a society. They were fully aware they came from somewhere else and held enthusiastically to the "heritage of Western civilization," but they wanted roots as well. They dreamed of becoming natives. These ideas shaped settler lives and the ways they made their living, but the land had its own imperatives, and in ways the settlers recognized and in ways they did not, it shaped them.

"The Best Poor Man's Country"

In the nineteenth century individual opportunity was the great fact and glittering hope of the settler societies, a dream erected on what seemed (or could be made to seem) the settler countries' unlimited expanse of fertile, vacant land and the industrial power that could transform it into farms. Even more than science mechanical energy fueled this dream. In North America the railroad engine, spouting black smoke and pulling a string of cars, became the icon of Progress, abolishing space and time, sweeping the wilderness away, and bringing in its wake smiling farms and civilization. That was rhetoric. Reality was the railroad connecting the periphery to the metropolis, bringing nature to the market. One of the first results of the connection was a set of wildlife slaughters on a scale never seen before. A century later and a continent away, Australian legislators could invoke the fate of the American buffalo and the passenger pigeon as a warning for their own nation, confident that people would know and take alarm.[2] Having helped the first wave profit by bringing wildlife and wood to market the railroad helped the second wave profit by transporting their wheat, corn, cattle, and wool. In the antipodes the railroad was, comparatively, less important. There, it was steamships and better sailing ships, as well as improving knowledge of winds and currents, that allowed Australia and New Zealand to ride to prosperity on a sheep's back.[3]

Americans tend to think of free land, an expanding frontier, and the chances it offered as their national heritage. It was theirs, but not theirs alone. Canada promised immigrants the same opportunities and established similar land policies in the Prairie Provinces around the rectangular grid, the promise of free land, and the lure of a railroad. Optimism ran just as high, though Canadian hopes focused more on settlement producing a milder climate than on its increasing the rainfall. In Australia, the settlers, in a continuing triumph of hope over experience, believed that it would rain in the interior and that if it did not plowing and tree planting would make it so. Each drought was only a "bad year." Australian legislatures echoed with speeches demanding that the squatters' vast estates (the inland sheep stations) be thrown open to settlement by sturdy yeoman farmers. The only thing more common was the squatters' success in beating back these schemes or using them to their own advantage. Even New Zealand offered a genteel version of opportunity—the chance to raise sheep in a purified British society ruled by the respectable middle class.

As the good land ran out the settlers called on science and technology to make more. In the American West and Australia the great hope was irrigation. Dams and canals would make the desert bloom with crops and small farms supporting virtuous families. In Canada plant and animal breeding would open the North to sturdy, hard-working farmers. Across the board settlers looked for development guided by science. While only the United States organized a national conservation program, everyone did something. Legislators from Western Australia to New Brunswick discussed dwindling forests and shortages of water, debated what agencies should be established, set aside reserves, and funded projects. Outside the legislatures, boosters continued to project dreams as grand as William Gilpin's. In the 1920s, for example, the Australia Unlimited movement held that the continent had no real deserts. It admitted that there was too little water in the Centre, but that was only on the surface. Nature in her beneficence had provided an unlimited underground supply. Geology would show where it was and bores (what Americans call wells) would bring it to the surface.[4] Several generations of Canadian politicians spoke with feeling about the storehouse of treasure that was the Canadian North, whose development would give the Dominion its rightful place among the great nations of the world. Parliament supported mining, lumbering, even reindeer raising in the Yukon and on Baffin Island.

Hopes rose and fell like some generations-long mental tide. After the schemes of the 1920s came those of the 1950s. Then the United States Bureau of Reclamation began a second phase of work on the Colorado River; farmers tapped the aquifers east of the Rockies; and others made plans (never carried out) to pipe water from the mouth of the Mississippi to the high plains of West Texas and from the Yukon to California. Canadians turned to northern rivers for electricity and the land for minerals and oil. On the mainland Australians built dams on the Murray-Darling, the continent's largest river system, and the island-state of Tasmania sought salvation—that is to say economic development—from hydropower. New Zealand succumbed to hydrofever as well. New technologies reshaped old industries. Getting resources from the forests progressed from cutting some trees to cutting all to cutting them on ever larger plots and on to wood chipping, a process that reduced everything from trees to undergrowth to pieces that could be processed into fibers. Now genetic manipulation promises either miracle crops to feed a growing population or Frankenfoods that will wreak havoc on humans and nature alike. Beyond that some groups advocate the exploration and mining of the moon and the asteroids, confident that outer space is our immediate future and glorious destiny—if only we will trust technology and the magic of the market.[5]

Plans showed the power of dreams but so did people's confidence. Optimism ran highest, perhaps, in the United States, where resources, climate, and technology made it seem anything could be done, and others shared the belief in an ever richer future. As recalled by Donella Meadows, one of the authors, criticism of the Club of Rome's report on the world system, *The Limits to Growth*, came "from the left and the right and the middle. The book was banned in the Soviet Union and investigated by President Nixon's staff. The Mobil Corporation ran ads saying 'growth is not a four-letter word.' Disciples of Lyndon LaRouche and the National Labor Caucus picketed our public appearances. Mainstream economists competed with one another to see who could write the most scathing reviews." Human ingenuity, they said, would always find a way around a lack of resources. People, in the words of one of the most fervent of optimists, Princeton economist Julian Simon, were the ultimate resource.[6] What Meadows found particularly disheartening was that everyone concentrated on what was seen as predictions of disaster. That, she said, was a mistake. *The Limits to Growth* "was not about prediction. It was about choice." The team had not written to "predict doom but to challenge the myth of growth as the answer to all problems."[7] True, but all the choices led away from a constantly expanding economy that gave more and more to everyone, and no one wanted to believe in a diminished future.

The Attractions of Knowledge

Knowledge fueled conquest, but it also supported understanding. From the eighteenth century organized knowledge and its institutions—roughly what we mean by science and scientific societies—were central to Anglo settlement and settler dreams. The settlers seized on natural history, "the study of the productions of the earth in their natural state, whether minerals, plants, or animals."[8] Peter Kalm, collecting for the great botanist Linnaeus in North America around 1740, found the core of a scientific society, including a botanical garden and a circle of naturalists. The British government put naturalists on its exploring ships, and their work soon influenced action. Captain Cook's reports encouraged the settlement of Australia and New Zealand, while the Lewis and Clark expedition gave Americans their first reports on the far west and three generations of surveys organized and publicized knowledge of the continent. Elsewhere, British officers, working for the Empire or a particular colony, did the same. With each generation the settlers' view grew. The first maps and reports showed outline—coasts, the mouths of rivers, indications of mountains. Later ones revealed the rivers' courses and the extent of mountains. Notes on forests, deserts, and prairies and indications of the soil, water, timber, and climate followed. Specialized fields added new pieces to the puzzle. Taxonomy arranged the fauna and flora, placed them in the "universal" intellectual structures of Western knowledge, and showed what was unique and noteworthy about each country's "natural productions." Geology described land formations, found mineral wealth, then estimated the size of deposits (legislatures, not surprisingly, funded geological surveys first).[9] Americans led the field, for obvious reasons. They had the largest population and the most money, and they could not turn to the British for aid or prestige. Elsewhere naturalists worked in the shadow of the British scientific establishment. Still, they worked, organizing their own societies, and their legislatures funded expeditions, collections, and then museums.

Natural history aided settlement, but it did more than that. In *Inventing Canada*, Suzanne Zeller argues that the "tasks of identification, inventory, and mapmaking [the central activities of natural history] gave form to the idea of a transcontinental national existence; they imparted to Canadians a sense of direction, stability, and certainty for the future."[10] They did elsewhere, too. Americans relied on scientific exploration and surveys to show them the continent, and maps and mineral surveys fueled the dreams of Manifest Destiny and American expansion. Other reports encouraged British authorities to establish an outdoor jail in New South Wales and private groups to fund the settlement of Western and South Australia and New Zealand. Even discussions of the limits to expansion rested on scientific reports. Those on the American Great Plains created "The Great American Desert," while those on the Prairie Provinces first discouraged, then overencouraged, settlement. In Australia more and more pessimistic reports on the interior led one scholar to describe nineteenth-century Australia as a "diminishing paradise."[11]

Settler societies appealed to knowledge, but so did settlers. Linnaeus, literacy, and cheap printing made natural history an amateur passion and allowed people to take part in the great adventure of exploring their land by collecting specimens and writing papers. Sending specimens to savants in Europe or—in North America—eastern institutions, they could establish social and intellectual ties to the metropolis. When specialized scientific disciplines displaced natural history from the forefront of science, amateurs found new activities appropriate to the new situation. In the late nineteenth century, as shooting birds for a cabinet became impractical or (to some) distasteful, a new kind of bird book appeared, one that helped people identify specimens in the bush rather than in the hand, and thirty years later a new generation of field guides served a continually growing audience. In North America there was Roger Tory Peterson's *Field Guide to the Birds* (1934). With its western supplement it covered the continent. Neville Cayley's *What Bird Is That?* (1931) did the same for Australia, and Perrine Moncrieff's *New Zealand Birds and How to Identify Them* (1925) for that country.[12] In the last twenty years environmental education has replaced natural history in the schools and field guides now take an ecological view, but the settlers still seek knowledge of their land through authoritative knowledge.

Becoming Native to This Place

There was as well that third dream, related to conquest and understanding but separate from them, of becoming native to the new land. It spoke to the common human wish to be at home in the land but against settler history, for the Anglos came as invaders or exiles or opportunists, defined themselves by conquest, and to find a home in the land tried to make the land like Europe or their dreams. That trend peaked in the nineteenth century and was most marked in the antipodes, where history and biology were most cooperative. Settled at a time when culture encouraged an interest in nature and technology allowed the settlers to import virtually anything, the southern countries were also depauperate, that is, had fewer species than theory suggested they should for their land mass, and mild climates. The extreme was New Zealand, which had, save two species of bats and whatever seals hauled out on the beaches, no native mammals at all. Faced with very odd plants and animals (odd at least to them), the homesick Australians brought in all the familiar ones. The New Zealanders looked at a land that seemed much like Britain and decided to make the changes needed to finish the job. In the north things were different. By the time technology allowed easy imports, the North American settlers, particularly those with the money to import new things, were not interested, for they had been born in the new country and were used to its plants and animals. When Anglophilia or the desire for novelty won out local conditions often imposed a veto. The climate (particularly in Canada) and the vigorous North American biota put a quick end to most of the introductions.

Beyond importing species, the settlers reshaped entire landscapes to their dreams of industry and leisure. Particularly where irrigation was necessary, the settlers dreamed of remaking the land into a garden. California and Victoria were the centers of this enthusiasm. Into the twentieth century, politicians, newspapers, and land salesmen depicted a constructed, harmonious, profitable, and fruitful landscape, in which independent growers (always white, middle-class, and respectable) raised fruits or vegetables for the market, using nonwhites for the hard labor required (Chinese, seen as a naturally docile, hardworking, peasant people, were often favored for this role).[13] Horticulture, alas, turned out to be just another business, and one plagued by all the usual problems, but the dreams remained and reappeared in promotions for suburbs after World War II. They were at the center of efforts to "sell" places like California and Florida as places to retire. Real estate advertisements showed the happy retired couple—white and middle class—emerge in the morning to pick oranges and grapefruit from the trees in their yard, contemplate with pride the tropical blossoms beside the house, and admire the palms—that symbol of exotic leisure—shading the street.

The land's role, when it was not raw material, was to serve as the antagonist that formed the settlers' character. That dominated American thinking from the formation of Daniel Boone's reputation in the 1780s—the prototype for the American frontier myth. The wilderness made him nature's nobleman and it was his home. His task, his destiny, was to open it to settlement. He lived, that is to say, to destroy what had made him and in flight from those he served.[14] The Australian bush legend, a century later, laid less stress on the contradictions of conquest but held, as strongly as the American version, that the struggle with nature forged individual virtue and national character. Even Australian children's literature told the story. The bush either "broke" the "new chum" or made a new man of him.[15] In Canada there was less talk of conquest, for it was clear that Canadians were not going to conquer their frontier in the North. Instead they made survival the touchstone of their identity in the land, and climate and weather, secondary elsewhere, became "major attributes of nationality."[16] The Canadian mythology spoke of Canada as a "Northern" nation, the cold shaping Canadian virtue and, providentially, protecting it from the corruption that lurked south of the border. In New Zealand there was little talk of a distinctive character shaped by the land, but speeches extolled the pioneer, the hard work that created farms, and the virtues of rural life.

As the rush for land slowed in the late nineteenth century the settlers more consciously sought an identity in the land based on living there rather than coming there. To that end they made their history the land's only history, began calling themselves natives, gave other names to the indigenous peoples, and used native plants and animals as symbols of the nation. In Australia the kangaroo became the preeminent animal emblem, in New Zealand the kiwi, with the silver fern as an important botanical marker. In Australia the new nature literature (New Zealand had too few people to support a literary community) appealed to the beauty of native scenes and the nostalgia of country childhoods and rural vacations.[17] Except for the Australians, who lacked Romantic scenery, the settlers enshrined spectacular landscapes in national parks. This too Americans see as their natural heritage, but arguments for Banff Hot Springs sound very American, one Canadian legislator asserting, for example, that anyone who had seen the area "and not felt himself elevated and proud that all this is part of the Dominion, cannot be a true Canadian."[18] The search for roots in native nature and local experience has only grown since then. There are now registries of historic sites, programs for local and regional history, folklore collections, and local museums.[19]

The Limits of Dreams

Dreams shaped lands but lands shaped dreams. Reality intruded on a large scale in the second half of the nineteenth century. Australians moved inward from the coast, and Americans and Canadians across the plains, with the conviction that everything on the land would bloom. Farmers in the Prairie Provinces, with a very un-Canadian optimism, even believed their presence and work would moderate the climate. That, and ideas about rain following the plow, turned out to be wishful thinking. Farmers found, often at considerable personal cost, where they could not live. Dry years in the 1880s drove South Australian wheat farmers back toward the coast. A decade later another drought ruined people on a broad arc from Queensland to South Australia. In North America drought on the western plains ruined hopes from Colorado to Alberta, sent farmers "back east," and made empty shells of entire towns. In a less spectacular fashion, early and late frosts set limits on Canadian farming. New Zealand escaped the collapse of these castles in the air but not the slower halt imposed by the lack of any more good land.

Even where the settlers reigned they did not fully rule. To make their pastures safe they poisoned, shot, and trapped every animal they could find, which got rid of the larger ones but not the smaller. The dingo continued to be a problem in most sheep-raising areas in Australia, and in North America the coyote not only survived but took advantage of the settlers' war against the wolf to expand its territory. It now ranges over large parts of the continent it never saw before Columbus. Other creatures adapted to the new conditions. Gophers and ground squirrels dug holes in pastures and the banks of irrigation canals as easily as in the virgin prairie. Mice multiplied in fallow fields. Birds feasted on grain. In Australia fruit-eating bats flocked to orchards. In Australia and New Zealand species brought from "home," freed from familiar ecological checks, multiplied out of control. The legendary case, of course, was the European rabbit. Introduced into Australia and New Zealand for sport, it quickly went from protected rarity to abundant game to natural disaster—the "gray blanket" or "rabbit menace." It was only the most conspicuous of a clutch that included not only introduced wild species but stock gone wild. Australia has, for instance, a large population of feral camels, descendents of ones imported for the construction of telegraph systems and railroads in the central desert. New Zealand had rabbits, the weasels and stoats brought in to control the rabbits, and the deer brought in for deer-stalking.

Accidental introductions added to the settlers' problems. As ocean traffic improved in speed and grew in volume it became easier for pest insects, weeds, and microorganisms to make the jump, and oceans that had been moats turned into highways. Finding monocultures and few natural enemies, the hitchhikers spread rapidly and at times caused enormous damage. The San Jose, or cottony-cushion, scale, brought into California around 1880, soon threatened the state's citrus industry. Entomologists brought it under control by finding and importing one of its natural enemies, an Australian ladybird beetle, but this and other pests forced the settler governments to guard their borders with agricultural quarantine and inspection services and fund scientific research on crop and stock diseases. Not only crops suffered; native species also fell to the invaders. Early in the twentieth century the chestnut blight, accidentally brought from Europe in infected timber, destroyed the American chestnut, a common eastern shade tree and a keystone species in the Appalachians. The bear population there went into a steep decline; ecosystems in the mountains changed and are still changing. In the 1950s Dutch elm disease devastated the native trees that were the emblem and ornament of small towns throughout the East and Midwest. Less obvious but no less damaging were plants like cheat and Russian thistle, which took over millions of acres of farm and range land.[20]

What happened to the dream of conquest happened to other dreams as well. The settlers could chart the land, describe and classify plants, animals, and soil, find minerals, measure the rain, and with ecology unravel at least some of the interrelationships among species and between species and the land. They could not fully understand the land or become natives. They could speak of themselves as such and celebrate their ties to the land, but the very fervor of their rhetoric betrayed them. That and the wistful way they looked to indigenous cultures showed they were still settling.

Confronting the Society, Confronting the Self

Old dreams faded but the settlers found new ones, among them environmentalism. This shift seems an odd perspective on a movement that opposed conventional ideas about our relationship to the land and drew much of its energy and passion from the failures and disasters of settlement, but just as surely as the ideas it rejected, environmentalism spoke to the wishes behind them and incorporated their goals. Like conquest it saw opportunities for the individual. Like the dream of understanding it looked to science as a way of coming to terms with the land. It acknowledged human power over nature but directed it toward the end of a more human life for all in a community rooted in and growing from the land. Like earlier dreams, it looked for a new society grounded in the new land. It subverted the stories of settlement and conquest that formed the official Anglo history, but it built on settler history, using established ideas even as it transformed them. Wilderness, for instance, incorporated ideas of masculinity and pioneer recreation. The Boundary Water Canoe Area, one of the first (administratively declared) wilderness areas, was a monument to the romance of the fur trade and stereotypes of masculinity. Bioregionalism drew on agrarianism and producer ideals of small-scale community. In Australia and New Zealand the bushwalking clubs that defended wild lands and scenery looked for inspiration to the Australian legend, exulting mateship, the skills of bush living, endurance, and the virtues of the nineteenth-century graziers' life.

Roots are evident even in such radical ideas as the belief that we have moral duties toward the land. The most influential statement of that idea, Aldo Leopold's land ethic, drew on American agrarianism and in particular Liberty Hyde Bailey's *The Holy Earth*.[21] The earth is holy, Bailey said, and we have therefore to "deal with it devotedly and with care that we do not despoil it, and mindful of our relations to all beings that live on it." Our situation is one of "obligation and service"—to others, future generations, and the earth itself. Our response can not be limited to public policy; it has to be personal and moral. "It would seem that a divine obligation rests on every soul." We need ties to the land, and "all people, or as many of them as possible, shall have contact with the earth and . . . the earth's righteousness shall be abundantly taught." That does not mean we all should go "back to the land." It does mean we have to look for ways by which people can find "personal satisfaction in the earth to which we are born, and the quickened responsibility, the whole relation broadly developed." We have to live with nature. "A useful contact with the earth places man not as superior to nature but as a superior intelligence working in nature as a conscious and therefore as a responsible part in a plan of evolution, which is a continuing creation." To meet that obligation requires that we look at the land in a new way. We have put our relation to the land "in the realm of trade." We must put it "into the realm of morals." "The morals of land management are more important than the economics of land management . . . [and] any line of development founded on accountant economics alone will fail." Leopold, though he appealed to ecology rather than Scripture, clearly wove this perspective into his argument.[22]

That was one side of the coin. On the other was environmentalism's fundamental opposition to key elements of settler culture and history, for it dismissed the "conquest of nature" as a destructive and self-destructive dream and saw continued economic growth as the road to disaster. Its critique was fundamental, so fundamental that environmentalists have not yet explored its implications, which may, and probably do, lead in directions that not even committed environmentalists fully appreciate. Consider: settler dreams made nature change and assumed nature would bear the pain of change. Individual settlers might, to be sure, suffer, might even die, but that was only the price of the society's crossing over to the Promised Land. The environmental dream demanded that the settlers change their hearts and their values, and in drastic ways. We could not establish a sustainable society, however defined, without discarding large parts of our lives, including ideas of success and accomplishment, and here the settlers and not nature would have to bear the pain. Environmentalists spoke of enlarging the boundaries of the community, taking into account the needs of nonhuman organisms. They appealed to Aldo Leopold's dictum that "[a] thing is right when it tends to preserve the integrity, stability and beauty of the biotic community" and "wrong when it tends otherwise."[23] That was a revolutionary sentiment in a society that was built around the ideal of the autonomous individual and the sanctity of private property, gave the community only the most restricted role, and often saw it as only the aggregate of individuals. Placing the long-term interests of the community—and a community that includes plants, animals, and the land as well as humans—would require us to rethink what we mean by the individual and the community and the relation between them. We might have to see the individual as constituted by relationships as much as by autonomy. In the same fashion, if continued growth was impossible we needed sources of satisfaction other than money and consumer goods. These changes strike to the heart of our identity and our society, and it is only in utopian fantasies, books like Ernst Callenbach's *Ecotopia* or Charles Reich's *The Greening of America*, that change on this order is either painless or easy.[24] Looked at in this way, building a society that would care for the land and make nature an emotionally significant part of our lives suggested individual agony and social upheaval on a grand scale. The environmental dream might wreak as much havoc in the settlers' minds as earlier dreams did on the land.

There is a certain poetic justice, or historical irony, in the settlers' dreams thus turning on them, and while it is too early to start appreciating that irony, there are signs the settler societies are grappling with the problems. In North America change was apparent in debates and actions that blurred the sharp line people commonly drew between nature and culture, in discussions of wilderness and attempts to find nature in daily life. Environmental justice challenged conventional belief by bringing people's bodies and living arrangements, including cities, into the "environment." In the antipodes discussions of "natives" and "native nature" acquired a new dimension, and everywhere settlers acknowledged more clearly (though not completely) indigenous peoples' ties to the land.

In North America its advocates established wilderness as a separate world, separated from humans by a great gulf. Legislation ratified the definition of wilderness as land that lacked evidence of permanent human occupation and change. So did wilderness writings and the iconic photographs of Ansel Adams and Eliot Porter, which showed a world without humans, beyond them and their concerns, a place people did not live but only came to as pilgrims in search of insight. Its defenders, in the courts and on the ground, concentrated on excluding industrial America, by lying down in front of bulldozers and living in redwood trees, if necessary. When William Cronon declared, in his essay "The Trouble with Wilderness," that "wilderness" was a name we gave to some part of the world outside us, wilderness defenders accused him of attacking the movement and wilderness.[25] Largely lost in the uproar was his point, which echoed Aldo Leopold, that we would not work to save what we did not love and would not love what we did not know or have in our lives. If we found nature only in wilderness we would not, in the end, find it there and we would not find wilderness compelling enough to work for. Nature had to be part of ordinary experience.

Others made the same point in different ways. In *Second Nature* Michael Pollan called for a new approach to nature, one suited to our lives and our society. He believed we had learned much from wilderness, and much that was valuable, but we needed a way to nature that was closer to home and gave us a way to work in nature. The garden, he thought, offered such an approach, a way to think about nature that let us act and taught us by the consequences of our acts, an approach that could lead us to nature and a marriage of nature and culture. In *The Thunder Tree* Robert Pyle described his childhood explorations of the High Line Canal near Denver, a bit of still wild nature near his suburban home, and how they led him to become a naturalist. He believed we needed to save the canal and areas like it, not as parks but as places where children could learn about nature through play and collecting plants and butterflies. In *The Meadowlands* Robert Sullivan carried the search for wildness into the swamps and dumps just east of New York City. Using the conventions of the natural history essay to describe the herons and the highways, the water plants and the trash, he mixed and subverted categories, fusing nature and culture in a way that spoke to urban experience but led beyond the city.[26]

People also translated ideas into daily action in ordinary lives. The sacred American lawn, with its monoculture of imported grass, retained its worshippers, but dissenters from the true faith became numerous enough to support nurseries and catalog companies specializing in native shrubs, flowers, and grasses. In arid and semiarid areas of the United States xeriscaping—the use of low-water, local plants instead of the imports that require irrigation—became an established niche among landscape companies. Enthusiasts tried to restore their backyards to the wild, make native prairies or woodlots, or provide resting and feeding places for birds or butterflies.[27] Australian nurseries sold native plants, and the streets of Canberra's newer suburbs were planted in native trees rather than the European or American ones that had been favored.[28] Amateur natural history enjoyed another surge in popularity. Where bird books once had the nature shelf in the local bookstore to themselves, now guidebooks covered every visible form of life and described local ecologies as well. National parks and nature museums provided guides to the area and—for the less ambitious—small sheets with pictures of common birds, plants, and butterflies.

Environmental justice showed another aspect of changing ideas—as well as some differences among the settler countries. American environmentalism started with issues of human health—Rachel Carson's treatment of pesticide residues made that a major concern in the early years—but its focus was wild nature. When the urban poor, often minorities, rallied against pollution in their neighborhoods under the banner of environmental justice, the mainstream movement was baffled and occasionally hostile, not seeing urban areas or people's bodies as part of the environment. Over the last decade a dialogue developed, one that called into question our ideas about what was nature, what culture, and how the two were related.[29] In Australia and New Zealand, though, there was not the same sharp division between nature and culture, and environmentalism never focused on wild nature, including from the start topics like urban housing, public health, and city planning. The first book on environmental law in New Zealand, for example, had no chapter on wildlife or the national parks because these topics were not among those "most likely to be encountered in practice."[30] Australian environmental histories made no distinction between the environments the settlers found and the ones they built.[31] In both countries organizations working for civic improvement, city parks, and soil conservation were early members of the environmental coalition, and the groups most concerned with the wild were the bushwalking clubs—the antipodean equivalent of hiking and trail clubs.[32] Wildlife societies were a minor component. Organized labor, which in North America was largely hostile to environmentalism, joined in early. Labor unions helped defend Australia's Great Barrier Reef in the 1970s.[33]

In the antipodes, discussions about what was "native" took a new direction. In the late nineteenth century, seeking a separate identity (within the British Empire, of course) the settlers made the kangaroo Australia's preeminent symbol, the personification of the nation in everything from editorial cartoons to patriotic posters, and in New Zealand the kiwi became their symbol—distinctive, found only in New Zealand, and easy to draw. Early in the twentieth century, introduced species came to be seen less as reminders of "home" than intruders destroying landscapes now regarded as a "national heritage" of native plants and animals. There followed a chorus of laments about the loss of "old Australia" and "primeval New Zealand."[34] In New Zealand, reaction, coupled with economic concerns, led to a government deer eradication campaign in the 1930s and after World War II, an extensive and coordinated campaign against rabbits. By the 1970s, about the time it became clear that these were not eliminating the species, sentiment shifted still further. In 1973 two ecologists noted that the Maori Rat, the *kirre*, was now being referred to as a "native" and had "even crept into the ranks of desirable native wildlife, vying with such elite as the tuatara and saddleback for protection on select island refuges. To what dizzier heights," they asked, "can an introduced rat with but squatter's rights aspire—and how much longer must later introductions await similar recognition? This country," they declared, "will come of age ecologically when Western man and his animal introductions are regarded as part of the natural environment."[35] In 1990 Carolyn King said the same thing in her *Handbook of New Zealand Mammals*. It was "time that the native and introduced mammals were treated in practice as resident species of equal status in the scientific sense," that we recognize that what exists is "a working, evolving community . . . [that] will continue to evolve according to natural processes largely beyond our control."[36] This view was a new idea, as King recognized, for studying weasels and stoats a few years before, she had found that many New Zealanders still saw these animals as unnatural horrors, bloodthirsty creatures from another land that preyed on the helpless, native, flightless birds.[37]

The dream of restoration was strongest in the southern countries, but it affected Americans as well. In the 1930s the National Park Service declared that exotics should be eliminated from the parks, which should show visitors landscapes as they were before Columbus—minus, of course, the Indians, whose presence was at odds with a pristine nature. By the 1970s park officials, under pressure from ecologists, came to see this goal as an impossible, even incoherent, ideal. It was not just that exotics could not be eliminated. A timeless, static land, unaffected by humans, was as great an illusion as conquest. The first whites had looked out on dynamic landscapes, many showing the influence of Indian fire, hunting, and planting. Their fires had, for example, created the open, parklike floor of Yosemite, which the first whites had taken as a wilderness paradise. The only way to have a pre-Columbian landscape was to kill everything and preserve it in place.

Life on the land also took on new dimensions as well. Borrowing from Romanticism and agrarianism but relying on ecology, people set out to develop a moral life in touch with the land and devoted to healing it, with bioregionalists like Wendell Berry, Gary Snyder, and Wes Jackson taking different paths, each appropriate to the area they called home.[38] They saw community in terms that included plants, animals, and the soil and tried to live in that way. A few sought an ecologically responsible life outside the orbit of conventional economics, but more looked for understanding without, fully, detaching themselves from the established society. In *Reading the Mountains of Home* John Elder described learning about the land and community around his home, Middlebury, Vermont, organizing his narrative and musings around an analysis of a poem by Robert Frost.[39] He appealed, though, to ecological knowledge and saw the land in that perspective, the community not as individuals but the web of connections among them. In North America life on the land was largely a matter of individual explorations, the loose ties of the bioregional movement providing less organization than paths for communication. Elsewhere the state and existing communities and their economies were important. In Australia, for instance, federal and local authorities supported the search for local and national heritage and placed more emphasis on learning about existing local communities and their established economies than new kinds of ties to the land.[40]

Environmental ideas went out from the community of committed environmentalists to the wider public debate. Thirty years ago environmental ethics was not even part of academic philosophy (just as the general run of historians did not recognize environmental history). Now terms like our "obligation to the earth" appear in newspaper editorials without explanation. Major religions ask what their traditions say about human responsibility for the environment and what we should do in response to current environmental problems. The Catholic bishops of the northwestern United States, for instance, published a pastoral letter on the degradation of the ecosystems of the Columbia River.[41] There was wider, though by no means universal, acceptance of indigenous peoples' spiritual relationship to the land as a basis for legal rights. In Canada the claims of the First Nations loomed as a political factor in natural resource development projects from the 1970s, and in the United States the sacredness of salmon was at least considered, while the federal government worked to accommodate Native Americans seeking to use eagle feathers (from a threatened species) in their ceremonies. Australian courts in the last decade recognized at least some Aboriginal land claims based on occupation and subsistence.[42]

All these considerations showed the environmental dream spreading through the culture, which was understandable. Old dreams did not speak to new times, and the times were certainly new. We faced great and grave problems, and environmentalism suggested a solution and did it from within the culture. It pointed past the cycles of creation and destruction that marked settler history and looked to science to lead us into a state of peace with the land and toward a society of human-scale communities where each person had a place and purpose and all had roots in the land. It was an alluring dream, and one far more generous than visions of conquest (if in a different way). Its advocates were intelligent and dedicated, and the existence of environmental problems added urgency and credibility to their work. This dream, though, was no more likely than earlier ones to appear full-blown on the land. We build with what we know, what we want, and what we have, but we do it within the limits of our power and our knowledge, the land has its own imperatives, and we cannot begin anew. Decisions made centuries ago bind and will bind us, and we must make more decisions and change the land further in the course of living. We have and must keep some old ideas even as we find new ones, and, for good or ill, creation and destruction will go on, and failure, unintended consequences, and partial victories will be our lot. This future is not a cheerful prospect. We all want a definite result, preferably a final one, but resolutions are final only in fiction and the grave. Any harmony we achieve cannot end our conversation with the land but only give it a direction. Each generation and each person must struggle with the realities of the situation and the conditions of life. We can only hope to dream dreams large enough to inspire us and wise enough to guide future generations, ones that speak to human needs, recognize human limits and nature's capacities, and provide for the continuing learning required if we are to live with as well as from the earth.

Afterword
Environmental History, Past, Present, and Future

Alfred W. Crosby

NVIRONMENTAL HISTORY is the story of humanity's interaction with its physical surroundings: that is, a narrative of humanity in geological, meteorological, and biological context, rather than, as is typical of the usual textbook history, a narrative of its political and military affairs. Environmental history has always existed (more than two thousand years ago Plato remarked on the effects of deforestation on the hills of Attica), but not as a recognized field of inquiry, with courses identified as such in the catalogue and chairs in the subject and professors sitting in them.

A half century ago when I wandered onto the slippery slope of an undergraduate major in history, environmental history did not exist in a formal sense. I went through four undergrad years and several graduate years without ever hearing of George Perkins Marsh or such living innovators as Fernand Braudel (who was French, anyway, and not worthy of consideration by an American student of American history). I got a doctorate without hearing a word on the Potato Famine or the boll weevil. I memorized a list of the kings of England and the names of the major battles of our Civil War, picked up my diploma, and took employment in, amazingly, an accredited college.

Now, I am glad to say, environmental history undeniably and officially does exist. We environmental historians are producing more books and journal articles than I can possibly read and are cultivating a goodly number of aspiring environmental historians. We actually have formal associations and conferences. There are even a few places where one can get a job as an openly environmental historian. We even have our own hero, Aldo Leopold, and our own heroine, the quasi-saintly Rachel Carson.

We have made considerable intellectual progress qualitatively. We no longer think of *Homo sapiens* as a little below the angels, à la the Eighth Psalm, but as a keystone species, that is, a creature whose numbers and behaviors are such as to profoundly influence—to enrich (I am thinking of cockroaches), to terminate (the passenger pigeon comes to mind)—the existence of a great number of other species. We are even beginning to think of ourselves as a keystone species before we think of ourselves as Americans, Chinese, Muslims, Presbyterians, and so forth, which stimulates useful cogitation. For example, the Sumerians of the BC era and citizens of California's central valley today, though obviously very different, are quite alike in important ways environmentally. The former irrigated and salinized their land; so do the latter. Iraq is not just a place where Saddam Hussein lived and ruled. It is a place where farmers have farmed for millennia and is, therefore, rife with lessons on what that can do to an environment.

Environmental history, although obviously a transnational subject, has an American tilt to it, with effects I'll discuss in a moment. The changes that European and African immigrants wrought in North America in the last few centuries have been no greater than humans have made in Iraq and many other lands, but much more abrupt, especially as pertains to that renowned feature of American history, the so-called frontier. We have detailed accounts and even photographs of, for example, the Sacramento River basin when it was markedly different from what it is now, but no such primordial data on, oh, the Rhone. No Frenchman feels guilty about the absence of herds of aurochs, gone from his country a millennium ago, but the absence of all but a few thousand of our bison haunts Americans. The obviousness of the environmental changes in North America have made many Americans into environmentalists, starting a century and more ago, and have provided historians with a tradition to work within. It is a tradition of nostalgia for the wild and guilt about its desecration, of suspicion about our exploitation of nature. There are admirable chapters in this book within that tradition. John Muir, were he still with us, and even Teddy Roosevelt (if he were not crafting political compromises), would be quick to bless Andrew Isenberg's exposé of hydraulic mining in California and Nancy Langston's chapter on the ineptness of attempts to tame the waters of the Great Basin. Muir might find Elizabeth Blackmar, more concerned with legal concepts than with actual dirt and water, somewhat bewildering, but she is no less concerned with the aggressions on the environment than the others in her part of this volume. A half millennium ago the conquistadores consulted priests for justification. Our equivalents check with their lawyers.

The three chapters just cited are admirable examples of the tradition of environmental history as it has been practiced since the Progressive era, a tradition that we can and must continue to follow for the simple fact that rivers, mountains, and fields are the lights, lungs, and livers of our ecosystem. But environment is more than countryside. Environmental historians have to get beyond their obsession that rivers, mountains, and fields are environment but concrete and bricks are not. We need to shift much of our attention to the city for the very good reason that that is where most of us live. The demands of the city dictate how our economies work and what demands we impose on the biosphere. This volume offers evidences that such a fresh appraisal of the history of our cities is well underway. Joel Tarr's insightful approach is flatly biological. He looks at cities as organisms, hence entities with metabolisms. To continue with this analogy, Sarah Elkind's chapter seems to me a study of urban pulmonary failure, while Ursula von Petz's describes an encouraging case of at least partial rehabilitation.

Another shortcoming of environmental history as practiced in the United States is its parochial nature. There is nothing wrong whatsoever with environmental history on the national or even local level, but we need to also widen our considerations. For instance, global warming may be largely an American product, but it is a global subject. I pause here to discuss the problems that can arise from a too narrow focus on the North American environmental experience. That tight focus is often the product of nothing more mysterious than the way our college and university history departments are staffed and managed and how our course catalogues are organized, but it is also a matter of scholarly preference. I am not complaining that American environmental historians are too patriotic. There is nothing any more wrong about loving one's country than one's spouse. My worry is that we American environmentalists spend too much time looking at history through American spectacles and thus encourage others to do likewise, with myopic effects that may surprise us and that we may not like. My worry about looking at the world through American glasses grows out of my conviction that the American environmental experience is exceptional. We citizens of the United States are environmentally much more fortunate than most other peoples. "From the mountains to the prairies, to the ocean flecked with foam," we have had a huge and varied expanse, most of a continent, to play with. In addition, the United States, except for Hawaii and Alaska, is entirely within the temperate zone, that is, we have, all in all and except for mountain tops and the driest deserts, a forgiving climate. American historians are apt to overlook and American citizens to underestimate our colossal luck and to credit our success to our economic philosophies and work habits, and then to look for others to follow our route to happiness. But the road is not so open nor so smooth for the others. We Americans chopped down our eastern forests and then migrated west to do the same, and the eastern forests, slurping up the generous rainfall of that part of the United States, have come back. New England has more woods than it did in 1800. Nantucket, where I live, was a sheep-ridden, treeless moor when Melville described it a hundred and fifty years ago. Nantucketers were planting "toadstools before their houses, to get under the shade in summer time." On the island, said Melville, "one blade of grass makes an oasis, 3 blades in a day's walk a prairie." Now the island has considerable woodlands and we have to resort to controlled burns to preserve our moors. Chop down trees in the African Sahel or the Amazonian basin, and the forests do not bounce back. The bared soil may well turn to hard laterite under the blazing sun or erode down to bedrock and run off to the sea under the battering of torrential rains. Chop down the trees of the taiga in boreal Alaska, Canada, Scandinavia, and Russia, and the trees may return, but you will have to check with your great-grandchildren to confirm that. Frigid climate reduces recovery to a slow walk.

Another of our commonly overlooked advantages is that the human footprint was shallow here when the European and African Americans arrived. I do not mean nonexistent—the pyramids at Cahokia and the canals of the Anasazi are clear indications that pre-Columbian Native Americans tinkered with their environments, but only locally and not profoundly, relative to what has happened since. We late-coming immigrants moved into a dwelling whose sinks were not filled with somebody else's garbage and whose deltas were not smothering in silt from pastures laid bare by predecessors' farming practices and livestock. To cite one example of the effects of that, the Mississippi and Missouri may have given us miseries but have been jolly comrades compared to China's Yellow River. We latecomers moved into a land and joined an ecosystem containing only a few of the microorganisms associated with the standard infections of heavy human and livestock populations. We eventually brought them all from the Old World, but we first established a firm foothold here. Moreover, these germs, being descendants of a few immigrants, were a narrow slice genetically and have, thereby, been easy to deal with, compared to, for instance, Corsica's anciently established malarial plasmodia.

We have had few problems with population size relative to our ability to feed ourselves. The Native Americans were here in considerable numbers circa 1500, especially in the Southeast, but not in tens of millions, and they declined in population precipitously upon contact with the invaders. The new immigrants arrived to displace them in the tens of millions but did so over a period of many decades; and because it was expensive to get here, European immigrants, with the stark exception of the Irish circa 1850, seldom debarked in rags with empty bellies. We have been able to feed ourselves quite well, except when we insisted on not doing so, as in the early years of the Virginia Colony. That generality may seem too rosy to historians of the American lower classes, but I suggest that they compare our hunger pangs to the full-out famines of India, China, Africa, and preindustrial Europe. Our poor have suffered malnutrition, but rarely from flat-out starvation. We have never had to use bulldozers to bury our victims of starvation.

Our population began small and then grew, first by natural means (even among the slaves; could there be a higher tribute to our environment than that?) and then by immigration. Our environmental advantages attracted millions upon millions of immigrants. Our wage scale has always been high—the law of supply and demand applies to labor as well as inanimate objects—but immigrants have kept it from rising so high as to lame our economy. And immigration and a growing population have guaranteed the economic stimulation of a large and expanding home market. We have subjugated the North American ecosystem, broken it like a colt, creating immense wealth, without paying or even facing up to the crushing ecological bill for our excesses—as yet. We have our wonderful continent to run away and hide in, shielded by our forgiving climate. When the European and African American pioneers crossed the Appalachians, they found themselves in the biggest expanse of excellent farm land on the planet, an expanse populated by small and shrinking numbers of Native Americans. When the Russians, in contrast, crossed the Urals, they found themselves in Siberia, a land of many riches, but inhospitable to most cultivation. When the Russians moved south into their breadbasket, the steppe, they found it occupied by a considerable population not in decline. In addition, I should point to the simple fact that the vast bulk of the former USSR and of Russia today is north of all our states but Alaska and has a vicious climate. A full listing of examples of the historical effects of our environmental advantages would break the binding of this book, so let me cite only two more. When in the 1930s drought hit the middle of our continent, turning cultivated fields into the Dust Bowl, the desperate Okies went—where? West to California, where they were mistreated and exploited but eventually prospered. When similar droughts have hit the Brazilian northeast, the victims have fled west into the Amazonian interior to lands with what is all in all a less hospitable climate than they were running from, lands where simply surviving has been a challenge. If somebody points out to us that Africa has a crushing burden of malaria, we are inclined to see that (like the problem of poverty in our own inner cities) as somehow the fault of the victims. Well-informed Americans may know that we once did suffer a lot of malaria from Pennsylvania on south and throughout most of the Mississippi valley and even in California, but now it is not a problem. Why? Because, we are too apt to presume, we implemented the relevant public health policies: drained swamps, sprayed insecticides, installed screens. Ah, but malaria was in full retreat long before we even knew that mosquitoes carried it and took actions on the basis of that knowledge. Malaria is now very rare here because . . . well, we are not absolutely sure why. Certainly our climate has been an essential factor. Our therapeutic winters knock back the mosquitoes every cold season, and they have to start from scratch every spring. Global warming may improve their lot.

Our luck has misled many of us, I think, to credit too much of our success to ourselves. It has even misled non-Americans to agree. Brute-force technology (Paul R. Josephson's phrase) is the way to go, we and those who may envy our successes are apt to think. If strip mining made West Virginia rich (did it? some say so), then let's do it only more so in Irian Jaya. The Chinese, in part because of our Hoover, Grand Coulee, and similar megadams, are building a colossal dam in the Yangtze gorge. Nature is exacting on Americans a price for such environmental arrogance and will extract higher prices for similar mistakes of others in less generous environments.

Environmental matters are usually transnational, as, happily, the chapters in this book illustrate. John McNeill's consideration of *Aedes aegypti* and James McCann's of maize carry us across national boundaries, climatic divisions, seas and oceans. Thomas Dunlap's consideration of Anglo settler culture in different lands teaches us not to jump to assumptions about the interactions of customs and physical surroundings. Paul Josephson presents us with Stalin's version of brute-force technology, a version that should shake even American faith in technology.

There is a solid argument in favor of the proposition that the greatest challenges facing humans in general in this new millennium are environmental in nature. Our species needs to learn and to understand its relationship with its physical and living surroundings. It needs the advice and counsel of environmental historians. This book signals a beginning of that process.

Notes

Challenges for Environmental History

1. Ted Steinberg, "Down to Earth: Nature, Agency, and Power in History," *The American Historical Review* 107, 3 (June 2002): 798–820.

2. Donald Worster, ed., *The Ends of the Earth: Perspectives on Modern Environmental History* (Cambridge: Cambridge University Press, 1988); William Cronon, ed., *Uncommon Ground: Rethinking the Human Place in Nature* (New York: Norton, 1995). For some of the response to Cronon, see the articles in *Wild Earth* 6, 4 (Winter 1996/97), especially "The Trouble with Cronon," 59–62.

3. William Cronon, *Nature's Metropolis: Chicago and the Great West* (New York: Norton, 1991).

4. Certainly, these directions are not brand new. Harold Innis was internationalizing the cod fishery in 1940. Sam Hays revealed the complexities and human frailties of the conservation movement in 1958. Roderick Nash revealed the changing constructs of wilderness in 1967. Carolyn Merchant has been working to bring gender, a key element of social history, into environmental history for two decades. See Harold Innis, *The Cod Fisheries: The History of an International Economy*, rev. ed. (Toronto: University of Toronto Press, 1978); Samuel Hays, *Conservation and the Gospel of Efficiency: The Progressive Conservation Movement, 1890–1920* (Cambridge: Harvard University Press, 1959); Roderick Nash, *Wilderness and the American Mind*, 3rd ed. (New Haven: Yale University Press, 1982); and Carolyn Merchant, *The Death of Nature: Women, Ecology, and the Scientific Revolution* (San Francisco: Harper & Row, 1980).

5. See, for instance, Joachim Radkau, "Exceptionalism in European Environmental History," *Bulletin of the German Historical Institute* 33 (Fall 2003): 23–44; and John McNeill's reply, "Theses on Radkau," *Bulletin of the German Historical Institute* 33 (Fall 2003): 45–52.

6. Richard Tucker, *Insatiable Appetite: The United States and the Ecological Degradation of the Tropical World* (Berkeley: University of California Press, 2000); Thomas Dunlap, *Nature and the English Diaspora: Environment and History in the United States, Canada, Australia, and New Zealand* (Cambridge: Cambridge University Press, 1999).

7. John McNeill, *Something New under the Sun: An Environmental History of the Twentieth-Century World* (New York: Norton, 2001).

8. Andrew Hurley, *Environmental Inequalities: Class, Race, and Industrial Pollution in Gary, Indiana, 1945–1980* (Chapel Hill: University of North Carolina Press, 1995); Cronon, *Nature's Metropolis*.

9. Jennifer Price, *Flight Maps: Adventures with Nature in Modern America* (New York: Basic Books, 1999); Cronon, *Uncommon Ground*.

10. Anne Whiston Spirn, "Constructing Nature: The Legacy of Frederick Law Olmsted," in *Uncommon Ground*.

11. Andrew C. Isenberg, personal communication to Kurk Dorsey, April 29, 2002.

12. Andrew C. Isenberg, *The Destruction of the Bison: An Environmental History, 1750–1920* (Cambridge: Cambridge University Press, 2000); Nancy Langston, *Forest Dreams, Forest Nightmares: The Paradox of Old Growth in the Inland West* (Seattle: University of Washington Press, 1995); Joseph E. Taylor, III, *Making Salmon: An Environmental History of the Northwest Fisheries Crisis* (Seattle: University of Washington Press, 1999).

13. Giovanna Di Chiro, "Nature As Community: The Convergence of Environment and Social Justice," in *Uncommon Ground*.

14. Steinberg, "Down to Earth"; Andrew C. Isenberg, "Historicizing Natural Environments: The Deep Roots of Environmental History," in *A Companion to Western Historical Thought*, ed. Lloyd Kramer and Sarah Maza (Malden, MA: Blackwell, 2002).

15. Ted Steinberg, *Acts of God: The Unnatural History of Natural Disaster in America* (Oxford: Oxford University Press, 2000).

Chapter 1: The Metabolism of the Industrial City

1. Eugene P. Odum, *Ecology and Our Endangered Life-Support Systems* (Sunderland, MA: Sinauer Associates, 1989), 17.

2. Another way of expressing the concept of society-nature interaction is to think of a society as making "colonizing interventions," where such interventions are "the sum of all purposive changes made in natural systems that aim to render nature more useful for society." Thus, metabolism and colonization are "intricately interwoven," reflecting aspects of society-nature interactions. See Verena Winiwarter, "Where Did All the Waters Go? The Introduction of Sewage Systems in Urban Settlements," in *Environmental Problems in European Cities in the 19th and 20th Century*, ed. Christoph Bernhardt (New York: Waxman, 2001), 107.

3. Mike Davis, *Ecology of Fear: Los Angeles and the Imagination of Disaster* (New York: Metropolitan Books, 1998); B. R. Stephenson, *Visions of Eden: Environmentalism, Urban Planning, and City Building in St. Petersburg, Florida, 1900–1995* (Columbus: Ohio State University Press, 1997); and Theodore T. Steinberg, *Acts of God: The Unnatural History of Natural Disasters* (New York: Oxford University Press, 2000).

4. Pittsburgh has also historically faced major problems from flooding. For a discussion of attempts to control the floods see Roland M. Smith, "The Politics of Pittsburgh Flood Control, 1908–1960," *Pennsylvania History* 42 (January 1975): 5–24, and 44 (January 1977): 3–24.

5. Richard C. Wade, *The Urban Frontier: The Rise of Western Cities, 1790–1830* (Cambridge: Harvard University Press, 1959), 95; Catherine E. Reiser, *Pittsburgh's Commercial Development, 1800–1850* (Harrisburg: Pennsylvania Historical and Museum Commission, 1951), 129; and Leland D. Baldwin, *Pittsburgh: The Story of a City* (Pittsburgh: University of Pittsburgh Press, 1938), 156.

6. Richard A. Sabol, "Public Works in Pittsburgh Prior to the Establishment of the Department of Public Works" (research paper, Department of History, Carnegie Mellon Uni-

versity, 1980), 5; Frank Kern, "History of Pittsburgh Water Works, 1821–1842" (research paper, Department of History, Carnegie Mellon University, 1982), 1–4.

7. Erwin E. Lanpher and C. F. Drake, *City of Pittsburgh: Its Water Works and Typhoid Fever Statistics* (Pittsburgh: City of Pittsburgh, 1930), 23–25. Extensive waste and leaky pipes plagued the system resulting in frequent water shortages.

8. James H. Thompson, "A Financial History of the City of Pittsburgh, 1816–1910" (Ph.D. diss., University of Pittsburgh, 1948), 44–45; Paul Studenski and Herman E. Kross, *Financial History of the United States* (New York: McGraw-Hill, 1952), 13.

9. Susan J. Kleinberg, *The Shadow of the Mills: Working-Class Families in Pittsburgh, 1870–1907* (Pittsburgh: University of Pittsburgh Press, 1989), 87–93.

10. Robin L. Einhorn, *Property Rules: Political Economy in Chicago, 1833–1872* (Chicago: University of Chicago Press, 1991), 104.

11. Clayton R. Koppes and William P. Norris, "Ethnicity, Class, and Mortality in the Industrial City: A Case Study of Typhoid Fever in Pittsburgh, 1890–1910," *Journal of Urban History* 2 (May 1985): 269–75.

12. Charles Davis, in discussion following Geo. H. Browne, "A Few of Pittsburgh's Sewers," *Transactions Engineers' Society of Western Pennsylvania* 1 (January 1880–June 1882): 229; Terry F. Yosie, "Retrospective Analysis of Water Supply and Wastewater Policies in Pittsburgh, 1800–1959" (Doctor of Arts diss., Carnegie Mellon University, 1981), 14–16, 48–49. The nuisances created led to municipal regulation of privies as early as 1816.

13. Davis, in discussion following Browne, "A Few of Pittsburgh's Sewers," 229.

14. Yosie, "Retrospective Analysis of Water Supply and Wastewater Policies in Pittsburgh, 1800–1959," 49. Before the availability of piped-in water, Americans had found various ways, such as the use of cisterns, wells, and local ponds, to provide a water supply for household plumbing. See Maureen Ogle, *All the Necessary Conveniences: American Household Plumbing, 1840–1890* (Baltimore: Johns Hopkins University Press, 1996).

15. Jacqueline Corn, "Municipal Organization for Public Health in Pittsburgh, 1851–1895" (Doctor of Arts diss., Carnegie Mellon University, 1972), 15–16; John Duffy, "The Impact of Asiatic Cholera on Pittsburgh, Wheeling, and Charleston," *Western Pennsylvania Historical Magazine* 47 (July 1964): 205, 208–9.

16. Browne, "A Few of Pittsburgh's Sewers"; and Davis in discussion following Browne, "A Few of Pittsburgh's Sewers," 214–49.

17. For a discussion of the conflict in Pittsburgh between engineers and the Board of Health see Davis, in discussion following Browne, "A Few of Pittsburgh's Sewers," 219–21.

18. Jon A. Peterson, "The Impact of Sanitary Reform upon American Urban Planning," *Journal of Social History* 13 (Fall 1979): 84–89.

19. Combined sewer overflow events are a frequent cause of bacterial pollution in the Pittsburgh-area rivers today.

20. The so-called street acts, passed by the city councils in 1887–1889, provided that street and lateral sewer improvements would be made on the petition of one-third of the abutting property owners in a neighborhood. All abutters, however, would be assessed for improvements. In 1891 the state supreme court declared these acts unconstitutional. See Thompson, "Financial History," 178–79; Yosie, "Pittsburgh Water Supply and Wastewater Policies," 112–13.

21. *Fourth Annual Report of the State Department of Health* (Harrisburg, PA: Wm. Stanley Ray, State Printer, 1911), 1476.

22. Quoted in Nancy Tomes, *The Gospel of Germs: Men, Women, and the Microbe in American Life* (Cambridge: Harvard University Press, 1998), 189–90.

23. Quoted in Koppes and Norris, "Ethnicity, Class, and Mortality in the Industrial City," 271. For a study of a similar situation in Pittsburgh's neighboring city of Allegheny, see Bruce W. Jordan, "The Allegheny City Water Works, 1840–1907," *Western Pennsylvania Historical Magazine* 70 (January 1987): 29–52. Pittsburgh annexed Allegheny in 1907.

24. James Otis Handy, "Sand Filtration of Public Water Supply," in *Proceedings of Engineers' Society of Western Pennsylvania* 13 (1897): 70–126.

25. C. E. Drake, "Statistics of Typhoid Fever in Pittsburgh," in *City of Pittsburgh: Its Water Works and Typhoid Fever Statistics,* 29–38.

26. See, for example, Pittsburgh Chamber of Commerce, *Sewage Disposal for Pittsburgh* (Pittsburgh, 1907); G. Soper, "The Sanitary Engineering Problems of Water Supply and Sewage Disposal in New York City," *Science* 25 (1907): 601–5; "Up Stream or Down Stream?" *New York Times,* September 25, 1910; C. D. Leupp, "To the Rescue of New York Harbor," *The Survey* (October 8, 1910), 89–93; Merchants Association of New York, *Committee on Pollution of State Waters: Protest against the Bronx River Valley Sewer* (New York, 1907); and *The Battle of the Microbes: Nature's Fight for Pure Water* (New York, 1908).

27. "The Unusual Prevalence of Typhoid Fever in 1903 and 1904," *Engineering News* 51 (1904): 129–30.

28. F. H. Snow, "Administration of Pennsylvania Laws respecting Stream Pollution," *Proceedings of Engineers' Society of Western Pennsylvania* 23 (1907): 266–83.

29. "Sewage Pollution of Water Supplies," *Engineering Record* 48 (1909): 117.

30. "The Greater Pittsburgh Sewerage and Sewage Purification Orders," *Engineering News* 63 (1910): 179–80; "Pittsburgh Sewage Purification Orders," *Engineering News* 63 (1910): 70–71; "The Sewerage Problem of Greater Pittsburgh," *Engineering Record* 61 (1910): 183–84; see, also, G. Gregory, "A Study in Local Decision Making: Pittsburgh and Sewage Treatment," *Western Pennsylvania Historical Magazine* 57 (1974): 25–42.

31. "The Most Important Sewerage and Sewage Disposal Report Made in the United States," *Engineering Record* 65 (1912): 209–12; "Pittsburgh Sewage Disposal Reports," *Engineering News* 67 (1912): 398–402.

32. Ibid., 400–401.

33. "The Pittsburg [sic] Sewage Purification Order: Letters from Commissioner Dixon and May Magee," *Engineering News* 67 (1912): 548–52.

34. Pennsylvania Commissioner of Health, *Eighth Annual Report* (Harrisburg: Wm. Stanley Ray, State Printer, 1913), 901–2; Gregory, "A Study in Local Decision Making," 41–42.

35. "The Pollution of Streams," *Engineering Record* 60 (1909): 157–59.

36. Comments were made about smoke in Pittsburgh as early as 1800. For a review of nineteenth-century developments, see John O'Connor, Jr., "The History of the Smoke Nuisance and of Smoke Abatement in Pittsburgh," *Industrial World* (March 24, 1913); Robert Dale Grinder, "From Insurgency to Efficiency: The Smoke Abatement Campaign in Pittsburgh before World War I," *Western Pennsylvania Historical Magazine* 61 (1978): 187–202.

37. Ibid., 2.

38. See, for example, J. W. Henderson, Bureau Chief, Pittsburgh Bureau of Smoke Regulation, "Smoke Abatement Means Economy," *Power* (July 24, 1917); R. Dale Grinder, "The Battle for Clean Air: The Smoke Problem in Post–Civil War America," in *Pollution and Re-*

form in American Cities, 1870–1930, ed. Martin V. Melosi (Austin: University of Texas Press, 1980), 89.

39. Victor J. Azbe, "Rationalizing Smoke Abatement," in *Proceedings of the Third International Conference on Bituminous Coal* (Pittsburgh, 1931) 2:603.

40. Osborn Monnett, *Smoke Abatement, Technical Paper 273, Bureau of Mines* (Washington, DC: Government Printing Office, 1923); H. B. Meller, "Smoke Abatement: Its Effects and Its Limitations," *Mechanical Engineering* 48 (November 1926): 1275–83.

41. Interview with Abraham Wolk, April 26, 1973, in "An Oral History of the Pittsburgh Renaissance," Archives of Industrial Society, University of Pittsburgh (hereafter cited as "Oral History"). Letters defending air pollution still appear in the Pittsburgh newspapers at times when tighter air pollution controls are discussed for industry.

42. Joel A. Tarr and Carl Zimring, "The Struggle for Smoke Control in St. Louis: Achievement and Emulation," in *Common Fields: An Environmental History of St. Louis,* ed. Andrew Hurley (St. Louis: Missouri Historical Society Press, 1997), 199–220; Oscar H. Allison, "Raymond R. Tucker: The Smoke Elimination Years, 1934–1950" (Ph.D. diss., St. Louis University, 1978).

43. "Cities Fight Smoke," *Business Week,* April 6, 1940, 33–34.

44. *Pittsburgh Press* and *Pittsburgh Post-Gazette,* February 3, 4, 12, 1941.

45. David L. Lawrence, "Rebirth," in *Pittsburgh: The Story of an American City,* 2nd ed., ed. Stefan Lorant (Lenox, MA, 1975). Lawrence himself was the boss of the county Democratic party. Wolk noted that in 1941 "Dave Lawrence never said a word to me against it." Noted in interview with Abraham Wolk, April 26, 1973, "Oral History." One commentator observed that it was important that Alexander, a physician, was prominently involved because "he was able to generate some real fear on the part of the people that maybe after all this was dangerous to health as well as being an economic proposition." Interview with William Willis, April 16, 1973, "Oral History." See, also, Dr. I. Hope Alexander, "Smoke and Health," United Smoke Council of Pittsburgh, 1941, H. John Heinz III History Center, Pittsburgh. Alexander noted that "The medical profession is in accord with the statement that smoke is a health menace of major proportions. . . . For the present, however, there are few scientific facts to definitely establish a case of cause and effect."

46. *Pittsburgh Press,* March 13, 1941.

47. See, for example, *Pittsburgh Press* and *Post-Gazette,* March 13, April 30, June 24, 1941; M. Jay Ream to _____, April 3, 1941, Civic Club Records; "Notes Taken on Smoke at Annual Meeting," May 8, 1941, Civic Club Records. See, also, "List of Organizations Co-Operating with Civic Club on Smoke Elimination," Civic Club Records.

48. The comment is that of John P. Robin, the mayor's executive secretary, in "Fourth Meeting of the Mayor's Commission for the Elimination of Smoke," March 12, 1941, 74, Pittsburgh City Council Archives.

49. "Hearings before the Pittsburgh Smoke Commission," April 15, 1941, 49, Pittsburgh City Council Archives.

50. "Hearings before the Pittsburgh Smoke Commission," April 15, 1941, 38–39, Pittsburgh City Council Archives.

51. See, for instance, "Proceedings of the Fifth Meeting of the Pittsburgh Smoke Commission," March 31, 1941, 23, 69–78, Pittsburgh City Council Archives; "Proceedings of the Sixth Meeting," April 7, 1941, 38–39, Pittsburgh City Council Archives.

52. Ibid., 19.

53. In addition to smoke, the suggested ordinance provided for enforcement against other air pollutants such as fly ash, noxious acids, gases, and fumes. This provision was also included in the St. Louis ordinance and represented an advance in air pollution control compared to earlier ordinances that had focused on dense smoke only.

54. *Pittsburgh Press*, July 7, 1941.

55. There are discussions of methods of enforcement by Dr. Sumner B. Ely in "Minutes," United Smoke Council, December 13, 1945; and in *Report of Stationary Stacks*, Bureau of Smoke Prevention, Department of Public Health, Pittsburgh, 1948, 9–10. See, also, interview with Albert Brandon, July 21, 1972, Renaissance Oral History Project, Archives of Industrial Society. Brandon was assistant city solicitor in charge of the enforcement of smoke control.

56. See "The United Smoke Council of the Allegheny Conference," in United Smoke Council Records; and "Minutes," United Smoke Council of Pittsburgh and Allegheny County, October 18, 1945, Heinz History Center.

57. "Minutes," United Smoke Council of Pittsburgh and Allegheny County, November 3, 1945, Heinz History Center.

58. *Pittsburgh Press,* February 2, 1948; United Smoke Council, *That New Look in Pittsburgh,* (n.p., n.d.), Heinz History Center.

59. The ordinance fell hardest on poor families, because fuel costs composed a larger percentage of their budget than for higher income groups, and because of their fuel-buying habits. The Bureau of Smoke Prevention attempted to educate low-income consumers as to the proper measures for firing smokeless coal rather than fining people for smoke violations. In 1948, for instance, only fifteen persons were summoned before magistrates for smoke violations, compared with 250 trucker violations.

60. City of Pittsburgh, Department of Public Health, Bureau of Smoke Prevention, *Report 1955* (Pittsburgh, 1955), 6.

61. "Lower cost to consumers and availability at all times," noted the Bureau of Mines in 1943, "are the principal factors favoring the use of coal." Arno C. Fieldner, *Recent Developments in Fuel Supply and Demand,* U.S. Department of the Interior, Bureau of Mines, November 1943, 11. For discussions of the high price and erratic supply conditions of natural gas in 1941, see transcripts of the Mayor's Commission for Smoke Elimination, March 12, 1941, 17–19, 60; for March 28, 1941, 7–8; and March 31, 1941, 74–76, all in Archives, Pittsburgh City Council.

62. See "Jobs for Inches," *Business Week,* December 29, 1945, 19; "Natural Gas Is on the Up," *Business Week,* March 13, 1948, 26; and *Annual Reports* of the Philadelphia Company (Equitable Gas Company), for 1946, 15; 1948, 16–17; 1949, 21–22. See also Christopher James Castaneda, *Regulated Enterprise: Natural Gas Pipelines and Northeastern Markets, 1938–1954* (Columbus: Ohio State University Press, 1993), 75–89, 118.

63. Data on household fuel use are available from the 1940 and 1950 Censuses of Housing. See U.S. Department of Commerce, Bureau of the Census, *Housing: Characteristics by Type of Structure, 16th Census of the United States* (Washington, DC: General Printing Office, 1945); and *Census of Housing: 1950,* vol. 1, *General Characteristics: 17th Census* (Washington, DC: General Printing Office, 1953).

64. The evidence suggests that the coal producers and miners were correct in warning that the smoke control law would hasten the loss of their domestic markets and their jobs.

Pittsburgh representatives of the United Mine Workers charged in the postwar period that there was a conspiracy in Pittsburgh to drive out coal in favor of natural gas. See *Pittsburgh Press*, December 21, 1945; March 8, 9, April 23, December 2, 5, 1947; and July 3, 1948. In its 1950 *Annual Report*, Pittsburgh Consolidation Coal noted that "It was obvious five years ago that in many of the areas into which our coal normally moved there would be a gradual decrease in the amount of coal used for domestic heating, as natural gas, with its greater convenience, found its way into their markets." In its 1949 *Annual Report,* the Equitable Gas Company, which served more households in Pittsburgh than any other gas utility, observed that smoke abatement legislation and the high cost of coal were increasing their domestic sales.

65. Joel A. Tarr and Sherrie Mershan, "Strategies for Clean Air: The Pittsburgh and Allegheny County Smoke Control Movements, 1940–1960," in *Devastation and Renewal: An Environmental History of Pittsburgh and Its Region,* ed. Joel A. Tarr (Pittsburgh: University of Pittsburgh Press, 2003).

66. Ibid., 169–73.

67. Ian Douglas, *The Urban Environment* (Baltimore: Edward Arnold, 1983), 93.

68. Robert A. Woods, "Pittsburgh: An Interpretation of Its Growth," in *The Pittsburgh District: Civic Frontage,* ed. Paul U. Kellogg (New York: Survey Associates, 1914), 19–20.

69. R. L. Duffus, "Is Pittsburgh Civilized?" *Harper's Monthly Magazine* 161 (October 1930): 537–45.

70. The following material dealing with the Nine Mile Run Valley draws heavily on Andrew S. McElwaine, "Slag in the Park," *Devastation and Renewal,* 174–92.

71. For a discussion of the effect of Olmsted's ideas about nature on Progressive Period reformers, see Paul Boyer, *Urban Masses and Moral Order in America, 1820–1930* (Cambridge: Harvard University Press, 1978), 220–51.

72. Frederick Law Olmsted, *Pittsburgh Main Thoroughfares and the Down Town District* (Pittsburgh: Pittsburgh Civic Commission, 1911), 119–20.

73. Roy Lubove, *Twentieth-Century Pittsburgh: Government, Business, and Environmental Change* (New York: Wiley, 1969), 53–56.

74. Citizens Committee on City Plan for Pittsburgh, *Parks: A Part of The Pittsburgh Plan* (Pittsburgh, September 1923), 64–71.

75. McElwaine, "Slag in the Park," 183–84; Anne Lloyd, "Pittsburgh's 1923 Zoning Ordinance," *Western Pennsylvania Historical Magazine* 57 (July 1974): 288–305; and Janet R. Daley, "Zoning: Its Historical Context and Importance in the Development of Pittsburgh," *Western Pennsylvania Historical Magazine* 71 (April 1988): 99–125.

76. McElwaine, "Slag in the Park," 184–85.

77. See "The Development of Nine Mile Run: A Brownfield Site in Pittsburgh" (unpublished paper, Studio for Creative Inquiry, Carnegie Mellon University, March 20, 1997) for technical details concerning the site. For zoning and protests by neighbors of the site, see McElwaine, "Slag in the Park," 186–89.

78. City of Pittsburgh, Dept. of City Planning, "Nine Mile Run Development Proposal," Pittsburgh, August 1982, Archives, Pittsburgh Dept. of City Planning; ibid., "Nine Mile Run Major Development Project," March 1987, Archives, Pittsburgh Dept. of City Planning; and GAI Consultants, Inc., "Nine Mile Run Development Traffic Study," Pittsburgh, 1988, Archives, Pittsburgh Dept. of City Planning.

79. John Paul and Molly Davidson-Welling, "Brownfield Development Case Study: Nine Mile Run" (unpublished report, Carnegie Mellon University, July 17, 1996).

80. McElwaine, "Slag in the Park," 190–91.

81. Ibid., 191–92.

Chapter 2: Los Angeles's Nature

1. Elbert D. Owen to Los Angeles City Council, August 17, 1943, and Emily K. Krug to Mayor Bowron, September 1944, both attached to Fletcher Bowron to J. W. Livingston, August 11, 1943, Los Angeles City Archives, Box A832, Communication 15399; Jerrie M. Rossen to Los Angeles City Council, September 17, 1944, Los Angeles City Archives, Box A851, Communication 18283; Fletcher Bowron to William L. Stewart, October 16, 1943, Fletcher Bowron Collection, Huntington Library, San Marino, CA; Frederic A. Kane to Los Angeles City Council, September 8, 1944, Los Angeles City Archives, Box A851, Communication 18283. Not all workers criticized industrial smoke. The CIO Local 132, representing utility workers at the butadiene plant, opposed the city's efforts to close down their plant. See "Butadiene Plant Closed," *Los Angeles Examiner*, October 24, 1943, Bowron Collection.

2. "City Hunting for Source of 'Gas Attack,'" *Los Angeles Times*, July 27, 1943, Bowron Collection; General Hospital Ward 400 to Los Angeles City Council, October 4, 1943, Elbert D. Owen to Los Angeles City Council, August 17, 1943, both in City Archives, Box A832, Communication 15399.

3. See Scott Hamilton Dewey, *Don't Breathe the Air: Air Pollution and U.S. Environmental Politics, 1945–1970* (College Station: Texas A & M Press, 2000). A number of other scholars have written excellent studies of Los Angeles and national air pollution efforts. See, for example, James E. Krier and Edmund Ursin, *Pollution and Policy: A Case Essay on California and Federal Experience with Motor Vehicle Air Pollution, 1940–1975* (Berkeley: University of California Press, 1977).

4. Isador A. Deutch, "Report on the 40th Annual Meeting of the Smoke Prevention Association," July 7–10, 1947, John Anson Ford Collection, Huntington Library.

5. Charles L. Senn to George M. Uhl, October 22, 1943, Ford Collection. Fumes were recorded on July 26, September 21, October 5, October 12, and October 25, 1943. In 1939, aviation authorities called L.A.'s haze "a serious menace to safe flying." See I. A. Deutch, "Various Aspects of Air Pollution Control" (paper delivered before the American Society of Heating and Ventilating Engineers, May 6, 1946, 1, in Ford Collection). As early as 1940, the city health department blamed industrial "smokes, gases and fumes" for bouts of eye irritation in the Los Angeles area. See Charles L. Senn to George M. Uhl, July 30, 1943, Ford Collection.

6. Charles L. Senn to George M. Uhl, October 22, 1943, Ford Collection; "End Ordered for Gas Fume Annoyances," *Los Angeles Times*, September 19, 1943, Bowron Collection. In accordance with these agreements, the Southern California Gas plant closed on September 21, and October 5, 1943.

7. "Move to Shut Down Gas Plant," *Los Angeles Herald Examiner,* no date, Bowron Collection; Bowron to City Council, September 20, 1943, City Archives, Box A832, Communication 15399; "Resolution Adopted by the Grand Jury of the County of Los Angeles," September 20, 1943, City Archives, Box A832, Communication 15399, supplement 3.

8. George M. Uhl to L.A. City Council, September 21, 1943, City Archives, Box A832,

Communication 15399; "City Hunting for Source of 'Gas Attack,'" *Los Angeles Times,* July 27, 1943, Bowron Collection.

9. "Steps Taken to Eliminate Gas Nuisance," *Los Angeles Examiner,* September 23, 1943; "Gas Plant Shuts Down in New Fume Outbreak," *Los Angeles Times,* October 1, 1943; "Rubber Plant Role Told by U.S. Official," *Daily News,* October 22, 1943; "Plenty Fumes but L.A. Gas Has Alibi," *Los Angeles Daily News,* October 1, 1943; "Gas Co. Has Alibi for Latest Batch of Smarting Eyes," *Los Angeles Daily News,* November 16, 1943, all in Bowron Collection.

10. Frederick A. Kane to Los Angeles City Council, September 8, 1944, City Archives Box A851, Communication 18283.

11. Sherrie M. Rossen to Los Angeles City Council, September 17, 1944, City Archives Box A851, Communication 18283.

12. Elbert D. Owen to Los Angeles City Council, August 17, 1943. Health-related complaints include General Hospital Ward 400 to Los Angeles City Council, October 4, 1943, and Emily Krug to Los Angeles City Council, September 1944, all in City Archives, Box A832, Communication 15399. This one city council file contains five letters from constituents complaining about industrial fumes. Many others are found in the Fletcher Bowron collection at the Huntington Library.

13. See, for example, "The Shame of the Smog," *Los Angeles Times,* September 26, 1946.

14. F. S. Wade to Los Angeles City Council, August 24, 1943, City Archives, Box A832, Communication 15399. One article that quotes Southern California Gas as accepting responsibility for the fumes problem is "Find Cause of Eye-Smarting Here," *Los Angeles Herald Examiner,* July 28, 1943, Bowron Collection.

15. F. S. Wade to Los Angeles City Council, August 24, 1943, City Archives, Box A832, Communication 15399.

16. "Find Cause of Eye-Smarting Here." Even at this early date, the newspaper reported that atmospheric conditions played a major role in creating the fume problem.

17. "Councilmen Persuaded to Drop Gas Suit," *Los Angeles Daily News,* October 27, 1943, Bowron Collection.

18. "War Fumes and War Rubber," *Los Angeles Times, Los Angeles Examiner, Los Angeles Herald Express, Los Angeles Daily News,* and *Citizen News,* October 18, 1943, Bowron Collection.

19. L.A. City Health Dept., "Progress Report on Smoke Elimination," August 25, 1943, Ford Collection; "Butadiene Plant Closed," *Los Angeles Examiner,* October 24, 1943, Bowron Collection.

20. "City to Take Fumes War to U.S. Court," *Los Angeles Daily News,* October 18, 1943, Bowron Collection.

21. "Law Ordered Drafted to Curb Fumes Nuisance," *Los Angeles Times,* September 9, 1944, Bowron Collection; Los Angeles Area Chamber of Commerce Board of Directors' Minutes, September 14, 1944, 77, Los Angeles Area Chamber of Commerce Collection, Regional History Center, University of Southern California, Los Angeles (hereafter cited as "LAACC Board Minutes" and "LAACC Collection").

22. Bradley Dewey to Los Angeles City Council, October 22, 1943, City Archives, Box A835, Communication 16028; "U.S. Rebukes City's Suit on Gas Fumes," *Los Angeles Daily News,* October 26, 1943; "Council Halts Suit to Close Butadiene Plant," *Los Angeles Times,* October 28, 1943; "Butadiene Gas Suit Dropped," *Los Angeles Examiner,* October 28, 1943, all in Bowron Collection.

23. "Find Cause of Eye-Smarting Here."

24. H. O. Swartout to Board of Supervisors, "Subject: The Smoke and Fumes Nuisances—Second Progress Report," September 27, 1944, 2–3, Ford Collection.

25. Ibid.

26. "The Smog Problem Discussed by H. O. Swartout," Los Angeles County Pollution Control, September 1945 (unpublished typescript), 4, Ford Collection; H. O. Swartout and I. A. Deutch, "The 'Smog' Problem" (unpublished typescript, September 1945), 4, Ford Collection.

27. "It Isn't ALL Fumes at Butadiene Plant," Los Angeles Times, November 1, 1943, Bowron Collection.

28. "The Fumes Nuisance Should Be Tackled Right," Los Angeles Times, October 7, 1943, Bowron Collection.

29. H. O. Swartout disputed the health hazards of smog. During one conference, he announced that the cigarette smoke inhaled by smokers in the room was far worse than L.A.'s worst smog. "Parley Agrees on Test Suit to Abate Fumes," Los Angeles Times, August 31, 1944, Bowron Collection.

30. George M. Uhl to Los Angeles City Council, September 21, 1943, City Archives, Box A832, Communication 15399; Swartout to Board of Supervisors, "Subject: The Smoke and Fumes Nuisances—Second Progress Report," 2–3.

31. Bowron to William L. Stewart, October 16, 1943, Bowron Collection.

32. In 1945, the Pico Post reported that County supervisors were delaying action on smoke and fumes ordinance until they could "iron out objections of the Chamber of Commerce and other interested parties to certain provisions in the ordinance." See "Smoke Ordinance Is Still under Discussion," Pico Post, August 23, 1945.

33. H. F. Dunton, president of the Altadena Property Owners League, as quoted in "D. A. Plans Test Suit in City's Smoke Fumes War," Los Angeles Daily News, August 31, 1944, Bowron Collection. In the 1940s and 1950s, the Altadena Property Owners League was one of the civic groups that most consistently demanded reductions in industrial smoke.

34. H. O. Swartout to Board of Supervisors, "Subject: The Fumes and Smoke Problem—Progress Report," August 1, 1944, 3, Ford Collection.

35. By 1945, H. O. Swartout clearly accepted industry's argument that aggressive smoke regulations would force Los Angeles to abandon its industrial economy. See Swartout to Franklin B. Cole, June 26, 1945, Ford Collection.

36. Franklin B. Cole to Preston Kline Caye, June 29, 1945, Ford Collection.

37. "Smoke 'Czar' Indorsed by 16 City Officials," Los Angeles Times, September 22, 1944; "4 Firms Cited over Fumes, Smoke in L.A.," Los Angeles Examiner, September 13, 1944, Bowron Collection.

38. "Types of Fuel May Be Decided to Curb Fumes," Los Angeles Times, October 19, 1944, Bowron Collection.

39. Swartout to Board of Supervisors, "Subject: The Fumes and Smoke Problem—Progress Report," 2; "Report to the Los Angeles Board of Supervisors by the L.A. County Smoke and Fumes Commission," March 13, 1944, 3, Ford Collection.

40. "Plenty of 'Fog' Faces Smoke Board," Los Angeles Daily News, October 20, 1943, Bowron Collection.

41. "City 'Smog' Laid to Dozen Causes," Los Angeles Times, September 18, 1944, Bowron Collection.

42. LAACC Board Minutes, September 14, 1944, 77, LAACC Collection.

43. "Three-Point Plan to Combat Fumes Offered," *Los Angeles Times*, October 7, 1944, Bowron Collection.

44. Dewey, *Don't Breathe the Air*, 44–45.

45. R. L. Daugherty to J. A. Ford, January 18, 1954, Ford Collection.

46. Los Angeles Area Chamber of Commerce Stenographers Reports, October 12, 1944, 8, LAACC Collection (hereafter cited as "LAACC Steno").

47. LAACC Board Minutes, September 14, 1944, 78, LAACC Collection.

48. Bowron to Wilton L. Halverson, November 2, 1944, Bowron Collection.

49. "County Grand Jury Acts on Smoke-Fumes Issue," *Los Angeles Times*, September 14, 1944.

50. Swartout to Board of Supervisors, "Subject: The Smoke and Fumes Nuisances—Second Progress Report," 2–3.

51. W. L. Stewart, Jr., to Louis C. McCabe, September 27, 1948, attachment to John M. Pierce to John Anson Ford, September 27, 1948, Ford Collection.

52. LAACC Steno, January 14, 1954, 1, LAACC Collection.

53. Bowron to Wilton L. Halverson, November 2, 1944, Bowron Collection.

54. Morris Pendleton speech before Los Angeles Area Chamber of Commerce Board of Directors, LAACC Steno, October 19, 1944, LAACC Collection.

55. "'Smog' Blankets City Again," *Los Angeles Times*, October 26, 1944.

56. See, for example, "Policy Statement of the Los Angeles Chamber of Commerce," September 29, 1955, Ford Collection.

57. LAACC Steno, October 12, 1944, 8, LAACC Collection; "The History, Legal and Administrative Aspects of Air Pollution Control in the County of Los Angeles," Report submitted to the Board of Supervisors of the County of Los Angeles, May 9, 1954, Bowron Collection. For more information on the industrial community's reactions to the APCD, see Dewey, *Don't Breathe the Air*, 43–45.

58. By 1945, the county office of air pollution control had thoroughly embraced a multipronged attack on air pollution. A report released in September of that year, outlining a proposed program of smoke reduction, not only cited the Chamber's successful voluntary industrial smoke reduction campaign but also outlined procedures for reducing smoke from railroads, diesel trucks, automobiles, buses, and the incineration of rubbish. See H. O. Swartout and I. A. Deutch, "The 'Smog' Problem," September 1945, 1–7, 12, Ford Collection.

59. *Los Angeles Times* editorial, May 18, 1947, as quoted in Harold Kennedy, "The History, Legal and Administrative Aspects of Air Pollution Control in the County of Los Angeles," Report submitted to the Board of Supervisors of the County of Los Angeles, May 9, 1954, 14, Bowron Collection.

60. Kennedy, "The History, Legal and Administrative Aspects of Air Pollution Control in the County of Los Angeles," 20.

61. W. L. Stewart, Jr., to Louis McCabe, September 27, 1948, Ford Collection; Dewey, *Don't Breathe the Air*, 44.

62. Dewey, *Don't Breathe the Air*, 45.

63. "Glendale Will Ask Permit to Build Incinerator," *Los Angeles Herald Express*, September 8, 1948, Bowron Collection. Some critics saw even McCabe's departure as evidence of an industrial conspiracy, insisting that McCabe lost his job because he took on the petro-

leum industry. See C. H. Matheny and Frank L. Alexander, "History of Los Angeles Smog: War Chemical Used on Battlefields Responsible," October 20, 1954 (unpublished type-script), Ford Collection. For more on McCabe's years at the APCD, see Krier and Ursin, *Pollution and Policy*, 65, 73–74.

64. Kennedy, "The History, Legal and Administrative Aspects of Air Pollution Control in the County of Los Angeles," 16.

65. Matheny and Alexander, "History of Los Angeles Smog"; Krier and Ursin, *Pollution and Policy*, 65.

66. "Gordon Larson Points to Auto Exhausts As Major Source of Smog in Hour-Long Special Broadcast Prepared by KNX News Bureau," January 15, 1954, 1–3, Ford Collection. McCabe had dismissed concerns about car exhaust as "folklore" because exhaust in L.A. never exceeded the concentrations considered unacceptable in mines and tunnels. Using the standards of industrial hygiene, cars could not logically be to blame, nor should public fears about car exhaust drive public policy, until confirmed by scientific study. So, in 1949, Mc-Cabe dismissed the empirical evidence upon which so many Angelenos based their accusations against the automobile: "the layman who experiences high concentrations of exhaust fumes from a bus only a few feet away" may believe that such exhaust is a major source of L.A.'s smog problem, but this was not born out by research.

67. Gordon P. Larson to Retail Clerks Union, Local 770, April 1, 1954, Ford Collection.

68. Louis McCabe, as quoted in Krier and Ursin, *Pollution and Policy*, 74.

69. "Methods Developed for Cleansing Air," *Los Angeles Times,* March 29, 1949; "Councilmen Asked to See Smog Control," *Citizen News,* December 2, 1950, Bowron Collection; "Smog Control Duty 'Shirked,'" *Los Angeles Examiner,* December 2, 1950, Bowron Collection; "'Worst' Smog Charges," *Los Angeles Herald,* December 1, 1950, Bowron Collection.

70. Gordon P. Larson to Retail Clerks Union, Local 770, April 1, 1954, Ford Collection.

71. Matheny and Alexander, "History of Los Angeles Smog," 2.

72. The Western Oil and Gas Association funded the Air Pollution Foundation and hired the Stanford Research Institute to carry out this research. Monterey Park Smog Committee, "Report to City Council," December 6, 1954; Arthur J. Will to county supervisors, "Subject: Study and Recommendations on Implementing the Operations of the Air Pollution Control District in the County of Los Angeles," October 11, 1954, 9; "Air Pollution Foundation, List of Contributors," August 25, 1955, all in Ford Collection.

73. Krier and Ursin, *Pollution and Policy*, 44. The number of cars grew from 871,773 in 1930 to 1,229,194 in 1940.

74. Robert L. Daugherty to Kenneth Hahn, October 14, 1954, Ford Collection; "Pioneer Agitator against Smoke Asks Fight 'Czar,'" *Pasadena Star News,* September 25, 1944. As John Anson Ford noted in 1955, Los Angeles officials' ability to control auto exhaust was limited by the fact that no devices existed to clean auto exhaust. See J. A. Ford to Gustav White, December 15, 1953, and Pure Air Committee, Inc., "Recommendations Submitted to Los Angeles Board of Supervisors," November 23, 1953, both in Ford Collection. Scott Dewey details the technical developments that ultimately reduced tailpipe emissions, and the ways that the automobile industry may have used research and patent monopolies to slow this technical progress, in *Don't Breathe the Air,* 57–82.

75. LAACC Board Minutes, September 22, 1955, 97, LAACC Collection.

76. For more on the automobile industry's resistance to designing these smog control devices, see Dewey, *Don't Breathe the Air,* 57–82.

77. "For Immediate Release," March 10, 1953, Kenneth Hahn Papers, Huntington Library.

78. See, for example, R. L. Daugherty to Francis H. Packard, June 20, 1955, Ford Collection.

79. "Statement by Supervisor Kenneth Hahn," October 21, 1953, Hahn Papers.

80. "D. A. Plans Test Suit in City's Smoke Fumes War," *Los Angeles Daily News*, August 31, 1944.

81. "Policy," *Citizen News*, September 21, 1943, Bowron Collection.

82. "Lesson," *Citizen News*, October 27, 1943, Bowron Collection.

83. LAACC Board Minutes, September 22, 1955, 97, LAACC Collection.

84. S. W. Royce to John Anson Ford, August 24, 1954, Ford Collection.

85. Marion Shanafelt to Herbert C. Legg, October 23, 1954, Ford Collection.

86. LAACC Steno, September 14, 1944, 11–12, LAACC Collection.

87. LAACC Steno, October 12, 1944, 8, LAACC Collection.

88. LAACC Board Minutes, May 27, 1948, 57, LAACC Collection.

89. P. K. Caye to LeRoy M. Edwards, November 26, 1945, attachment to H. F. Holley to George J. Murray, December 21, 1945, Ernest East Collection, Southern California Automobile Club Archives, Los Angeles, CA.

90. "Brief of 'Smog' Meeting Held in the Pasadena City Hall, October 9, 1945," Ernest East Collection, 12: 1 "1945 Correspondence," Southern California Auto Club Archives; "Mayor Calls on Jury for Smog Investigation," *Los Angeles Times*, September 11, 1949. For a particularly pointed editorial, see "No Progress Being Made in Ridding City of Fumes Evil," *Los Angeles Herald Express*, January 25, 1945, Bowron Collection.

Chapter 3: The Environmental Transformation of the Ruhr

1. As Françoise Choay, the French architectural historian, put it during a visit in the 1980s.

2. A rather simple building code prescribed a limit in height equal to the width of the street.

3. In 1864, to compensate for a lack of open space in densely populated built-up Leipzig, a physician, Dr. Ernst Innocenz Hauschild, founded a "Verein zur Förderung der Jugendpflege, des Familienlebens, der Volkserziehung und Volksgesundung," which around 1900 led to the founding of *allotment gardens,* named after the pedagogue and physician Dr. Daniel Gottlob Moritz Schreber.

4. The most impressive visualization of this movement is the illustration of *Lichtgebet* (Light Prayer) from 1910 to 1922 by Fidus (Hugo Hoeppener).

5. The German romantic movement in art from the early nineteenth century, still a preindustrial period, was reappraised through the oeuvre of Caspar David Friedrich, whose paintings were exhibited in a major exposition in 1906 in Berlin. His landscape paintings were known for supposedly portraying unadulterated, real German *nature.*

6. Just how much old German traditions about forests and nature influenced this movement is a question that needs to be discussed separately because of its complexity. Germany in the early Middle Ages could lay claim to a Roman tradition in urbanization west along the Rhine and south along the Danube, but the other parts of the country were developed simply by clearing woodland and making it arable. Even beyond this commercial-agricultural polarity, city and region (*Stadt und Land*) were very much opposites in law, social structure,

and land ownership patterns. Nevertheless, nature was always present, the dark woods a source of danger as well as a place of myths or a place of simple life. A "culture of cities" developed only slowly, and it came later with the Hanseatic League. Not having a capital like London or Paris, the German emperor moved from palace to palace or visited his imperial cities in his decentralized country.

7. This work actually consists of four books: *Die bürgerliche Gesellschaft* (The civilian/bourgeois society), 1851; *Land und Leute* (Land and people), 1853, a treatise about the social function of peasant society; *Familie* (The family), 1855; and *Wanderbuch* (Book of wanderings), 1869. Three years earlier Friedrich Engels had published his essay about the situation of the working class in Manchester.

8. Wilhelm Heinrich Riehl, "Die grossen Städte," in *Lesebuch für Baumeister*, ed. Fritz Schumacher (1853; reprint, Berlin: Henssel Verlag, 1941), 296.

9. Wolfgang Riedel, "Homo Natura: Zum Menschenbild der Jahrhundertwende," in *Die Lebensreform: Entwürfe zur Neugestaltung von Leben und Kunst um 1900,* ed. Kai Buchholz et al., vol. 1 (Darmstadt: Haeusser, exhibition catalog, 2001), 105–8.

10. Schallmayer was a medical doctor. With his brochure of 1891 he opened the German debate about eugenics as a battle against degeneration—as opposed to Darwin, who proposed a positive natural selection for an evolutionary society. Schallmayer was followed by Alfred Ploetz, also a medical doctor, who became the founder of the race-based eugenics movement.

11. Jürgen Reulecke, *Das Ruhrgebiet und die "Volksgesundheit"* (Bochum: Stiftung Bibliothek des Ruhrgebiets; reprint, Essen: Klartext, 2001); Sheila Weiss, *Race Hygiene and National Efficiency: The Eugenics of Wilhelm Schallmayer* (Berkeley: University of California Press, 1987).

12. Alfred Lichtwark, the famous director of the Hamburg Kunsthalle and another outstanding figure in the reform debate, also belonged to this organization.

13. Town planning was a relatively new discipline in Germany. Camillo Sitte's plea for "art in town planning" appeared in *Der Städtebau nach seinen kunstlerischen Grundsätzen* (Vienna: C. Graeser, 1889), followed by Ebenezer Howard's *Garden Cities of Tomorrow* in various editions between 1898 and 1902 (London: Swan Sonnenschein, 1902); both were instant successes. Carl Henrici, an admirer of Sitte, had been appointed to a chair in architecture in 1875 at Aachen Technische Hochschule, and beginning in the 1880s he started to teach town planning. In 1903 a monthly journal, *Der Städtebau (Town Planning)*, was founded by Camillo Sitte and Theodor Goecke. At the Technical University of Berlin between 1907 and 1913, an annual series of lectures on town planning (Städtebauliche Vorträge) became a famous institution. National and international exhibitions followed.

14. Robert Schmidt, *Denkschrift betreffend Grundsätze zur Aufstellung eines Generalsiedlungsplanes für den Regierungsbezirk Düsseldorf (rechtsrheinisch)* (Essen, 1913), 42.

15. Unfortunately, Osthaus's activities were halted by the onset of World War I, and he died in 1921.

16. Charles Eliot, *Charles Eliot: Landscape Architect* (Cambridge, MA: Riverside Press; reprint, Boston: Houghton, Mifflin, 1902); Werner Hegemann, *Der Staedtebau nach den Ergebnissen der Allgemeinen Staedtebau-Ausstellung in Berlin nebst einem Anhang: Die Internationale Staedtebau-Ausstellung in Düsseldorf,* 2 vols. (Berlin: Wasmuth, 1911 and 1913).

17. Hegemann had studied in Charlottenburg (Berlin), Munich, Paris, London, and Philadelphia. He had conducted housing studies for New York and Philadelphia in 1905. In

1909 he was asked to work for the exhibition "Boston 1915," thus coming in contact with many planners and architects. In 1910 he became the organizer for the Städtebau-Ausstellung in Berlin and then Internationale Städtebau-Ausstellung at Düsseldorf. He published several books on American planning, such as *The American Vitruvius* and later, together with Elbert Peets, *Civic Art*. With Peets he ran a studio in Milwaukee for seven years, and he lectured many times in the United States and South America. From 1924 to 1933 he was managing editor for *Wasmuths Monatshefte für Baukunst und Städtebau*, and later *Der Städtebau*, Berlin. Because of his attacks on Hitler he emigrated to New York in 1933, where he died three years later. See Christiane Crasemann Collins, "Werner Hegemann (1881–1936): Formative Years in America," *Planning Perspectives* 11 (1996): 1–21.

18. Schmidt, 56.

19. Schmidt, 5.

20. Schmidt, 101.

21. Schmidt, 30.

22. Franziska Bollerey, Gerhard Fehl, and Kristiana Hartmann, eds., *Im Grünen wohnen—im Blauen planen: Ein Lesebuch zur Gartenstadt.* Stadt Planung, Geschichte, 12 (Hamburg: Christians, 1990), 74–77.

23. Peter Hall, *The World Cities*, 4th ed. (London: Weidenfels and Nicolson, 1972), 122; Ursula von Petz, "The German Metropolitan Region: The Ruhr Basin," in *Mastering the City: North European City Planning, 1900–2000*, ed. Koos Bosma and Helma Hellinga, vol. 1 (Rotterdam: Netherlands Architecture Institute, 1997), 56–65; Petz, "Ruhr Basin 1920: Wirtschaftsplan für den Ruhrkohlenbezirk," in *Mastering the City*, vol. 2, 184–91; Petz, "Robert Schmidt and the Public Park Policy in the Ruhr District, 1900–1930," *Planning Perspectives* 14, 2 (1999): 163–82.

24. Heinz Wilhelm Hoffacker, *Entstehung der Raumplanung, Konservative Gesellschaftsreform und das Ruhrgebiet* (Essen: Klartext, 1989), chap. 1.

25. Claudia Bruch, "Zink, Blei und Schwefel," in *Landschaftsverband Rheinland*, Schwer Industrie (exhibition catalog) (Essen: Klartext, 1997), 31.

26. Bruch, 33.

27. Already since around 1900 it was possible to designate special *Landhausviertel* in their plans. This term referred to industry-free areas for large middle-class houses, which would be kept free from environmental degradation.

28. For example, in an institute in the city of Hadamar (one of six centers of euthanasia), ten thousand children, women, and men were killed in 1941 by gas and forty-five hundred children, women, and men between 1942 and 1945 by medical murder. See Gedenkstaette Hadamar, www.hlzhessen.de/gedenkstaetten/texte/gedenkstaeten/hadamar.html.

29. See Petz, *Stadtsanierung im "Dritten Reich,"* vol. 45 (Dortmund: Dortmunder Beiträge zur Raumplanung, 1987), back cover. There are many quotations of this kind in this period, but one can also find them earlier.

30. Another reason why housing conditions worsened so dramatically since the 1890s was that it became much more favorable for the private sector to invest in the stock market than in the building sector, and rental housing always required tiresome administration. See Lutz Niethammer, "Ein langer Marsch durch die Institutionen: Zur Vorgeschichte des preussischen Wohnungsgesetzes von 1918," in *Wohnen im Wandel: Beiträge zur Geschichte*

des Alltags in der bürgerlichen Gesellschaft, ed. Lutz Niethammer (Wuppertal: Hammer, 1979), 363–84.

31. The war ended in May 1945.

32. *Revier* was by then an antiquated expression for the Ruhr area, but even now it is sometimes still used.

33. The articles were written either by K. G. Mellinghoff or R. Ungewitter.

34. A contract lasting until the year 2000 stipulating that every ton of mined coal received a government subsidy of one German penny shows how long the policy of protecting the industry lasted. And even after that date the mining industry remains highly subsidized.

35. For example, Konrad Meyer, one of the most important and radical Nazi planners, the man responsible for the notorious Generalplan Ost, spent only a year in jail and later held a chair for agriculture and regional planning at Hanover University. Thus, he not only taught the next generation of planners but also was able to remain in close contact with the Academy of Research and Regional Planning (Akademie für Raumforschung und Landesplanung), the successor of the relevant Nazi institution.

36. The heritage laws in Germany are state laws. Northrhine Westphalia adopted its law only in 1984, but nevertheless the sensibility toward industrial heritage and the listing of a steel plant or extraction tower as an object of heritage has meanwhile become officially accepted.

37. Up to then no university was located in the Ruhr. Düsseldorf had an academy, Aachen the technical institute, and the University at Münster offered the classical mix of sciences. In coordination with the 1966 plan and based on a strong political will finally to improve the region's educational capacity, five new universities were founded. The University of Dortmund had a new planning department organized as an interdisciplinary faculty—the first of its kind in Germany.

38. A regional plan had not existed before the mid-1920s, when the first plan was developed by the SVR.

39. The historic governments always had opposed the SVR, as had the two original professional landscape associations in the Rhineland and Westphalia. In German these were called *Landschaftsverbände,* where *Landschaft* or landscape was understood in the sense of historic territory and not as a reflection of nature.

40. Some of these companies had closed long before any awareness of environmental damage became significant.

41. Walter Gropius, quoted in Wolfgang Welsch, "Orte des Menschen?" (paper read at the conference Baukultur in Deutschland, Cologne, December 3–5, 2001).

42. Welsch uses the term *Menschenwelt,* 21.

43. Welsch.

44. Draft of May 2004.

Chapter 4: Of REITS and Rights

Jessie Alpaugh helped me gather mall stories. I thank William Leach, Jeffrey Sklansky, Eliza Byard, Hilary Botein, and Lara Vapnek for their valuable comments on a draft.

1. Adam Rome, *The Bulldozer in the Countryside: Suburban Sprawl and the Rise of American Environmentalism* (New York: Cambridge University Press, 2001), 221–30; William Leach, *Country of Exiles: The Destruction of Place in American Life* (New York: Pantheon,

1999), 31–90. For the number of shopping centers, see the Web site of the International Council of Shopping Centers, www.icsc.org/srch/rsrch/cope/current/index.html.

2. Government Accounting Office, "Community Development: Local Growth Issues— Federal Opportunities and Challenges: Report to Congressional Requesters," GA1.13: RCED-00-178/RCED-OO-178 (September 2000), 78, purl.access.gpo.gov/GPO/LPS51611. The Government Accounting Office conducted several studies of sprawl, and although GAO investigators were generally skeptical of sprawl's dangers, they offered a working definition of its characteristics: low-density development, dependent on automobiles, with segregated land uses (e.g., commercial, industrial, residential); long distances and poor access between housing, jobs, and schools; and consumption of land occurring at a faster rate than population growth, especially consumption of agricultural and environmentally sensitive lands; ibid., appendix 5, 90. See also GAO, "Community Development: Extent of Federal Influence in 'Urban Sprawl' Is Unclear," GAO/RCED-99-87 (April 30, 1999), purl.access.gpo.gov/ LPS11471. The Environmental Protection Agency (EPA) has more aggressively identified the ecological burdens of sprawl; documents from regional studies in the 1990s can be found on the EPA Web site (e.g., www.epa.gov/ARD-5/sue/brochure/page4.htm), along with links to the extensive Smart Growth institutional and organizational network that has defined itself in opposition to sprawl.

3. Kenneth Jackson, *Crabgrass Frontier: The Suburbanization of the United States* (New York: Oxford University Press, 1985); Andres Duany, Elizabeth Plater-Zyberk, and Jeff Speck, *Suburban Nation: The Rise of Sprawl and the Decline of the American Dream* (New York: North Point Press, 2000), includes a useful bibliography. See also Tom Daniels, *When City and Country Collide: Managing Growth in the Metropolitan Fringe* (Washington, DC: Island Press, 1998).

4. Rome, *The Bulldozer in the Countryside*. Samuel Hays, in *Beauty, Health and Permanence: Environmental Politics in the United States, 1955–1985* (New York: Cambridge University Press, 1987), also sees middle-class consumers as a key constituency of the environmental movement but places greater emphasis on their desire to enjoy nature in national parks. See also Robert Gottlieb, *Forcing the Spring: The Transformation of the American Environmental Movement* (Washington, DC: Island Press, 1993).

5. Thomas Bethel, *The Noblest Triumph: Property and Prosperity through the Ages* (New York: St. Martin's Press, 1998), 272.

6. The property rights movement can be taken as a general rubric for a broad, primarily libertarian political campaign that has produced numerous books and articles on its notions of free-market environmentalism as well as property rights. For the early structuring of environmental debates around property rights, see Rome, *The Bulldozer in the Countryside*, 230–47. Key or representative texts of the property rights movement include Richard A. Epstein, *Takings: Private Property and the Power of Eminent Domain* (Cambridge: Harvard University Press, 1986); Peter Huber, *Hard Green: Saving the Environment from the Environmentalists: A Conservative Manifesto* (New York: Basic Books, 1999); Richard Pipes, *Property and Freedom* (New York: Knopf, 1999); Terry Anderson and Donald R. Leal, *Free Market Environmentalism* (1993; reprint, New York: Palgrave, 2001); and a steady stream of law review articles and books by Bruce Yandle and associates, funded by the Political Economy Research Center. For the rise and legal strategies of the antienvironmentalist, antidevelopment property rights movement in the 1980s, see Douglas T. Kendall and Charles P.

Lord, "The Takings Project: A Critical Analysis and Assessment of the Progress So Far," *Boston College Environmental Affairs Law Review* 25, 509 (Spring 1998); Harvey M. Jacobs, *Who Owns America? Social Conflict over Property Rights* (Madison: University of Wisconsin Press, 1998). On the intersection of the property rights movement and the so-called Wise-Use movement (stewardship), see John Echeverria and Raymond Booth Eby, eds., *Let the People Judge: A Reader on the Wise Use Movement* (Washington, DC: Island Press, 1995); and Philip D. Brick and McGreggor Cawley, eds., *A Wolf in the Garden: The Land Rights Movement and the New Environmental Debates* (Lanham, MD: Rowman and Littlefield, 1996). For the politics of antienvironmentalism, see Hays, *Beauty, Health and Permanence,* 287–328; and Mark Dowie, *Losing Ground: American Environmentalism at the Close of the Twentieth Century* (Cambridge: MIT Press, 1995).

7. Thomas Hanchett, "Financing Suburbia: Prudential Insurance and the Post–World War II Transformation of the American City," *Journal of Urban History* 26, 3 (March 2000): 312–28; Thomas Hanchett, "U.S. Tax Policy and the Shopping Center Boom," *American Historical Review* 101, 4 (October 1996): 1082–110. Geographer David Harvey has developed theoretical models for thinking about the relation of finance capital and real estate in *The Limits to Capital* (Oxford: Blackwell, 1982); *The Urbanization of Capital* (Oxford: Blackwell, 1985); and *The Urban Experience* (Oxford: Blackwell, 1989).

8. Aldo Leopold, *A Sand County Almanac, and Sketches Here and There* (1949; reprint, New York: Ballantine, 1968), 237–61.

9. Ed Coppola of the Macerich Co., quoted in "Strategic Buys Build Portfolio," *Chain Store Age Executive* 76, 5 (May 2000): 100.

10. John Carpenter, "Schaumburg Built It and They Came," *Chicago Sun-Times,* September 15, 1996, 16.

11. Entrepreneurs' biographies often change from one news article to another. These versions are taken from Stephanie Strom, "Martin Bucksbaum, 74, Pioneer in Shopping Center Development," *New York Times,* July 10, 1995, D-11; Paula Kepos, ed., *International Directory of Company Histories* (Detroit: St. James Press, 1988, 1999), 8:355–57 (Simon); 27:399–402 (Simon); 10:159–62 (DeBartolo). The best study of the design and construction of early shopping centers is Richard Longstreth, *City Center to Regional Mall: Architecture, the Automobile, and Retailing in Los Angeles, 1920–1950* (Cambridge: MIT Press, 1997). See also Lizabeth Cohen, "From Town Center to Shopping Center: The Reconfiguration of Community Marketplace in Postwar America," *American Historical Review* 101 (October 1996): 1050–81; and for a more anecdotal history, William Severini Kowinski, *The Malling of America* (New York: William Morrow Company, 1985). For the basics of the industry, see Mary Alice Hines, *Shopping Center Development and Investment* (New York: Wiley, 1988).

12. "Small Concerns Are Frozen Out of Shopping Centers, Panel Is Told," *Wall Street Journal,* December 19, 1961, 30.

13. Ann Burkhart, "Lenders and Land," *Missouri Law Review* 64 (Spring 1999): 273.

14. On the lending policies of commercial banks in the 1950s and 1960s, see Harold van B. Cleveland and Thomas F. Huertas, *Citibank, 1812–1970* (Cambridge: Harvard University Press, 1985); and John Donald Wilson, *The Chase: Chase Manhattan Bank, N.A., 1945–1985* (Boston: Harvard Business School Press, 1986).

15. Burkhart, "Lenders and Land," 273–74; James Grant, *Money of the Mind: Borrowing and Lending in America from the Civil War to Michael Milken* (New York: Farrar, Straus & Giroux, 1992), 352–53.

16. Hanchett, "U.S. Tax Policy and the Shopping-Center Boom of the 1950s and 1960s," 1082–110.

17. Hanchett, "Financing Suburbia," 313.

18. "Equitable Life Puts Business Real Estate Loans above $3 Billion," *Wall Street Journal*, June 22, 1965, 13.

19. Financial Report, Supplement to Annual Report of Teachers Insurance and Annuity Association of America (hereafter cited as TIAA AR) for 1950, 5.

20. Financial Report, Supplement to TIAA AR for 1952, 9.

21. Financial Report, Supplement to TIAA AR for 1952, 4; TIAA AR for 1965, xx. In the 1980s, mortgages had declined to roughly 40 percent of the total portfolio of assets, but those mortgages were overwhelmingly for commercial properties. See Financial Report, Supplement to TIAA AR, 1979–1980.

22. Ibid., 4.

23. TIAA AR for 1960, 9.

24. TIAA AR for 1972, 4; "Melville Shoe to Double Rate of Store Openings over the Next 5 Years," *Wall Street Journal,* September 24, 1965, 15.

25. TIAA AR for 1965, 12; see also the account of Faneuil in Paul Doocey, "Twelve Who Dared," *Shopping Centers Today* 12, 5 (May 1991): 52–53.

26. TIAA AR for 1971, 12.

27. Debra Hazel, "TIAA Reaffirms Commitment to Retail despite Mall of America Offer," *Shopping Centers Today* 19, 8 (August 1998): 1.

28. Joel Seligman, "Another Unspecial Study: The SEC's Market 2000 Report and Competitive Development in the United States Capital Market," *Business Lawyer* 50, 485 (February 1995).

29. See, for example, TIAA AR for 1982, 12–13; TIAA AR for 1983, 12–14.

30. Michael A. Schill, "The Impact of the Capital Markets on Real Estate Law and Practice," *John Marshall Law Review* 32, 269 (Winter 1999), provides a clear summary of the law and economy of REITs. For an overview of changing legal rules and statistics, see the Web site of the National Association of Real Estate Investment Trusts, the main lobbying organization for REITs: www.nareit.com/faxondem/211.html.

31. Some developers moved in and out of REITs; the Bucksbaums organized their company as a REIT in 1970, liquidated the REIT in 1984, and went public again in 1993; www.generalgrowth.com/company/history.html. Michael Schill finds the number of equity REITs increased from 25 in 1984 to 197 in 1997, despite numerous mergers and acquisitions after the 1988–1989 recession: "Impact of the Capital Markets on Real Estate Law," 277. For inside summaries of the history of REITs as their value peaked in the mid-1990s, see David Harzell, Charles Wurtzebach, and David E. Watkins, "Combining Publicly Traded Real Estate Securities with Privately Held Portfolios," *Real Estate Finance* 12, 3 (Fall 1995): 26–40; Phillip S. Scherrer and Timothy Mathison, "Strategies for Investing in Real Estate Investment Trusts," *Business Credit* 97, 10 (November 1995): 38.

32. Schill, "Impact of Capital Markets on Real Estate Law," 273–74. Thomas F. Watten, "Divide and Price," offers an excellent succinct history of securitization, *Urban Land* 57, 6 (June 1998): 71–74, 99.

33. Burkhart, "Lenders and Land," 276. On the impact of deregulation on the 1980s boom more generally, see Barney Warf, "Vicious Circle: Financial Markets and Commercial Real Estate in the United States," in *Money, Power and Space,* ed. Stuart Corbridge, Ron Martin, and Nigel Thrift (Cambridge, MA: Basil Blackwell, 1994), 309–26.

34. On the development of commercial mortgage-backed securities, see "A New Breed of Bond," *Institutional Investor* 20, 3 (March 1995): 69.

35. Phoebe Moreo and Joe Rubin, "CMBS: Crossing the Bridge," *Urban Land* 57, 10 (October 1998): 82, 102.

36. "Long Awaited Mall Opens," UPI, July 18, 1984 (indexed through Lexis/Nexis). On the battle over the Fox River Mall, see Joshua Hausman, "The Building of the Fox River Mall" (unpublished paper, May 1998, copy in the possession of the author); and William E. Hauda, "Public Intervenor Plans Lawsuit to Block Appleton Shopping Mall," UPI, December 4, 1981 (indexed through Lexis/Nexis); see also, UPI Regional News articles indexed through Lexis/Nexis, dated September 24, 1982; February 14, 1983; March 19, 1983.

37. A search for newspaper coverage of opposition to malls on the Lexis/Nexis index for the 1980s and 1990s turns up numerous instances both of the use of environmental arguments by residents who have a broad range of social as well as ecological concerns, and of coalitions between organized proenvironmental groups and local activists. See, for example, efforts to block a new mall in the river bottoms of Hazelwood, Missouri: letters from Carl Fisher and Councilwoman Pat Jackson, *St. Louis Post-Dispatch,* May 4, 2000, B-6; Margaret Gillerman, "Coalition for the Environment Joins Foes of Hazelwood Mall," *St. Louis Post-Dispatch,* May 15, 2000, North, 3. In another example, Ohio environmental officials warned locals who "dreaded extra traffic" from a new mall that "we're only going to be able to respond to questions related to wetlands": Janet Tebben, "EPA Plans Hearing on Shopping Center Plan," *Cleveland Plain Dealer,* May 2, 2000, B-3. For a critical assessment of the same trend, see Debra Hazel, "The Perilous Path to Zoning," *Chain Store Age Executive* 69, 5 (May 1993): 76.

38. On the Attleboro mall fights, see Christine A. Klein, "Note: Bersani v. EPA: The EPA's Authority under the Clean Water Act to Veto Section 404 Wetland-Filling Permits," *Environmental Law* 19, 389 (Winter 1988); Stephen M. Rose, "Municipal Regulation of Wetland Use in Massachusetts: A Case Study," *New England Law Review* 24 (Summer 1990): 1322–27; Roberta Gratz, "Malling the Northeast," *New York Times Magazine,* April 2, 1990, 34; Anthony Flint, "Developer Hit with $200,000 Fine," *Boston Globe,* June 2, 1989, 43; Diane Dumanoski, "Supreme Court Action May End Battle of Sweeden's Swamp," *Boston Globe,* March 21, 1989, Metro, 23; and "Still Shopping at the Top: Simon Buys 14 New England Malls," *Providence Journal Bulletin,* February 26, 1999, 16 (quotation). On developers backing grassroots opposition to their competitors, for example, see Ellen Barry, "'Grass-Roots' Bid to Block Mall Had Secret Backer," *Boston Globe,* May 16, 1999, B1; or Mary Clark, "Vote on Proposed Prospect Village Is Delayed after Lengthy Hearing," *Louisville Courier-Journal,* September 12, 1990, in which one developer charged that another "was using the wetlands issue 'to hold this development hostage.'"

39. For overviews of the Simon and DeBartolo firms, including their conversion into REITs, see *International Directory of Company Histories,* 8:355–57(Simon); 27:399–402 (Simon); 10:159–62 (DeBartolo). For General Growth Properties, see Stephen Fitch, "Eating Your Own Children," *Grid* 2, 4 (July 2000): 66–67.

40. Stephanie Anderson Forest and Richard A. Melcher, "Can REITs Climb Out of the Rubble," *Business Week,* April 26, 1999, 40.

41. Fitch, "Eating Your Own Children," 66–67; Anna Robatan, "General Growth Turns 50," *Shopping Centers Today* 24, 3 (March 2004): 1; "Growing Season: Iowa's Eastern Hub Gets Superregional Center," *Chain Store Age Executive* 74, 9 (September 1998): 159.

42. "Merger Makes Simon Debartolo No. 1," *Chain Store Age Executive* 73, 5 (May 1997): 80 (quotation); Debra Hazel, "Megamergers Hit the Mall," *Chain Store Age Executive* 72, 5 (May 1996): 43.

43. "Strategic Buys Build Portfolio," *Chain Store Age Executive* 76, 5 (May 2000): 100.

44. "Top 25 Owners," *Shopping Center World* (August 2000); "Top Retail Firm," NREI Leadership Awards, *National Real Estate Investor* 42, 6 (June 2000).

45. Leslie Berkman, "Laguna Hills Mall Up for Sale As Part of $1-Billion Portfolio," *Los Angeles Times*, July 6, 1989, 5.

46. Lawrence S. Kaplan, "Pressure to Perform," *Urban Land* 57, 10 (October 1998): 84–85, 104–6.

47. Pyramid Cos., founded by Robert J. Congel and based in Syracuse, gained its reputation as a rogue developer after it was charged with buying through generous campaign contributions the support of the Poughkeepsie town council for its proposed Galleria in 1985. It subsequently used threats of lawsuits to cower residents and officials of Rockland County, New York, who opposed the construction of its Palisades Center in Nyack. Gratz, "Malling the Northeast."

48. The prodevelopment disposition of local political leaders, most of whom do not need to be bribed, is well explained in John R. Logan and Harvey Molotch, *Urban Fortunes: The Political Economy of Place* (Berkeley: University of California Press, 1987).

49. PricewaterhouseCoopers, "Greyfield Regional Mall Study," January 2001, Congress for the New Urbanism, http://env.org/malls/.

50. Edward Starkie, Leland Consulting Group, "Smart Development Program: Financial Capital Serivices," Report to the Oregon Department of Transportation, 1997, 11, www.smartgrowth.org/pdf/smartcap.pdf.

51. Rick Fulman, "Taking Malls to the Market: TIAA-CREF Pulls Several Major Properties off the Auction Block," *Pension and Investments*, March 22, 1999, 39. As it turned out, the Simon Property Group bought half of TIAA's stake and took over a larger share of the mall's debt. Melissa Levy, "Megamall Manager Becomes Part Owner," *Minneapolis Star-Tribune*, November 10, 1999, 1D.

52. "Top 25 Lenders List," *Shopping Center World* (August 2000).

53. Prospectus, TIAA Real Estate Account, May 1, 2001, 2.

54. Ibid., 5.

55. Brad A. Maurer, "Environmental Liabilities Pose Problems for Real Estate Investment Trusts," *Real Estate Finance Journal* 13, 2 (Fall 1997): 16–20; J. Kent Holland, Jr. and William McElroy, "Environmental Liability Insurance or Property Transactions," *Real Estate Finance Journal* 13, 1 (Summer 1997): 12–20.

Chapter 5: Floods and Landscapes in the Inland West

1. Giles French, *Cattle Country of Peter French* (Portland, OR: Binfords and Mort, 1964), 42.

2. David L. Shirk, "The cattle drives of David Shirk from Texas to the Idaho mines, 1871 and 1873: reminiscences of David L. Shirk, wherein are described his two successful cattle drives from Texas, in company with George T. Miller. His later experiences as a cattleman in eastern Oregon during the terrible depredations of hostile Indians and the range warfare with Pete French," from the original manuscript and related papers, now in the University of Oregon Library, ed. Martin F. Schmitt (1956), 128. For detailed descriptions of presettle-

ment conditions along the Blitzen River, see the useful reconstruction of General Land Office survey notes completed by Stephen Dow Beckham, "Donner und Blitzen River, Oregon: River Widths, Vegetative Environment, and Conditions Shaping Its Condition, Malheur Lake to Headwaters" (unpublished paper submitted to Eastside Ecosystem Management Project, 1995, on file at the Interior Columbia Basin Ecosystem Management Office, Walla Walla, WA).

3. Prim Ortega, "Testimony in the Matter of the Determination of the Relative Rights to the Use of the Waters of Donner und Blitzen River, a Tributary of Malheur Lake," vol. 8, original evidence, May 16, 1931, Harney County Courthouse, Clerk's Office, Burns, OR, 322.

4. Blitzen Valley Land Company, company prospectus, "General Description of the Property Owned by the Blitzen Valley Land Company Formerly Known As the French-Glenn Property in Harney County, Oregon," William Hanley, President, February 25, 1913, Hanley Company Papers, Oregon Historical Society, MSS 378, Box 4.

5. James Brandon, testimony, in Treadwell and Rand, "Brief in Support of Claims of Pacific Live Stock Company," 95, "In the Matter of the Determination of the Relative Rights to the Waters of Silvies River and Its Tributaries, a Tributary of Malheur Lake," Circuit Court of the State of Oregon for Harney County, testimony taken 1918, findings dated October 19, 1923, Harney County Courthouse, Burns, Oregon.

6. Henry Miller, letter to H. N. Fulgham, January 30, 1892, Knight Library Special Collections, University of Oregon.

7. The lawyer asked Prim Ortega if Peter French was putting up hay as early as 1877. Ortega replied: "Yes, he put up some but he did not put up very much, you know, at that time, they did not have to, you know, stock never got poor. There was lots of grass all over the range; but he put up a little, you know. Enough if he wanted to keep up stock, to work stock, or something like that, he would feed; he did not have to cut much hay at that time." Ortega, "Testimony," 336.

8. Myron Angel, rancher, cited in Margaret Lo Picollo, "Some Aspects of the Range Cattle Industry of Harney County, Oregon, 1870–1900" (master's thesis, Department of History, University of Oregon, June 1962).

9. John H. Lewis, "Irrigation in Oregon," USDA Office of Experiment Stations Bulletin 209 (Washington, DC: Government Printing Office, 1909), 29.

10. Peter K. Simpson, *The Community of Cattlemen: A Social History of the Cattle Industry in Southeastern Oregon, 1869–1912* (Moscow, ID: University of Idaho Press, 1987), 60.

11. "'A great change is taking place in the physical condition of our section of country,' said State Senator Cogswell of Lake County to a reporter of the Oregonian last week. 'The water of many of the lakes is subsiding, due in a measure to drawing it off for irrigating purposes, and also, to natural causes. Not over four square miles of the original bed of Warner Lake is now covered with water. In 1865 there was seven feet of water on it. . . . In Warner valley, a few days ago, 300 tons of hay were burned; in 1874 the spot where the fire took place was surveyed as Warner Lake. Goose Lake has subsided five feet since 1869. . . . Lake Malheur of Harney county registers eight feet lower than at any period within the memory of the oldest inhabitant.'" *East Oregon Herald*, March 28, 1889, 2.

12. W. A. J. Sparks, the reform-minded U.S. land commissioner, moved to disallow all swamp claims in Oregon; indictments were brought, but few claims reverted to the government. Simpson, *Community of Cattlemen*, 77.

13. *East Oregon Herald*, February 5, 1889, 4.

14. French, *Cattle Country of Peter French,* 153–56; Simpson, *Community of Cattlemen,* 80.

15. In 1937 alone, refuge staff built over 150,966 cubic yards of levees and dikes, set 95 miles of barbed wire, cleared out 83,938 cubic yards of channels, laid 34,680 cubic yards of riprap, and set out 35 separate water control structures. John Scharff, "Report of Activities Fiscal Year 1937, Malheur Migratory Waterfowl Refuge," Refuge files, Malheur National Wildlife Refuge, Princeton, OR, 12.

16. Ann Vileisis, *Discovering the Unknown Landscape: A History of America's Wetlands* (Washington, DC: Island Press, 1997), 180.

17. H. S. Davis, address to 1934 annual meeting of the American Fisheries Society, quoted in Christopher Hunter, *Better Trout Habitat: A Guide to Stream Restoration and Management* (Washington, DC: Island Press, 1991), 7.

18. Interview with Forrest Cameron, project director, Malheur National Wildlife Refuge, and Gary Ivey, wildlife biologist, Malheur National Wildlife Refuge, July 25, 1996. The "Annual Narratives" and the "Quarterly Narratives" from 1935 to 1996, stored in the Malheur National Wildlife Refuge Station Library, provide a good record of changing management practices.

19. In 1944, Congress allotted substantial funds for the Soil Conservation Service's drainage and irrigation work, and memos clarified that drainage and irrigation were "technical conservation practices." Vileisis, *Discovering the Unknown Landscape,* 196.

20. Ibid., 197.

21. Ibid.

22. Ibid., 201. The Fish and Wildlife Service and the Soil Conservation Service adopted a memorandum of understanding, in which federal and state wildlife agency recommendations were supposed to be incorporated into watershed plans. Local soil conservation districts had final say, however, and channelization soon began in earnest.

23. Vileisis, *Discovering the Unknown Landscape,* 245.

24. USDA Economic Research Service, "Report on Water and Related Land Resources Malheur Lake Drainage Basin Oregon" (Salem, OR: USDA Economic Research Service, Forest Service, and Soil Conservation Service, April 1967), 119.

25. Ibid., 87.

26. For spraying of 2,4-D and 2,4,5-T, see Herbert Fletcher and Harold B. Elmendorf, "Phreatophytes—A Serious Problem in the West," in *Water,* U.S. Department of Agriculture Yearbook of Agriculture (Washington, DC: Government Printing Office, 1955), 427. One of the first studies to draw scientific attention to the "waste" posed by phreatophytes was O. E. Meinzer, "Plants As Indicators of Ground Water," U.S. Geological Survey Water Supply Paper 577 (Washington, DC: Government Printing Office, 1927). See the extensive review of the scientific literature by T. W. Robinson, "Phreatophytes," U.S. Geological Survey Water Supply Paper 1423 (Washington, DC: Government Printing Office, 1959), 1–84. In 1970, the Forest Service botanist C. J. Campbell urged managers to consider the possible ecological importance of phreatophytes, but his caution was largely ignored for two decades. See C. J. Campbell, "Ecological Implications of Riparian Vegetation Management," *Journal of Soil and Water Conservation* 25 (1970): 49–52.

27. As the 1955 Yearbook of Agriculture put it, "Men who have studied the problem throughout the West realize that a large part of the water consumed by phreatophytes could be put to beneficial use by replacing the phreatophytes with crops, grass, or other beneficial vegetation." Fletcher and Elmendorf, "Phreatophytes," 424.

28. In Idaho, carp were introduced in the 1880s and 1890s as a food source; see Mark Fiege, *Irrigated Eden: The Making of an Agricultural Landscape in the American West* (Seattle: University of Washington Press, 1999), 57. However, the refuge biologist Harold Duebbert wrote that carp were introduced into the Silvies River watershed in the 1920s but gives no source; see Harold F. Duebbert, "The Ecology of Malheur Lake and Management Implications," Refuge leaflet # 412, USDI Fish and Wildlife Service, Bureau of Sport Fisheries and Wildlife (Washington, DC: U.S. Department of the Interior, November 1969), 15.

29. USDI Fish and Wildlife Service, Malheur National Wildlife Refuge, *Quarterly Narrative Report September to December 1955*, Refuge files, Malheur National Wildlife Refuge, Princeton, OR, 2.

30. Ibid.

31. Ibid., 11–12. The Quarterly Report detailed the elaborate process: "toxicant was placed in the Blitzen River beginning on October 15 at Page Dam, approximately 40 miles above the mouth. The material was introduced directly into the steam from 55-gallon steel drums on the basis of 2 1/2 pints of toxicant per acre-foot of water passing a given point. Additional drums were placed at Grain Camp Dam and near refuge headquarters. Known as drip stations, these drums poured toxicant into the river at a constant rate. The current carried the material through the entire course of the stream below Page Dam. Toxic water began entering the lake the evening of October 16. On October 17, the lake was sprayed by a contractor using flagmen and a converted TBF navy torpedo bomber which carried 640 gallons of toxicant, which was used without dilution. The aircraft treated a strip of water 400 feet wide with a 100 foot overlap and flew at an elevation of 235' above the water's surface. Spraying was done first north to south and then east and west with a total of 3.64 pints of toxicant being applied per surface acre. This dosage was considerably above that recommended by the manufacturer. . . . The various sloughs, lakes and marshes of the Blitzen Valley were treated by a small aircraft or by hand back pump cans."

32. USDI Fish and Wildlife Service, Bureau of Sport Fisheries and Wildlife, "Carp Control Project at Malheur Lake, Oregon 1955–1956," Refuge files, Malheur National Wildlife Refuge, Princeton, OR (1957), 35.

33. USDI Fish and Wildlife Service, Malheur National Wildlife Refuge, *Annual Narrative 1977*, Refuge files, Malheur National Wildlife Refuge, Princeton, OR, 9; USDI Fish and Wildlife Service, Malheur National Wildlife Refuge, *Annual Narrative 1987*, 19.

34. Not only carp died in these control programs, of course, for rotenone kills most fish and kills many of them more quickly and thoroughly than it kills carp. As the 1957 report read: "The effects of the toxicant in the upper treated portion of the main Blitzen River were evident within one hour from the time of introduction, when a number of rainbow trout, whitefish, small shiners, dace, squawfish, and suckers were killed. The reaction of carp to the toxicant was much slower, as expected." What about all these other species? From today's perspective, one immediately wonders under what moral or scientific calculus can one kill all aquatic species, just to increase food for ducks? What about the native fish in the basin? Eradicating native fish was, of course, nothing new. In 1950, Scharff had authorized replacing native fish in refuge waters with sport fish to make the refuge more attractive to sport anglers. He reported that "In 1952 and 1953 Boca Lake was rehabilitated with rotenone by Service biologists and stocked with rainbow trout in an effort to establish a source of spring-spawning rainbow trout eggs. The experiment failed to produce the desired results. However, the stocking program for the Blitzen River has produced excellent sport fishing for

rainbow trout which grow up to 20 inches in length in these waters." Note the language: the lake was "rehabilitated," as if native fish species were criminal, language akin to the Bureau of Reclamation's use of "reclamation" to mean the eradication of native ecosystems. USDI Fish and Wildlife Service, "Carp Control Project," 1957, 15, 42.

35. E. R. Jackman and John Scharff, *Steens Mountain in Oregon's High Desert Country* (Caldwell, ID: Caxton Printers, 1967), 16.

36. U.S. Army Engineer District, Portland, Corps of Engineers, "Survey Report on Silvies River and Tributaries, Oregon" (Portland, OR: U.S. Army Engineer District, 1957), 1.

37. Ibid., 6.

38. Ibid., 12.

39. Ibid., 29.

40. Ibid., 29.

41. Ibid., 56.

42. Ibid., 60.

43. Ibid., 66. The Army Corps of Engineers finally recommended that the project not be carried out because local water rights were still contested.

44. In 1964, a flood had caused $2,486,000 worth of damage in the basin, the most expensive yet. Local feelings, therefore, were strong about the need for flood control, at least during early public hearings in 1969. However, the army noted that by the 1976 public hearing, ranchers were presenting concerns about the usual issues: the cost of stored water, the acreage limitation imposed by a federal project, and the potential changes in ranching practices. See U.S. Army Corps of Engineers, Walla Walla District, "Silvies River and Tributaries, Oregon: Feasibility Report for Water Resources Development" (Walla Walla, WA: Walla Walla District Corps of Engineers, February 1977), 10.

45. For cost calculations, see ibid., 34. The high annual costs in the 1977 estimates were driven partly by the higher initial charges for the project construction, as well as annual payments on the $1150-per-acre cost of draining land and creating an irrigation distribution system (converted over an expected one-hundred-year life of the project at 6 1/8 percent interest).

46. Ibid., syllabus.

47. Ibid., 32.

48. Robert Raleigh, superintendent of Squaw Butte Experiment Station, letter to Col. C. J. Allaire, December 14, 1976, U.S. Army Engineer District, Portland, Corps of Engineers, "Survey Report on Silvies River and Tributaries, Oregon," app. 2, 17.

49. H. R. Stivers, acting regional director of the Bureau of Reclamation, letter to Col. C. J. Allaire, district engineer, Walla Walla, no date but between December 14, 1976 and January 26, 1977, U.S. Army Engineer District, Portland, Corps of Engineers, "Survey Report on Silvies River and Tributaries, Oregon," app. 2.

50. Ibid.

51. Raleigh to Allaire, letter, 19.

52. Since records have been kept, the normal lake level maximum has been 4,093 feet above sea level. Of course, normal lake levels do not mean a great deal, for in a closed basin the level varies each year depending on snowfall and patterns of snow melt. Cristin R. Mandaville, "A Swamp in the Desert: Theory, Water Policy, and Malheur Lake Basin" (M.S. thesis in geography, Portland State University, 1996), 64.

53. U.S. Army Corps of Engineers, "Final Version, Malheur Lake Flood Damage Reduc-

tion Feasibility Study and Environmental Impact Statement," Walla Walla District, U.S. Army Corps of Engineers (Walla Walla, WA: Walla Walla District Corps of Engineers, April 1987).

54. Ibid., 2–4.

55. Gayland T. Arp, "The Flooding of Malheur Lake: The Problems and Solutions" (unpublished manuscript, Refuge files, Malheur National Wildlife Refuge, Princeton, OR, December 9, 1986), 6; Pauline Braymen, *Burns Times Herald*, October 29, 1986, 15.

56. Arp, "The Flooding of Malheur Lake," 11.

57. Ibid.

58. Mandaville, "A Swamp in the Desert," 65.

59. Arp, "The Flooding of Malheur Lake," 6.

60. U.S. Army Corps of Engineers, "Reconnaissance Report, Malheur Lake, Oregon" (Walla Walla, WA: Walla Walla District Corps of Engineers, August 29, 1985), 17.

61. Ibid., 33.

62. U.S Army Corps of Engineers, "Final Version," 3–13.

63. U.S. Army Corps of Engineers, "Reconnaissance Report," 7. According to Squaw Butte's own inflated estimates of hay value in 1977, meadow hay was worth $20 per ton, and meadows without irrigation could produce .75 ton per acre, so at 50,000 acres of hay lost, that comes to $750,000. The highest estimate for the value of hay lost over the entire flooding came to $1,200,000.

64. The canal would have been seventeen miles long with a fish barrier to "minimize movement of carp and Tui chub from Malheur Lake into the Malheur River system." U.S. Army Corps of Engineers, "Final Version," 3–9.

65. Ibid., summary.

66. Ibid., 2–9. Malheur Lake quality was usually better than Harney and Mud lakes, because Malheur Lake normally would get flushed into the other two slightly lower-lying lakes during higher waters. Concentrations of most dissolved solids were normally ten times higher in Harney Lake than Malheur lake, but the very high lake levels meant some mixing of the lakes had occurred, and this poorer quality water would have been flushed into Malheur River if the canal had been completed.

67. USDI Fish and Wildlife Service, Division of Ecological Services, "Planning Aid Letter on the Malheur Lake Flood Control Project," Portland (April 10, 1985), U.S Army Corps of Engineers, "Final Version," C-13.

Chapter 6: The Industrial Alchemy of Hydraulic Mining

1. Frederick Jackson Turner, "The Significance of the Frontier in American History," *American Historical Association Annual Report* (1893): 199–227. For the icon of the prospector, see Janice T. Driesbach, Harvey L. Jones, and Katherine Church Holland, *Art of the Gold Rush* (Berkeley: University of California Press, 1998); see also Andrew C. Isenberg, "California, the West, and the Nation," *Reviews in American History* 29 (March 2001): 62–71.

2. Walter Prescott Webb, "The American West: Perpetual Mirage," *Harper's Magazine* 214 (May 1957): 25–31.

3. Donald Worster, "Hydraulic Society in California: An Ecological Interpretation," *Agricultural History* 56 (July 1982): 503–15.

4. See David Igler, *Industrial Cowboys: Miller & Lux and the Transformation of the Far West, 1850–1920* (Berkeley: University of California Press, 2001); Igler, "The Industrial Far

West: Region and Nation in the Late Nineteenth Century," *Pacific Historical Review* 69 (May 2000): 159–92; Stephen J. Pitti, *The Devil in Silicon Valley: Northern California, Race, and Mexican Americans* (Princeton: Princeton University Press, 2003), 51–77; Gray Brechin, *Imperial San Francisco: Urban Power, Earthly Ruin* (Berkeley: University of California Press, 1999); Igler and Brechin drew on the arguments of, among others, Rodman Paul, *California Gold: The Beginning of Mining in the Far West* (Cambridge: Harvard University Press, 1947).

5. David J. St. Clair, "The Gold Rush and the Beginnings of California Industry," in *A Golden State: Mining and Economic Development in Gold Rush California*, ed. James J. Rawls and Richard J. Orsi (Berkeley: University of California Press, 1999), 185–208.

6. See Graeme Bannock, R. E. Baxter, and R. Rees, *The Penguin Dictionary of Economics*, 3rd ed. (New York: Penguin, 1984), 166–67.

7. Of the nearly $525 million invested in manufacturing in the United States in 1850, only a little over $1 million was invested in the West—all of it in California. By 1900, only 4 percent of manufacturing capital was invested in the West. Inter-University Consortium for Political and Social Research, *Study 00003: Historical Demographic, Economic, and Social Data, U.S. 1790–1970* (Ann Arbor: ICPSR). For the shortages of capital and labor in mid-nineteenth-century California, see Robert Glass Cleland and Osgood Hardy, *March of Industry* (Los Angeles: Powell, 1929), 50, 134.

8. For labor in the nineteenth-century West, see Igler, *Industrial Cowboys*, 122–46; Gunther Peck, *Reinventing Free Labor: Padrones and Immigrant Workers in the North American West, 1880–1930* (New York: Cambridge University Press, 2000); Howard Lamar, "From Bondage to Contract: Ethnic Labor in the American West, 1600–1890," in *The Countryside in the Age of Capitalist Transformation: Essays in the Social History of Rural America*, ed. Steven Hahn and Jonathan Prude (Chapel Hill: University of North Carolina Press, 1985), 293–324.

9. See Donald J. Pisani, *Water, Land, and Law in the West: The Limits of Public Policy, 1850–1920* (Lawrence: University Press of Kansas, 1996); Charles F. Wilkinson, *Crossing the Next Meridian: Land, Water, and the Future of the West* (Washington, DC: Island Press, 1992).

10. For Americans' preference for relatively cheap technologies, see Alexander James Field, "Land Abundance, Interest/Profit Rates, and Nineteenth-Century British and American Technology," *Journal of Economic History* 43 (June 1983): 405–31.

11. Otto von Geldern, *An Analysis of the Problem of the Proposed Rehabilitation of Hydraulic Mining in California* (Yuba City, CA, January 3, 1928), 4.

12. B. S. Alexander and W. M. Pierce, "Testimony Taken by the Committee on Mining Debris, As Reported to the Assembly," 22nd Session, 1877–1878, *Appendix to the Journals of the Senate and Assembly of the 22nd Session of the Legislature of the State of California*, vol. 4 (Sacramento: F. P. Thompson, 1878), 28, 148.

13. For the geological formation of the Sierra Nevada, see John McPhee, *Assembling California* (New York: Farrar, Strauss & Giroux, 1993), 12–36; Elna Bakker, *An Island Called California: An Ecological Introduction to Its Natural Communities*, 2nd ed. (Berkeley: University of California Press, 1984), 146–48, 183–84; Allan A. Schoenherr, *A Natural History of California* (Berkeley: University of California Press, 1992), 73–75; Crane S. Miller and Richard S. Hyslop, *California: The Geography of Diversity* (Mountain View, CA: Mayfield, 1983), 51–56; Edward J. Tarbuck and Frederick K. Lutgens, *Earth Science*, 4th ed. (Columbus, OH: Charles E. Merrill, 1985), 189–92.

14. Joseph Pownall, Mariposa Diggings, CA, to Dr. O. C. Pownall, May 1850, Joseph Pownall Collection, Huntington Library, San Marino, CA (hereafter cited as HUN).

15. Joseph Pownall to Dr. O. C. Pownall, May 1850, Joseph Pownall Collection.

16. For too much water, see John H. Eagle, Gold Hill, Placer County, to Margaret H. Eagle, May 11, 1853, John H. Eagle Correspondence, HUN; Seymour D. Beach, Rattlesnake, CA, to Amos Parmalee Catlin, April 3, 1855, Amos Parmalee Catlin Papers, Box 2, HUN. For too little, see Beach, Rattlesnake, CA, to Catlin, April 5, 1855, July 18, 1855, and August 27, 1855, Catlin Papers, Box 2, HUN; John T. Kincade, Secret Ravine, CA, to James Kincade, April 8, 1855 and May 24, 1855, John Thompson Kincade Papers, HUN.

17. Maureen A. Jung, "Capitalism Comes to the Diggings: From Gold-Rush Adventure to Corporate Enterprise," in *A Golden State*, 52–77.

18. Ira B. Cross, *Financing an Empire: History of Banking in California* (Chicago: S. J. Clarke, 1927), 1:121–23, 172–83.

19. Gerald D. Nash, *State Government and Economic Development: A History of Administrative Policies in California, 1849–1933* (Berkeley: Institute of Government Studies, 1964), 9–10, 30, 91–95.

20. F. Halsey Rogers, "'Man to Loan $1500 and Serve as Clerk': Trading Jobs for Loans in Mid-Nineteenth-Century San Francisco," *Journal of Economic History* 54 (March 1994): 34–63.

21. Pownall, "History of Tuolumne County Water Company," c. 1880, Pownall Collection.

22. G. H. Mendell, "Report upon a Project to Protect the Navigable Waters of California from the Effects of Hydraulic Mining," 47th Cong., 1st sess., 1882, H. Ex. Doc. 98, 13.

23. "Annual Review of the Mining Interests of California," *Mining Magazine and Journal of Geology* 2 (April 1861): 138. For hydraulic mining technology, see Hunter Rouse, *Hydraulics in the United States, 1776–1976* (Iowa City: Institute of Hydraulic Research, 1976), 50–52.

24. Rossiter Raymond, *Silver and Gold: An Account of the Mining and Metallurgical Industry of the United States* (New York: J. B. Ford, 1873), 17.

25. "Mines and Mining," *Marysville Herald*, January 27, 1854, 2.

26. B. Silliman, *Reports on the Blue Tent Consolidated Hydraulic Gold Mines of California, Limited* (London: D. P. Croke, 1873), 13; George Black, *Report on the Middle Yuba Canal and Eureka Lake Canal, Nevada County, California* (San Francisco: Towne and Bacon, 1864), 8; John S. Hittell, *The Resources of California* (San Francisco: A. Roman & Co.; New York: W. J. Widdleton, 1874), 17; Titus Fey Cronise, *The Natural Wealth of California* (San Francisco: H. H. Bancroft, 1868), 547; Kincade, Secret Ravine, CA, to James Kincade, December 28, 1856, Kincade Papers.

27. For a discussion of the place of technology in labor history, see Donald MacKenzie, "Marx and the Machine," *Technology and Culture* 25 (July 1984): 473–502. Marx wrote, "The machine, which is the starting point of the industrial revolution, supersedes the workman, who handles a single tool." Karl Marx, *Capital*, vol. 1, *A Critical Analysis of Capitalist Production*, ed. Frederick Engels, trans. Samuel Moore and Edward Aveling (New York: International Publishers, 1967), 355.

28. The effort to impose such control is a hallmark of large technological systems. See Thomas P. Hughes, "The Evolution of Large Technological Systems," in *The Social Construction of Technological Systems: New Directions in the Sociology and History of Technology*, ed. Wiebe E. Bijker, Thomas P. Hughes, and Trevor J. Pinch (Cambridge: MIT Press, 1987), 53.

29. Malcolm Rohrbough, *Days of Gold: The California Gold Rush and the American Nation* (Berkeley: University of California Press, 1997), 125–27.

30. *James W. Tartar v. The Spring Creek Water and Mining Company,* 5 California 399 (1855). See also *Irwin v. Phillips,* 5 California 140 (1855).

31. *William Parsons v. The Tuolumne County Water Company,* 5 California 43 (1855).

32. *E. Hoffman et al. v. The Tuolumne County Water Company,* 10 California 413 (1858).

33. *Wolf et al. v. St. Louis Independent Water Company,* 10 California 541 (1858).

34. See Morton Horwitz, *The Transformation of American Law, 1785–1850* (Cambridge: Harvard University Press, 1976).

35. A. L. Williams, *Description of the Property of the Yuba Hydraulic Gold Mining Company* (Cincinnati: Moore, Wilstack, & Baldwin, 1867); Hamilton Smith, Jr., *An Account of the Operations of the North Bloomfield Gravel Mining Company* (San Francisco, 1875); Silliman, *Blue Tent Gold Mines,* 11–13; W. M. R. Wood, "California: Its Mining and Industrial Resources" (1864), 10–18, Bancroft Library, University of California, Berkeley; "Annual Review of the Mining Interests of California," 140.

36. See *Edwards Woodruff v. North Bloomfield Gravel Mining Company,* 18 F9 753 (1884).

37. John Muir, quoted in *Prospectus of the Cataract and Wide West Hydraulic Gravel Mining Co.* (San Francisco: Fluto & Co., 1876), 4–6.

38. Cronise, *Natural Wealth of California,* 547. See also Hittell, *Resources of California,* 81; Black, *Middle Yuba Canal,* 4.

39. Taliesin Evans, "Hydraulic Mining in California," *Century Magazine* 25 (June 1883): 328, 333–34.

40. "Transactions of the California State Agricultural Society, 1870 and 1871," *Appendix to the Journals of the Senate and Assembly of the Nineteenth Session of the Legislature of the State of California,* vol. 3 (Sacramento: T. A. Springer, 1872), 20–21.

41. "Accumulation of Tailings," *Placer Herald,* April 6, 1872, 3; W. H. Drum, "Testimony Taken by the Committee on Mining Debris," 77.

42. A. T. Arrowsmith, James H. Keyes, J. H. Jewett, and Joseph Johnson, "Testimony Taken by the Committee on Mining Debris," 4–5, 80–82, 100, 105, 141.

43. "Report of the Commissioners of Fisheries of the State of California, 1870 and 1871," *Appendix to the Journals of the Senate and Assembly of the Nineteenth Session of the Legislature of the State of California,* vol. 2 (Sacramento: T. A. Springer, 1872), 8; "Report of the Commissioners of Fisheries of the State of California for the Years 1876 and 1877," *Appendix to the Journals of the Senate and Assembly of the Twenty-Second Session of the Legislature of the State of California,* vol. 3 (Sacramento: F. P. Thompson, 1878), 5; see also Hittell, *Resources of California,* 193.

44. *James H. Keyes v. Little York Gold Washing and Water Company* (1879), 15–16. N. S. Hanlin and W. H. Drum, "Testimony Taken by the Committee on Mining Debris," 77, 137–38. See also Address of George Cadwalader, Delivered at Sacramento, February 28 and March 1st, 1882, on the Case of the *State of California vs. Gold Run Hydraulic Mining Co.* (Sacramento: H. S. Crocker & Co., 1882), 43. A federal study in 1891 reported that over forty thousand acres of farmland on the Feather, Bear, and Yuba rivers were destroyed by slickens. "Mining Debris in California," 51st Cong., 2nd sess., 1891, H. Ex. Doc. 267, 14.

45. Von Geldern, *Hydraulic Mining,* 9.

46. "California in '49 and '74," *Placer Herald,* January 16, 1875. Hittell, *Resources of California,* 328.

47. *Facts concerning the Quicksilver Mines in Santa Clara County, California* (New York: R. C. Root, Anthony, & Co., 1859), 7; *The Quicksilver Mining Company* (New York: Sun Job Printing House, 1868), 18; *The Quicksilver Mining Company* (New York: Sun Job Printing

House, 1869), 5; *The Quicksilver Mining Company* (New York: E. S. Dodge & Co., 1871), 13; *The Quicksilver Mining Company* (New York: Wm. F. Jones, 1873), 5; *The Quicksilver Mining Company* (New York: D. Murphy's Son, 1874), 7; *The Quicksilver Mining Company* (New York: D. Murphy's Son, 1875), 5; *The Quicksilver Mining Company* (New York: D. Murphy's Son, 1876), 6; *The Quicksilver Mining Company* (New York: D. Murphy's Son, 1877), 6; Hennen Jennings, *The Quicksilver Mines of Almaden and New Almaden: A Comprehensive View of Their Extent, Production, Costs of Work, Etc.* (1886), 9.

48. William V. Wells, "The Quicksilver Mines of New Almaden, California," *Harper's New Monthly Magazine* 27 (June 1863): 27–39.

49. U.S. Environmental Protection Agency, *Health Effects of Mercury and Mercury Compounds*, vol. 5, *Mercury Study Report to Congress*, EPA-452/R-97-007 (December 1997), ES 1-9.

50. Augustus Jesse Bowie, Jr., *A Practical Treatise on Hydraulic Mining in California* (New York: D. Van Nostrand, 1885), 244–45; J. Ross Browne, *Resources of the Pacific Slope* (San Francisco: H. H. Bancroft, 1869), 151; Silliman, *Blue Tent Gold Mines*, 11.

51. Rossiter Raymond, *Mineral Resources of the States and Territories West of the Rocky Mountains*, 40th Cong., 3rd sess., H. Ex. Doc. 54 (Washington, DC: Government Printing Office, 1869), 10; Hittell, *Resources of California*, 329.

52. Hittell, *Mining in the Pacific States*, 145.

53. R. H. Stretch, Charles Waldeyer, and Hamilton Smith, Jr., *Reports on the Spring Valley Hydraulic Gold Mining Company, Comprising the Cherokee Flat Blue Gravel and Spring Valley Mining and Irrigating Company's Property* (New York: John J. Caulon, 1879). For gold in the debris, see also Janin, "Report on the Excelsior Water and Mining Company," 8.

54. "Accumulation of Tailings," *Placer Herald*, April 6, 1872, 2.

55. *The Bear River Tunnel Company* (Boston: Alfred Mudge & Son, 1881), 10, 16–17.

56. U.S. Environmental Protection Agency, *Mercury Study Report to Congress*, ES 1-9.

57. "Report of the Commissioners of Fisheries of the State of California for the Years 1876 and 1877," 13.

58. Robert L. Kelley, *Gold vs. Grain: The Hydraulic Mining Controversy in California's Sacramento Valley* (Glendale, CA: Arthur H. Clark, 1959), 116.

59. Richard J. Orsi, "The Octopus Reconsidered: The Southern Pacific and Agricultural Modernization in California, 1865–1915," *California Historical Quarterly* 54 (Fall 1975): 200–202.

60. M. Catherine Miller, *Flooding the Courtrooms: Law and Water in the Far West* (Lincoln: University of Nebraska Press, 1993), 6.

61. *The Bear River and Auburn Water and Mining Company v. The New York Mining Company* 8 California 327 (1857).

62. Ibid.

63. Lester L. Robinson and James O'Brien, "Testimony Taken by the Committee on Mining Debris," 16–20.

64. Ibid., 3–5.

65. Kelley, *Gold vs. Grain*, 106.

66. "Industrial Condition of the Slope," *Alta California* (April 1, 1878), 1.

67. *Woodruff v. North Bloomfield.*

68. Donald J. Pisani, *From Family Farm to Agribusiness: The Irrigation Crusade in Cali-*

fornia and the West, 1850–1931 (Berkeley: University of California Press, 1984), 9; Rodman Paul, *The Far West and Great Plains in Transition, 1859–1900* (New York: Harper, 1988), 227.

69. Decker-Jewett Bank Papers, California State Library, Sacramento, California.

70. Kelley, *Gold vs. Grain*, 229–40.

71. Donald E. Trimble, *The Geologic Story of the Great Plains* (Bismarck, ND: Theodore Roosevelt Nature and History Association, 1980), 39–40.

72. John Muir, *My First Summer in the Sierra* (Boston: Houghton Mifflin, 1944), 157.

Chapter 7: West Africa's Colonial Fungus

1. See Alfred Crosby, *The Columbian Exchange: Biological and Cultural Consequences of 1492* (Westport, CT: Greenwood Press, 1972). A few scholars have claimed that maize in the Old World predated 1492, citing early Portuguese references to *milho zaburro* on the West African coast. See M. D. W. Jeffreys, "The History of Maize in Africa," *South African Journal of Science* (March 1954): 197–200; and M. D. W. Jeffreys, "The Origin of the Portuguese Word Zaburro As Their Name for Maize," *Bulletin de L'Institute Français de Afrique Noire, Serie B, Sciences Humaines* 19, 1–2 (January–April 1957): 111–36.

2. Jeffreys, "The History of Maize in Africa," 198. In this quotation the common mistranslation of the Portuguese *milho zaburro* as maize (as opposed to sorghum, an indigenous African grain) is not a factor. The reference to *mehiz* and to the grain's resemblance to chickpeas points to maize as the cereal described.

3. M. D. W. Jeffreys, "How Ancient Is West African Maize," *Africa* 33, 2 (1963): 121. Jeffreys cites a translation by Lains e Silva. Also, see Frank Willett, "The Introduction of Maize to West Africa: An Assessment of Recent Evidence," *Africa* 32, 1 (1962): 11. Robert Harms tells me that the French slaving ship *Diligent* called in at Sao Tomé December 1731–January 1732, where it took on cassava flour and "une Demy gamelle De mil," as food for the middle passage. The latter may be maize rather than millet since maize is elsewhere described as a major provision for such vessels calling at Sao Tomé. It is not clear why the *Diligent* did not take on maize, though perhaps the harvest was delayed.

4. Dominique Juhé-Beaulaton, "La diffusion du maïs sur les côtes de l'or det des esclaves aux XVII et XVIII siècles," *Review françois d'histoire d'outre-mer* 77 (1990): 188–90.

5. For forest fallow system, see Kojo Amanor, *The New Frontier, Farmer's Response to Land Degradation: A West African Study* (London: Zed Books, 1994), 175.

6. See James C. McCann, "Maize and Grace: Corn and Africa's Changing Landscapes, 1500–1999," *Comparative Studies in Society and History* (April 2001): 253, 263.

7. C. L. M. Eijnatten, *Towards the Improvement of Maize in Nigeria* (Wageningen, Netherlands: H. Veermen and Zonen N.V., 1965), 25.

8. See McCann, "Maize and Grace," 266–68.

9. Dr. G. A. C. Herklots (Secretary of State for Colonial Agricultural Research) to D. Rhind (Secretary for Agriculture and Forestry Research, West African Inter-Territorial Secretariat, Accra), July 24, 1951, records of the Colonial Office, Public Records Office, Kew, England (hereafter cited as CO) 927/189/7.

10. "Rust (fungus)," *Microsoft Encarta Encyclopedia 99,* encarta.msn.com.

11. Rusts are funghi, which propagate via spores that travel by wind or on living plant tissue, alternating between uredospore and teleutospore stages of virulence and dormancy, respectively. I am grateful to my colleague Professor Gillian Cooper-Driver, professor emeritus, Boston University and the National University of Lesotho.

12. Van Eijnatten, *Towards the Improvement of Maize in Nigeria,* 70; D. Rhind, J. M. Waterson, and F. C. Deighton, "Occurrence of *Puccinia polysora* Underw. in West Africa," *Nature* 169 (1952): 631; for Gold Coast losses, see D. Rhind, "Report to Secretary for Agricultural and Forestry Research, West-African Inter-Territorial Secretariat," Accra, October 24, 1951, CO 927/189/7. Estimates of losses seem to have been guesswork since colonial agricultural officers had no mechanisms for crop production beyond the losses to rust on test plots.

13. "Memorandum on Maize Rust Disease in West Africa," by D. Rhind, Secretary for Agricultural and Forestry Research, June 18, 1951, transmitted by Chief Secretary's Deputy, West African Inter-Territorial Secretariat to Governor, Nigeria; O.A.G. Gold Coast; Governor, Sierra Leone; O.A.G. Gambia, CO 927/189/7.

14. Rhind, "Memorandum on Maize Rust Disease."

15. Rhind, "Memorandum on Maize Rust Disease."

16. The first meeting of the Maize Rust Research Unit took place on March 4, 1953. See G. A. C. Herklots memo "Rust Disease of Maize in West Africa," July 18, 1951, CO 927/189. Geoffrey Herklots, Ph.D., was the secretary for the Committee for Colonial Agriculture, Animal Health, and Forestry Research founded in June 1945. Significantly, the Moor Plantation Research Station eventually evolved into the International Institute for Tropical Agriculture (IITA), part of the current CGIAR (Consulative Group for International Agricultural Research) system. For actions of the Maize Rust Research Unit see CO 927/277.

17. Rhind to Wiltshire, June 18, 1951, CO 927/189/7.

18. Webster to Herklot (Colonial Office), July 27, 1951, CO 927/189/7. The 1948 Economic Cooperation Act established the ECA as a branch of the State Department to administer the European Recovery Program (Marshall Plan). The ECA eventually evolved into the U.S. Agency for International Development (USAID) in 1961. My thanks to Sarah Phillips for this information.

19. Jenkins was in charge of all government maize breeding programs in the United States.

20. Herklots to Rhind, July 24, 1951, and Herklots Minutes of October 29, 1951, CO 927/189.

21. Rhind et al., "Occurrence of *Puccinia polysora,*" 631.

22. Beginning in 1943 the Rockefeller Foundation had spearheaded efforts in international crop research in Mexico that eventually resulted in the mid-1960s in the worldwide CGIAR.

23. W. R. Stanton and R. H. Cammack, "Resistance to the Maize Rust, *Puccinia polysora* Underw." *Nature* 172 (1953): 505–6.

24. Waterston to Rhind, September 24, 1953, CO 927/277.

25. Norman Borlaug, "A Case of Stable Balanced Biotic Relationship between Maize and Its Two Rust Parasites," *Conference on the Biology of Rust Resistance in Forest Trees,* USDA Forest Service (Washington, DC: U.S. Department of Agriculture, 1969), 618–19.

26. Van Eijnatten, *Towards the Improvement of Maize in Nigeria,* 5.

27. Van Eijnatten, *Towards the Improvement of Maize in Nigeria,* 618–19.

28. Borlaug, "A Case of Stable Balanced Biotic Relationship," 619. Here, he ignores evidence from African colonial research efforts on test plots that no African maize types showed any resistance.

29. I am grateful to Dr. Brian Spooner of the Mycology Department at the Royal Botan-

ical Gardens at Kew for this example. James Webb pointed out the case of the "brown bug" from his work on Sri Lanka.

Chapter 8: When Stalin Learned to Fish

1. Frederick Whymper, *Fisheries of the World* (London: C. Cassell, 1884), 333–34.

2. A. V. Terent'ev, "Russkii prioritet v mekhanizatsii rybnoi promyshlennosti," *Rybnoe khoziaistvo* 11 (1950): 7–10.

3. A. Kiselev and A. I. Krasnobaev, *Istoriia murmanskogo tralovogo flota, 1920–1970* (Murmansk: Murmanskoe knizhnoe izdatel'stvo, 1973), 18–25.

4. This biography of Knipovich is taken from P. I. Usachev, ed., *Sbornik, Posviashchennyi nauchnoi deiatel'nosti pochetnogo chlena Akademii nauk SSSR, zasluzhennogo deiatelia nauki i tekhniki, Nikolaia Mikhailovicha Knipovicha* (Moscow-Leningrad: Pishchepromizdat, 1939), 5–12.

5. On this attitude toward science and politics in the United States during the Progressive Era, see Samuel Hays, *Conservation and the Gospel of Efficiency: The Progressive Conservation Movement, 1890–1920* (Cambridge: Harvard University Press, 1959).

6. See also O. A. Grimm, *Nikol'skii rybovodnyi zavod* (St. Petersburg: P. P. Soikin, 1902).

7. N. M. Knipovich, *Ekspeditsiia nauchnopromyslovykh issledovanii u beregov murmana*, vol. 1 (St. Petersburg: Khudozhestvennaia pechat', 1902), 8–15.

8. Ibid., 1–6.

9. Knipovich turned to the Caspian Sea herring for studies between 1903 and 1912. World War I, the Russian revolution, and the civil war interrupted field research but gave Knipovich the chance to pour through the data he had gathered. He produced several outstanding works in this time including *Hydrological Research in the Caspian Sea* (1921). During the civil war some research was completed on better use of salt to preserve fish more effectively and cheaply to supply the Red Army. Otherwise, the industry remained mired in the nineteenth century with individual fishermen using human and wind power.

10. N. M. Knipovich, *Kaspiiskoe more i ego promysly* (Berlin: Z. I. Grzhebin, 1923), 72–90. Not long before his death in 1938 he published *The Hydrology of the Seas and of Salt Waters*. He had over 125 published works, many of them in German journals. His legacy is the great PINRO.

11. Tatiana Pashkova, "Iz pleiady istinnykh uchenykh," *Pybnyi murman*, March 5–11, 1999, 9; and "Pamiati Nikolaia Mikhailovicha Knipovicha" (unpublished article, 1999). My thanks to Dr. Pashkova for showing me the Knipovich Institute Museum and sharing her work on Knipovich with me.

12. Kiselev and Krasnobaev, *Istoriia murmanskogo tralovogo flota, 1920–1970*, 32–33.

13. Ibid., 42–52.

14. N. Kuznetsov and F. Paromov, *Tekhnika rybolovstva* (Arkhangelsk: Sevkraigiz, 1934), 3–6.

15. M. F. Mikhov, *Trallovoe delo* (Leningrad: Sevgosrybtrest, 1930), 3–6, 9, 61–69, 75–76.

16. Kiselev and Krasnobaev, *Istoriia murmanskogo tralovogo flota, 1920–1970*, 66–69.

17. Kuznetsov and Paromov, *Tekhnika rybolovstva*, 3–6.

18. N. E. Skorniakov et al., *Na traulerakh v Barentsovom more* (Moscow: Glavsevmorput, 1946), 151–56.

19. On the development of the PINRO research fleet, see M. L. Zaferman and A. I. Mukhin, *Nauchnyi flot PINRO* (Murmansk: PINRO, 1996); and M. L. Zaferman, *Ocherki*

gidronavtiki (Murmansk: PINRO, 1996). My thanks to Dr. Zaferman for sharing his excellent research with me. See also Skorniakov et al., *Na traulerakh v Barentsovom more*, 166–69, 179–83.

20. Julia Laius, "Uchenye, promyshlenniki i rybaki: nauchno-promyslovye issledovaniia na Murmane, 1898–1933," *Voprosy istorii estestvoznaniia i tekhniki* 1 (1995): 64–81.

21. P. L. Pirozhnikov, "Gosudarstvennyi nauchno-issledovatel'skii institut ozernogo i rechnogo rybnogo khoziaistva," *Rybnoe khoziastvo* 9 (1960): 7–12.

22. K. E. Babaian, "Stalinskii plan preobrazovaniia prirody i zadachi rybnoi promyshlennosti," *Rybnoe khoziaistvo* 1 (1953): 6.

23. A. G. Libergal, ed., *Stakhanovskoe dvizhenie v rybnoi promyshlennosti* (Moscow: Vlast sovetov, 1935), 9–25.

24. K. E. Babaian, "Zadachi rybokhoziaistvennogo osvoeniia vodokhranilitshch," *Rybnoe khoziaistvo* 10 (1953): 4–11.

25. R. I. Tsiunchik, "Sovetskoe prudovoe khoziaistvo," *Rybnoe khoziaistvo* 11 (1952): 41–47.

26. Iu. S. Sergeev, "Organizatsiia lova ryby na Rybinskom vodokhranilishche," *Rybnoe khoziaistvo* 10 (1956): 25–27; and V. I. Vladimirov, "Usloviia razmnozheniia prokhodnykh ryb v Dnepre v pervyi god ego zaregulirovaniia Kakhovskoi GES," *Rybnoe khoziaistvo* 8 (1957): 70–73.

27. I. V. Baranov, "Termicheskie i gidrokhimicheskie usloviia zimovki ryb v Gor'kovskom i Kuibyshevskom vodokhranilishchakh v pervyi god ikh sushchestvovaniia," *Rybnoe khoziaistvo* 12 (1957): 65–69.

28. G. N. Mikhalchenkov, "Iz opyta proektirovaniia prudovykh rybovodnykh khoziaistv," *Rybnoe khoziaistvo* 11 (1960): 11–15.

29. N. S. Strogakov, "Belikie stroiki kommunizma i peredelka prirogy promyslovykh ryb," *Rybnoe khoziaistvo* 12 (1952): 23–25; and R. I. Tsiunchik, "Sovetskoe prudovoe khoziaistvo," *Rybnoe khoziaistvo* 11 (1952): 41–47.

30. M. M. Gurov, "Rezul'taty peresadki osetrovykh v Tsimlianskoe vodokhranilishche," *Rybnoe khoziaistvo* 11 (1960): 16–21.

31. A. T. Diuzhikov, "Mechenie i peresadka osetra iz nizhnego b'efa Kuibyshevskogo gidrouzla v vodokhranilishche," *Rybnoe khoziaistvo* 11 (1958): 20–21.

32. N. Ia. Emel'ianov, "Bol'shoe vnimaniia obleseniiu krupnykh vodokhranilishch," *Lesnoe khoziaistvo* 12 (1958): 25–27.

33. N. I. Kozhin, "Problema vosproizvodstva rybnykh zapasov v sviazi s gidrostroitel'stvom," *Rybnoe khoziaistvo* 12 (1950): 19–23.

34. G. V. Nikol'skii, "Stroitel'stvo glavnogo Turkmenskogo kanala i voprosy rybnogo khoziaistva," *Rybnoe khoziaistvo* 12 (1950): 24–26.

35. Alfred Crosby, *Ecological Imperialism: The Biological Expansion of Europe, 900–1900* (Cambridge: Cambridge University Press, 1986).

36. Kozhin, "Problema vosproizvodstva rybnykh zapasov v sviazi s gidrostroitel'stvom," 19–23.

37. A. V. Lukin, "Rybokhoziaistvennoe osvoenie Kuibyshevskogo vodokhranilishcha," *Rybnoe khoziaistvo* 8 (1958): 22–24.

38. N. I. Nikoliukin, "O tselesoobraznosti zarybleniia stalingradskogo vodokhranilishcha ribridom belugi so sterliad'iu," *Rybnoe khoziaistvo* 3 (1960): 18–20.

39. V. S. Tanasiichuk and P. N. Khoroshko, "O nereste osetrovykh nizhe Stalingrada v sviazi s ustroistvom iskusstvennykh nerestilishch," *Rybnoe khoziaistvo* 9 (1958): 18–20.

40. S. P. Fedin, "Ob otritsatel'nom vliianii promyshlennogo zagriazneniia na rybnoe khoziaistvo Kakhovskogo vodokhranilishcha i putiakh ego ustraneniia," *Rybnoe khoziaistvo* 9 (1957): 74–76.

41. "Okhrana i vosproizvodstvo rybnykh zapasov—vazhneishaia narodnokhoziaistvennaia zadacha," *Rybnoe khoziaistvo* 11 (1956): 1–5.

42. A. N. Baluev, "Skhema rybokhoziaistvennykh meropriiatii v Volg-Kaspiiskom raione," *Rybnoe khoziaistvo* 10 (1956): 48–51.

43. M. E. Lur'e, Ia. I. Gandel'man, and Iu. M. Dziubenko, "Refrizheratornye priemno-transportnye suda s mashinnym okhlazhdeniem," *Rybnoe khoziaistvo* 8 (1952): 19–21.

44. K. K. Sarakhanov, *Kryl'ia semileti* (Murmansk: Murmansk Inizhnoe izdatel'stvo, 1960): 48–52.

45. Ibid.

46. "Okhrana i vosproizvodstvo rybnykh zapasov—vazhneishaia narodnokhoziaistvennaia zadacha," *Rybnoe khoziaistvo* 11 (1956): 1–5.

47. Vladil Lysenko, *A Crime against the World*, trans. Michael Glenny (London: Victor Gollancz, 1983): 49, 230.

48. On the politics, ideology, and myths of the Soviet Far North and the importance of the northern sea route to Arctic resource development, see John McCannon, *Red Arctic* (New York: Oxford University Press, 1998).

49. D. M. Skripal', ed., *Narodnoe khoziaistvo murmanskoi oblasti za 50 let Sovetskoi vlasti* (Murmansk: Murmanskoe knizhnoe izdatelstvo, 1967), 14.

50. M. Drozdov, "Glavnyi rybni tsekh," *Pravda*, February 16, 1969, 2.

51. "Obagatit' rybnuiu promyshlennost' novymi mashinami," *Rybnoe khoiaistvo* 7 (1946): 1–3.

52. V. Voronin, "Mimo stola," *Komsomolskaia pravda*, April 26, 1968, 2; and "Ministr otvechaet studentam," *Komsomolskaia pravda*, December 15, 1968, 2.

53. S. Gudkov, "Morskoe assorti," *Komsomolskaia pravda*, August 8, 1969, 2; and M. Kolesnikov, "Nachinaetsia s moria," *Pravda*, December 15, 1983, 2.

54. B. Kostin and A. Sabov, "Ne chudovishche morskoe," *Komsomolskaia pravda*, September 26, 1968, 2; B. Misiuk, "Zatianuvshaiasia degustatsiia," *Trud*, December 19, 1978, 2; and Mark Barinov, "Skol'ko ryby v more?" *Sovetskai rossiia*, May 29, 1969, 4.

55. Z. Belevskaia, "Siurprizy okeana," *Sovetskaia rossiia*, July 8, 1984, 2; Iu. Balakirev and V. Frid'ev, "Lozhka pavnodushiias' bochku sel'dei," *Sotsialisticheskaia industriia*, July 25, 1984, 2; and "Rybka zolota, banka zhestianaia," *Komsomolskaia pravda*, February 18, 1979, 2.

56. E. Fel'dman, "Vas zhdut v 'Okeane,'" *Pravda*, May 27, 1976, 3; "Rybolovnyi flot i rybnye produkty," *Izvestiia*, January 28, 1969, 2.

57. Ia. Bratslaver, "Ulov iz obshchikh slov," *Komsomolskaia pravda*, December 3, 1970, 2; "Komu sdat' ulov?" *Pravda*, February 28, 1974, 3; and G. Borodulin, "Pochemu traulery zhdut vygruzki," *Pravda*, March 14, 1971, 3.

58. G. Sytykh, "Bumazhnaia karusel' vokrug rukavichki," *Izvestiia*, August 4, 1983, 1; V. Martyshkin, "Odezhda rybaka," *Trud*, August 4, 1983, 1; V. Sungorkin, "Posle puska ostanovit'?" *Sovetskaia rossiia*, April 1, 1983, 2; Iu. Kirinitsiianov, "Krugi na vode," *Pravda*, Au-

gust 5, 1984, 2; V. Voronin, "Dyry v nevodakh," *Komsomolskaia pravda*, August 12, 1969, 2; V. Safronov, "Chto rybaku po dushe," *Sovetskaia kul'tura*, August 24, 1984, 2; and Reuter Wire Report, March 29, 1984.

59. "Russia Will Curb Fishing Catches off New England," *International Herald Tribune*, October 23, 1973.

60. *Izvestiia*, January 21, 1981, 2.

61. Lysenko, *A Crime against the World*, 151.

Chapter 9: Yellow Jack and Geopolitics

1. Philip Curtin, *The Plantation Complex* (New York: Cambridge University Press, 1991).

2. Christopher Duffy, *Siege Warfare: The Fortress in the Early Modern World, 1494–1660* (London: Routledge & Kegan Paul, 1979); Geoffrey Parker, *The Military Revolution: Military Innovation and the Rise of the West, 1500–1800* (Cambridge: Cambridge University Press, 1996).

3. Military matters are covered in the greatest detail by Christian Buchet, *La lutte pour l'espace caraïbe et la façade atlantique del'Amérique centrale et sud*, 2 vols. (Paris: Librairie de l'Inde, 1991); in Paul Butel and Bernard Lavallé, eds., *L'espace caraïbe: théâtre et enjeu des luttes impériales, XVIe–XIXe siècle* (Bordeaux: Maison des Pays Ibériques, 1996); and in Juan Zapatero, *La guerra del Caribe* (San Juan: Instituto de Cultura Puertoriqueña, 1964).

4. See George K. Strode, ed., *Yellow Fever* (New York: McGraw-Hill, 1951), the last comprehensive study of yellow fever. More recent work includes a far greater understanding of the genetics of the yellow fever virus: Jari Vainio and Felicity Cutts, *Yellow Fever* (Geneva: World Health Organization, 1998); Thomas P. Monath, "Yellow Fever," in *Tropical Infectious Diseases*, ed. Richard Guerrant, D. H. Walker, and P. F. Weller (Philadelphia: Churchill Livingstone, 1999), 1253–64; Donald Cooper and Kenneth Kiple, "Yellow Fever," in *The Cambridge World History of Human Disease*, ed. Kenneth Kiple (New York: Cambridge University Press, 1993), 1100–1107; A. D. Barrett and Thomas Monath, "Epidemiology and Ecology of Yellow Fever Virus," *Advanced Virus Research* 61 (2003): 291–315; P. F. da Costa Vasconcelos, "Febre amarela," *Revista da Sociedade Brasileira de Medicina Tropical* 36 (2003): 275–93.

5. The gruesome symptoms of yellow fever have the happy effect of making historical diagnosis less problematical than in most other cases. Whereas from seventeenth- and eighteenth-century descriptions it is normally impossible to tell a case (or an epidemic) of malaria from one of typhus, the black vomit is a unique signature.

6. Monath, "Yellow Fever," 1262.

7. Gerald L. Mandell, John E. Bennett, and Raphael Dolin, *Principles and Practice of Infectious Disease* (Philadelphia: Churchill Livingstone, 2000), 2:1716.

8. Theodore Tsai, "Yellow Fever," in *Hunter's Tropical Medicine and Emerging Infectious Diseases*, ed. G. T. Strickland (Philadelphia: Saunders, 2000), 272–75. Its sister virus, dengue, has evolved in multiple directions very rapidly over the past two hundred years. See W. J. Tabachnik, "Arthoropod-Borne Emerging Disease Issues," in *Emerging Infections*, ed. R. M. Krause (San Diego: Academic Press, 1998), 413.

9. It is indeed an anthropocentric conceit to conceive of yellow fever as a human disease. Recent research shows that humans are not entirely necessary: A. aegypti mothers can transmit the virus directly to their daughters ("vertical transmission"). Vainio and Cutts, *Yellow Fever*, 30; Monath, "Yellow Fever," 1263.

10. This crucial (if accurate) detail comes from A. Ramenofsky, "Diseases of the Ameri-

cas, 1492–1700," in *The Cambridge World History of Human Disease,* 325. She cites Henry Rose Carter, *Yellow Fever: An Epidemiological and Historical Study of Its Place of Origin* (Baltimore: Williams & Wilkins, 1931). Why, how, and when *A. aegypti* might have developed this preference for clay-bottomed water vessels is a mystery. Perhaps clay pots release useful nutrients into water that assist in the nutrition of mosquito larvae, and over the long history of pottery in West Africa, *A. aegypti* came to exploit this opportunity. But this would seem to require badly fired pots, and in any case *A. aegypti* larvae normally feed on bacteria and protozoa associated with organic detritus. The modern literature on *A. aegypti* does not mention any such preference, but it may be that with the rise of plastic in the last fifty years mosquitoes have so few opportunities to breed in clay vessels that it is rarely observed and so not reported. My colleague in the Georgetown University Biology Department Peter Armbruster has guided me through the thickets of mosquito-ology. Useful information on *A. aegypti* can be found in the Bible of mosquito studies, A. N. Clements, *The Biology of Mosquitoes,* 2 vols. (Dordrecht: Kluwer Academic, 2004); in R. C. Christopher, *Aedes aegypti, the Yellow Fever Mosquito: Its Life History, Bionomics, and Structure* (Cambridge: Cambridge University Press, 1960); and for laymen, in Andrew Spielman and Michael D'Antonio, *Mosquito* (New York: Hyperion, 2001).

11. These details come from William C. Black, "Evolution of Arthropod Disease Vectors," in *Emerging Pathogens: Archaeology, Ecology, and Evolution of Infectious Disease,* ed. Charles Greenblatt and Mark Spigelman (New York: Oxford University Press, 2003), 51.

12. This figure refers to today's populations; the vector competence of *A. aegypti* might conceivably have been different centuries ago. Mark Nathan Cohen and Gillian Crane-Kramer, "The State and Future of Paleoepidemiology," in *Emerging Pathogens,* 88.

13. Had yellow fever established itself in Brazil prior to 1630, it is unlikely that the Dutch conquest of half of the captaincies of Brazil could have taken place, because the Dutch West India Company sent thousands of nonimmunes to the port cities of Brazil.

14. David Watts, *The West Indies: Patterns of Development, Culture and Environmental Change since 1492* (Cambridge: Cambridge University Press, 1987), 219–23, 399–405, 434–43.

15. It is likely that the deforestation and soil erosion associated with sugar increased the amount of swampland too, which would have improved conditions for the anopheles mosquito, the vector of malaria.

16. See Manuel Moreno Fraginals, *El ingenio: Complejo económico-social cubano del azucar,* 3 vols. (Havana: Editorial de Ciencias Sociales, 1978).

17. James Goodyear, "The Sugar Connection: A New Perspective on the History of Yellow Fever," *Bulletin of the History of Medicine* 52 (1978): 5–21.

18. It is possible that yellow fever outbreaks occurred in San Juan, Puerto Rico, in 1598 and in Brazil in 1623. See Kenneth Kiple, "Disease Ecologies of the Caribbean," in *Cambridge World History of Human Disease,* 499. Francisco Guerra, "The European-American Exchange," *History and Philosophy of the Life Sciences* 15 (1993): 313–27, asserts that yellow fever struck Yucatan in 1523 and Guadeloupe in 1635 and again in 1640, but these diagnoses remain most uncertain.

19. Medical science has not detected any mechanism for this, as it has for inherited immunity to falciparum malaria among people of West African descent. The idea of heritable resistance to yellow fever is controversial. The latest World Health Organization study of yellow fever concludes, "It is uncertain whether the apparent increased resistance of blacks re-

flects acquired immunity or is due to genetic factors" (Vainio and Cutts, *Yellow Fever*, 30). The evidence of differential morbidity and mortality between blacks and others in historical yellow fever epidemics is strong. Kenneth Kiple, *The Caribbean Slave: A Biological History* (New York: Cambridge University Press, 1985), 163.

20. To judge by modern vaccination programs in Africa, a population with 60 percent immunes does not reliably confer herd immunity but one with 80 percent will. See the unpublished paper of the World Health Organization WHO/EPI/GEN/98.08, 3, National Library of Medicine, Bethesda, MD.

21. To be more exact, the most vulnerable were populations of young adults who had grown up, and whose ancestors for millennia had grown up, outside of yellow fever zones and possibly dengue fever zones. Apparently there is some cross-protection for survivors of one or another of the flaviviruses (Vainio and Cutts, *Yellow Fever*, 30; Tasi, "Yellow Fever," 272–75). There is some evidence that southern Chinese, who have no experience of yellow fever but have survived dengue fever, are also resistant to yellow fever. People from India, when translated to the Caribbean in the nineteenth century, seem to have shown greater resistance to yellow fever. Yellow fever has never been recorded anywhere in Asia or the South Pacific, for which there is no explanation. Perhaps it is connected to the prevalence of dengue: just as in the Caribbean populations who came from dengue zones seem to have shown a stronger resistance to yellow fever, so possibly dengue survivors carry sufficient cross-protection against yellow fever that the disease could not establish itself in Asia.

22. Buchet, *La lutte pour l'espace caraïbe*, 2:1129.

23. These figures are for deaths. Far more men fell ill and were useless as soldiers or sailors. The data come from Buchet, *La lutte pour l'espace caraïbe*, 2:730, 783–84.

24. Richard Harding, *Amphibious Warfare in the Eighteenth Century: The British Expedition to the West Indies, 1740–1742*, Studies in History No. 61 (London: Royal Historical Society), 3–4; Buchet, *La lutte pour l'espace caraïbe*, 1:515–26. Julián de Zulueta, "Health and Military Factors in Vernon's Failure at Cartagena," *Mariner's Mirror* 78 (1992): 127–41, takes the view that yellow fever did not decide the battle, which was won by Spanish tenacity and lost by British blundering. He argues that yellow fever became truly serious among British troops only after they had failed in an attempt to take one of Cartagena's forts by storm. True enough, but they attempted it rashly, without proper preparation, because of Vernon's dread of the building epidemic. The mortality among the colonials continued after Cartagena. In Alan Gallay, ed., *Colonial Wars of North America, 1512–1763, An Encyclopedia* (New York: Garland, 1996), 105, less than 10 percent of the colonials returned home. Among the survivors under Vernon's command was a Virginian named Lawrence Washington, whose plantation—Mt. Vernon—he named for his admiral before he passed it on to his more famous half-brother, George.

25. A medical account of this campaign is Thomas Dancer, *A Brief History of the Late Expedition against Fort San Juan, So Far As It Relates to the Diseases of the Troops* (Kingston: Douglas & Aikman, 1781). Dancer recommended opium and malt liquors as treatment for yellow fever (42, 48). "Diary of Surgeon Leonard Gillespie on HMS *Majestic* at Martinique, 1794–1795," Public Record Office, London (hereafter cited as P.R.O.), ADM 101/102/9, also relates the disease experience of the San Juan expedition.

26. Biblioteca Nacional (Madrid), ms 10,421, "Processo dada al Gobernador de la Habana Juan de Prado" (1765). In the 192 folios recording this trial the view was repeatedly expressed that Havana, if competently defended, would withstand all attacks, for example, fol.140: "invencible seguridad de la Plaza."

27. Celia María Parcero Torre, *La pérdida de la Habana y las reformas borbónicas en Cuba (1760–1773)* (Madrid: Junta de Castilla y León, 1998), 48, 60–62.

28. Forty-four letters from de Prado are in Seville's Archivo General de Indias, Sección Ultramar, legajo 169. His siege diary appears in Jacobo de la Pezuela, ed., *Diccionario geográfico, estadístico, histórico de la Isla de Cuba* (Madrid: Mellado, 1863), 3:27–51.

29. "General Return of Officers, Sergeants, Drummers, and Rank and File . . . from the 7th June to 18th October 1762," P.R.O., CO 117/1, f. 155.

30. "Estimate of the Expenses of the Fortifications at the Havana," P.R.O. CO 117/1, f. 275.

31. S. Johnson, "Thoughts on the Late Transactions Respecting Falkland's Islands," in his *Political Writings*, ed. Donald Greene (New Haven: Yale University Press, 1977), 10:374.

32. British Library, Additional Mss. 23,678, fol. 17 (1747).

33. Figures vary. These come from Richard Price and Sally Price, introduction to *Narrative of a Five Years Expedition against the Revolted Negroes of Surinam*, by John Gabriel Stedman (Baltimore: Johns Hopkins University Press, 1988), xxvi and lxxxvi. Stedman himself (607) thought that only 100 of 1,200 survived. The Dutch forces numbered closer to 1,650 than 1,200. Wim Hoogbergen, *The Boni Maroon Wars in Suriname* (Leiden: E. J. Brill, 1990), 104.

34. Stedman, *Narrative of a Five Years Expedition*, 607. The italics are in the original.

35. These figures are from Christopher Duffy, *Soldiers, Sugar, and Seapower: The British Expeditions to the West Indies and the War against Revolutionary France* (Oxford: Oxford University Press, 1987), 334. Duffy notes that battle deaths were trivial compared to disease deaths and that yellow fever was the greatest killer of all.

36. Quoted in C. L. R. James, *The Black Jacobins* (New York: Vintage Books, 1989), 314. See p. 299 for Toussaint's statement: "the rainy season will rid us of our foes." James provides no sources for these quotations. Denis Laurent-Ropa, *Haiti: Une colonie française, 1625–1802* (Paris: L'Harmattan, 1993), 323, gives fifty-four thousand as the total number of French troops lost in Haiti, with eight thousand survivors. A contingent of Swiss mercenaries some eight hundred strong lost all but eleven men; Swiss mercenaries never consented to go overseas again. Danielle Anex-Cabanis, "Mort et morbidité aux Antilles lors de l'expédition de Saint-Domingue: Notes à propos des mercenaires suisses," in *Mourir pour les Antilles,* ed. Michel Martin and Alain Yacou (Paris: Editions Caribéennes, 1991), 187.

37. Printed in Antonio Rodríguez Villa, *El teniente general Don Pablo Morillo, Primer Conde de Cartagena, Marqués de la Puerta (1778–1837)* (Madrid: Editorial América, 1908–1910), 3:442–43. According to Mark Elvin, the Bai people of Yunnan (southwestern China) understood that there was a link between anopheles mosquitoes and malaria during the Ming dynasty, and some Chinese learned of it too. Elvin, *The Retreat of the Elephants: An Environmental History of China* (New Haven: Yale University Press, 2004), 262.

38. Julio Albi, *Banderos olvidadas: el ejército realista en América* (Madrid: Ediciones de Cultura Hispánica, 1990), 403–5.

39. See Margaret L. Woodward, "The Spanish Army and the Loss of America, 1810–1824," *Hispanic American Historical Review* 48, 4 (1968): 586–607.

40. Whether this practice actually bred more mosquitoes I cannot say. The health history of the Panama Canal appears in J. A. Le Prince and A. J. Orenstein, *Mosquito Control in Panama* (New York: Putnam, 1916); and M. D. Gorgas and B. J. Hendrick, *William Crawford Gorgas: His Life and Work* (New York: Doubleday, Page, 1924).

Chapter 10: Creation and Destruction in Landscapes of Empire

1. The term "neo-Europe" is from Alfred Crosby, *Ecological Imperialism* (New York: Cambridge University Press, 1986).

2. Remarks of E. C. M. Fox, in Australian Parliament, House of Representatives, *Hansard*, 58 (May 2, 1968).

3. On the process in Australia see Geoffrey Blainey, *The Tyranny of Distance,* rev. ed. (South Melbourne: Macmillan, 1982).

4. Edwin J. Brady, *Australia Unlimited* (Melbourne: George Robertson, 1918).

5. The curious should look up the Artemis Project and the L-5 Society on the Internet.

6. Julian Simon, *The Ultimate Resource* (Princeton: Princeton University Press, 1981); Donella Meadows et al., *The Limits to Growth: A Report for the Club of Rome Project on the Predicament of Mankind* (New York: Universe Books, 1974).

7. Donella Meadows, *The Global Citizen* (Washington, DC: Island Press, 1991), 11, 32.

8. Asa Gray, *How Plants Grow* (New York: American Book Company, 1858), 2.

9. Anne Marie Milbrooke, "State Geological Surveys of the Nineteenth Century" (Ph.D. diss., University of Pennsylvania, 1981).

10. Suzanne Zeller, *Inventing Canada* (Toronto: University of Toronto Press, 1987), 9.

11. Ross Gibson, *Diminishing Paradise* (Sydney: Angus and Robertson, 1984).

12. Frank M. Chapman, *Color Key to North American Birds* (New York: Appleton, 1903); J. A. Leach, *An Australian Bird Book* (Melbourne: Whitcombe and Tombes, 1911); Roger Tory Peterson, *Field Guide to the Birds* (Boston: Houghton Mifflin, 1934); Neville Cayley, *What Bird Is That?* (Sydney: Angus and Robertson, 1931); Perrinne Moncrieff, *New Zealand Birds and How to Identify Them* (Auckland: Whitcombe and Tombes, 1925).

13. Ian Tyrrell, *True Gardens of the Gods* (Berkeley: University of California Press, 1999); and David Vaught, *Cultivating California* (Berkeley: University of California Press, 1999).

14. On American myths see Richard Slotkin, *Regeneration through Violence* (Middletown, CT: Wesleyan University Press, 1973); John Mack Faragher, *Daniel Boone* (New York: Henry Holt, 1992).

15. Russel Ward, *The Australian Legend,* 2nd ed. (Melbourne: Oxford University Press, 1978); Brenda Naill, *Australia through the Looking-Glass: Children's Fiction, 1930–1980* (Melbourne: Melbourne University Press, 1982).

16. Margaret Atwood, *Survival* (Toronto: Anansi, 1972); Gaile McGregor, *The Wacousta Syndrome* (Toronto: University of Toronto Press, 1985); Carl Berger, "The True North, Strong and Free," in *Nationalism in Canada,* ed. Peter Russell (Toronto: McGraw-Hill, 1966), 4.

17. This was clearest in Australia, where a literary tradition treating nature only began in these years. See, for instance, Donald Macdonald, *Gum Boughs and Wattle Bloom* (Melbourne: Cassell, 1888).

18. Quoted in W. F. Lothian, *A History of Canada's National Parks* (Ottawa: Environment Canada and predecessor agencies, 1977–87), 1:4.

19. For cases see Stephen Dovers, ed., *Environmental History and Policy: Still Settling Australia* (South Melbourne: Oxford University Press, 2000).

20. Charles Elton, *The Ecology of Invasions by Animals and Plants* (London: Methuen, 1958).

21. Liberty Hyde Bailey, *The Holy Earth* (1915; reprint, Ithaca: New York College of Agriculture, 1980).

22. On Leopold's use of Bailey see small brown notebook in Box 1, 9/25/10-7, Diaries and Journals, U.S. Forest Service diaries; Miscellaneous, 1899–1916, Aldo Leopold Papers, College of Agriculture, University of Wisconsin Archives, Madison. Leopold used quotations from Bailey, apparently from this notebook, in his *Game Management* (New York: Scribner, 1933), 21. Quotations from Bailey in this paragraph are 13, 13, 14, 19, 23, 51, 13, 35.

23. Aldo Leopold, *A Sand County Almanac* (1949; reprint, New York: Ballantine, 1970), 262.

24. Ernst Callenbach, *Ecotopia* (1975; reprint, New York: Bantam, 1977); Charles Reich, *The Greening of America* (New York: Random House, 1970).

25. *Wild Earth* 6 (Winter 1996–1997) was devoted to articles discussing Cronon. The debate still goes on. See Philip Cafaro, "For a Grounded Conception of Wilderness and More Wilderness on the Ground," *Ethics and the Environment* 6, 1 (2001): 1–17; William Cronon, "The Trouble with Wilderness: Or, Getting Back to the Wrong Nature," in *Uncommon Ground: Rethinking the Human Place in Nature,* ed. William Cronon (New York: Norton, 1995), 69–90.

26. Robert Pyle, *The Thunder Tree* (New York: Lyons Press, 1993), is a good example of individual commitment and the local campaign that grew out of it. See also Gary Nabhan, *Cultures of Habitat* (Washington, DC: Counterpoint, 1997); Michael Pollan, *Second Nature: A Gardener's Education* (New York: Atlantic Monthly Press, 1991); Robert Sullivan, *The Meadowlands: Wilderness Adventures on the Edge of a City* (New York: Scribner, 1998).

27. Sara Stein, *Noah's Garden* (Boston: Houghton Mifflin, 1993). On this literature see the nature shelves in any chain bookstore.

28. Information on Canberra from Libby Robin and Tom Griffiths, Australian historians.

29. See, for instance, Giovanna Di Chiro, "Nature As Community: The Convergence of Environment and Social Justice," in *Uncommon Ground,* 298–320. A more recent treatment is Christopher Foreman, *The Promise and Peril of Environmental Justice* (Washington, DC: Brookings Institution, 1998).

30. D.A.R. Williams, *Environmental Law* (Wellington: Butterworth of New Zealand, 1980), ix.

31. Geoffrey Bolton, *Spoils and Spoilers* (Sydney: Allan and Unwin, 1981).

32. Libby Robin, *Defending the Little Desert* (South Carleton: Melbourne University Press, 1999). On organizations, see Australian Conservation Foundation, *Green Pages, 1991–1992* (Melbourne: Australian Conservation Foundation, 1992).

33. For discussion, see James D. Proctor, "Whose Nature? The Contested Moral Terrain of Ancient Forests," *Uncommon Ground,* 269–97; and Richard White, "Are You an Environmentalist or Do You Work for a Living?" in *Uncommon Ground,* 171–85.

34. H. H. Finlayson, *The Red Centre* (Sydney: Angus and Robertson, 1935), 16, gives an example. On New Zealand see Leonard Cockayne, "Botanical Survey of Kapiti Island," Department of Lands and Survey (Wellington: Government Printer, 1907), 2.

35. J. A. Gibb and J. E. C. Flux, "Mammals," in *The Natural History of New Zealand: An Ecological Survey,* ed. Gordon R. Williams (Wellington: Reed, 1973), 365.

36. Carolyn King, *Handbook of New Zealand Mammals* (Auckland: Oxford University Press, 1990), 9.

37. Carolyn King, *Immigrant Killers* (Auckland: Oxford University Press, 1984), 125.

38. For a sample see Gary Snyder, *The Practice of the Wild* (Berkeley, CA: North Point, 1990); Wes Jackson, *Becoming Native to This Place* (Lexington: University Press of Kentucky,

1994); Wendell Berry, *The Unsettling of America: Culture and Agriculture* (San Francisco: Sierra Club, 1977), 19. A more recent statement is his "Back to the Land," *Amicus Journal* 20 (Winter 1999): 37–40.

39. John Elder, *Reading the Mountains of Home* (Cambridge: Harvard University Press, 1998).

40. See Dovers, *Environmental History and Policy,* on these efforts. On the background to this work see Tom Griffiths, *Hunters and Collectors* (Melbourne: Cambridge University Press, 1996).

41. See *High Country News* 32, 17 (September 11, 2000): 1. A recent example of the literature is Dieter T. Hessel and Rosemary Radford Reuther, eds., *Christianity and Ecology* (Cambridge: Harvard University Press and Harvard Center for the Study of World Religions, 2000).

42. Ken Gelder and Jane M. Jacobs, *Uncanny Australia: Sacredness and Identity in a Postcolonial Nation* (Carleton South: Melbourne University Press, 1998).

Contributors

ELIZABETH BLACKMAR is professor of history at Columbia University, author of *Manhattan for Rent, 1785–1850*, and coauthor with Roy Rosenzweig of *The Park and the People: A History of Central Park*.

ALFRED W. CROSBY, professor emeritus, University of Texas at Austin, won the Ralph Waldo Emerson Prize from Phi Beta Kappa for *Ecological Imperialism: The Biological Expansion of Europe, 900–1900*. He is a fellow of the Academy of Finland, American Academy of Arts and Sciences, and the American Philosophical Society.

JEFFRY M. DIEFENDORF is professor of history at the University of New Hampshire. An urban historian, he is the author of *In the Wake of War: The Reconstruction of German Cities after World War II*, and editor of *Rebuilding Europe's Bombed Cities* and *Rebuilding Urban Japan after 1945*.

KURK DORSEY teaches history at the University of New Hampshire. His book *The Dawn of Conservation Diplomacy: U.S.-Canadian Wildlife Protection Treaties in the Progressive Era* was cowinner of the Stuart L. Bernath Book Prize from the Society for Historians of American Foreign Relations.

THOMAS DUNLAP, professor of history at Texas A&M University and three-time winner of the Theodore Blegen Award (given annually by the Forest History Society for the best article in forest, conservation, and environmental history), has written *DDT: Scientists, Citizens, and Public Policy; Saving America's Wildlife; Nature and the English Diaspora: Environment and History in the United States, Canada, Australia, and New Zealand*; and, most recently, *Faith in Nature: Environmentalism As Religious Quest*. He is currently working on a history of field guides to birds in the United States.

SARAH S. ELKIND, an associate professor at San Diego State University, teaches courses in urban, environmental, and political history. She examined the politics of public works and environmental crises in *Bay Cities and Water Politics: The Battle for Resources in Boston and Oakland* and in *The Public Good: Environment, Politics, and Culture in America*. Her current research investigates political influence and the definition of the public good that shaped environmental policy in post–World War II America.

ANDREW ISENBERG is associate professor of history at Temple University in Philadelphia. He is the author of *The Destruction of the Bison: An Environmental History, 1750–1920.*

PAUL JOSEPHSON teaches history at Colby College, where he also directs the Science, Technology, and Society Program. He has written several books, with *Resources under Regimes: Technology, Environment, and the State* the most recent.

NANCY LANGSTON is associate professor in the Nelson Institute for Environmental Studies and the Department of Forest Ecology and Management at the University of Wisconsin-Madison. She is author of *Where Land and Water Meet: A Western Landscape Transformed,* and *Forest Dreams, Forest Nightmares: The Paradox of Old Growth in the Inland West,* winner of the 1997 Charles Weyerhaeuser Prize (Forest History Society).

JAMES C. MCCANN is professor of history and associate director of the African Studies Center at Boston University. He is author of *People of the Plow: An Agricultural History of Ethiopia,* and *Green Land, Brown Land, Black Land: An Environmental History of Africa.* His book *Maize and Grace: Africa's Encounter with a New World Crop* will be published by Harvard University Press in spring 2005.

J. R. MCNEILL is professor of history and holder of the Cinco Hermanos Chair of Environmental and International Affairs at Georgetown University. He is the author of *Something New under the Sun: An Environmental History of the 20th-Century World,* which won two book prizes and was translated into six languages.

URSULA VON PETZ is a professor at the University of Dortmund, where she teaches planning history and theory, and urban planning. She has been a visiting lecturer at the University of Architecture at Venice and Ferrara, and for several years she was a visiting professor at the Technical University in Aachen. An elected member of the German Academy of Urban and Regional Planning, she is the author of *Stadtsanierung im "Dritten Reich"* and numerous articles on planning history in Germany, especially in the Ruhr area.

JOEL A. TARR is the Richard S. Caliguiri university professor of history and policy at Carnegie Mellon University. His main research interests are in the history of urban environmental pollution and urban technological systems. Most recently he is the author of *The Search for the Ultimate Sink: Urban Pollution in Historical Perspective,* and editor of *Devastation and Renewal: An Environmental History of Pittsburgh and Its Region.*

Index

A. aegypti. *See* Aedes aegypti
Aboriginals, 209, 224
absentee ownership, 92, 98; by institutional investors, 82, 83, 84, 86, 97; and real estate investment trusts, 78, 89, 90, 95
adaptive management, 120–21
Aedes aegypti: breeding of, 198–99, 201, 202, 206, 269n10; and yellow fever, 194, 197, 198, 268n9, 269n12. *See also* mosquitoes
Africa, 230, 231, 270n30; maize in, 140, 144–48; maize rust in, 139, 140, 148, 157–58. *See also* East Africa; South Africa; West Africa
Agent Orange, 100, 109
air pollution, in Los Angeles: 8, 11, 12; and civic groups, 38–39, 40, 44; controls in, 39, 41; gas attacks, 38, 40, 41, 44; haze, 40, 42, 48, 240n5; and household incinerators, 44, 45, 47, 50; nonindustrial sources of, 12, 39, 40, 44–49; and the oil industry, 39, 46, 47–48; and public health, 38, 41, 43–44, 47, 240n5; and rubbish disposal, 39, 41, 44–47, 243n58; smoke control programs for, 40, 46, 50; voluntary smoke reduction program for, 40, 44, 46, 50, 243n58; and wartime production, 12, 38, 42–44, 45, 46. *See also* automobile emissions; fumes; Los Angeles Chamber of Commerce; Los Angeles County Air Pollution Control District; smog; Southern California Gas
Air Pollution Control District. *See* Los Angeles County Air Pollution Control District
Allegheny County, 25, 30, 31, 32

Allegheny River, 12, 18, 21, 32
All-Union Polar Research Institute of Fish Economy (PINRO), 167, 170–71, 184, 190, 265n10
All-Union Scientific Research Institute of Lake and River Fisheries (VNIORKh), 172, 180
American frontier, 4, 122, 123, 208, 210, 215, 227
American rust: disappearance of, 144, 156; identification of, 153, 154, 158; spread of, 143, 148, 157–58. *See also* maize rust; *Puccinia polysora; Puccinia sorghi*
Anglo settlements, 207–9, 212, 214, 218, 231. *See also* Australia; Canada; New Zealand; United States
Anti-Debris Association, 132–33
Aral Sea, 172, 175, 179
Archangel, 165, 168, 169, 192
Arctic Ocean, 167, 185, 187, 189
Army Corps of Engineers, 92, 107, 175; canal project in Malheur National Wildlife Refuge, 79, 116–18, 258n64, 258n66; and environmental concerns, 79, 117, 118; reservoir project in Malheur National Wildlife Refuge, 112–15, 257n43, 257n45
Arts and Crafts movement, 56, 57
Atlantic Scientific Research Institute of Fish Economy and Oceanography (AtlantNIRO), 184, 189
AtlantNIRO. *See* Atlantic Scientific Research Institute of Fish Economy and Oceanography
Australia: Aboriginals in, 209, 224; bioregional movement in, 223–24; environ-

DATE DUE

MAR 2 3 2009			